TURNING HEADS

Royal
Museum of
Fine Arts
Antwerp

Nico Van Hout
Koen Bulckens
Michael W. Kwakkelstein
Lizzie Marx
Friederike Schütt

TURNING

KMSKA

HEADS

HANNIBAL

CONTENTS

FOREWORD

This is the most comprehensive exhibition devoted to one of the most innovative categories of art in sixteenth- and seventeenth-century Europe: paintings of the human face. These head studies were emphatically not portraits. They were made in order to inform the production of the most prestigious art forms of the day – grand narrative paintings, depicting subjects drawn from biblical and classical history and mythology – and were produced by some of the greatest Northern European Baroque artists, including Peter Paul Rubens, Rembrandt van Rijn and Johannes Vermeer. These images, full of personality and character, bring the peoples and emotions of the seventeenth century to life. In these works, every face tells a powerful story.

Art historians know these works as 'tronies', from the Old Dutch word for face. Essentially, a 'tronie' is a depiction of a face. It could serve as a head study that a master painter could use to vary the figures in a densely populated composition, or it could be a finished piece that served a market fascinated by the characterful heads. These are often small, but always stunningly painted works. Unlike much of the art produced by a busy workshop, these head studies were by the hand of the master.

The 'tronie' has been particularly associated with Rembrandt and his friend Jan Lievens. As young men in their twenties, they worked so closely together that it can be hard to distinguish who painted what. In what may have been a shared studio, they posed models (sometimes friends, close relatives, or even the artists themselves) in striking and exotic costumes, including showy jewellery, ornamental helmets and lavish textiles. These heads, however, were not the invention of the brilliant artists from Leiden.

We can trace the evolution of this artistic genre during the sixteenth century in paintings which increasingly show the human face in a variety of striking expressions, some exaggerated, others natural. These were a particular feature of Rubens's activity. Highly worked head studies enabled him to produce large paintings efficiently which, although the work of many hands, convincingly represent his 'house style'. Many other artists used this genre in their own way, throughout the seventeenth century. The exhibition, and the accompanying publication, follow the evolution of these heads through several themes, including works that were used in the workshop, heads that were decorated with varying costumes, faces covering the spectrum of expression, and works that evoke the most exquisite effects of light and shadow.

We would like to thank Dr Nico Van Hout (Head of Collections), Dr Koen Bulckens (Curator, Old Masters) and Veerle De Meester (Exhibition Manager) at the Royal Museum of Fine Arts Antwerp (KMSKA) who have worked tirelessly on this project. The exhibition owes its genesis to Nico, whose research on Rubens's study heads for the *Corpus Rubenianum* is well known. We are grateful to the whole KMSKA team contributing to the exhibition with enthusiasm and energy. *Turning Heads* would not have been possible without the State Indemnity granted by Jan Jambon, Minister-president of Flanders and Flemish Minister for Foreign Policy, Culture, Digitisation and Facilities, and Toerisme Vlaanderen, as well as the generosity of exhibition partners DCA and Nationale Loterij. At the National Gallery of Ireland, the exhibition is curated by Dr Lizzie Marx (Curator of Dutch and Flemish Art) and Dr Brendan Rooney (Head Curator), working closely with Kim Smit (Head of Collections and Research), Lynn McGrane (Head of Exhibitions and Collection Services) and Mia Shirreffs (Exhibition Coordinator). We are grateful to all the Gallery team who have worked on the exhibition with passion and dedication. In addition, we would like to acknowledge the essential role of our Board of Governors and Guardians, and its Chair, Mary Keane. We acknowledge the significant contributions made to this project by Sean Rainbird, former Director of the National Gallery of Ireland and Dr Adriaan Waiboer, former Head of Collections and Research. We warmly thank Catherine Martin TD, Minister for Tourism, Culture, Arts, Gaeltacht, Sport and Media and her officials for their essential ongoing support, including the State Indemnity scheme.

Luk Lemmens,
KMSKA Chairman

Carmen Willems,
KMSKA Managing Director

Caroline Campbell,
National Gallery of Ireland Director

Tronies displayed a wide variety of facial expressions. Representations of basic emotions such as joy, fear, anger and sadness, they could also include odd character traits. It was believed that viewers would experience the same emotions they saw portrayed.

(DETAIL FIG. 86)
Peter Paul Rubens,
Head Study of a Man,
s.d., oil on panel,
Liechtenstein Museum
Vienna, GE 113

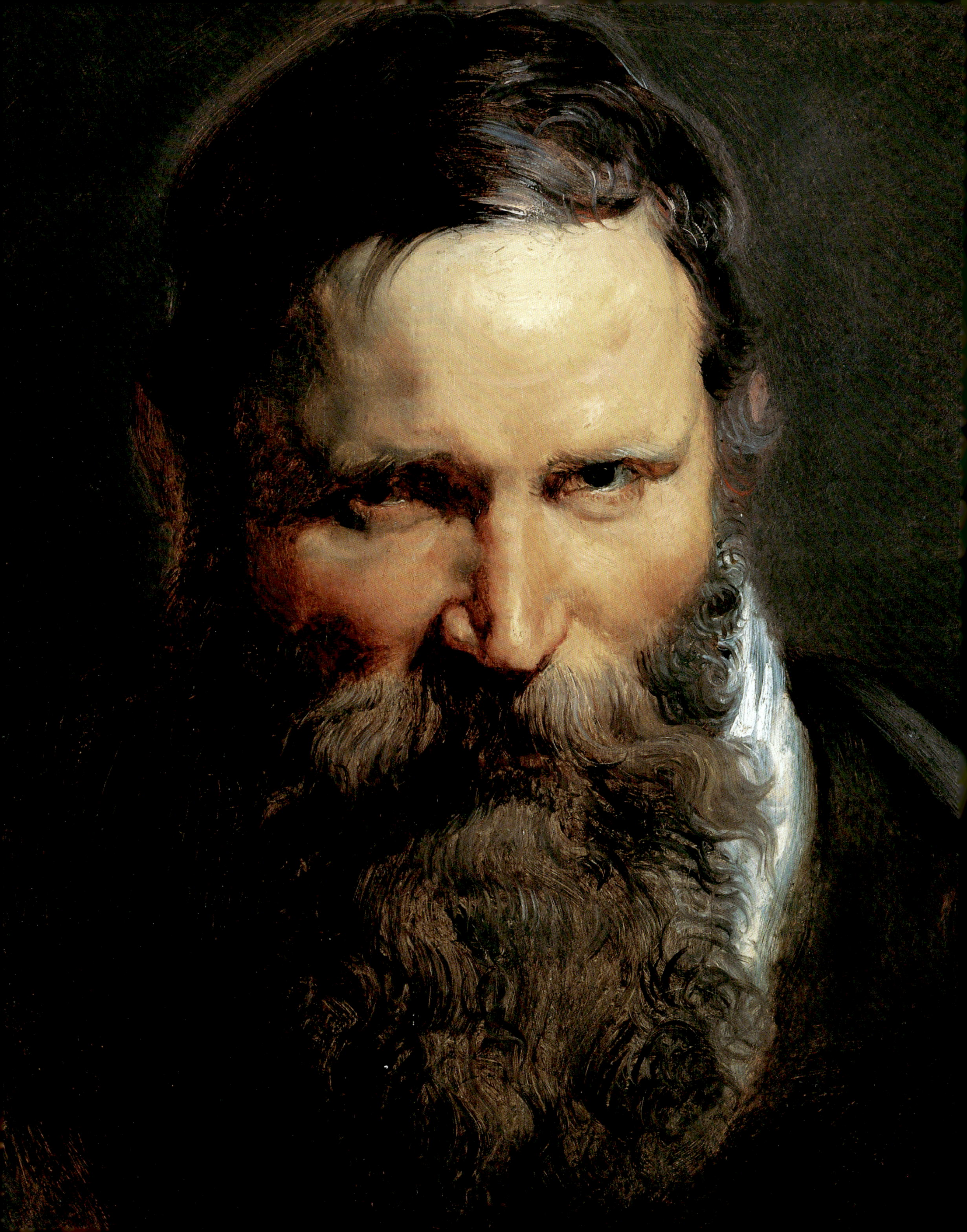

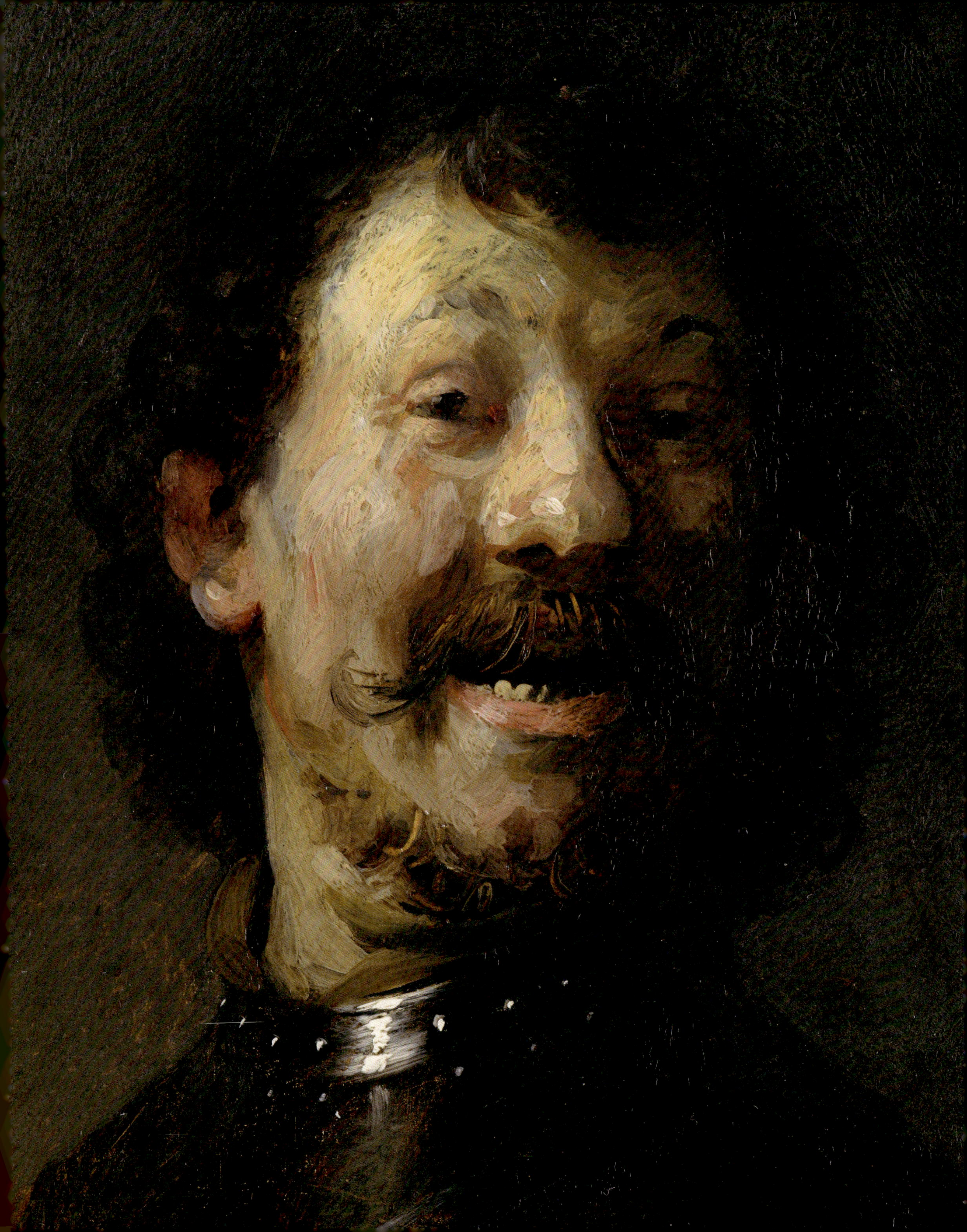

TRONIES

An Introduction to their Character and Origins

Koen Bulckens & Nico Van Hout

This book is about 'tronies' in paintings such as Rembrandt's *The Laughing Man* (Fig. 11). Tronies zoom in on a face, depicted against a monochrome background. They are mostly small pictures, meaning the heads are life-size or smaller, and appear to be painted from a live model. Lastly, and most importantly, the identity of the sitter is irrelevant in a tronie: Rembrandt based this picture on his own likeness, for example, posing before a mirror as he painted. His main aim, however, was for the work not to be recognised as his self-portrait. In pictures such as *The Laughing Man*, the real subject is the face itself, its form and expressive powers.

The term 'tronie' has a wide currency and poses no problem in generalised statements, such as those above. Its precise definition, however, has been the cause of much debate.[1] The features of a genre can be notoriously difficult to define, and this is especially true here. There are pictures which could pass as a tronie, as well as something else, such as a genre painting with a single figure. Other works greatly resemble tronies but deviate from the format in one crucial aspect. These problems of categorisation are, in part, related to disagreement about where and when tronies originated, and which works can therefore serve as their prime examples.

This essay seeks to bring clarity to both issues. The first part explores the characteristics of the genre. We shall explore tronies in relation to other painted faces – such as portraits, head studies, and history and genre paintings – highlighting the differences and similarities between them, as well as issues in interpreting them. In so doing, we map several grey areas around the category 'tronies'. This is, in our view, more valuable than defining it in terms of black and white. The second part studies the origin of tronies. The majority of publications place this in the early seventeenth century, when tronies suddenly flooded the art market of the Dutch Republic. We believe, however, that significant precedents were painted earlier, in sixteenth-century Antwerp. For the first time, we integrate these works into a wider history of the genre.

(DETAIL FIG. 11)
Rembrandt,
The Laughing Man,
1629–1630, oil on
copper, Mauritshuis,
The Hague, 598

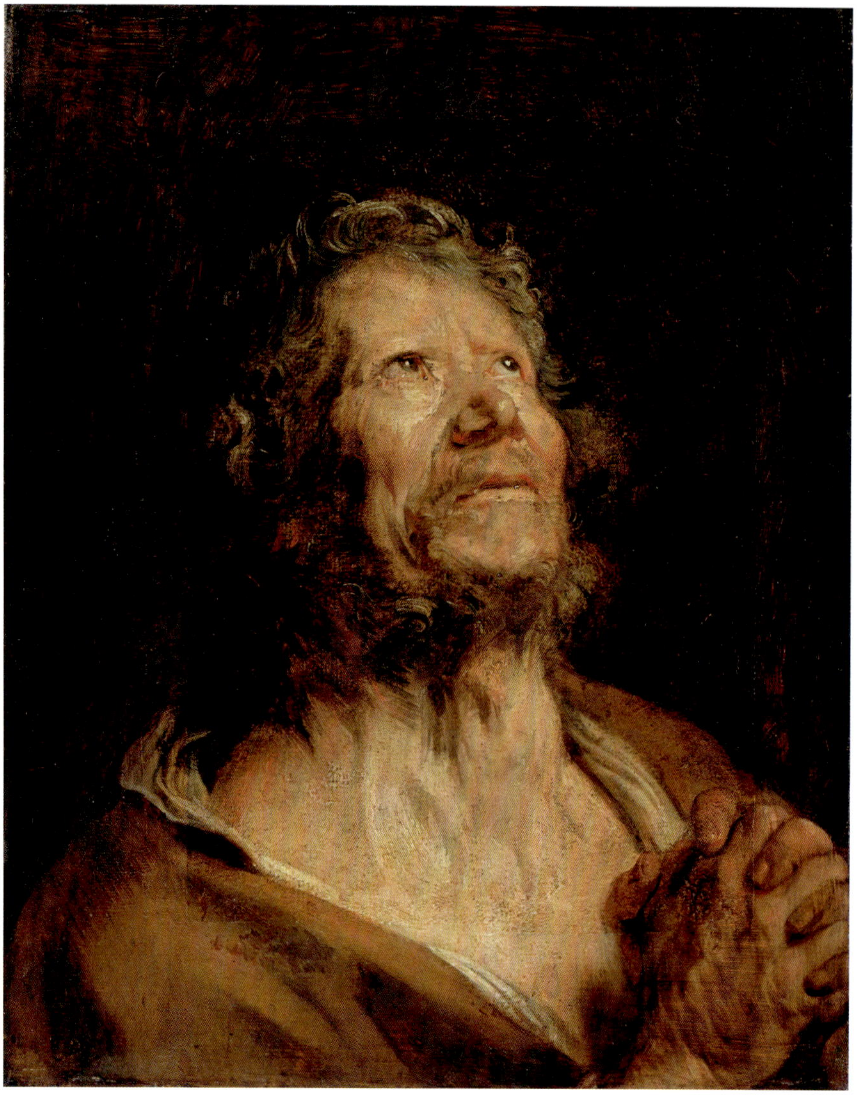

A Recent Problem

Before diving into the troubled definition of tronies it should be noted that this matter is a relatively recent phenomenon. From the late Middle Ages until the nineteenth century the word simply meant 'face' in Dutch.[2] The term also had a broad and uncomplicated meaning in early modern sources on art, including correspondence, court cases, or inventories of art collections. In these contexts, 'tronie' referred to any sculpted, printed, but most often painted depiction of the human face. These included heads of peasants, fools and soldiers, as well as apostles, emperors or figures from classical mythology. They could be preparatory studies intended for use inside the workshop, as well as proper art works which would be displayed in picture galleries. There was no specific definition of the genre in contemporary art theory, which in itself is significant. Though they were popular and at times figured in esteemed collections, tronies were not considered the most ambitious form of painting.[3]

In the twentieth century, this broad definition posed a problem for art historians. Some painted faces had a function or meaning which was clearly different from others. This prompted scholars to devise a workable version of the concept. In this process, tronies were juxtaposed with other painted faces – specifically portraits, head studies, and single-figure history paintings and genre paintings – aiming to articulate each category precisely.[4] Since the artists who painted these faces did not follow theorised formulae, however, some of these distinctions would have made little sense to them. Whereas the early modern notion of a tronie was extremely inclusive, we may now have swung too far the other way.

The Many Faces of Abraham Grapheus

As noted above, we do not believe that it is productive to aim to decide definitively on the border between tronies and their alleged opposites. Instead, we shall pursue a more nuanced analysis of their relationship. For this purpose, we refer to a range of depictions of one sitter, Abraham Grapheus. Grapheus was the messenger of the Antwerp Guild of Saint Luke and, in this capacity, a well-known figure in the city's art world. He also regularly modelled for painters in different types of pictures. In the paragraphs which follow, different genres of images of Grapheus's face are juxtaposed with what is here considered a tronie of him by Anthony van Dyck (Fig. 1).[5] We start with simple distinctions before moving on to more complex issues of categorisation.

FIG. 1
Anthony Van Dyck, with additions by Jacques Jordaens the Elder, *An Apostle with Folded Hands*, c. 1618–20, oil on paper laid on panel, Gemäldegalerie, Berlin, 790F

Tronies are Not Portraits[6]

Portraits are the most broadly known paintings of faces. They preserve the likeness of a specific individual. We find them in different media in cultures across time and space. In European Old Master paintings, portraits followed a range of conventions and codes with regard to pose, costume and attributes. These aspects all contributed to fashioning the subject's identity for posterity. The portrait of Abraham Grapheus by Cornelis de Vos shows these dynamics at play (Fig. 9). The work was painted for the chambers of the Antwerp Guild of Saint Luke, where artists gathered and held their banquets. Grapheus is wearing a fine ruff and proudly boasts the Guild's silver on his chest. His pose, the outward gaze, and one hand holding one of the Guild's golden cups, were carefully crafted to convey an air of spontaneity. The image displays Grapheus as a dignified member of the Guild.

Portraits were generally painted from a live model, the artist copying the sitter's face from nature. The same is true for tronies. Whereas portraits were typically painted on commission from the sitter, tronies were made at the artist's own initiative and for the open market. More importantly, the resulting image had a different meaning. Let us take the tronie of Grapheus (Fig. 1) by Van Dyck as a comparison. Van Dyck in this image abandons the conventions of Old Master portraiture entirely. Viewers consequently would not be concerned with the sitter's social identity, at least not in the first place. Rather, they may have marvelled at how the expression was rendered, and the response this provoked.[7] Contemporaries also appreciated tronies as the result of artistic skill, resulting in a life-like image sometimes executed in sketchy brushwork, in turn seen as a display of artistic virtuosity.[8] Lastly, some faces may have served as examples through the connotations they held, such as wisdom or piety.[9]

Portraits are about the 'who', while tronies are about the 'what'.[10] Both genres historically held a different significance and show clear visual differences. Making the distinction poses no problems in the majority of cases, although exceptions exist.[11]

Tronies are Not Head Studies

Another prevalent type of face painted from life is a head study. Such studies, mostly painted in oils and sketchy brushwork, were made in preparation for larger compositions. The faces were thus inserted into narrative scenes, generally derived from biblical and classical texts. Additionally, head studies were an important didactical tool in large workshops. Students copied them often over the course of their apprenticeship.

The difference between a head study and a tronie lies in function. Artists made tronies to sell them, after which they would make their way to a collector's gallery. A head study, by contrast, served its ends inside the workshop. In some cases, the difference between a tronie and a head study is clear immediately. *Two Head Studies of Abraham Grapheus* (Fig. 10), for example, due to its composition and extremely rough brushwork, is obviously not a standalone work. With others, such as *Head Study of Abraham Grapheus*, in Douai (Fig. 51), the difference is less apparent. The latter head shows the same vivid manner regularly found in tronies painted for the market, such as our example by Van Dyck. We can be confident, however, that the Douai panel functioned as a head study, since we know several paintings for which it was the prototype.[12]

The resemblance between tronies and head studies brings us to a problem of interpretation. While these works had different purposes for the artists who made them, we cannot always tell them apart. Complicating matters further, one and the same object could also have held both functions. This is in fact believed to have been the case with our Grapheus tronie. The central part of this picture was once a preparatory head study, kept inside the workshop as a model. In a later stage, the support was expanded and the clasped hands were added, so that the study could be sold as an autonomous art work.[13]

Tronies are Not History Paintings

The large compositions in which artists inserted head studies are known as history paintings. History painting was the highest-value good for an early modern artist. Depicting different people convincingly in a pictorial space demanded true artistry, a command of both perspective and anatomy. There also exist what have been labelled 'single-figured history paintings'.[14] Rather than showing multiple figures, these pictures concentrate on one specific character from a story. Sometimes such a figure is shown in a spatial setting, such as the prophet in his cave in Rembrandt's *Jeremiah Lamenting the Destruction of Jerusalem* (Fig. 102). In other instances the context was omitted, resulting in a half-length or bust depiction against a monochrome background. These figures can be linked to their story by way of costume or attributes. There are several examples of single-figured history paintings featuring Grapheus as a model.[15] In *The Apostle Peter* (Fig. 3), for example, the keys and yellow and blue cloak give away that he represents Christ's prime apostle. With *The Apostle Andrew* (Fig. 2) the X-shaped cross allows us to identify the depicted disciple.

It should also be noted, however, that apart from the significant attributes or costume elements, tronies and single-figure history paintings resemble one another closely. As was the case with head studies, there emerges an issue of interpretation due to the similarity between both types of picture. Meaningful costumes or attributes are all we have to go on to make the distinction in some cases. If we do not recognise the significance of these elements, therefore, we fail to see the artist's intent.

A man holding keys dressed in blue and yellow unmistakably represents Peter, although the situation is more ambiguous in other works.[16] Incidentally, Van Dyck's Grapheus tronie has been considered a biblical figure by some authors. Like other Antwerp paintings with a figure praying or reading against a dark background, the work has at times been labelled 'an apostle'. This identification would disqualify the painting as a tronie. Due to the absence of attributes, however, we contend that Grapheus in this picture did not represent an apostle for Van Dyck. In this sense it differs, in our view, from single-figure history paintings such as the *Peter* and *Andrew*. It is still worth remembering that Van Dyck himself would have referred to all three works as 'tronies'.

A Concluding Complication: Tronies and Genre Paintings

The relationship between tronies and other categories of picture was relatively straightforward up to this point, although several possible problems around interpretation have been noted. The boundary between tronies and genre paintings discussed in the following paragraphs is more ambiguous. As we shall see, 'genre painting' is like 'tronie', an anachronistic art historical concept. It should therefore be kept in mind that neither category is set in stone.[17]

Whereas history paintings imagined great deeds by prominent people, another category of works depicted the everyday lives of common and anonymous folk. These include pictures of fairs or taverns, peasants or fishermen. They were mostly painted on a small scale, while history paintings were large. Different types of paintings from everyday life were first developed in sixteenth-century Antwerp.[18] These were, however, only considered as a group and

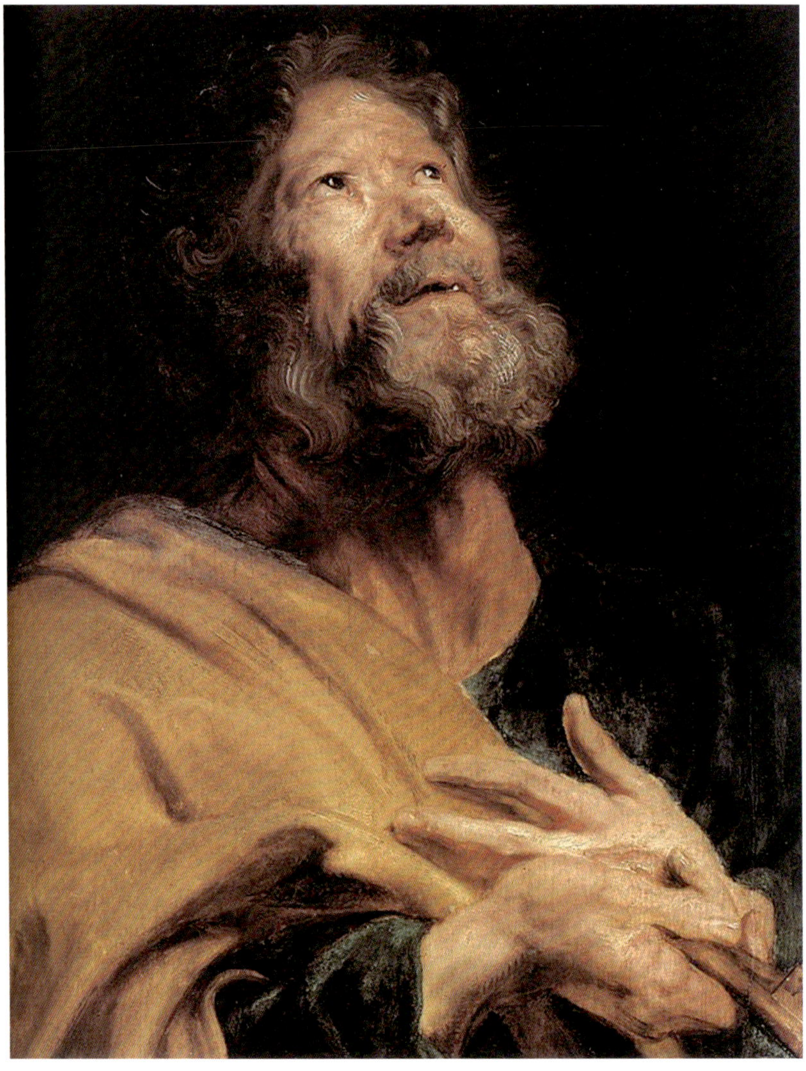

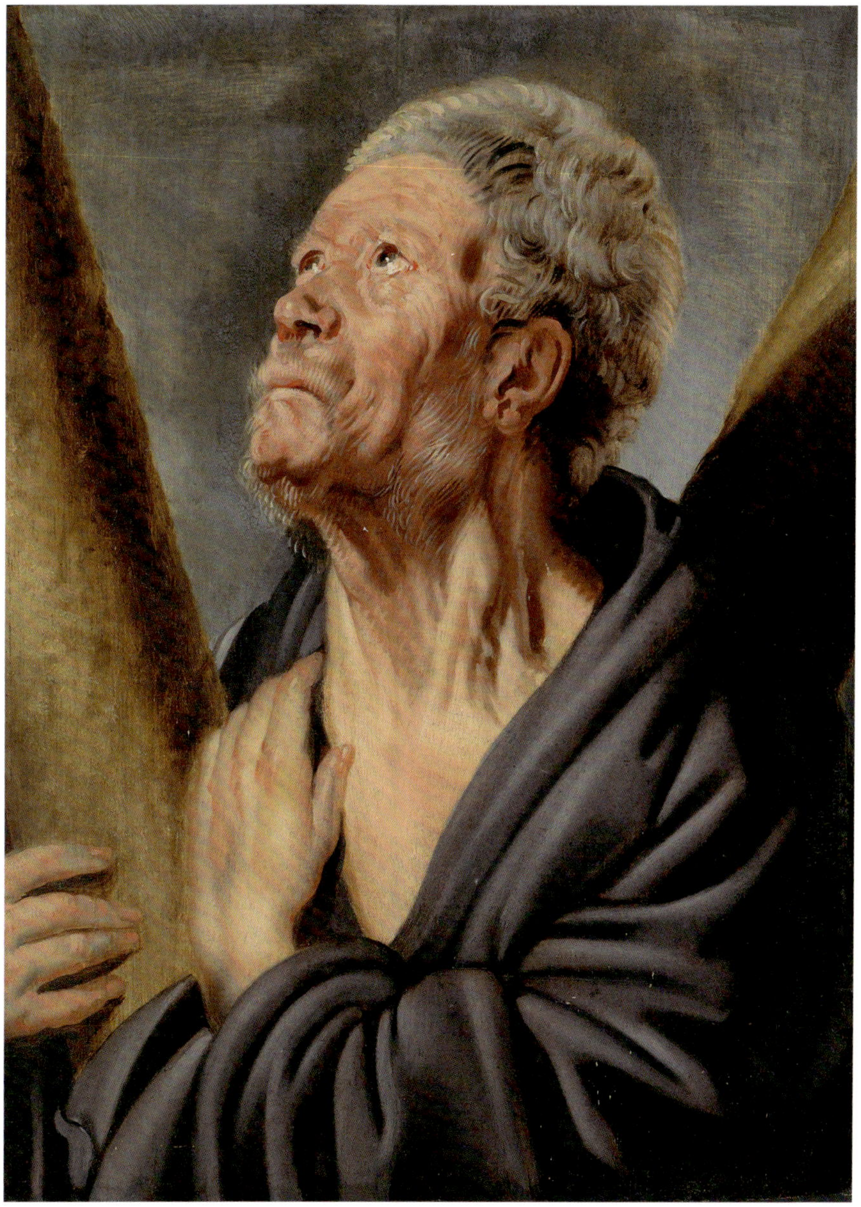

labelled 'genre paintings' in the seventeenth century.[19] Genre painting was then ranked lower than history painting as it was believed to be less challenging artistically and to have less moral value. Though the hierarchy of genres has long been abandoned, genre painting has remained the commonplace term for scenes of everyday life.

As with history paintings, one variant of genre paintings has been described as 'single-figured genre works'. This in turn has different subtypes. Some show the figures in context, like the *Fisher Boy* by Frans Hals (Fig. 4). He is shown at half-length, carrying a fishing net on his shoulder, standing in the dunes which give way to the sea in the distance. In others, we encounter only the figure's head against a monochrome background, the earliest examples of which were produced in Bruegel's circle in the sixteenth century. His *Head of a Peasant Woman* (Fig. 13) is a good example. The picture has the compositional focus on the face which is the hallmark of tronies. Nonetheless, scholars differ on the status of such works: some describe them as tronies, while others insist they must be genre paintings.[20]

The key arguments of the second camp, as in our comparison between tronies and history paintings, concerns the identity of the depicted figures. Tronies and genre paintings are related in their association with anonymous people rather than with famous heroes or rulers. The people they display have no names. A perceived difference between both is that tronies depict real people, while genre paintings show stereotypes of social groups.[21] We take issue with this distinction, however. Compare, for example, Bruegel's *Head of a Peasant Woman* to the *Head of a Woman* (Fig. 14) by Michael Sweerts, a picture universally accepted as a tronie.

FIG. 2
Attributed to Jacques Jordaens, *The Apostle Andrew*, (1616–1622), oil on panel, private collection. Auction Vienna, Dorotheum, 29.04.2014, lot 535

FIG. 3
Anthony Van Dyck, *The Apostle Peter*, (1613–1621), oil on panel, Hermitage, St Petersburg, ??-556

One could argue that they both reference social groups thanks to their headgear. The same can be said about both the *Head of a 'Landsknecht'* by Pieter Brueghel the Younger (Fig. 5) and a quintessential Rembrandt-style tronie such as *Tronie of a Young Man of African Origin Wearing a Yellow Feathered Beret* (Fig. 74). The depiction of stereotypes is not a fundamental marker for distinguishing tronies from genre paintings.

Apart from the subject (a real person versus a stereotype), stylistic differences have been advanced to disqualify works in the Bruegel tradition as tronies. The above-mentioned pictures by Sweerts and Rembrandt indeed look different from those by Bruegel and his son. The former have often been described as naturalistic, while the latter can be said to border on caricature. Some believe the reason for this is that Sweerts and Rembrandt worked from the live model, while the Bruegels, and other artists in their slipstream, followed artistic conventions and formulae.[22] Whether this was indeed the case or not can never be verified, although it should be noted that some authors do not agree, maintaining that the Bruegel heads were also painted from life.[23] More importantly, the naturalistic mode of the seventeenth-century works should not, in our view, be considered a defining characteristic of the tronie format. Rather, it reflects the stylistic fashions of the time. In other words, we believe that seventeenth-century naturalism was the language into which Bruegel's sixteenth-century idea was translated.

This temporal issue is important. Authors who reject Bruegel's work as a tronie do so on the grounds of perceived differences with seventeenth-century examples. If we accept that tronies originated at an earlier point, the category would include the Bruegel-like works. Our juxtaposition of genres (tronies versus genre paintings), has thus brought us to the question of when tronies originated. The origins of tronies are therefore further investigated in the next part.

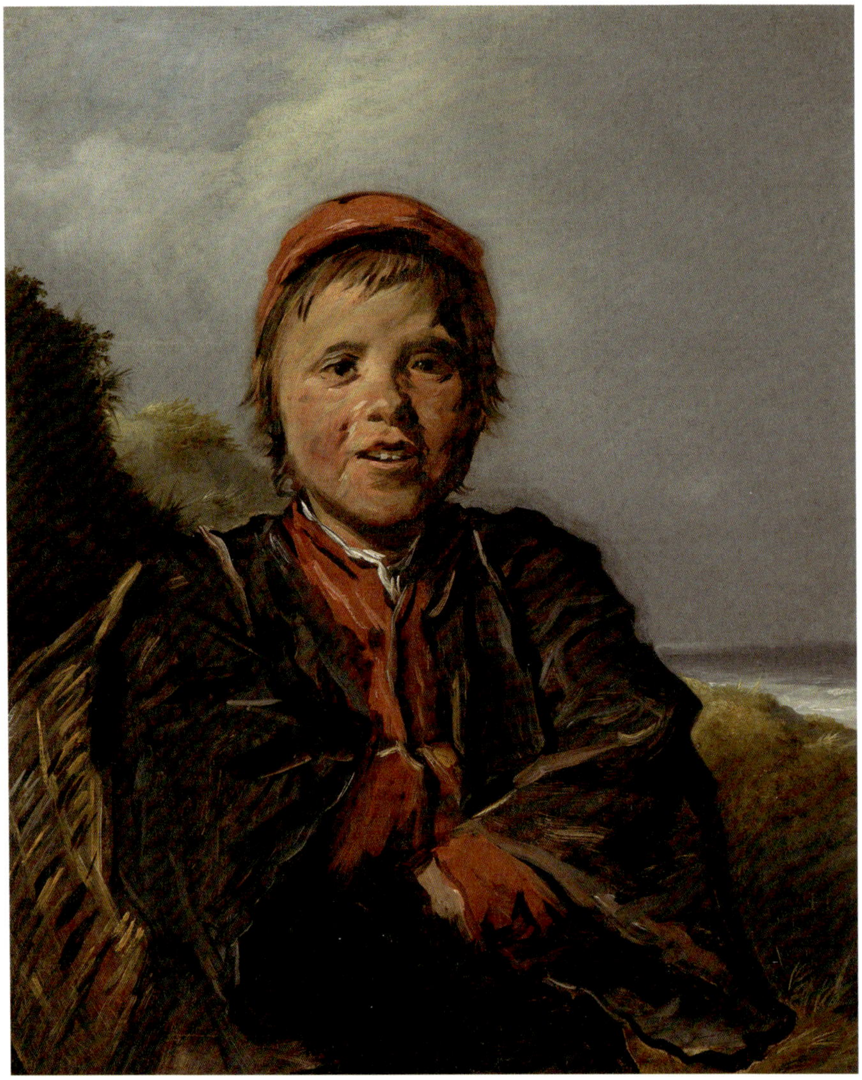

FIG. 4
Frans Hals,
Fisher Boy, s.d.,
oil on canvas, KMSKA,
Antwerp, inv. 188

FIG. 5
Pieter Brueghel
the Younger,
Head of a 'Lands-knecht', s.d.,
oil on panel,
private collection

Origins

The authoritative view on the origin of tronies is that they evolved out of head studies in the early seventeenth century.[24] Artists such as Rubens then painted heads from life as a workshop aid, and these studies allegedly inspired Dutch artists, such as Rembrandt, to paint faces which they could sell on the market. This position is elaborated below, where we contend that head studies were indeed an important element in the development of the tronie. In the following section, however, we add two important qualifications to this hypothesis. Firstly, the earliest instances of tronies were, in our view, painted in the sixteenth century, meaning that the Dutch works constitute a second, albeit more substantial, wave in the genre. Secondly, we highlight several more important preconditions for tronies to emerge, moving beyond the formal inspiration by head studies. The result is an enriched view of the early history of the genre.

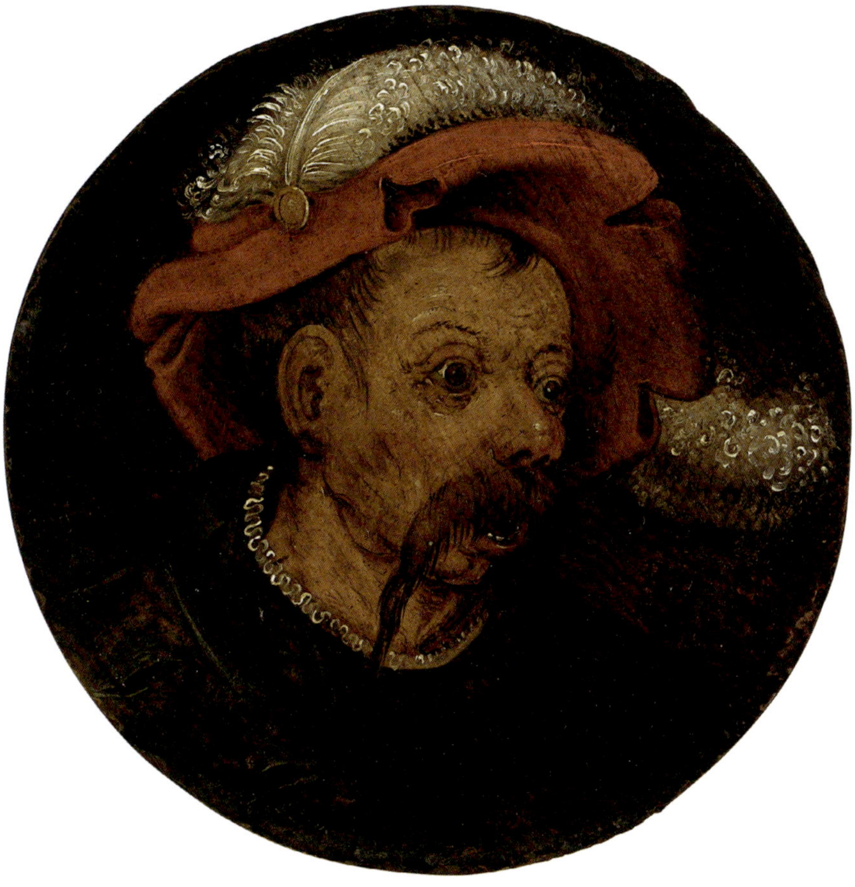

The Influence of Study Heads in the Early Seventeenth Century

The production of autonomous tronies in the United Provinces was significantly stimulated by Frans Hals, Jan Lievens and Rembrandt in the period immediately following the end of the Twelve Years' Truce (1609–1621). In the course of those economically flourishing years, Rubens, Jordaens and their assistants in Antwerp created hundreds of large-scale history paintings, for which they drew heavily on head studies. The latter were essential to the functioning of the studio and so were kept with the artist.

The border between the Northern and Southern Netherlands was reopened during the truce, and not only merchants but also artists made use of their restored freedom of movement. Rubens, for instance, visited the United Provinces in the summer of 1612,[25] accompanied by other Antwerp artists, including Jan Brueghel the Elder and Hendrick van Balen.[26] One reason for his trip might have been to seek out a high-quality engraver or engravers capable of turning his compositions into prints. First and foremost, however, it was Rubens's admiration for Hendrick Goltzius – the engraver who had so brilliantly translated the mythological and Italian formal language into print – that encouraged him to make the journey north.[27] Goltzius's business model must also have appealed to Rubens: the Haarlem artist kept tight control of the concept, design and publication of his prints, hiring engravers to transpose his own compositions onto the copper plate under his supervision. As a painter, meanwhile, Goltzius seems to have been swiftly impressed by Rubens's talent.[28] The Flemish master had already secured his reputation internationally by that time and is sure to have exerted a considerable attraction on young Dutch artists. Rubens acquired several assistants during his trip to the Dutch Republic: the painters Pieter Soutman (1593/1601–1657) from Haarlem[29] and Arnout Vinckenborch (1590–1620) from Alkmaar,[30] the engravers Lucas Vorsterman the Elder (1595/6–1674/5) from Zaltbommel, and Boëtius Adamsz. Bolswert (1570/90–1633) and Schelte Adamsz. Bolswert (1586–1659) from Bolsward.

We know that Frans Hals was present in Antwerp in October and November 1616,[31] and it is hard to imagine that during this extended stay in the city of his birth he did not pay a visit to the most important living artist in the Low Countries. A large number of vividly painted study heads were circulating in Rubens's studio at the time. It is likewise entirely plausible that Hals was impressed during his stay by the bold and expressive brushwork of Jacques Jordaens. In, or shortly after 1616, the Leiden painter and printmaker Jacques de Gheyn III (1596–1641) made drawings of two head studies by Rubens,[32] and he too is likely to have closely examined the oil studies in the Antwerp master's studio on the Wapper.

In 1618, Rubens was engaged in negotiations with Sir Dudley Carleton, the English ambassador to The Hague, concerning the exchange of a number of his paintings for sculptures in the envoy's collection. Rubens appointed the Haarlem painter and art dealer Frans Pietersz. de Grebber (1573–1649) to accompany the goods as they were transported between the cities. De Grebber's son Pieter (1595–1652), a pupil of Goltzius, was working in Antwerp in 1618.[33] Interestingly, the young artist quoted one of Rubens's head studies in his *Belshazzar's Feast*, now in Kassel,[34] and also in his *St Paul Reading*[35] (both c. 1625). There is also a suggestion in the art literature that Jan Lievens visited Antwerp in 1625.[36] It is not known whether Rembrandt ever travelled to the Flemish city.

When Rubens made the journey to the United Provinces for a second time (19 July–6 August 1627), he did not meet with diplomats, as had been his intention, but instead with artists. We know that he visited Honthorst in Utrecht and that the young Joachim von Sandrart accompanied him to see Abraham Bloemaert and Cornelis van Poelenburch, before Rubens continued on to Amsterdam and other Dutch cities.[37] It cannot be ruled out that Rubens could have met the young Rembrandt during that trip, which remains a tantalising hypothesis.

Sixteenth-Century Precedents: Their Preconditions and Afterlife

The tsunami of tronies on the Dutch art market in the seventeenth century is a captivating trend. A case could be made for viewing these works as a whole, as a distinct art-historical phenomenon which unfolded within a specific geographical context and network, marked by certain formal characteristics. In our view, however, they cannot be considered in complete isolation from experiments which took place in sixteenth-century Antwerp, such as the above-discussed heads by Bruegel. Apart from an overall resemblance to seventeenth-century counterparts, the sixteenth-century works were created, sold and displayed under similar circumstances. Moreover, they formed part of seventeenth-century visual culture.

Pushing the origins of tronies back to sixteenth-century Antwerp means that we cannot assume that the genre evolved naturally out of head studies.[38] While the latter were an important inspiration for the genre in Rembrandt's day, they were not the sole instigator. Pictorial genres, as has often been noted in histories of landscape painting, do not develop in a linear fashion from a single starting point.[39] We propose instead to view tronies as the result of the confluence of favourable market conditions, ongoing intellectual and artistic fascinations with physiognomy and expression which may, in conclusion, relate to a biological predisposition in humans for faces.

Sixteenth-century Antwerp had a booming art market, catering to a discriminating local as well as international clientele. Such a situation is conducive to innovation. Artists began to experiment, trying new formulae in the hope that they could bring them commercial success. Indeed, many new genres in painting saw the light of day in Antwerp around this time, including landscapes, still lifes, and market or tavern scenes.[40] They were gradually diversified by followers in the decades, sometimes centuries, which followed. The earliest tronies should be considered a part of this larger context. It is relevant that beneficial market dynamics also marked the Dutch Republic in the seventeenth century, when Rembrandt and his colleagues gave new life to the genre. Tronies were a particularly interesting format for experiment for artists. Due to their small scale, meagre compositional demands, and sometimes sketchy finish, they did not require substantial production time or costs in raw materials.[41] Moreover, tronies were a safe subject at a time when conflict over religious images plagued the Low Countries.[42] For collectors, on the other hand, the little works must have appealed as affordable samples of artistic mastery.[43]

Pictures like Bruegel's *Head of a Peasant Woman* (Fig. 13) rank among the earliest experiments in the genre. The work can be seen as the result of converging artistic traditions. Quinten Massys was an Antwerp artist who devoted great attention to the morphology and expressive powers of the human face. He often showed grotesque heads in his narrative tableaux, which were the result of significant effort. Massys's altarpiece for the Joiners' Guild (Fig. 17), for example, includes several heads created by Leonardo da Vinci, although it remains unclear how he obtained the prototypes.[44] Massys also showed remarkable faces individually and up close, in works such as the so-called *Ugly Duchess* and its pendant *An Old Man* (Fig. 16). The compositional scheme of these pictures

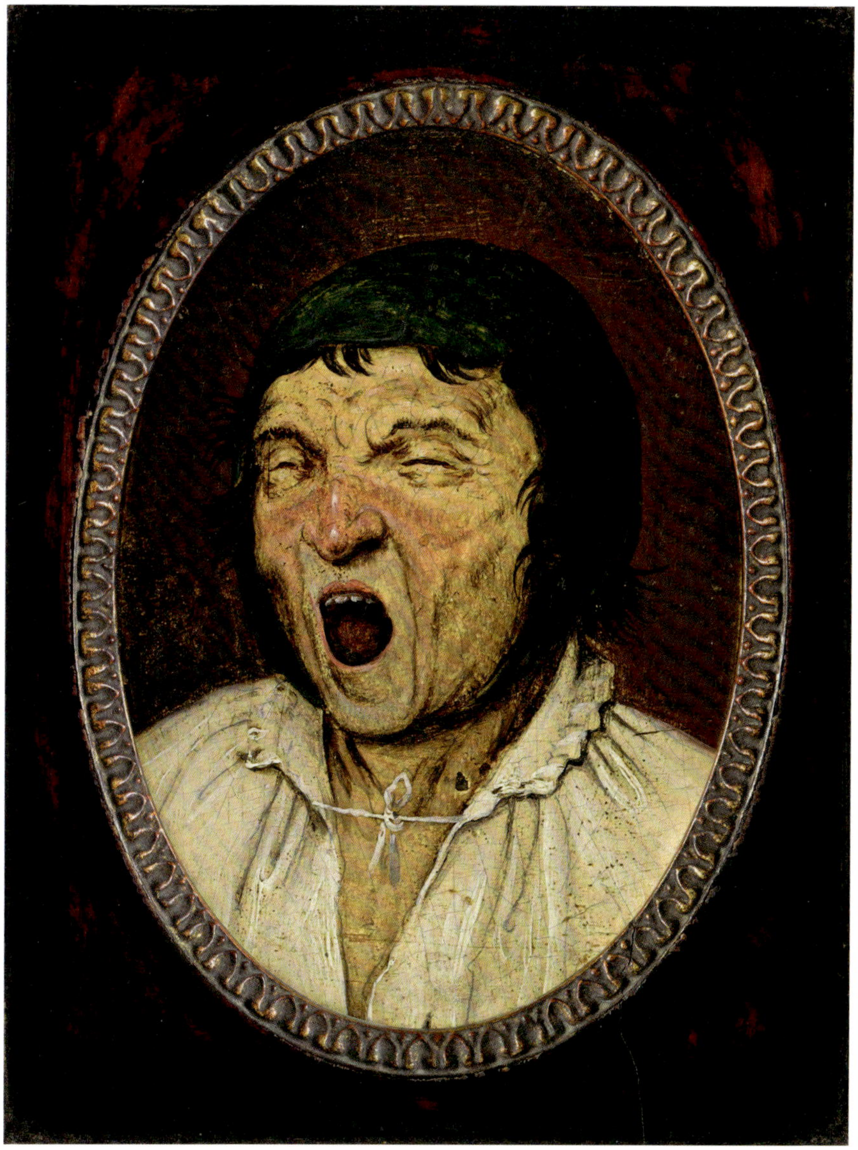

FIG. 6
After Pieter Bruegel the Elder, *The Yawner*, end of the sixteenth century, oil on panel, Royal Museums of Fine Arts, Brussels, inv. 6509

was inspired by the tradition of portraiture. Scholars have described them as parodies of this genre.[45] Apart from an artistic engagement with faces, the artistic interest in everyday life was an important precondition for the earliest tronies. Bruegel was a leading figure in this context. Many of his densely populated compositions showed peasants in full length, at work and at weddings. From there, it was but a small step to depict a single peasant's head up close. Around the same time, lastly, the Antwerp painter Frans Floris used preparatory study heads in his bustling workshop. He apparently sold several of these works to contemporaries, who displayed them in their collections.[46]

Importantly, the sixteenth-century tronies had not disappeared from view when the new wave of tronies arrived in the early seventeenth century. There was a true Massys revival in Antwerp at this time, leading to a renewed interest in the artist's work, the erection of a monument in his honour and a book-length biography.[47] The author of this text marvelled at the facial expressions in Massys's compositions.[48] Around the same time there were mentions of Pieter Bruegel tronies, some of whose paintings were housed in famous collections. Rubens, for example, owned twelve Bruegels, five of which were tronies, or heads of anonymous figures.[49] Moreover, Bruegel's eldest son, Pieter the Younger, continued to produce tronies from his father's designs. *The Yawner* (Fig. 6), of which Rubens apparently also owned a version, is an example of such a repetition. Lastly, Bruegel has been credited as the inventor of a series of 72 prints which showed pairs of heads of peasants, 'moors' and 'a wild man' (Fig. 9). They were first engraved around 1564/65 by Joannes van Doetecum the Elder (1530–1605) and Lucas van Doetecum (d. 1573/89), and remained popular during the seventeenth century as study material among artists in the Low Countries.[50] Such works must have been a reference for the artist producing tronies in the seventeenth century, as well as for the clients buying their work. This does not mean that the earlier pictures functioned as direct prototypes. It is noteworthy, still, that an earlier generation had already made the point that a painting of an individual unnamed face could be art too.

The rise of seventeenth-century tronies has been linked to an increase in attention to the face in contemporary art theory.[51] Authors such as Karel van Mander (1604) and Franciscus Junius (1637) indeed dwelled on its expressive powers at greater length than their predecessors. This perspective has been interpreted as fundamental for the appreciation of tronies as a new genre. Importantly, however, theoretical interest in faces was not foreign to the sixteenth century. Physiognomy – the pseudo-science of telling a person's character by way of their face – had been practised since Antiquity, and there was a steady stream of treatises on the method from the fifteenth century onwards. This culminated in the famous work by Giambattista della Porta (1585), eagerly studied by artists. We also find reflections of the Platonic assumption that beautiful faces reflected a just personality, and grotesque ones moral inferiority. The physiognomy of peasants, for example, in fifteenth-century literature, was discussed in negative terms and connected to their alleged bad and impulsive behaviour. These comments have been linked to the Bruegel tradition.[52] In several of his popular publications, Erasmus of Rotterdam, who was in the orbit of Massys, described the face as the mirror of the mind, an idea with precedent in classical texts.[53] Lastly, at around the turn of the sixteenth century, artists such as Leonardo da Vinci and Albrecht Dürer explored the morphology of the human face in both their work and writings.[54]

In other words, there was already a significant tradition of thinking about faces at the time Massys, Bruegel and Floris experimented with painting their heads. This context was not static. Ideas about character, emotions and their relation to the face evolved over the early modern period.[55] Some tronies may therefore

FIG. 7
Face-pareidolia
https://nl.pinterest.com/pin/291959988350599474/

FIG. 8
Johannes or Lucas van Doetecum (possibly), after Pieter Bruegel the Elder, *Susanna Smuls and Leuye Joost*, 1612–52, etching and engraving, Rijksmuseum, Amsterdam

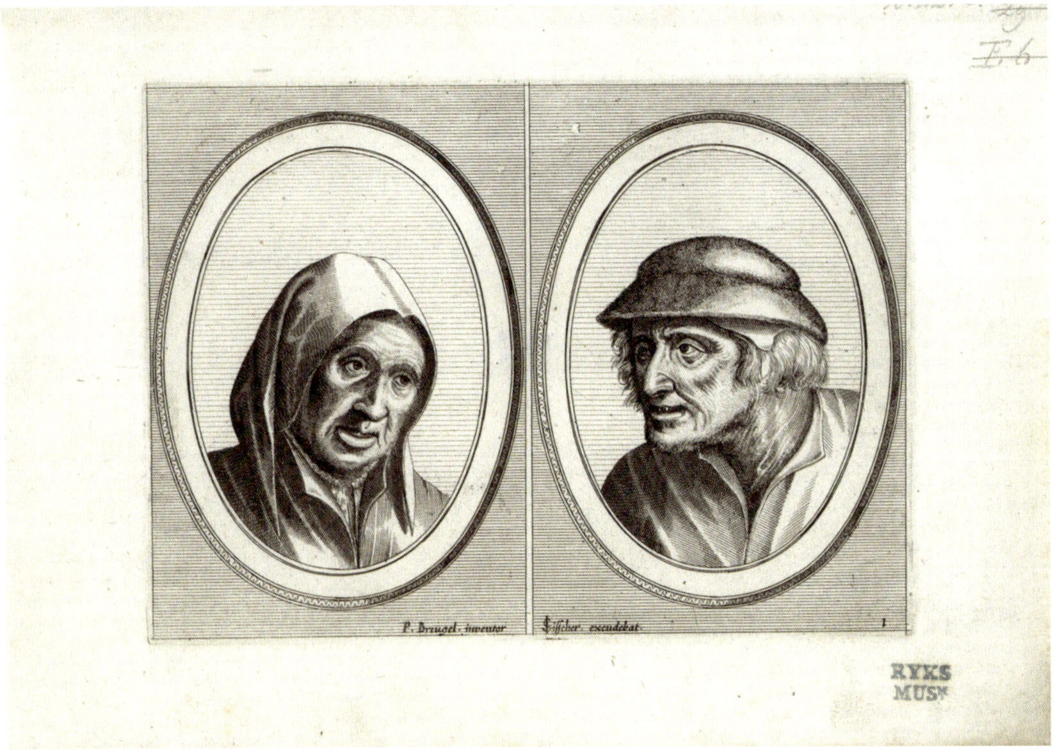

have provoked different associations at different points in time. It is nonetheless significant that the face remained the mediator of these changing views.

In conclusion, the centrality of the face was not an exclusive characteristic of early modern European painting and literature. Faces are prevalent in the visual and material record of cultures across time and space.[56] In this sense, tronies can be considered a symptom of a much wider phenomenon. Moreover, the manifold representations of heads – ranging from ritual masks to tronies and emojis – have a broad appeal. Perhaps a biological explanation may tentatively be advanced for this, dare we say, 'universal' fascination.

Contemporary research in neuroscience makes clear that a significant portion of our brain is devoted to 'reading' faces.[57] These mechanisms are thought to be rooted in our deepest instincts. As pack animals, evaluating whether we know a person and what their expression displays, could be essential for survival. This attention to faces in the real world has an effect in our reading of two-dimensional images of faces. A well-known experiment tracking eye movements has shown that viewers of a figurative composition, including humans, focus first on the heads and hands.[58] Apparently, these elements are subconsciously considered essential to deciphering what is going on. Lastly, 'pareidolia' is our tendency to recognise faces in everyday objects or images of them, such as a letter box (Fig. 7). Our brain, psychologists believe, structures such stimuli as a face because it is especially equipped for reading faces.[59]

Since some of these perceptual mechanisms appear to be present in primates, it is not unreasonable to assume that they were shared by early modern Europeans. The preprogrammed disposition for faces may also have been a factor in the emergence of tronies, as well as their enduring popularity.

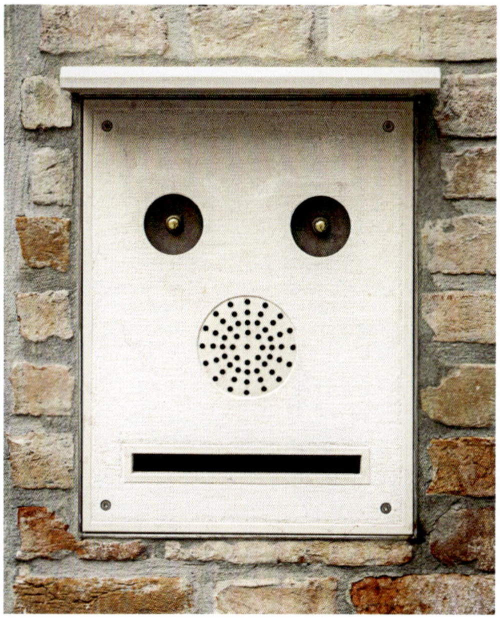

1 Two monographs have been devoted to tronies: Hirschfelder 2008 and Gottwald 2011. These books are very thorough, gathering key scholarship and sources, and listing many examples of tronies. They were therefore used as points of reference throughout this present contribution. An important difference in our position compared with these earlier authors, it should be noted, is that we insist on the blurred edges of tronies as a genre, whereas they aimed to define the category rigidly. The works of art cited in this introduction are also dis-cussed in the subsequent essays in this book. A reference to recent scholarly literature on them can be found in the endnotes to these essays.

2 'tronie' in S.n. 2007. For a brief etymology, Gottwald 2011, 11–13.

3 As explained in more detail below, history painting was considered the greatest possible challenge for an artist. This showed multiple figures in full length in a spatial setting, whereas tronies showed the face of a single figure.

4 The studies of Hirschfelder (2008) and Gottwald (2011) follow this approach of negative definition.

5 In Barnes *et al.* 2004, 45, no. I, 29, the work has been labelled 'an apostle with folded hands' and tentatively identified as 'a Penitent Peter (?)'.

6 This juxtaposition was a starting point for Hirschfelder 2008, esp. Chapter II.3

7 Hirschfelder 2008, Chapter V.

8 The emulation of sketched brushwork in tronies is a central point in Gottwald's (2011, esp. pp. 127 ff) analysis of the genre. See also Hirschfelder 2008, 340–43 and 347 ff on the 'painterly' (*schilderachtige*) aspects of the genre. It should be added that there are also tronies, such as Vermeer's, in which the vivid brushwork is not a prominent characteristic.

9 Suggested in Hirschfelder 2008, 310 ff.

10 Therefore, in Belting's (2017, 199–201) conception, tronies resemble masks (representing something) more than portraits (representing someone).

11 See e.g. the cases explored in Hirschfelder 2009, 49–59.

12 E.g. *Offering to Ceres* in the Museo Nacional del Prado (Fig. 52) and *The Tribute Money. Peter Finding the Silver Coin in the Mouth of the Fish* in the Statens Museum for Kunst, Copenhagen, both painted by Jordaens.

13 The brushwork of this second stage has been attributed to Jacques Jordaens in Von Bode 1906, 264–265.

14 As defined in De Vries 1989.

15 Importantly, these are 'history paintings' for which Grapheus modelled, and not 'historical portraits' (or '*portraits historiés*') of Grapheus. The latter are a type of portrait painting in which the sitter is dressed as a fictional character or historical figure. On this phenomenon, see the contributions in Manuth *et al.* 2016.

16 Cf. Hirschfelder 2008, 310. The author argues that tronies reference costumes from figures in history paintings, and that this reference may communicate the same values (e.g. wisdom) associated with those figures in their original context.

17 Problems of categorisation are evident in the studies by Hirschfelder and Gottwald. The former includes depictions of peasants (2008, 158–162, as an 'excursus') and shepherds (2008, 190–191) in her discussion of tronies, while acknowledging such works are also genre paintings. According to the latter (2011, 113), the 'first tronie', created by Rembrandt, was also a single-figured genre painting.

18 On this subject, see Silver 2006. Continuities in genre imagery between sixteenth-century Antwerp and the Dutch Republic of the seventeenth century, were further explored in De Clippel 2006.

19 For an introduction to the early history of the category, see Kleinert 2006, 23–26; Van der Coelen and Lammertse 2015, esp. 10–11.

20 It is notable that authors who focus mainly on sixteenth-century painting readily consider these works tronies. See e.g. Muylle 2001; Silver 2006, 199 ff. By contrast, Hirschfelder and Gottwald, whose work is chiefly concerned with the seventeenth century, dismiss them as examples of the genre. Their arguments are explored below. It is important to note that they also consider seventeenth-century Bruegel-like pictures, such as those by the artist's son Pieter the Younger, as genre works.

21 Hirschfelder 2008, 40, 60. Gottwald (2011, 78) links the Bruegel examples to the category of genre painting rather than tronies without motivation.

22 See especially Hirschfelder 2008, 40–42 ff.

23 E.g. Sellink 2012, 257. The author refers to a passage in Karel van Mander (1604, fol. 233v), in which it is stated that Bruegel travelled the countryside and mingled with peasants to observe their clothing and behaviour. Van Mander also writes that Bruegel 'made many faces from life' (*makende veel ghesichtkens nae t'leven*). However, it is important in the present context that Van Mander states explicitly that these were done 'in pen' (*met de Pen*), and not in oil on panel, like the Munich tronie.

24 This is the central argument of Gottwald 2011.

25 Van Gelder 1950–1951, 120; De Smet 1977, 199–200.

26 The visitors from Antwerp found themselves suddenly 'arrested' in a village near Haarlem by artists from this city in disguise. In the celebrations that followed, they drank a toast to 'friendship and favour' (*vriendschap ende foy*). The event was recorded in a poem by Balthazar Gerbier marking the death of Hendrick Goltzius in 1617. See Hymans 1882, 402; Hirschmann 1920, 118–119.

27 Other engravers from Goltzius's circle had previously made prints from Rubens, including Jacob Matham and Willem Buytewegh. Vermeylen and de Clippel 2012, 149.

28 Sluijter 1991, 396, no. 24.

29 Barrett 2012, 24–51.

30 Duverger 1973, 242–245.

31 Van Thiel-Stroman 1989–1990, 19; *Idem*. n.d.: 377, doc. 17 and 378, doc. 22.

32 Van Hout 2020, 171–173, nos. 57–58.

33 Van Thiel-Stroman 2006, 163–164 and 168.

34 Van Hout 2020, 81–86, no. 7.

35 Hemmer 2015, 205–206.

36 Schnackenburg 2001, 107.

37 Von Sandrart 1675, 291, Chapter XVI.

38 Head studies were used in some sixteenth-century Antwerp workshops: that of Frans Floris, discussed in Nico Van Hout's contribution to this book, is a well-known example. However, these early head studies are, in our view, not the only instigator of the early tronies.

39 For example, Büttner 2006 emphasises a broad range of visual precedents and shifting ideas which exercised a joint influence on the emergence and development of landscape painting. Vermeylen 2001, by contrast, takes an economic stance, highlighting that the increased demand on the art market of sixteenth-century Antwerp triggered innovations. A helpful biological metaphor for the emergence and survival of new genres is introduced in Silver 2006, introduction.

40 This context is explored in detail by Silver 2006.

41 Tronies were considered an especially fruitful format for experiment in a recent study on Vermeer: Libby *et al.* 2022.

42 Emphasised in Gottwald 2011, 132.

43 This is argued for seventeenth-century examples in Hirschfelder 2008, 239.

44 See the contribution by Michael Kwakkelstein in this book.

45 Capron 2023. In a discussion of Massys as a painter of faces, his *Bagpiper* (Yale University Art Gallery, inv. 2020.37.5, Silver 1984, 219–220, no. 30 'a drunkard') and *Head of an Old Man* (Museu Nacional d'Art de Catalunya, inv. 064998-000, Silver 1984, 221, no. 33) also deserve mention. Both are cropped to a format resembling that of a tronie. Silver posits that the latter may be a fragment, though a technical study which could positively confirm or deny this remains lacking.

46 Wouk 2018: chapter 6, esp. 237-39.

47 See Pousão-Smith 2001.

48 Van Fornenbergh 1658, 16–18. The sixteenth- and seventeenth-century literary appreciation of facial expression in the oeuvres of Massys and Bruegel has been studied by Jan Muylle (2001, 174 ff; 2002; 2011).

49 De Clippel 2004, 315: 'two little faces on a round panel, by Bruegel the Elder' (*deux petits visages en rondeaux, du vieux Breugel*), 'a yawner, by Bruegel the Elder' (*Vn baailleur, du vieux Breugel*) and 'the face of a beggar, by the said Bruegel [the Elder]' (*Vn visage d'vn geux, en rond, du dict Breugel*).

50 The popularity of the series, of which several editions appeared, is stressed in Muylle 2001, 174–204, esp. 194; De Clippel 2004, 332, note 55.

51 An overview of these valuable connections can be found in Hirschfelder 2008, 321–349; Gottwald 2011, 19–26.

52 Vandenbroeck 1984, 106–108; Muylle 2002, 115 ff.

53 Erasmus' observations on physiognomy have been connected to Massys's oeuvre in Schütt 2021, 18–22.

54 On Leonardo, see the contribution by Michael Kwakkelstein in this volume. Panofsky 1955, 265–273 remains a key introduction to Dürer as an anatomist and physiognomist.

58 Bos (2010), for example, argues that seventeenth-century theories on emotions (e.g. Descartes) influenced thoughts about the morphology of the face.

59 An excellent study on the plurality of faces in visual and material culture, as well as intellectual traditions on them, is Belting 2017.

57 An accessible introduction to this topic with references to key research is Bruce and Young 2012, 37–44. The authors are presently completing a new edition of this volume. See also Little *et al.* 2011, the introduction to a thematic issue on 'Face perception: social, neuropsychological and comparative perspectives'.

58 Yarbus 1967, 191. Faces attracted attention during a free examination of the picture, but the author's core argument is that viewers directed their gazes elsewhere when given specific cues.

59 Recent studies have observed that the brain regions activated in face-pareidolia are the same that are active in the perception of real faces, Akdeniz, Toker and Atli 2018; Palmer and Clifford 2020. This implies that face-pareidolia has evolved from an attention to real-world faces.

FIG. 9
Cornelis de Vos,
Portrait of Abraham Grapheus, 1620,
oil on panel, KMSKA,
Antwerp, inv. 104

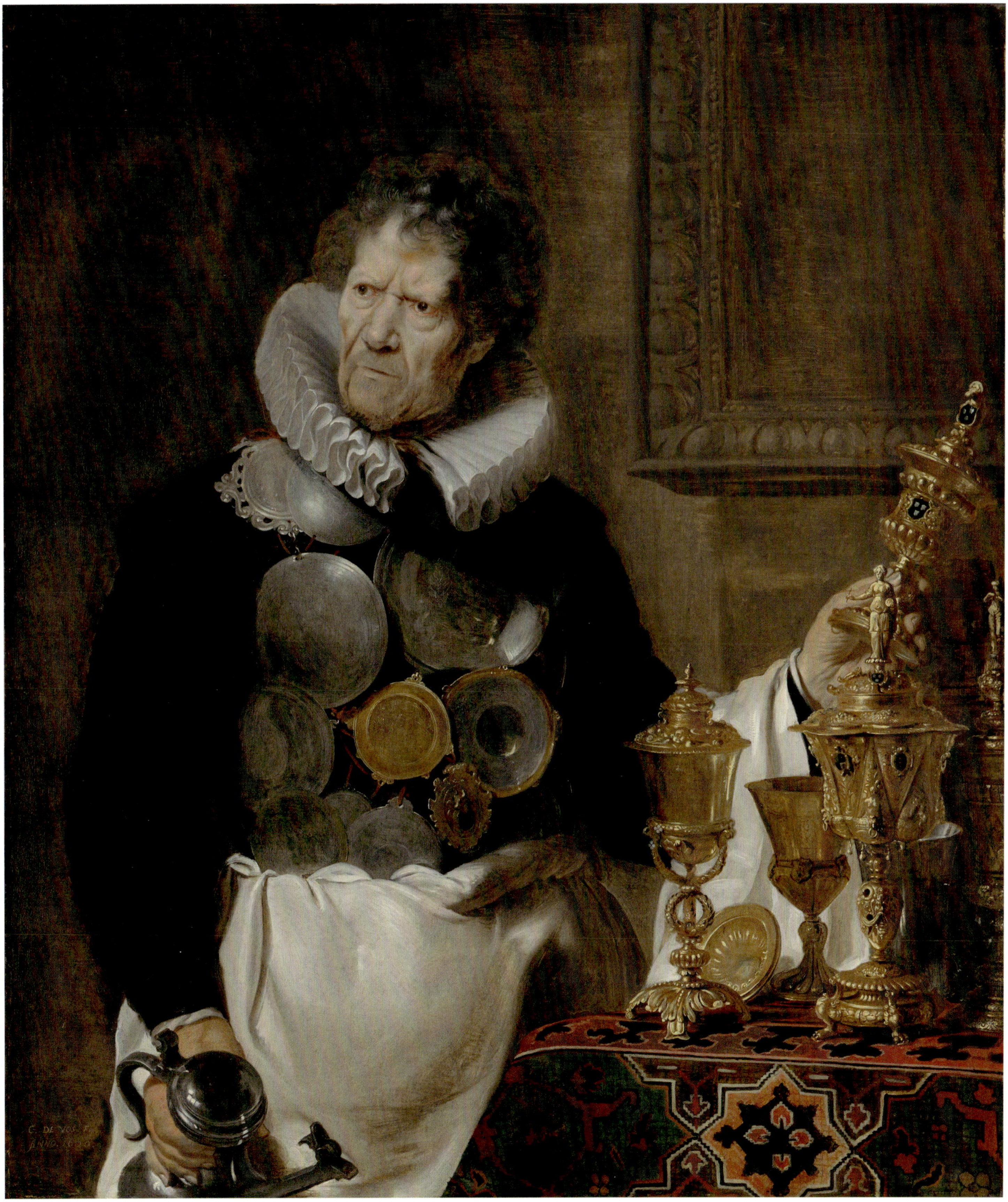

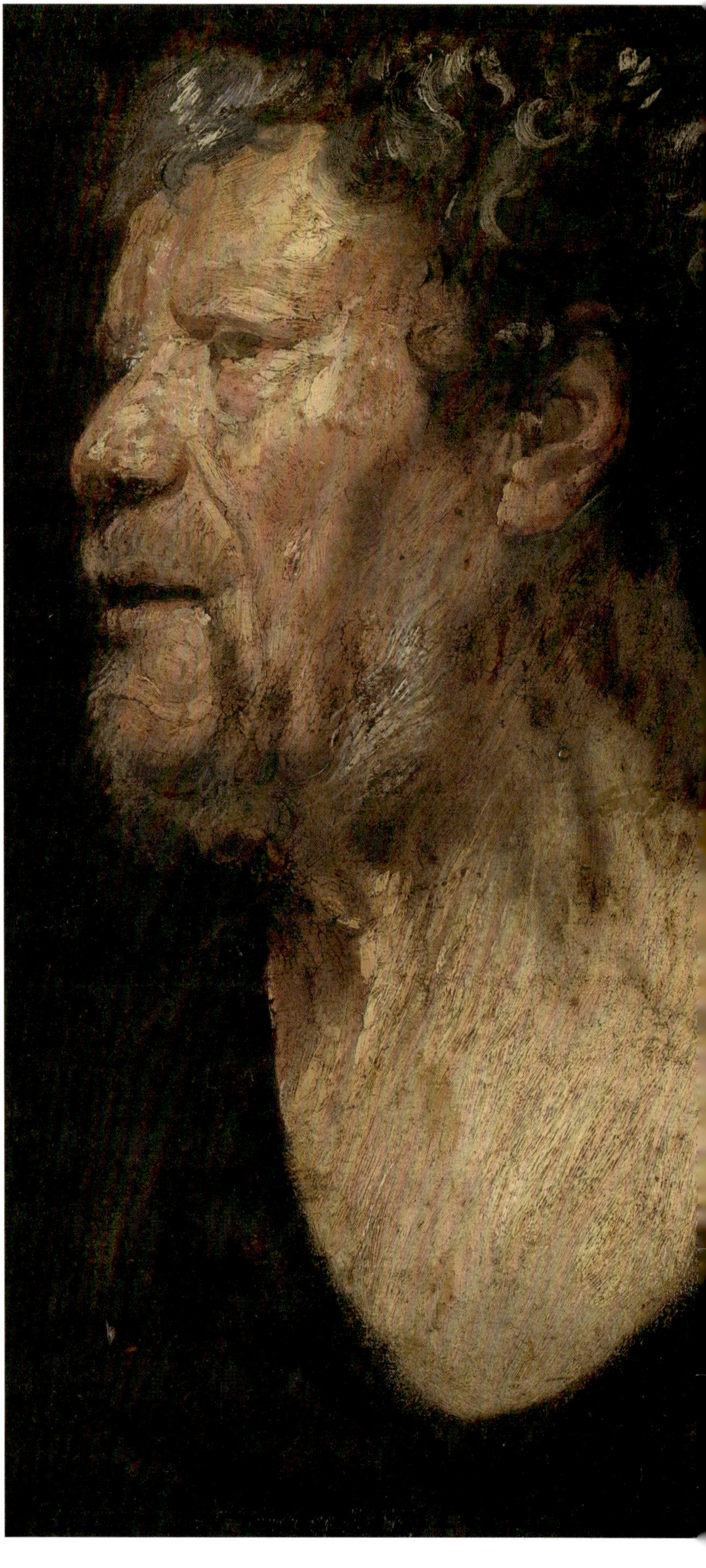

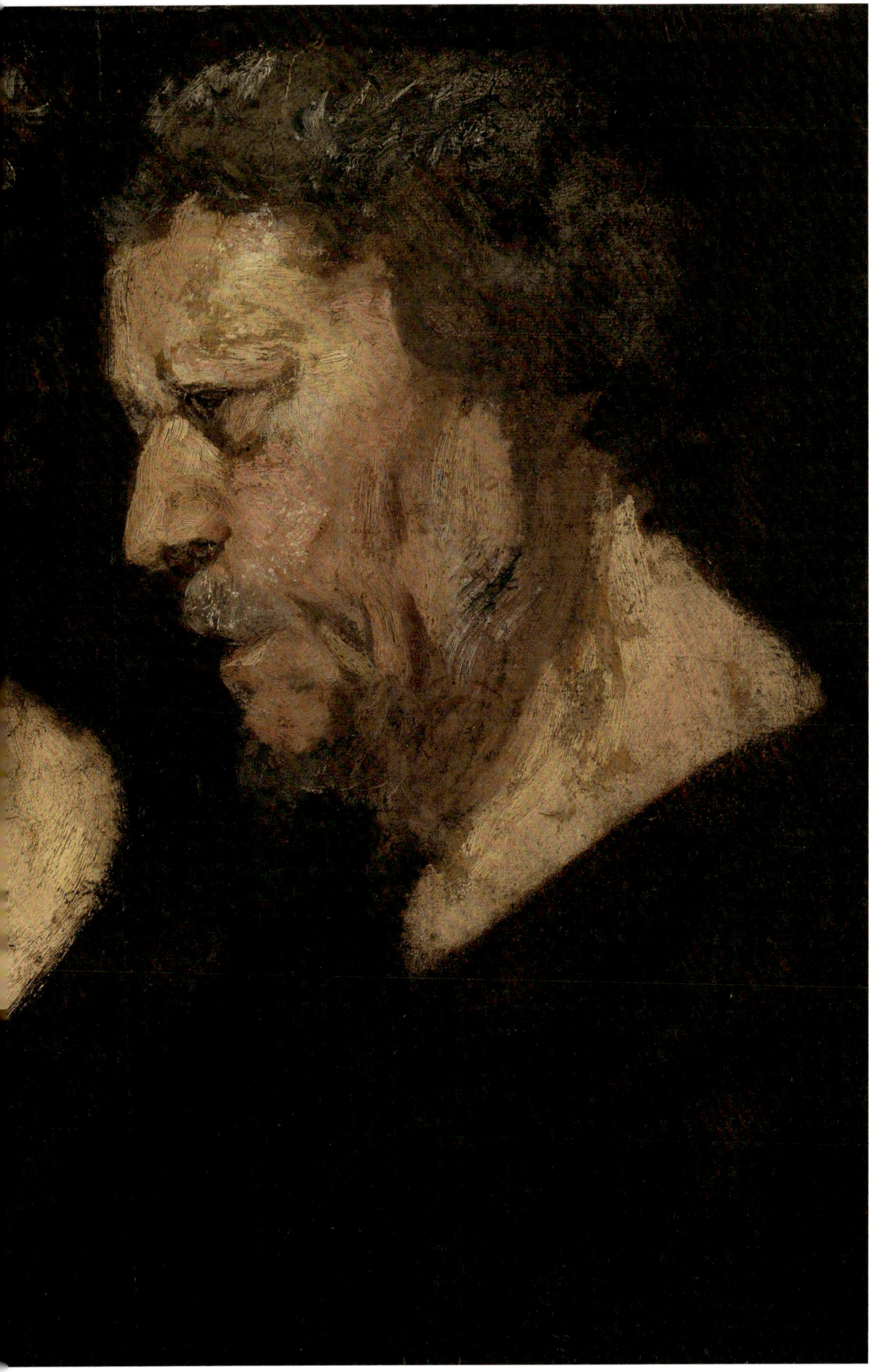

FIG. 10
Jacques Jordaens the Elder, *Two Head Studies of Abraham Grapheus*, c. 1620–21, oil on paper, glued on panel, Museum voor Schone Kunsten, Ghent, 1899-B

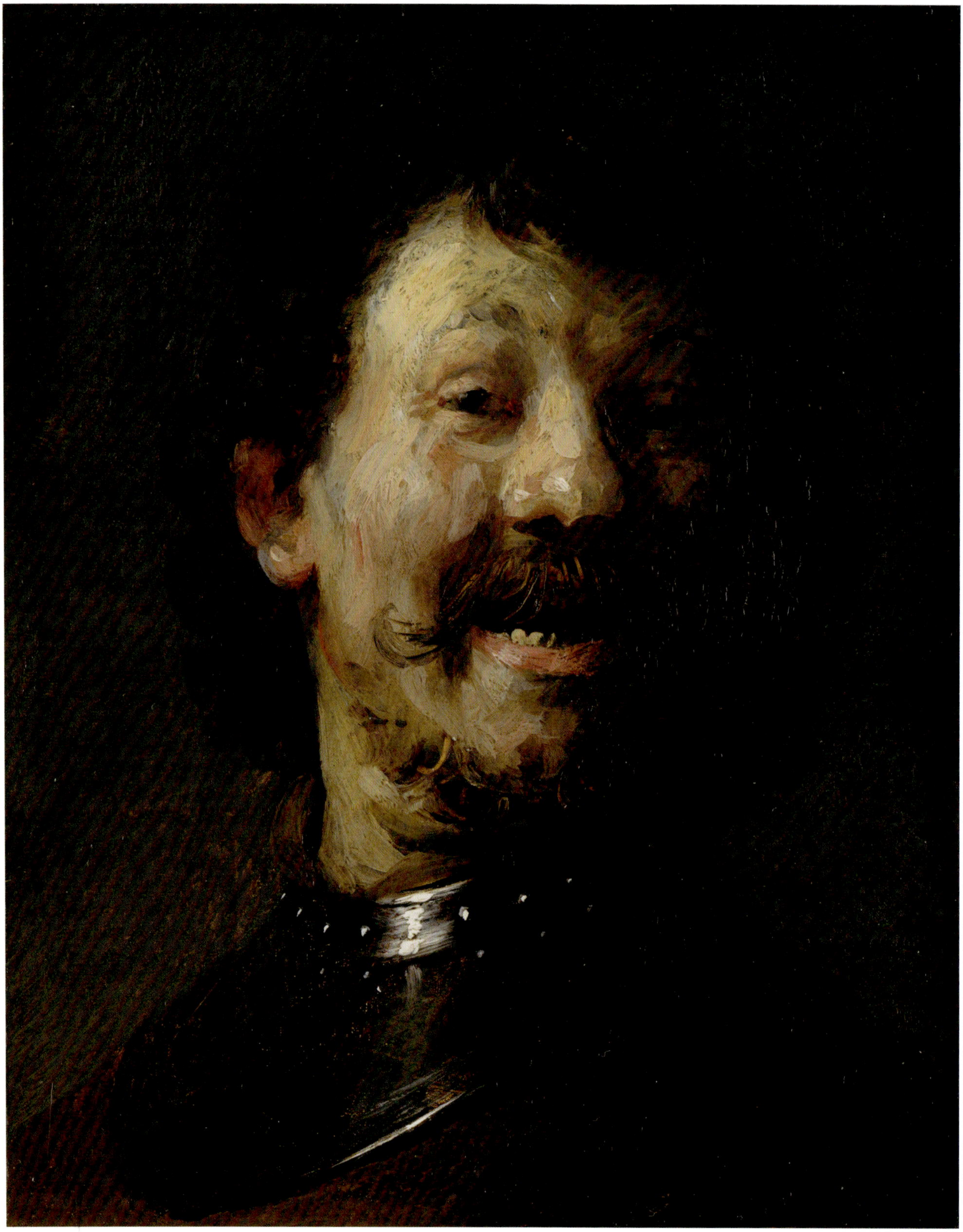

FIG. 11
Rembrandt,
The Laughing Man,
1629–1630, oil on
copper, Mauritshuis,
The Hague, 598

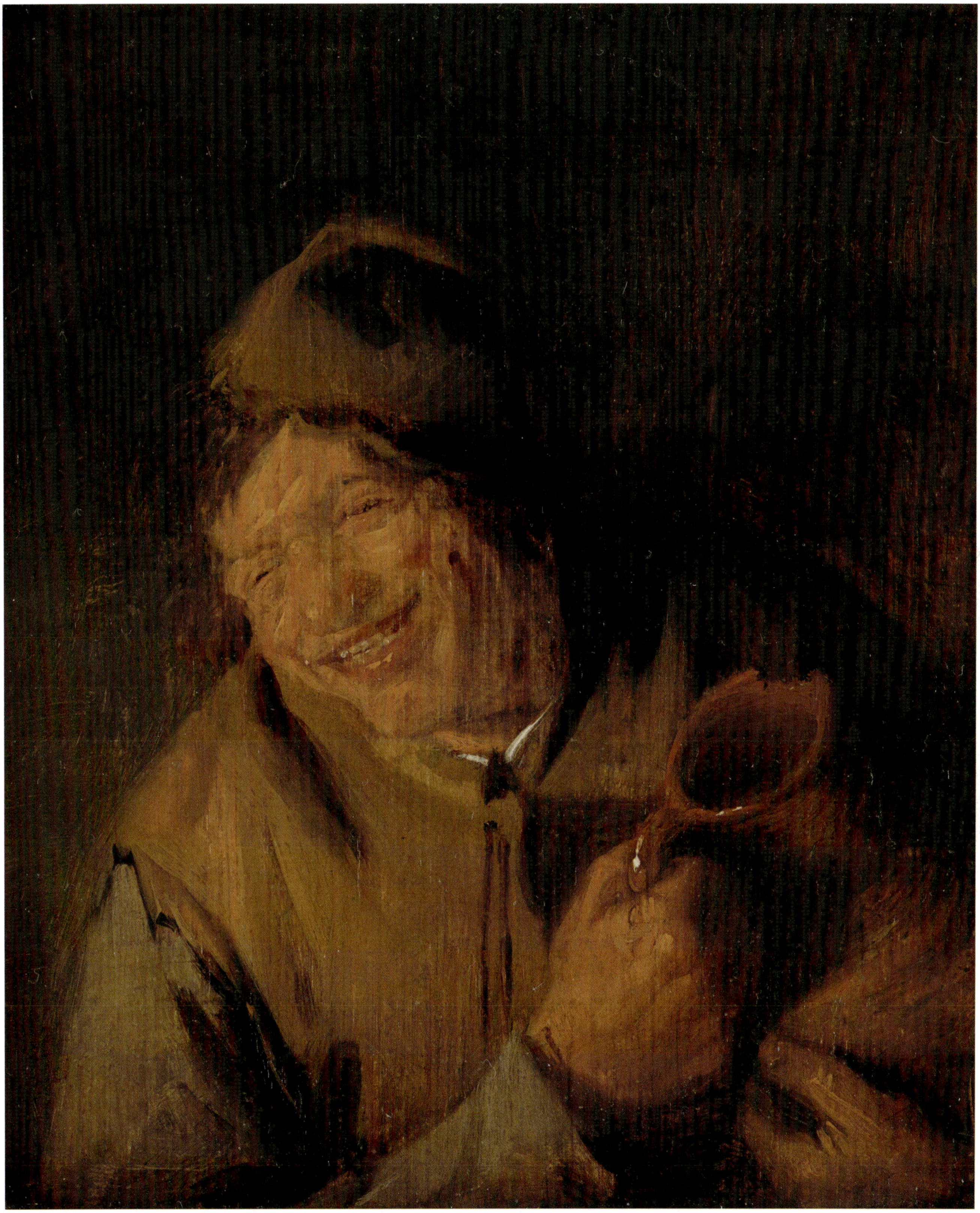

FIG. 12
Adriaen van Ostade,
The Merry Peasant,
c. 1646, oil on panel,
Rijksmuseum,
Amsterdam, SK-A-302

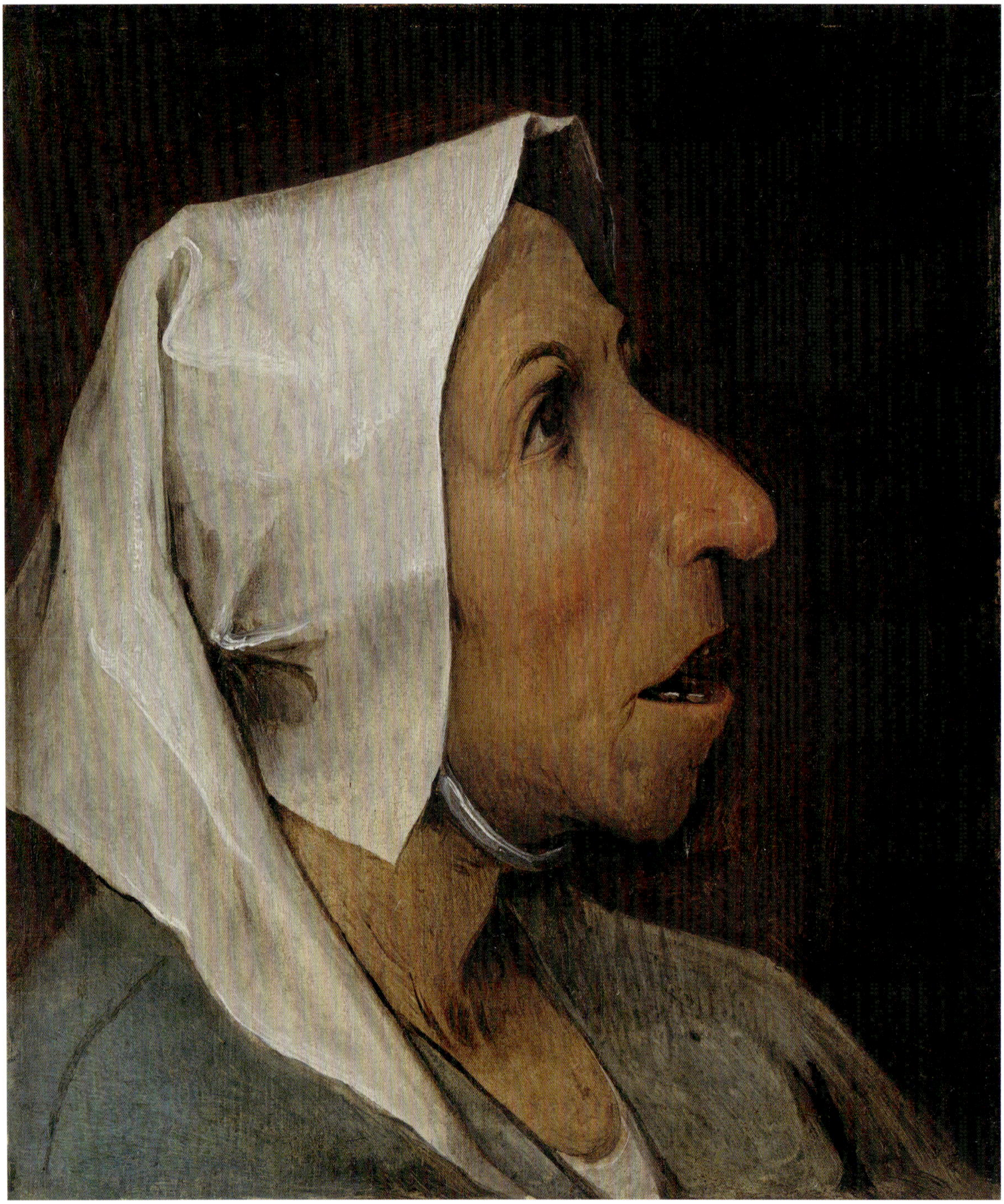

FIG. 13
Pieter Bruegel the Elder, *Head of a Peasant Woman*, s.d., oil on panel, Bayerische Staatsgemäldesammlungen, Alte Pinakothek, München, 7057

FIG. 14
Michael Sweerts, *Head of a Woman*, c. 1654, oil on panel, The J. Paul Getty Museum, Malibu, 78.PB.259

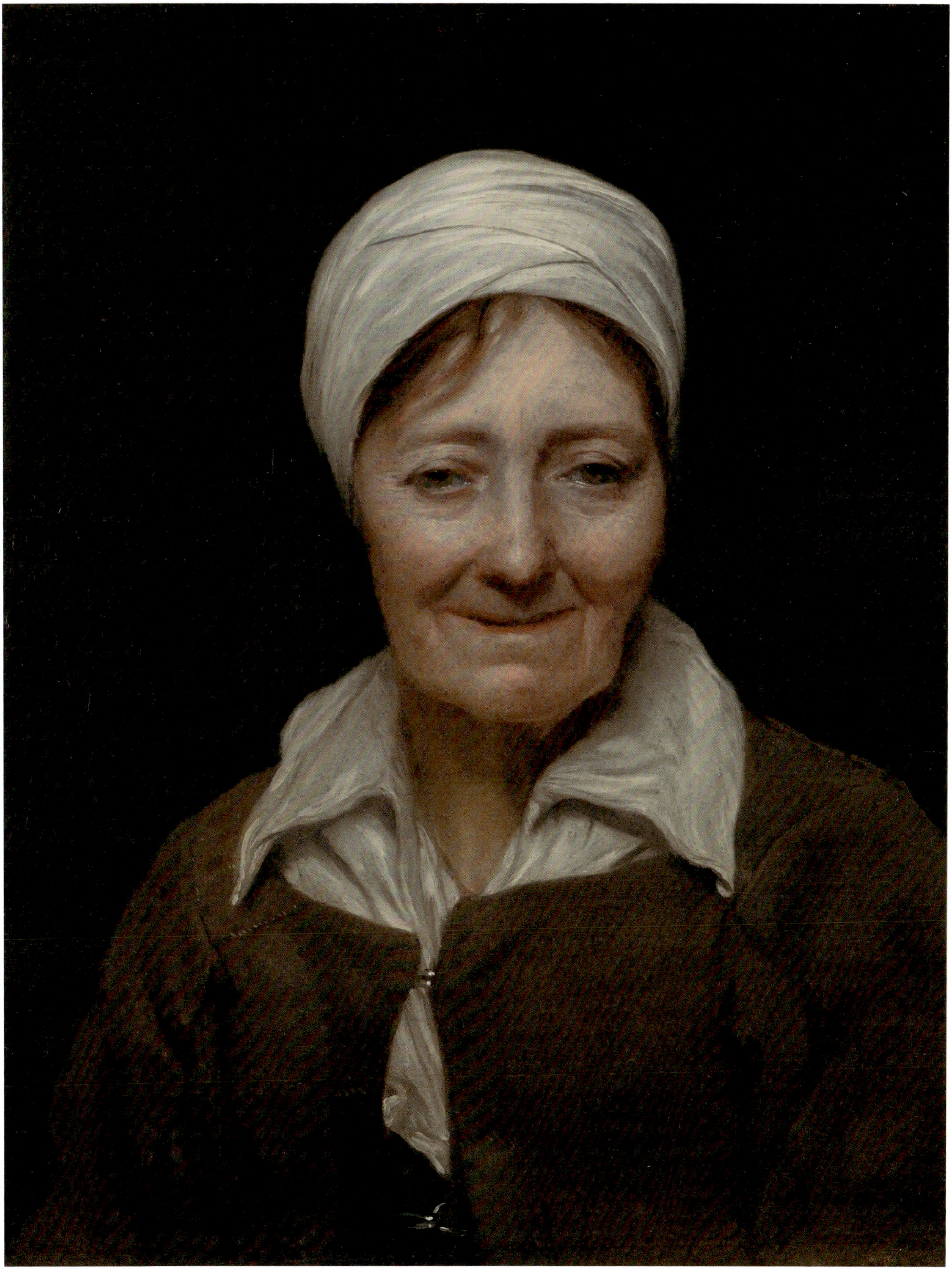

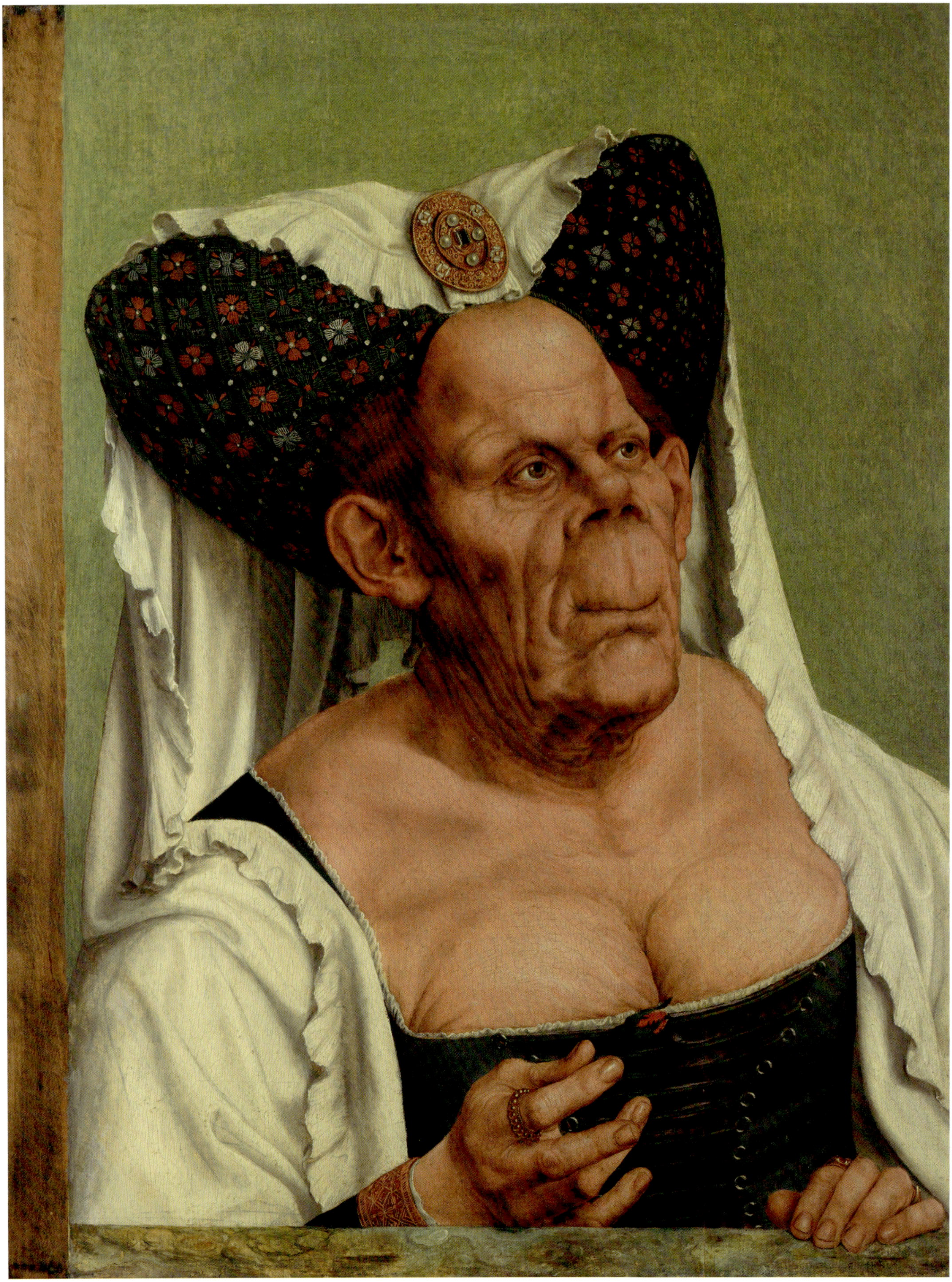

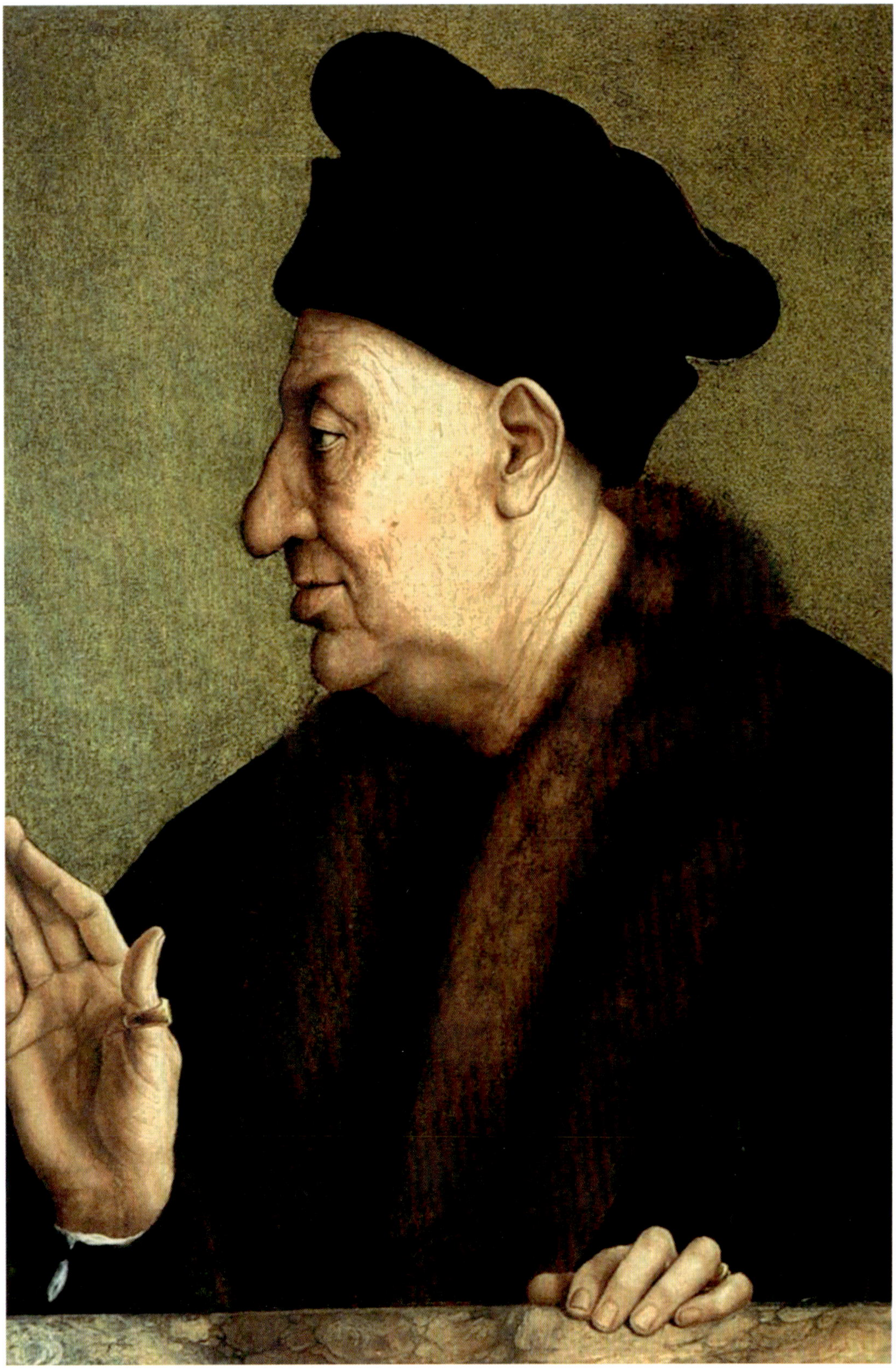

FIG. 15
Quinten Massys,
The Ugly Duchess,
c. 1513, oil on panel,
National Gallery
London, NG5769

FIG. 16
Quinten Massys,
An Old Man,
c. 1513, oil on panel,
private collection,
New York

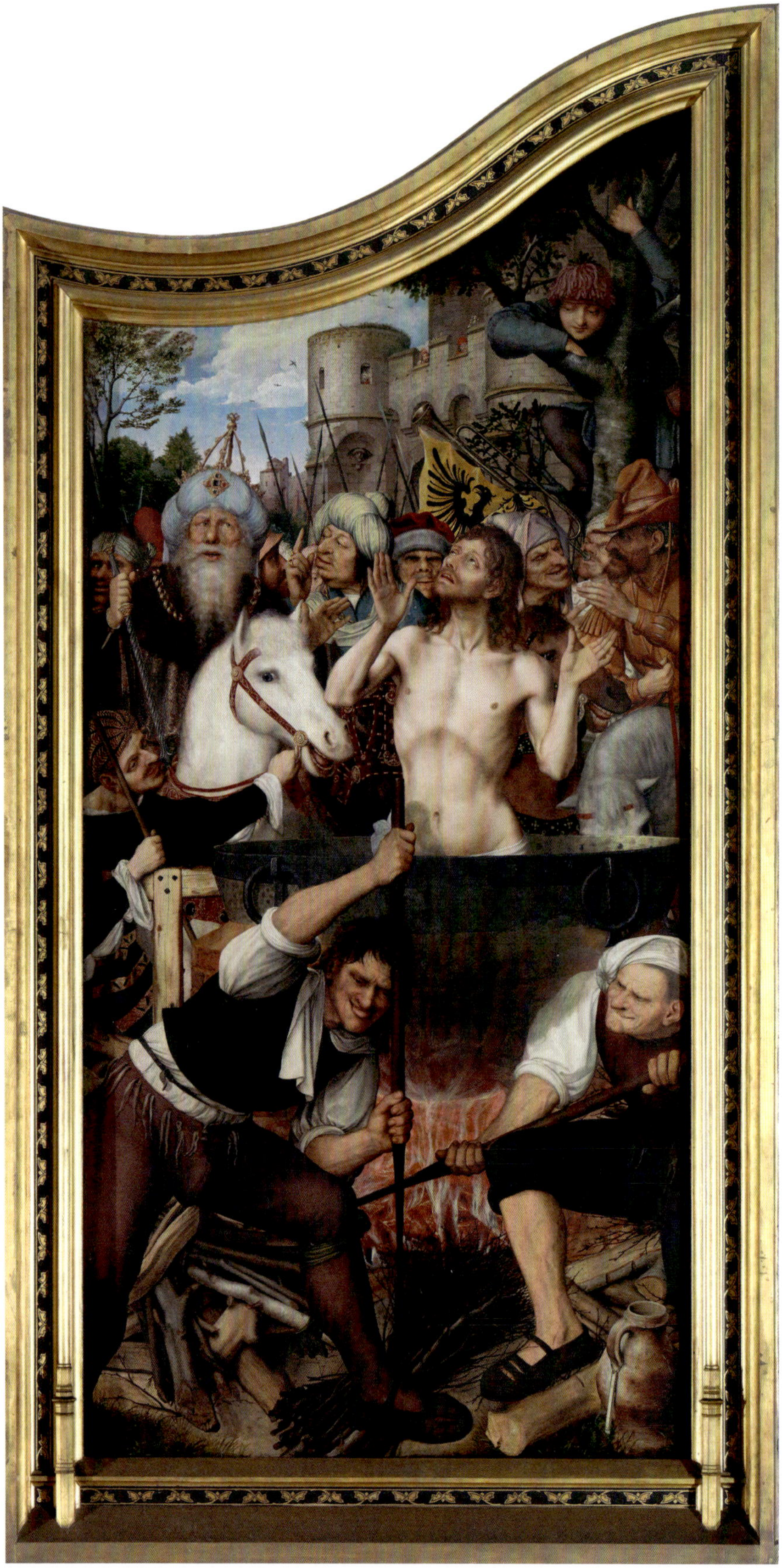

FIG. 17
Quinten Massys,
The Martyrdom of Saint John (right wing),
(1511), oil on panel,
KMSKA, Antwerp,
inv. 248

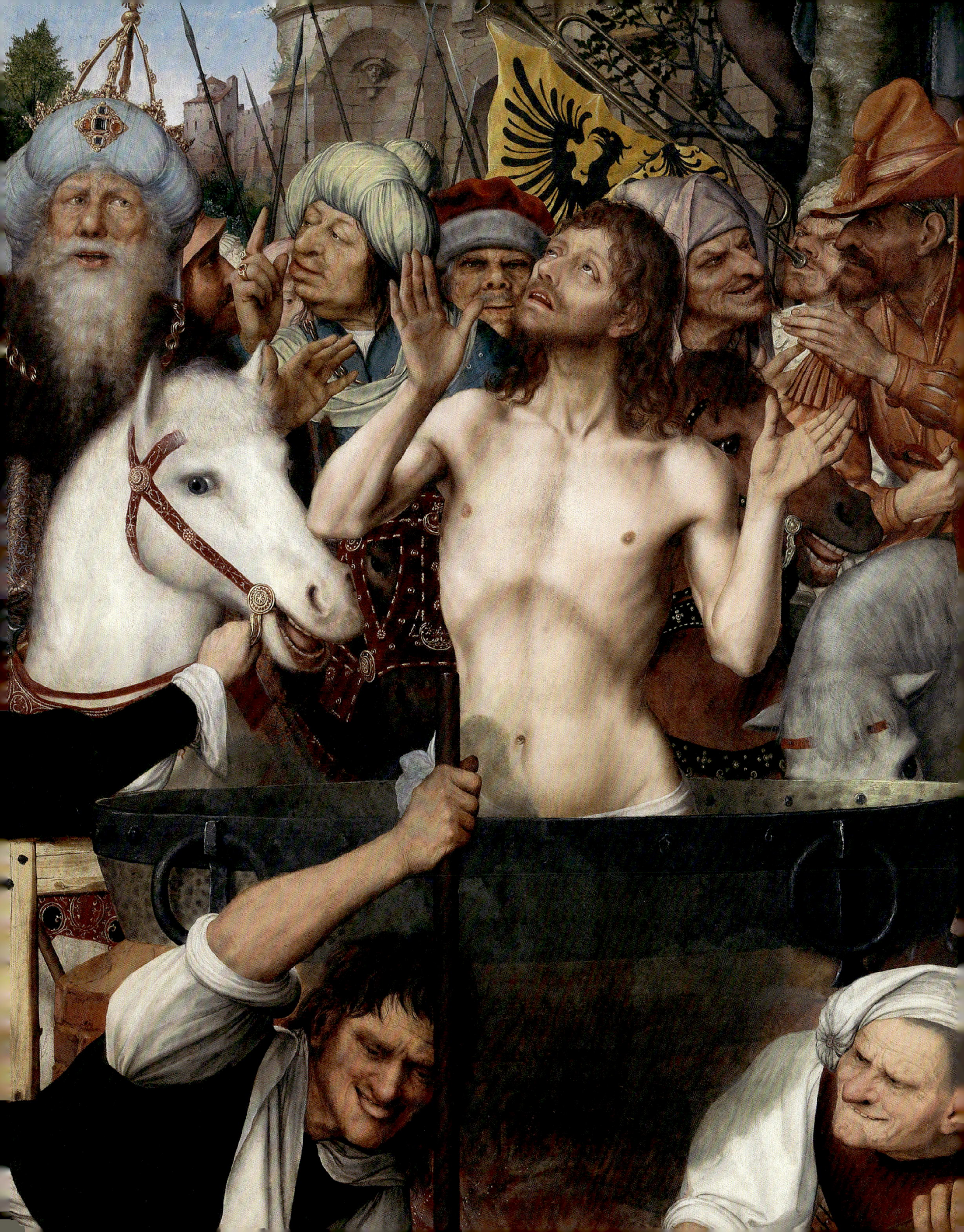

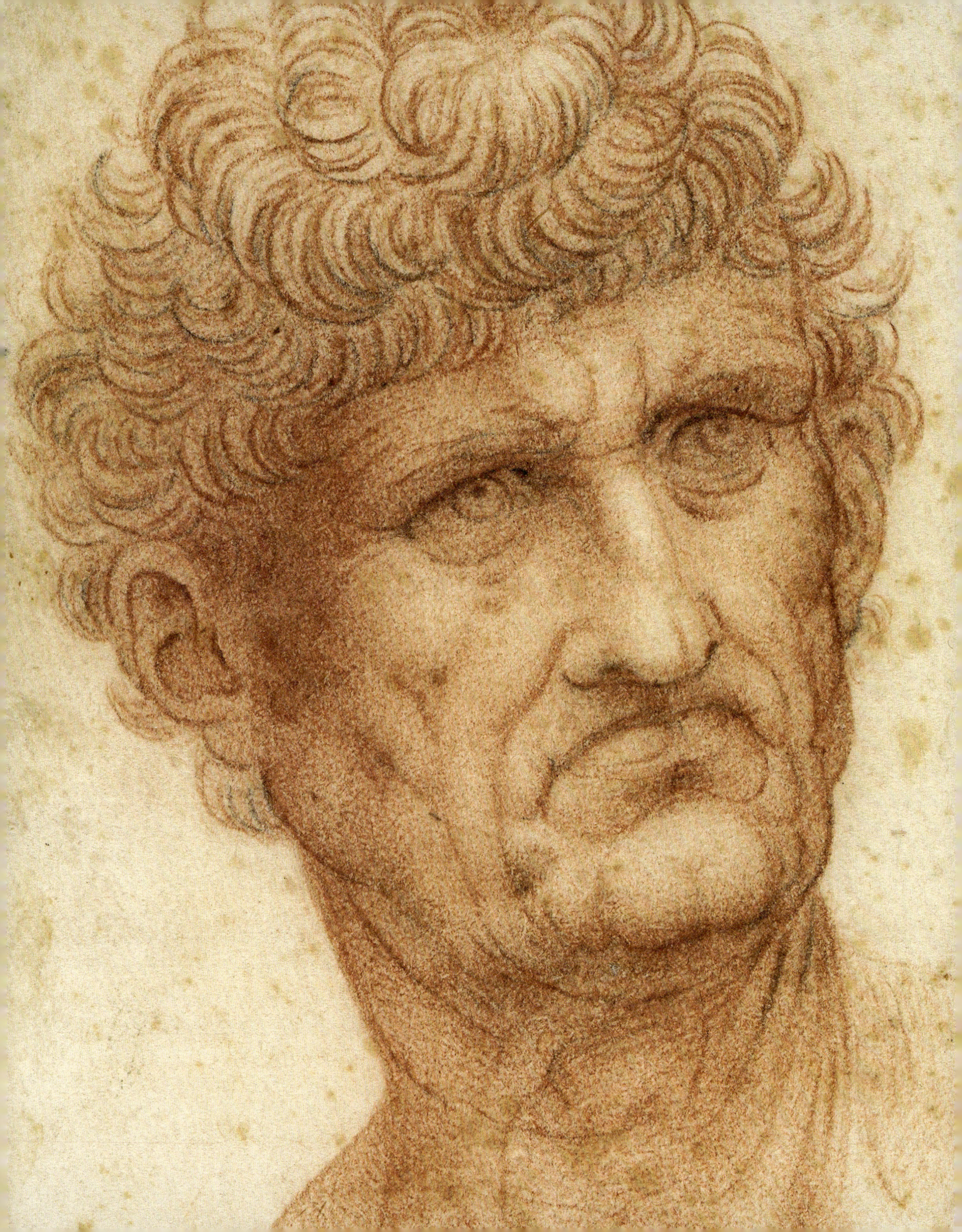

HEADS IN HISTORIES

From Likeness to Type in Verrocchio, Leonardo, Dürer, Massys and a Follower of Bosch

Michael W. Kwakkelstein

Among the Old Master drawings preserved at the Royal Library in Turin is a red chalk drawing by Leonardo da Vinci (1452–1519) depicting the head of an old man with bushy eyebrows, long wavy hair and a flowing beard seen in three-quarter view (Fig. 18). The drawing would never have achieved the status of one of the world's most famous drawings had it not been endlessly published and advertised as the artist's self-portrait during the last years of his life.[1] The melancholy or sorrowful expression of the man represented in the drawing has often led Leonardo's biographers to speculate about his inner life so as to compensate for the fact that his vast written legacy contains very little information about his personal life.[2] Doubts, however, have sometimes been raised about the identity of the sitter. Some scholars have pointed out that the old man's face bears little resemblance to that of Leonardo in the only known portrait of the artist made from life, while others have argued that it corresponds to a facial type that Leonardo employed in varying contexts throughout his career. Moreover, it has been noted that the style and technique of the drawing suggests a dating not to circa 1515/17, as is commonly assumed, but rather to the 1490s when Leonardo was in his forties.[3]

Accepting a much earlier date for the drawing than the final years of Leonardo's life makes it indeed difficult to understand why he would have depicted himself as old and bearded at a time when, in Italy, beards were considered "the preserve of the barbarous, Germans, Orientals, figures from ancient history, mythology and biblical times, philosophers, hermits, and penitents."[4] These are compelling arguments that undermine the idea of a self-portrait that the Milanese painter and author Giuseppe Bossi (1777–1815) had introduced at the beginning of the nineteenth century when the now-famous drawing resurfaced.

Verrocchio: two head types

Leonardo's drawings attest to his special interest in physiognomy and its expressive power. In addition to drawing portraits, of which only a few have survived, Leonardo enjoyed drawing old men and women with monstrous faces in bust-length profile. Though most of these bizarre types are imaginary and are meant to be humorous, some sketches of profile heads that occur amidst his notes reveal a special interest in the physical changes that occur with old age, especially those caused by edentulism.[5] A third category of head studies consists of drawings

(DETAIL FIG. 28)
Francesco Melzi (after Leonardo da Vinci), *Head of a Man in Three-quarters to the Right*, s.d., Gallerie dell'Accademia, Gabinetto dei disegni e stampe, Venice, 262

with studies of heads of male and female figures of common or idealised beauty that reveal a close dependence on head types in the work of Leonardo's teacher, the Florentine sculptor Andrea del Verrocchio (1435–1488).

From the beginning of his career as an artist, Leonardo adopted not only Verrocchio's ideal of female beauty, but also his use of two classically inspired antithetical facial types: one representing a youth of epicene beauty, and the other depicting a mature, stern-looking man with an aquiline nose and a prominent chin.[6] Both types are derived from ancient coins: the handsome youth bears a close resemblance to the profile portrait of Antinous but also to that of Alexander the Great, whereas the stern type of old man is based on the portrait of the aged Emperor Galba.[7] On a large double-sided sheet with studies of heads in profile, dated to circa 1478, Leonardo illustrated both these classicising types, juxtaposing them to their variants, both male and female, so as to explore the contrasts in facial characteristics due to differences in age (Fig. 19).[8]

Comparable drawing exercises feature a double-sided sheet that once belonged to a Verrocchio sketchbook.[9] The verso of this sheet includes a large study of the vigorous head of an old man, seen in near frontal view, whose features and expression resemble those of Galba (Fig. 20). On comparing this head study by Verrocchio with the head type that recurs, viewed from different angles, in Leonardo's drawings, it becomes immediately apparent that it reflects a sculptural model, and that this model provided the prototype on which Leonardo based many of his depictions of the Galba type (Fig. 21).[10]

Verrocchio employed Galba's aged and vigorous head type mostly for his sculpted figures of warriors – ancient or contemporary.[11] Leonardo followed this example but, in his own drawings and paintings, he extended the use of this ancient motif beyond that of the representation of warriors. In so doing, he changed the appearance of the Galba type by either aging a figure up (Fig. 23) or down (Fig. 25), lending it a beard (Fig. 24), giving it a full head of classically curled hair (Fig. 27), or transforming it into an absurdly deformed head (Fig. 29).[12]

Leonardo applied the same method to vary the appearance of the Antinous/Alexander the Great type (Fig. 26). As evidenced by his depictions of, for example, the *Angel of the Annunciation,* known from a copy (Kunstmuseum, Basel), St John the Evangelist in the *Last Supper* (Refectory of Santa Maria delle Grazie, Milan),

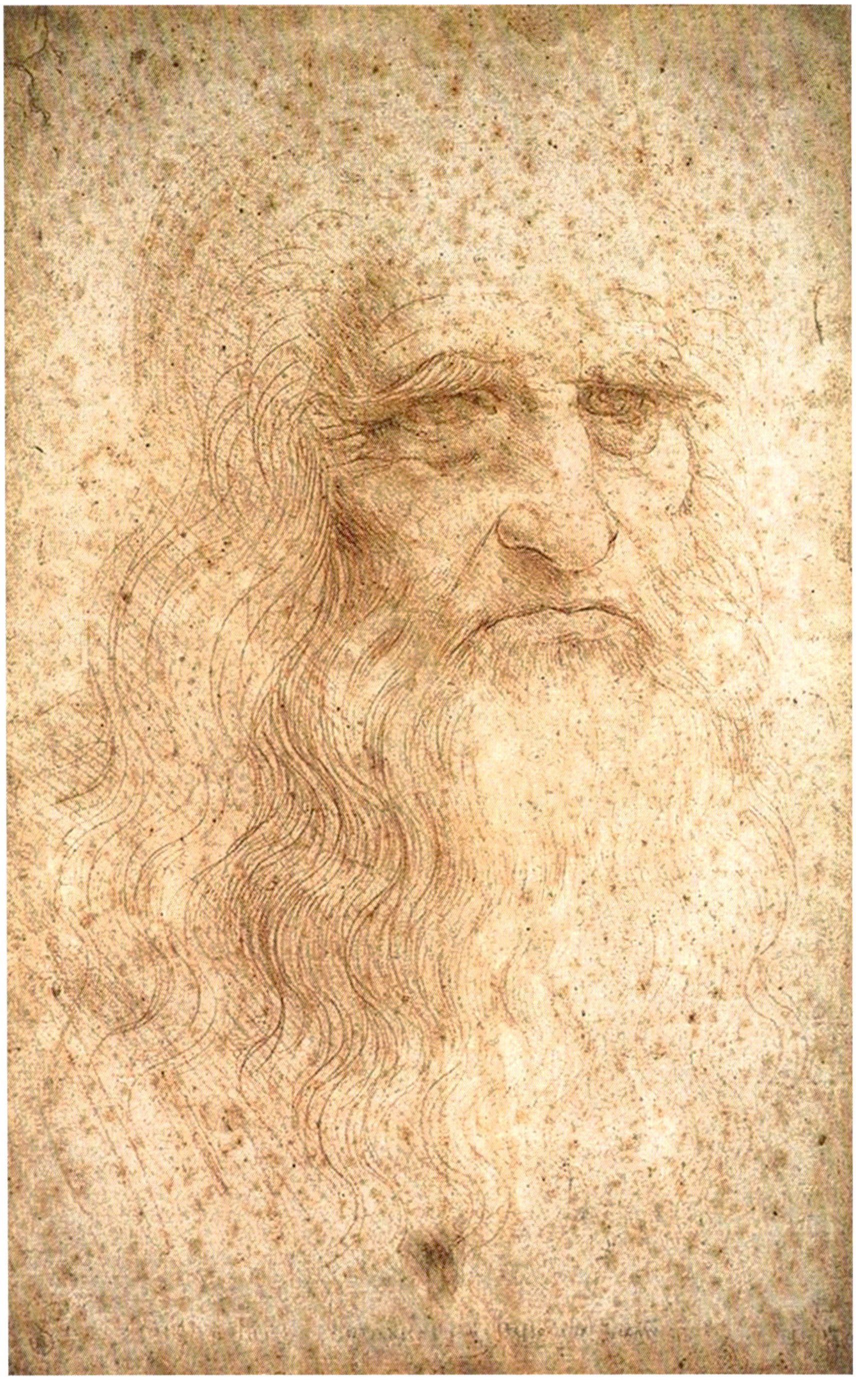

FIG. 18
Leonardo da Vinci, *Self-portrait* (?), c. 1490, 1517–1518, red and black chalk on paper, Biblioteca Reale, Turin, D.C. 15571

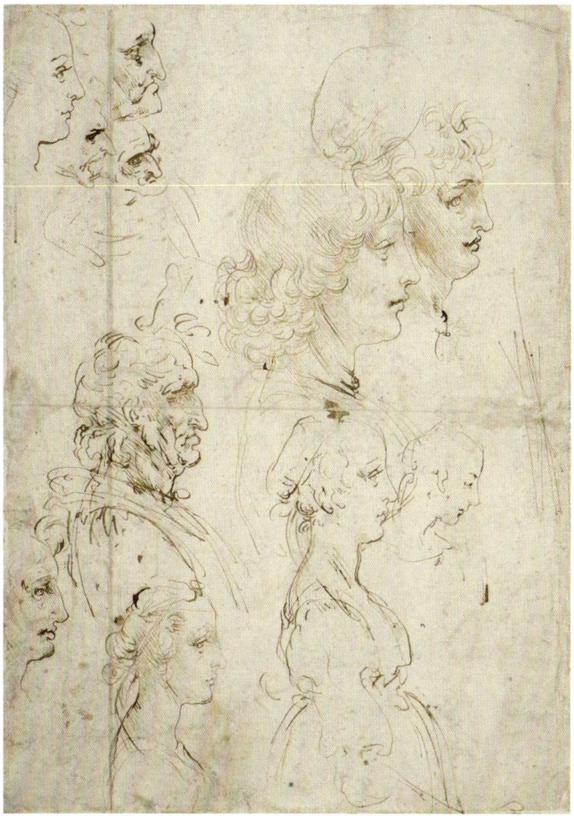

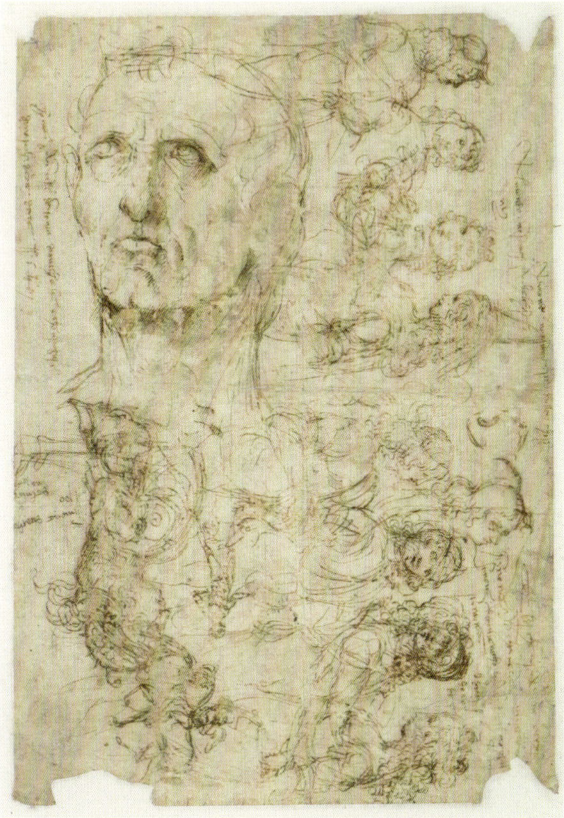

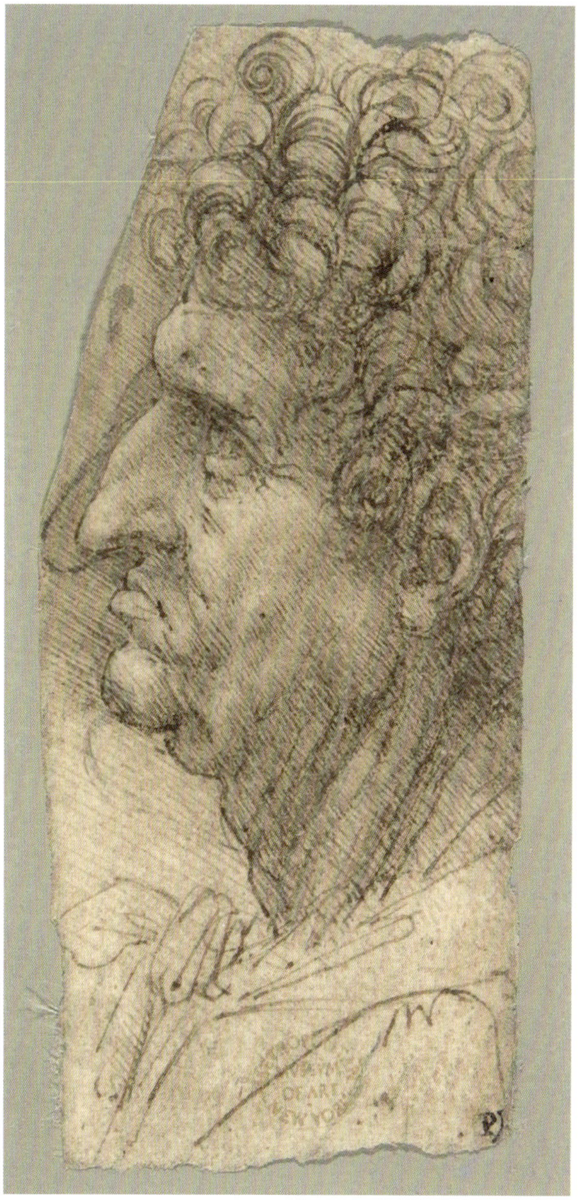

FIG. 19
Leonardo da Vinci, *Heads in Profile*, c. 1478–80, pen and ink on paper, The Royal Collection, Windsor, RCIN 912276 verso

FIG. 20
Andrea del Verrocchio and assistant, *Figure Studies*, s.d., silverpoint, pen and brown ink and wash on a pink prepared paper, National Galleries of Scotland, Edinburgh, D642 (verso)

FIG. 21
Leonardo da Vinci, *Head of a Man in Profile Facing to the Left*, 1491–1494, pen and brown ink, over soft black chalk, The Metropolitan Museum of Art, New York, 10.45.1

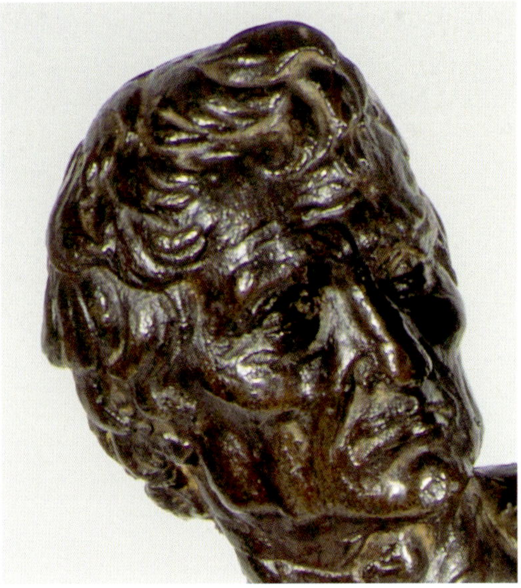

FIG. 22
Andrea del Verrocchio, *Nude Male, called 'Il Pugilatore'* (detail), s.d., bronze, Museo Nazionale del Bargello, Florence, bronzi 288

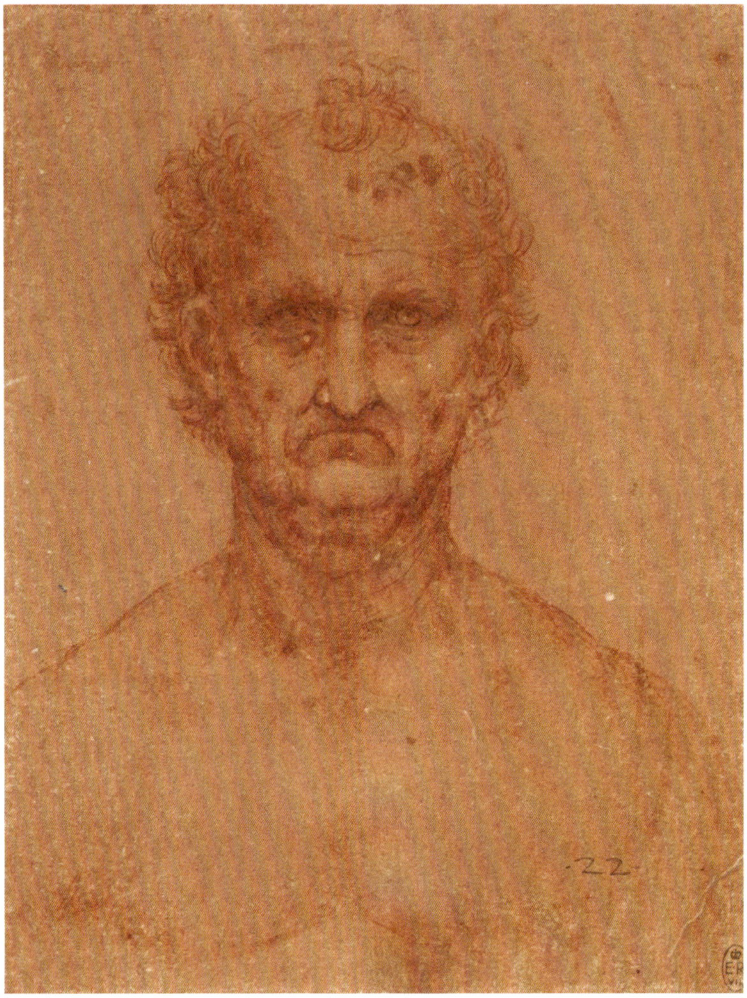

FIG. 23
Leonardo da Vinci, *The Bust of a Man*, c. 1505–10, red chalk with touches of black chalk on pale red prepared paper, The Royal Collection, Windsor, 912503

Leda (The Royal Collection, Windsor, inv. 912518) and *St John the Baptist* (Musée du Louvre, Paris), he used this facial type for both male and female figures. Since these figures share the same youthful age, the differences are primarily marked by varying hairstyles and the direction of the figure's gaze.[13] The fact that St John the Baptist's facial type and expression bear a close resemblance to those of the young woman depicted in the painting known as the *Mona Lisa* (Musée du Louvre, Paris), shows that Leonardo also applied this ideal and interchangeable type to portraiture.[14]

Working with two facial stereotypes for his depictions of male figures meant that when Leonardo designed a multi-figure composition such as the *Last Supper,* he achieved variety mostly by juxtaposing heads modelled on the Antinous/Alexander the Great type to those modelled on the Galba type, whose appearance he changed by varying age, facial expression, hair and beard style.[15] That he had previously followed the same procedure for the depiction of the heads of the figures in the *Adoration of the Magi* of 1481 (Gallerie degli Uffizi, Florence), supports the view that repetition and adaptation are typical of his design method.[16] It is this working method that explains the close resemblance between, for example, the head and face of the second apostle from the right in the *Last Supper* and that of the old man in the Turin drawing, and between the head of the old man immediately to the right of the Christ Child in the *Adoration of the Magi* and that of a figure illustrated in a drawing that has generally been accepted as a preparatory study for the figure of St Peter in the *Last Supper*.[17]

Given these considerations regarding Leonardo's design method, the possibility cannot be ruled out that the Turin drawing is indeed a self-portrait, but not one that faithfully records Leonardo's likeness. By advancing the age of the prototype head of Galba and adding long hair, a long beard, bushy eyebrows and a melancholic expression, Leonardo may have had in mind the image of an ancient sage or philosopher, perhaps one he admired or even identified with.[18] The drawing would then represent a study of a type of character comparable to, for example, the type of character Leonardo illustrated in bust-length format in several drawings that have been dated to around 1508/10 (Fig. 24).[19]

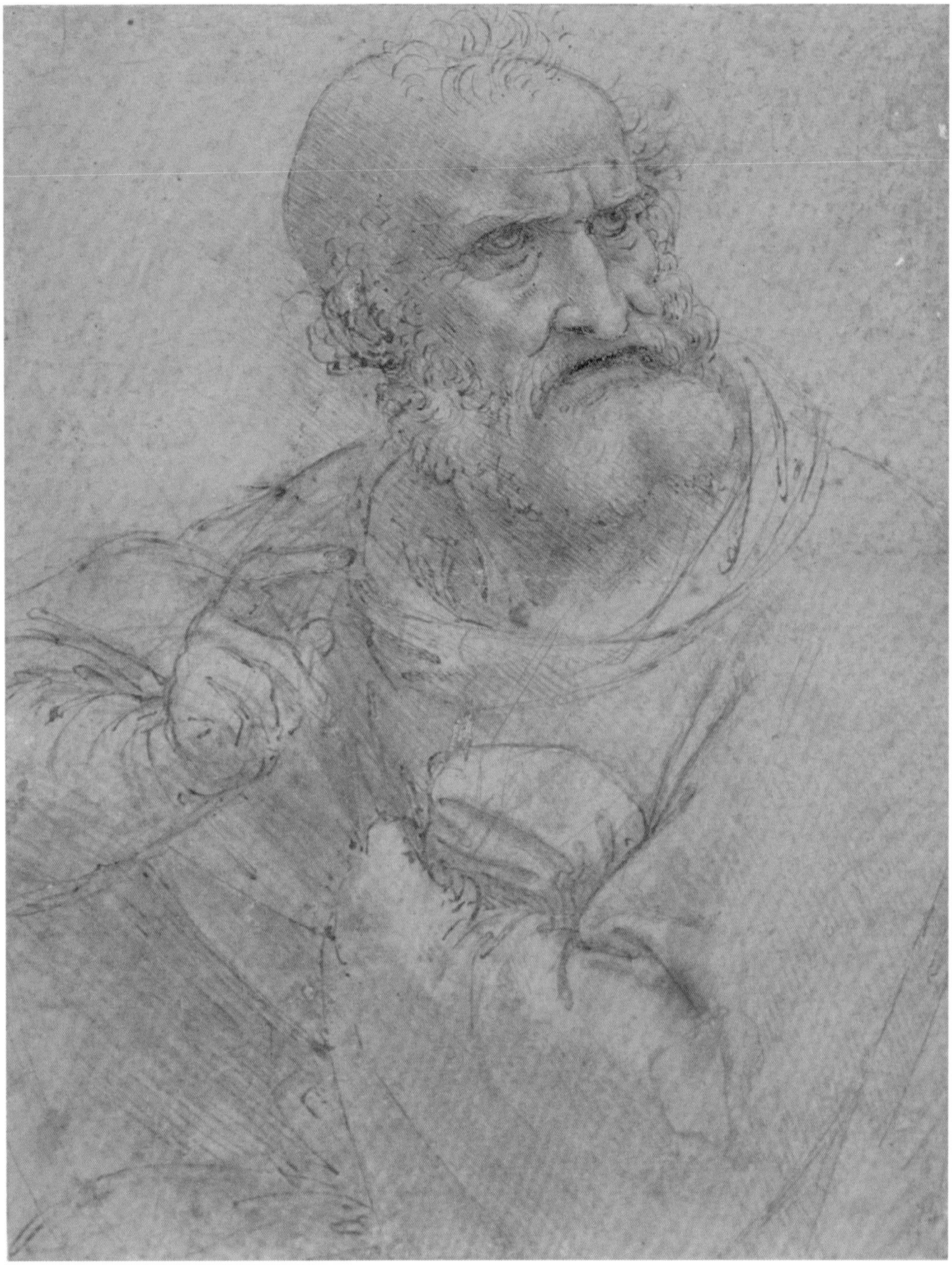

FIG. 24
Leonardo da Vinci, *Half-length figure of an Apostle*, 1493–1495, silverpoint, pen and brown ink on a blue prepared paper, Graphische Sammlung Albertina, Vienna, 17614

Fierce men

Considered as a group, these drawings, also executed in red chalk, perhaps best illustrate Leonardo's typical practice of modifying the age and features of the Galba type to explore how these changes create a different character head. Interestingly, instead of imitating the sculptural head mentioned above, Leonardo turned his attention to another sculptural model from Verrocchio's studio: a bronze figure of a nude warrior (Fig. 22).[20] In age, facial type and expression, the figure's square-shaped, weathered face with its sunken cheeks, heavy eyebrows and dimpled chin closely correspond to that of the mature or old man Leonardo illustrated in these drawings. This connection becomes especially clear when comparing the head of Verrocchio's warrior with the head illustrated in a drawing by Leonardo that is known only in a copy (Fig. 28). In the lost drawing, Leonardo had also copied the figure's head tilt.[21]

Furthermore, the bust-length format Leonardo adopted in these drawings suggests a dependence on marble reliefs with the isolated head or bust in profile of a Roman emperor or hero from Antiquity that Desiderio da Settignano (1429–1464) and Mino da Fiesole (1428–1464) had carved in Florence during the 1460s.[22] Leonardo must have greatly admired this innovative and highly successful sculptural genre because, during the second half of the 1470s, he produced a carefully executed metal-point drawing with a study of the bust-length likeness of Darius III, King of the Persians (d. 330 BC) that is generally assumed to reflect a now-lost relief by Verrocchio.[23]

The fact that these sculptural reliefs celebrate Roman emperors and ancient commanders known for their military prowess and victories suggests that the male figure Leonardo depicted in these drawings belongs to a similar class of fierce men.[24] This interpretation is supported by the laurel wreath with which the figure is crowned in a drawing in Turin (Royal Library, inv. 15575 D.C.), whereas in the frontal study of this figure (Fig. 27) the combination of a wreath of ivy leaves and a lion's head sketched in the lower right-hand corner likewise alludes to military victory.[25] Moreover, by matching the man's menacing gaze with that of the lion, Leonardo sought to underline his choleric nature. According to physiognomic theory, with which Leonardo was familiar, a man whose head and face resemble that of a lion is stout hearted and magnanimous, but also irascible and insidious.[26]

Furthermore, the man's emphatically threatening grimace, as illustrated in the frontal study

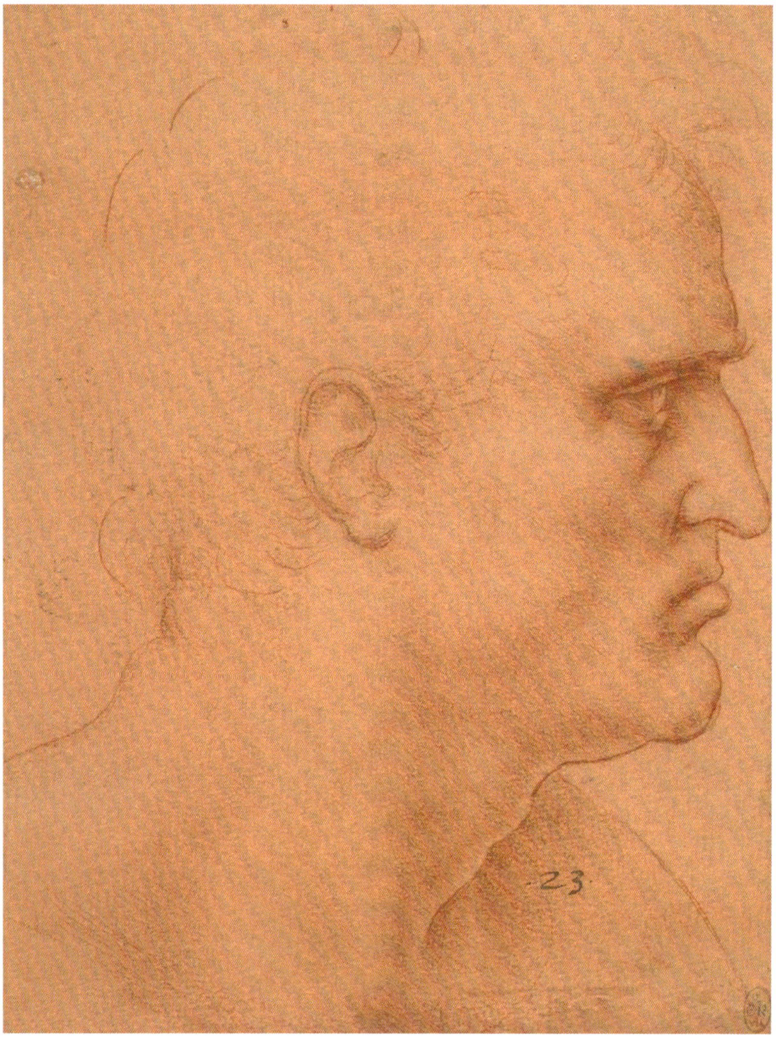

(Fig. 23), recalls the ferocious expression of Verrocchio's ideal portrait of the *condottiere* Bartolomeo Colleoni (1395–1475). When visiting Venice in 1500, Leonardo must have seen Verrocchio's equestrian monument to Colleoni.[27] Having adopted Verrocchio's design method from an early stage, Leonardo immediately noticed how the sculptor had adapted the likeness of Colleoni to conform to that of Emperor Galba, whose vigorous features and stern expression he had exaggerated to heighten the expressive power with which the figure's physiognomy conveys Colleoni's martial character.[28]

Physiognomic types

Leonardo's keen interest in the physical expression of human character is the subject of an anecdote recounted by the Ferrarese poet and author Giambattista Giraldi Cinthio (1504–1573). In his *Discorsi intorno al comporre de' Romanzi,*

FIG. 25
Leonardo da Vinci, *The Head of St Bartholomew*, c. 1495 or later, red chalk on red prepared paper, The Royal Collection, Windsor, 912548

FIG. 26
Leonardo da Vinci, *The Head of a Youth*, s.d., red chalk, touches of white chalk, on orange-red prepared paper, The Royal Collection, Windsor, 912554

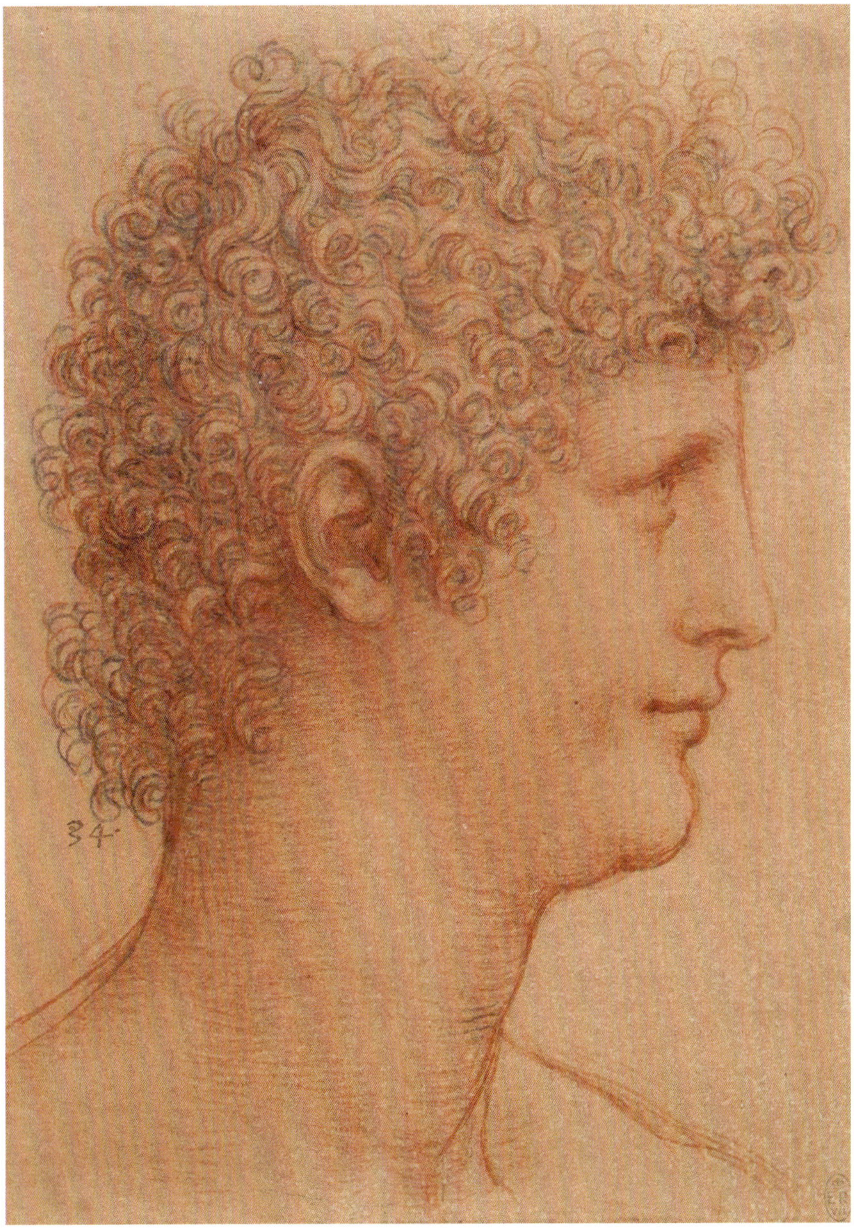

delle Comedie, e delle Tragedie, written in 1549 (published in Venice in 1554), Cinthio relates how Leonardo designed the bodily appearance of the human figures in his paintings, especially of those he depicted in the *Last Supper*. He wrote: "whenever he wanted to paint some figure, he considered first its quality and its nature, that is, whether that person should be noble or plebeian, joyous or stern, upset or gay, old or young, of irate or tranquil mind, good or evil; and then, knowing its being, he went where he knew persons of such quality congregated and observed diligently their faces, manners, habits and bodily movements. Having found that which seemed to him befitting to what he envisaged to create, he drew it with his stylus in the little notebook that he always kept at his belt. And after doing this many, many times; then, when he had collected as much as he considered was required for the image he wished to paint, he set about portraying it and succeeded marvellously in doing so."[29]

According to Cinthio, Leonardo set about portraying the type of character he wished to paint only after collecting as many life drawings as he considered was required to create such an image. From Cinthio's account we learn that Leonardo was much less concerned with depicting figures with individualised faces than with creating composite images of physiognomic types to convey individual temperament or moral character. Yet in his travel diary, the secretary to Luigi, Cardinal of Aragón (1474–1519), Antonio de Beatis, who visited Leonardo in Amboise in 1517, claims that the figures in the *Last Supper* are "portraits from life of several people of the Court and of Milanese of that time, of true stature".[30] Though Leonardo's notes attest to his use of living models to study a body part he deemed appropriate for a figure in the mural, the apparent lack of facial variety and the degree of idealisation that characterise the figures in the *Last Supper*, suggest that his use of life drawings was limited to introducing some changes to the appearance and expression of his two facial stereotypes to differentiate the faces of the apostles and Christ, and render them more lifelike without diminishing the grandeur of their classicising air.[31]

The truthfulness of Cinthio's account of Leonardo's working method is confirmed by the artist's notes on painting that generally reflect his own practice. On various occasions, Leonardo urged the painter to study and draw how, in life, people express their emotions and intentions through bodily movements and facial expressions. To ensure that the expressive actions of the figures would be convincing in narrative painting, Leonardo advised the painter to observe decorum or propriety, since people of different sex, age, rank, status, temperament and character behave differently when expressing their emotions. It is when he comments upon the issue of variety that he manifests an interest in the relationship between man's permanent character and his physical appearance, in particular that of his face: "Depict your faces so that they do not all have the same [type of] countenance, as one sees done in most cases, but give them different countenances, according to ages, complexions and natures, either bad or good."[32]

Leonardo's belief in the interrelation between the form of man's body and his soul or character was based on his familiarity with medical texts on humours and complexions, and writings on physiognomics.[33] At the time, physiognomic theory enjoyed considerable popularity because it claimed to offer readers knowledge that would enable them to draw conclusions about someone's character and inclinations based on bodily movements and the specific characteristics of that person's physical appearance. Since the oldest known text on physiognomics was believed to have been written by Aristotle, the doctrine had attracted the attention of prominent mediaeval scholars such as Michael Scot (c. 1175–c. 1235), Roger Bacon (c. 1219/20–c. 1292), Jean Buridan (c. 1301–c. 1358) and Albertus Magnus (c. 1200–1280) who wrote their commentaries on it.[34] Regardless of whether a text on physiognomics has been written by a learned physician, an astrologer, or a natural or humanist philosopher, it invariably contains a catalogue of a fixed set of bodily features whose varying shapes and dimensions were supposed to correspond to certain traits of character. Traditionally, the most detailed attention is devoted to the interpretation of the "signs" of the face.[35]

Leonardo, whose library included writings on physiognomics, dismissed the theory as deceptive (*falace*) on the grounds of its divinatory claims.[36] Yet he fully recognised the relevance of its premise to painters and reminded himself to write on physiognomy, or 'filosomia' as he called it.[37] As we have seen, Leonardo urged the painter to depict faces in accordance with a figure's distinctive type of complexion and inner nature, "either bad or good". This kind of advice reflects not only Leonardo's general belief in the relationship between human character and bodily characteristics, but it also points to his

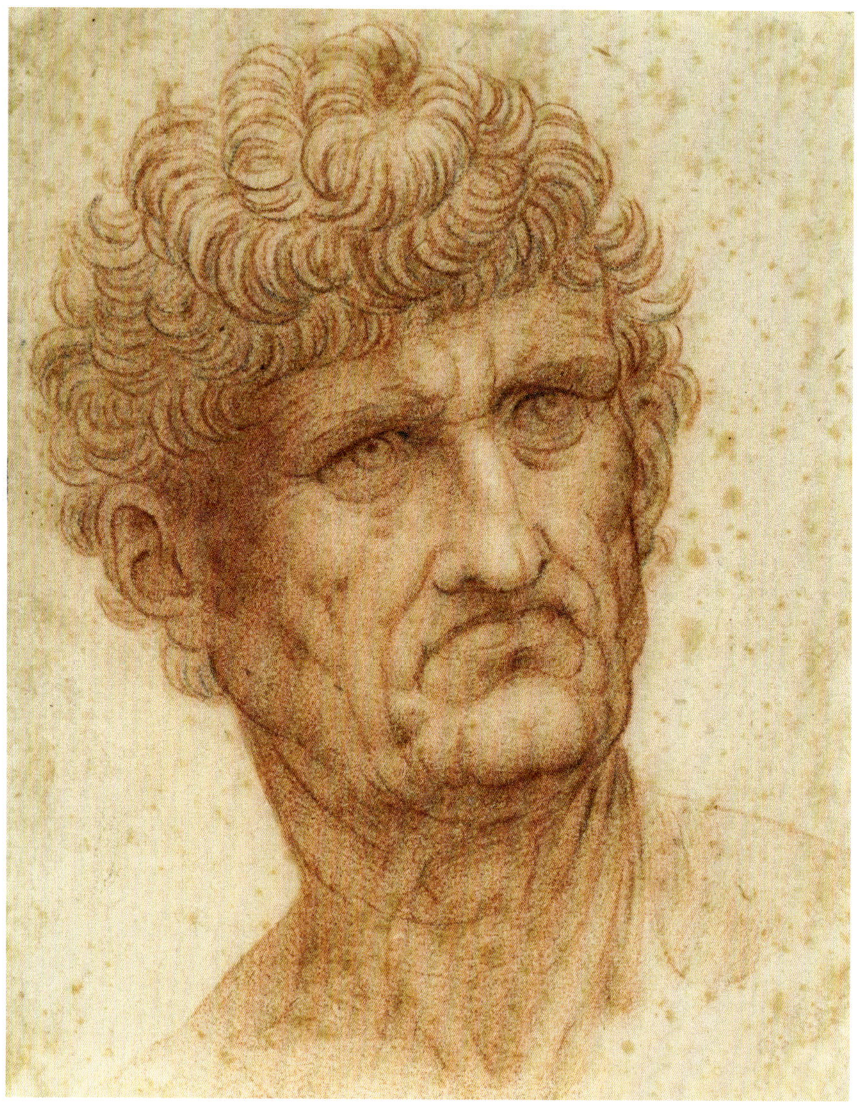

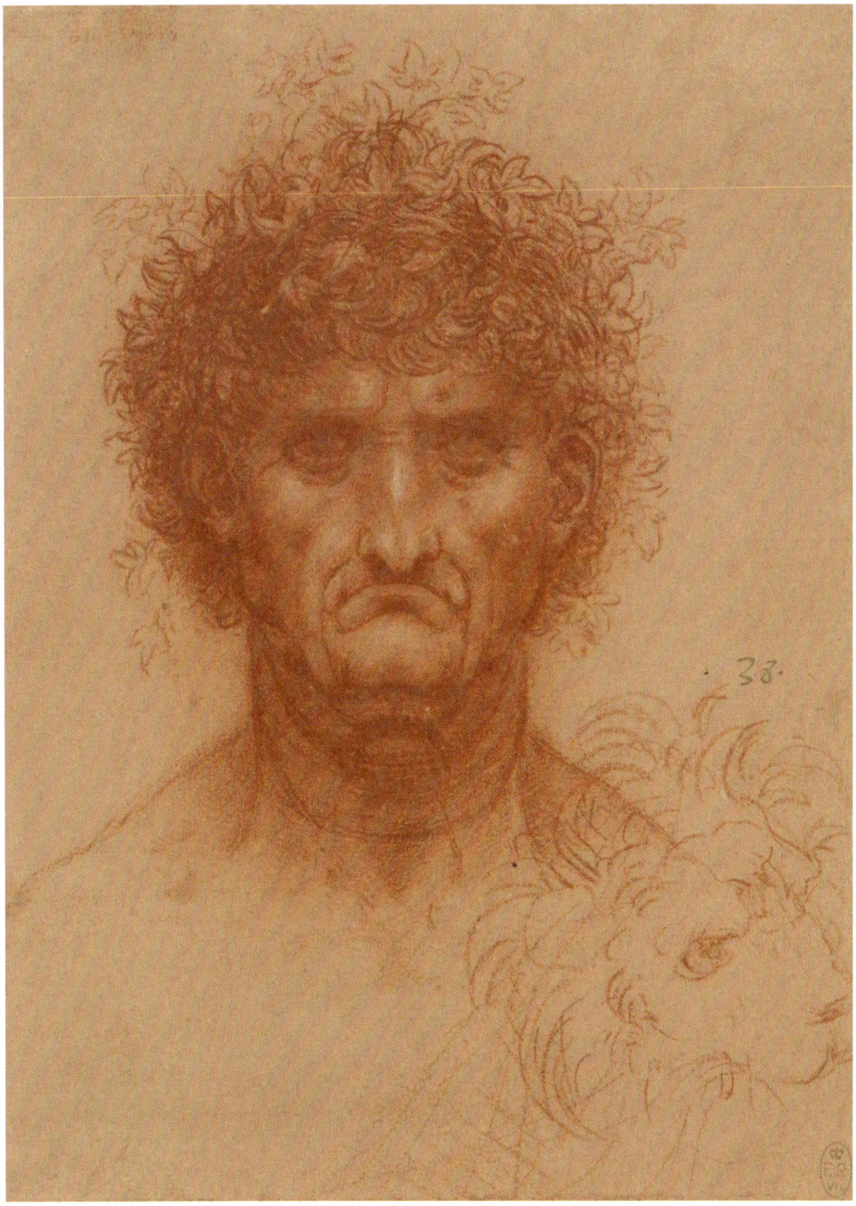

FIG. 27
Leonardo da Vinci, *The Bust of a Man and the Head of a Lion*, c. 1510, The Royal Collection, Windsor, 912501

FIG. 28
Francesco Melzi (after Leonardo da Vinci), *Head of a Man in Three-quarters to the Right*, s.d., Gallerie dell'Accademia, Gabinetto dei disegni e stampe, Venice, 262

awareness of the painter's ability to represent human nature through physiognomic typology. The importance Leonardo attached to the bodily expression of character and emotions was inextricably linked to his concept of painting as an art form that possesses the power to prompt an emotional response in the viewer: "If the painter wishes to see beauties that would enrapture him, he is master of their production, and if he wishes to see monstrous things which might terrify or which would be buffoonish and laughable or truly pitiable, he is their lord and god."[38]

Leonardo's concern with the emotive power of painting led him to devise various visual strategies to enhance its overall impact on the viewer. One of these strategies was the juxtaposition of figures of opposite bodily appearances. In a note on the importance of figural variety in narrative painting, Leonardo urges the painter always to depict various antithetical types and as closely juxtaposed as possible, having "the ugly next to the beautiful, the large next to the small, the old next to the young, the strong next to the weak".[39] The reason for this, as he explains in another note, is that such contrasts heighten the expressive force of each figure individually because "beauty and ugliness seem more powerful through one another".[40] Although Leonardo made numerous drawings of the heads of decrepit or monstrous old men and women, he never included such hideous head types in his painted works to contrast with a head type of idealised beauty.[41]

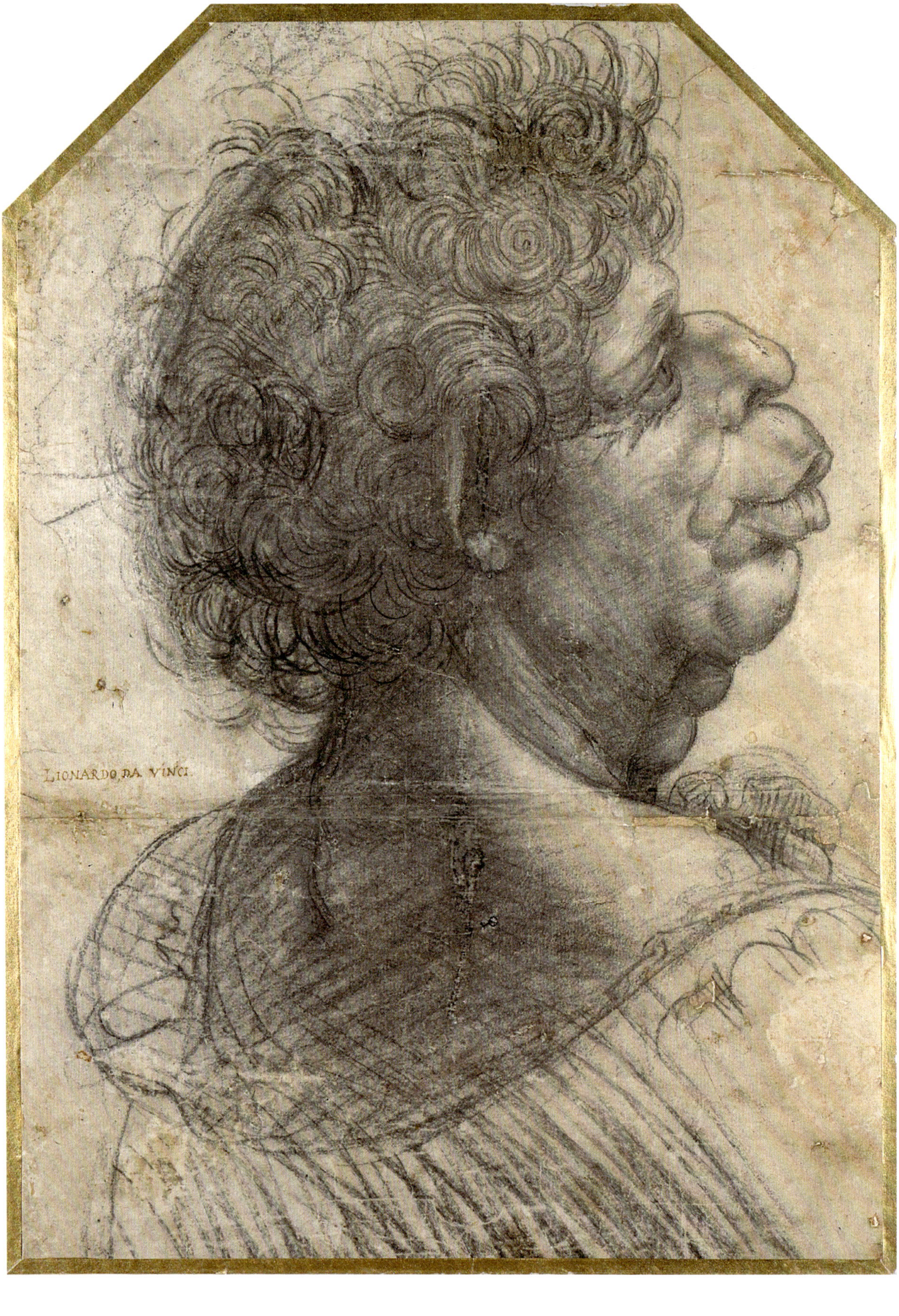
LIONARDO DA VINCI

Dürer and a follower of Bosch

In 1506, while in Venice, Albrecht Dürer (1471–1528) produced a painting representing *Jesus among the Doctors* (Fig. 31). In a letter to his friend Willibald Pirckheimer (1470–1530), dated 23 September 1506, he referred to it as a picture "the like of which I have yet never painted".[42] Of the many characteristics of this painting that may have prompted Dürer to make this comment, it is the prominent presence of an old man with a monstrous face that stands out. The fact that, in a devotional painting, Dürer included a monstrosity as the embodiment of evil and juxtaposed it with the idealised face of the youthful Christ, suggests the influence not only of Leonardo's ideas on physiognomical diversification and contrasts in narrative painting, but also of his drawings of monstrous head types.[43] While no direct relation can be established between the doctor's monstrous face and Leonardo's types, the figure's close proximity to the idealised head of Christ suggests that Leonardo's ideas on the expressive force of painting had inspired Dürer to explore new ways to enhance the overall emotive effect and visual impact of his work.

A similar interest in the expressive force of images of facial ugliness within the context of a Christian narrative is reflected in a painting of *Christ Carrying the Cross* that has been attributed to a follower of Hieronymus Bosch (Fig. 30).[44] Whereas in Dürer's painting, only one of the six male figures surrounding Christ is portrayed with a truly hideous face, in *Christ Carrying the Cross* (Museum voor Schone Kunsten, Ghent) the faces of nearly all the men grouped around Christ are frighteningly repulsive. In addition, their ugliness, the aggressive expression of some of these figures, further emphasises their vile and malevolent nature. Since the painting has been dated to circa 1530/40, it is often assumed that copies after Leonardo's drawings of old men and women with monstrous faces provided a source of inspiration for the anonymous painter.[45] However, no exact correlations can be established between the head types in the Ghent picture and those illustrated in Leonardo's drawings. Instead, it seems more likely that the painter was inspired by the figures of Christ's tormentors in works by Hieronymus Bosch that depict Passion scenes, such as his *Ecce Homo, Christ Carrying the Cross* and *The Crowning with Thorns*. These paintings all feature similarly closely grouped figures of angry, grimacing, hideous old men, seen either frontally or in profile.[46]

Massys

Discussions on the possible influence of Leonardo's bizarre head types on northern painters have centred also on the work of Quinten Massys (1465/66–1530).[47] His most famous adaptation of a monstrous head type invented by Leonardo that is known only through a copy drawing, is represented by a painting of *An Old Woman*, known as 'The Ugly Duchess' (Fig. 15).[48] The painting has been dated to around 1513 and forms the counterpart to a portrait-like painting, *Portrait of an Old Man* (private collection), seen in profile to the left, whose facial features are not deformed but common to old age. The fact that these paintings, recently referred to as 'A Grotesque Couple', were conceived as a pair reinforces the theory that Massys borrowed the idea and motifs from Leonardo's drawings or copies of them.[49]

Today, most of Leonardo's humorous drawings depicting busts and heads of old men and women with grotesquely deformed faces turn up as loose and small-scale fragments illustrating a single figure. However, before a sixteenth-century collector cut these small but carefully finished drawings of comic types out of the sheet of paper, many of them were juxtaposed, forming a couple of a man and a woman facing each other in profile, as numerous early copies suggest.[50] By adopting the format of contemporary double portraits in which husband and wife face each other in profile, Leonardo mocked his fellow human beings by portraying them not as young, beautiful, decorous and fashionable, but as old, decrepit, monstrous and sometimes immodest types wearing outdated clothes and headgear. These attributes allow us to establish

FIG. 29
Leonardo da Vinci, *Bust of a Man with a Grotesque Head*, 1482–1499, Christ Church Picture Gallery, Oxford, 33

that Leonardo targeted men belonging to different social classes, ranging from friars to rulers, and from poets to citizens of high status and function in public life.[51] Like Leonardo, Massys adopted the conventional format of the double portrait to paint the likenesses of an imaginary old man and an imaginary old woman who, because of her extreme ugliness, exposed cleavage and outdated attire and headgear, was undoubtedly intended to be the object of ridicule and laughter.[52]

One wonders what kind of viewer response Leonardo envisaged when, in around 1503/05 while in Florence, he represented the bust-length figure of a man with a monstrous face in an almost life-size cartoon that is pricked for transfer (Fig. 29).[53] The large dimensions and characteristics of this drawing suggest that it originated in connection with a project for a painting. Moreover, the cartoon appears to be a fragment of a larger design which raises the question as to what context the figure may have belonged.[54]

In the case of a Passion scene, such as 'Christ as the Man of Sorrows' or 'Christ Carrying the Cross', the figure's hideous appearance would have provided a powerful contrast to that of Christ, and elicited a strong sense of disgust and condemnation in the viewer.[55] On the other hand, if the composition were to include exclusively ugly or monstrous figures and Leonardo had brought it to completion, such a secular scene would have undoubtedly provided an important stimulus to the development of satirical painting as a genre, both in Italy and in the North.[56] The impact would not have been less had Leonardo conceived the monstrous figure in the cartoon as the male companion to a similarly portrait-like image of an old and monstrous woman and brought the work – or two pendant paintings – to completion, as Massys did a decade later with his 'Grotesque Couple'.

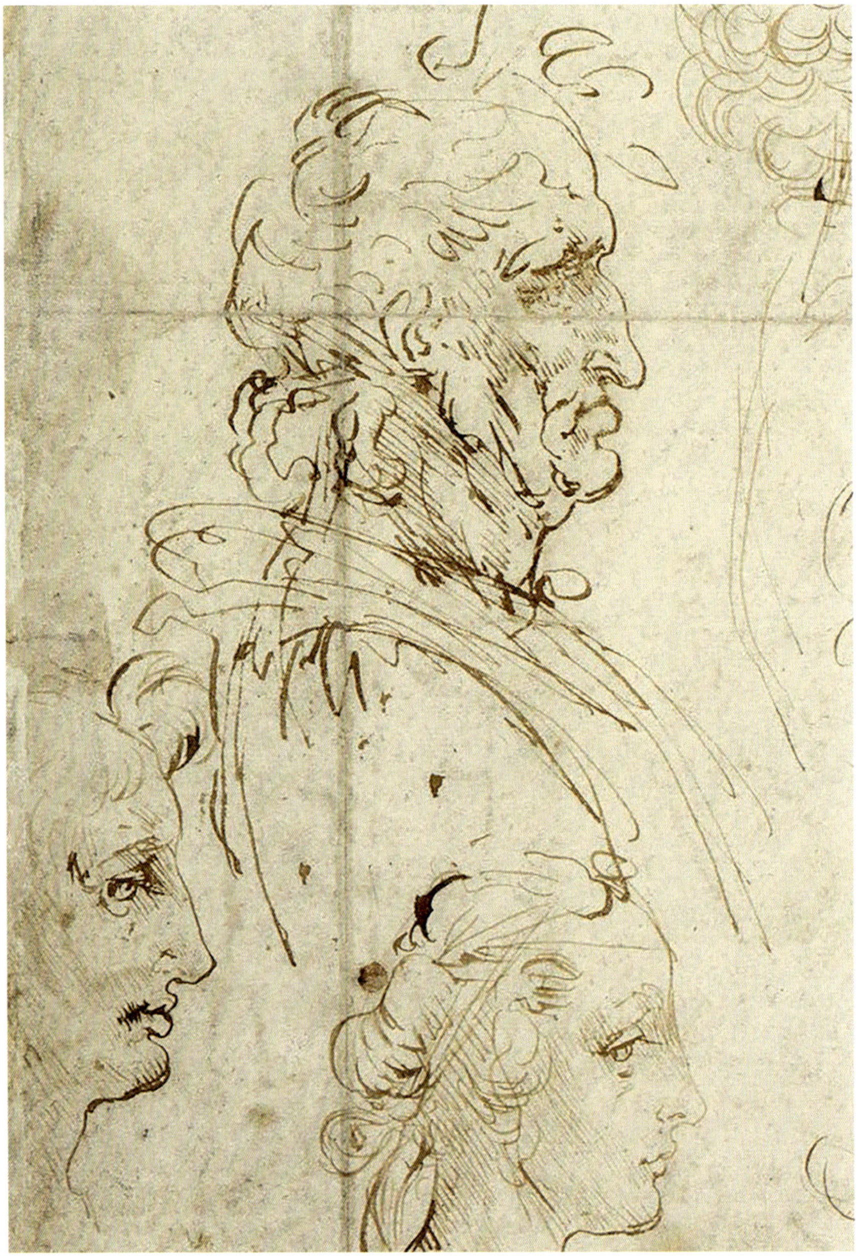

(DETAIL FIG. 19)
Leonardo da Vinci, *Heads in Profile*, c. 1478–80, pen and ink on paper, The Royal Collection, Windsor, RCIN 912276 verso

1 For recent discussions of the Turin drawing, see Pedretti in Florence 2006, pp. 107–108, cat. no. II.a; Salvi in Turin 2011, pp. 106–108, cat. no. 1.19; Salvi in Turin 2019, pp. 189–193, 389, cat. no. 50; and Bambach 2019, vol. I, pp. 26–34.

2 Bramly, 1991, p. 19; Arasse 1998, pp. 28–30; Nicholl 2004, pp. 12–13; and Isaacson 2017, p. 453: "… the face displays different mingled emotions each time you look at it: strength and vulnerability, resignation and impatience, fatalism and resolve. The tired eyes are contemplative, the down-turned lips are melancholy."

3 Dating the drawing to the first half of the 1490s, Bodmer, 1931, p. 398, ruled out the possibility that it could be Leonardo's self-portrait. Similar doubts have been expressed by Lange 1911, p. 13, n. 1; Gombrich 1976 (1954), p. 70; Payne 1979, p. 213; Roberts in London 1989, p. 46; Turner 1993, p. 11; Brown 1994, p. 76; Kwakkelstein 2014 (1994), p. 112; Clayton in London 2002, p. 112; Nathan in Zöllner 2019 (2003), p. 368; Villata in Florence 2005, p. 110. Following Carlo Pedretti's dating and interpretation of the drawing, Paola Salvi (as in note 1) has upheld the view that the Turin drawing represents Leonardo's self-portrait and that it can be dated to c. 1515/17. Bambach 2019, vol. I, p. 30; vol. II, p. 291, argues for a dating to around 1500/05. Although the author (vol. I, pp. 31–32) recognises that the old, bearded man "is somewhat of a physiognomic type in Leonardo's drawings", she is willing to accept that "the face rendered in the Turin drawing is portrait-like in its conception of detail, in its sense of intimacy, in its relatively unforgiving individualization of features, and in its poignant psychological grandeur. This is a man physically burdened by the power of his inner vision and intellect, as is indicated by his gaze of absorption."

4 Cited after Clayton in London 2002, p. 110.

5 From an inventory Leonardo compiled of his works during the early 1480s, it can be inferred that he practised drawing portraits and had drawn heads of young and old men. The list also includes such items as "many heads of old men", "a head of a gypsy" and "a head of an old man with a long chin" that may well refer to drawings made from memory. The inventory is given in Richter 1970, vol. I, p. 387–388, § 680 (*Codex Atlanticus*, fol. 888r). For Leonardo's portrait drawings, generally assumed to have been done from life, see Clayton in London 2002, pp. 101–113; Syson in London 2011, pp. 228–229, cat. no. 59; and by Salvi in Turin 2019, pp. 378–380, nos. 37, 38. Leonardo's carefully finished drawings of the busts of old men and women with monstrous faces are the fruits of his imagination as he exaggerated the shape of observed forms to depict despicable figures with absurdly deformed features. These bizarre head types reflect not only his interest in the expressive power of monstrous physiognomy, but also the pleasure he derived from mocking his fellow human beings by emphasising their ignorance and folly. See Kwakkelstein 2019, 2023.

6 As pointed out by Thiis 1913, pp. 154–156; Clark 1988 (1939), pp. 46; 121–124; Popham 1994 (1945), pp. 39–40; Gombrich 1976 (1954), pp. 68–70; and Gombrich 1986, pp. 108–112. Verrocchio's most influential depictions of these antithetical types were represented by a pair of two marble reliefs that he produced during the 1470s, one with the ideal profile portrait of Alexander the Great (356–323 BC), the other with that of Darius III, King of the Persians (d. 330 BC). See Parmiggiani in Florence 2019, pp. 102–105, cat. nos. 2.6 and 2.7; and Luchs, May, Smith in Washington 2019, pp. 140–142, cat. no. 9.

7 Gombrich 1976 (1954), p. 70, pointed to Leonardo's use of coins of the Galba and Nero type. Meller 1963, p. 54, observed that Verrocchio's so-called Old Warrior type "depends upon antique profiles of Galba, the most pronouncedly martial of the Roman emperors". For Leonardo's use of a Roman coin of the Antinous type, see Kwakkelstein in Haarlem 2018, p. 36. Fig. 6. On Leonardo's study of ancient coins, see Cunnally 1993.

8 For an analysis of Leonardo's working method, as reflected in the drawings on both sides of the Windsor sheet, see Clayton in London 2002, pp. 16–19 (cat. no. 1); and Eisenberg 2019, pp. 20–22.

9 For a recent discussion of the drawings on both sides of the sheet from Verrocchio's sketchbook, see Melli in Washington 2019, pp. 260–263, cat. no. 39.

10 This connection has hitherto not been recognised. That the head in Verrocchio's drawing reflects a sculptural model was suggested by Cadogan 1983, p. 385; Bambach in New York 2003, p. 266; and Melli in Washington 2019, p. 263. Verrocchio's workshop contained naturalistic plaster casts of body parts and sculptural heads of old men that allowed pupils to copy these three-dimensional models from whatever angle they wished. See Eisenberg 2019, pp. 5–6. Following Verrocchio's practice, Leonardo produced heads of old men in clay, now lost, that enabled his pupils to practise drawing from sculpture and assimilate his types, see Kwakkelstein 2014 (1994), pp. 105–112.

11 See note 6 above (ideal portrait of Darius III), note 26 below (ideal portrait of Bartolomeo Colleoni) and Butterfield 1997, p. 115, Fig. 144 (the figure of a soldier in the *Beheading of St John the Baptist*). Plutarch, *Parallel Lives*, 1926, vol. XI, p. 271, XXIX, concludes his life of Galba by saying that "in arms and camps, indeed, he was an 'imperator' of a severe and ancient type". It is not unreasonable to assume that Verrocchio was familiar with Plutarch's characterisation of Galba. Ancient portraits of Galba depict the emperor as an aged man with a vigorous head, strongly marked features and a stern expression which may explain why Verrocchio adopted Galba's head for his representation of ancient warriors. For Plutarch's influence in fifteenth-century Italy, see Pade 2007.

12 The drawing is illustrated in Kwakkelstein 2018, p. 126 (cat. no. 19). It was Thiis 1913, pp. 154–157, who first pointed to Leonardo's habit of working with two facial stereotypes. See also Clark 1988 (1939), pp. 121–124; Popham 1994 (1945), pp 39–41; Gombrich 1976 (1954), pp. 68; 70–77; and more recently Eisenberg 2019, pp. 16–17; and Bambach 2019, vol. III, pp. 133–136. The Master of the Pala Sforzesca (active in Milan in the 1490s) copied this procedure from Leonardo. In a group of drawings that illustrate the head of an old man from different angles, the anonymous artist changed the man's appearance by changing his hairstyle, ranging from baldness to a full head of curly hair. See Kwakkelstein 2014 (1994), fig. 103–111.

13 Kwakkelstein 2014b, pp. 57–58. For a discussion of the origins and meaning of a type of youthful, idealised and androgenous male that recurs in the work of Leonardo and his Milanese followers, see Corry 2013.

14 Gombrich 1976 (1954), pp. 69–70: "The Mona Lisa passes as a portrait and is at the same time a type that recurs in Leonardo's vocabulary, a type, we may assume, applied to an individual." See also Brown 1983. The women in Leonardo's portraits and narrative painting all share the same youthful age and idealised beauty. In Florence at the time of Lorenzo de' Medici (1449–1492), the ideal of female beauty was influenced by the Petrarchan ideal of beauty. This ideal, associated above all with the virtue of chastity, determined the degree of idealisation that is characteristic of Florentine female portraiture of that period. See Tinagli 1997, pp. 73–77; and Kirkham in Washington 2001, pp. 49–61; and Woods-Marsden in Washington 2001, pp. 64–87.

15 Commenting on the recurrence in Leonardo's work of two facial stereotypes, Clark 1988 (1939), p. 70, observed that "even in his most conscious creations, even in the *Last Supper*, they remain, as it were, the armature round which his types are created". For Leonardo's use of facial stereotypes, see Gombrich 1976 (1954); Gombrich 1986; Kwakkelstein 2014b; Zöllner 2022.

16 Nathan 2002; Kwakkelstein 2014b.

17 Kwakkelstein in Haarlem 2018, p. 181, cat. no. 59.

18 Planiscig 1927, p. 143, pointed out that Leonardo's so-called self-portrait recalls late fifteenth-century imaginative portraits of Aristotle and argued that Leonardo modelled his face on that of the Stagirite.

19 For a recent discussion of these drawings, see Bambach 2019, vol. III, pp. 133–136.

20 Butterfield 1997, 2001, first attributed the statuette to Verrocchio. The attribution is accepted by Luchs and Smith in Washington 2019, pp. 118–120, cat. no. 4 (c. 1470/80). The bronze figure has hitherto not been connected to Leonardo's head studies of the so-called warrior type.

21 For a recent discussion of the copy drawing, see Kwakkelstein in Venice 2019, pp. 234–236, cat. no. 59.

22 For a discussion of this sculptural genre, see Caglioti 2008 and Caglioti 2011 (with emphasis on Verrocchio).

23 For Leonardo's drawing, see Chapman in London 2010, pp. 204–205 (cat. no. 50); Barone and Kemp 2010, pp. 48–49, no. 6. For Verrocchio's Darius relief, see note 6, above.

24 Meller 1963, pp. 55–58, first advanced the theory that Leonardo's drawings are connected to a heroic portrait of the Milanese nobleman and *condottiere* Gian Giacomo Trivulzio (1440/1–1518). This theory has not been unanimously accepted, see Clayton in London 2002, p. 60, cat. no. 20; p. 64, cat. no. 22 ("a wild man was Leonardo's ostensible subject"); Bambach 2019, vol. III, p. 134.

25 For a recent discussion of the Turin drawing, see Salvi in Turin 2019, pp. 355–356, cat. no. 11. In his comments on ivy, Pliny (*Nat. Hist.* Bk 16.62) reports that "Alexander had come back victorious from India with his army wearing wreaths of ivy, because of its rarity, in imitation of Father Liber".

26 "Leo fortis audax heros iracundus… liberalis magnanimus insidiosus", cited after Meller 1963, p. 59, note 22.

27 For a discussion of Verrocchio's equestrian monument to Colleoni, see Butterfield 1997, pp. 159–183.

28 Meller 1963, pp. 62–63, argued that Verrocchio enhanced the force and aggressiveness of Colleoni's expression to emphasise the ferocious side of the lion type of man that, according to the doctrine of physiognomy, was held to embody both ferocity and magnanimity.

29 English translation cited after Kwakkelstein 2014 (1994), p. 75 (original text reproduced on pp. 117–118). Cinthio probably received this information from his father, Cristoforo, whom he credited as the source of another anecdote about the working method Leonardo followed in creating the head of Judas in the *Last Supper*. Leonardo's fascination with the bodily expression of human character and emotions was fuelled by the naturalistic rendering of these qualities in the depictions of the human figure in the art of Verrocchio, including his drawings of 'burlesque Morris dancers'. See Melli in Washington 2019, p. 95; and Nuttall 2021 (for Verrocchio's drawings of comic-grotesque figures).

30 De Beatis 1905, p. 176: "Li personaggi di quella ['una cena picta al muro da messer Lunardo Vinci'] son de naturale retracti de più persone de la corte et di Milanesi di quel tempo, di vera statura." De Beatis also claims to have seen Leonardo's mural painting in Milan.

31 Richter 1970, vol. I, p. 381, § 667: "Cristo. Giova[n] co[n]te, quello del cardinale del Mortaro." [Christ. Count Giovanni, the one with the Cardinal of Mortaro]; vol. II, p. 352, § 1403: "Alessandro Carissimo, da Parma per la ma[no] di xpo." [Alessandro Carissimo of Parma, for the hand of Christ].

32 Pedretti and Vecce 1995, vol. II, p. 260, § 287: "Fa che i visi non sieno d'una medesima aria, come nei più si vede operare; ma fa diverse arie, secondo l'etadi e complessioni, e nature triste o buone." Closely related to this advice and the working method described by Cinthio is Leonardo's advice: "when you make a figure, think well about what it is you want it to do, and see that the work is in keeping with the figure's aim and character". Cited after Kwakkelstein 2014 (1994), p. 76. Leonardo may have borrowed these remarks from Filarete's *Treatise on Architecture* (c. 1460), of which he owned a manuscript copy. Filarete urges artists who wish to be praised for their works to always consider the gender, age, nature and status of a certain figure to avoid depicting it with inappropriate bodily characteristics and animated movements. See Filarete ed. Spencer 1956, vol. I, pp. 306–307 (bk xxiii, fols. 179r-v).

33 Kemp 2006 (1981), pp. 142–144; Kwakkelstein 2014 (1994); Laurenza 2001.

34 Kwakkelstein 2014 (1994), p. 41.

35 Aristotle ed. Hett 1936, p. 137:

"The most favourable part for examination is the region round the eyes, forehead, head and face." Kwakkelstein in Haarlem 2018, pp. 39–41.

36 Pliny, *Nat. Hist.* XXXV, xxxvi, 88, describes physiognomists as men "who prophesy people's future by their countenance". The relevant passage is reproduced in Pedretti and Vecce 1995, vol. II, p. 262, § 292. For the titles on physiognomics in Leonardo's library, see Kwakkelstein 2014 (1994), p. 46, n. 85; Laurenza 2021, p. 290, Versiero in Vecce 2021, pp. 304–396.

37 Pedretti and Vecce 1995, vol. II, p. 263: "Vero è che li segni de' volti mostrano in parte la natura degli uomini, di lor vizii e complessioni…". See Kwakkelstein 1991, p. 130, n. 13; Laurenza 2001, p. xiv. Clayton in London 2002, p. 64.

38 Pedretti and Vecce 1995, vol. I, p. 138, §. 13: "Se'l pittore vol vedere bellezze che lo innamorino, lui è signore di generarle, e se vol vedere cose mostruose che spaventino, o che sieno buffonesche, e risibili, o veramente compassionevoli, lui n' è signore et dio …" English translation cited after Kemp-Walker 1989, p. 32. Even outside the context of his notes on the so-called 'Paragone' or rivalry of the arts, Leonardo placed great importance on the emotive power of painting, see his note as given in Pedretti and Vecce 1995, vol. I, p. 221, § 188. Furthermore, as a writer of precepts on painting, Leonardo drew inspiration from certain passages in Leon Battista Alberti's short treatise on painting (written in 1435). In these passages Alberti pointed to the emotive power of narrative painting and provided his reader with some examples of how certain emotional states can be recognised. Alberti ed. Grayson 1972, pp. 80–81. In his writings, Leonardo makes no reference to Alberti's book on painting, nor does it appear in the various lists he compiled of the books he owned. However, parts of its contents were accessible to him through Antonio Averlino's [Filarete] *Treatise on Architecture* (written in the early 1460s), a copy of which he owned. See Vecce 2021, pp. 237–239.

39 Ibid, p. 221, § 187: "Dico anco che nelle istorie si debbe mischiare insieme vicinamente i retti contrari, perché danno gran paragone l'uno a l'altro; e tanto più quanto saranno più propinqui, cioè il brutto vicino al bello, e 'l grande al piccolo, e 'l vecchio al giovane, il forte al debole; e così si varia quanto si po' e più vicino." English translation cited after Kemp-Walker 1989, p. 220.

40 Pedretti and Vecce 1995, vol. I, p. 204, § 139: "Le bellezze con le bruttezze paino più potenti l'una per l'altra."

41 The only antithetical types that feature a multi-figure composition such as the *Adoration of the Magi,* are men of opposite ages, that is either youthful or old. See Zöllner 2022.

42 "Auch wist, daz mein tafell fertig ist, awch ein ander quar, des gleichen jch noch nie gemacht hab". Cited after Schawe in Vienna 2003, p. 338.

43 Bialostocki 1959, p. 32. Schawe in Vienna 2003, p. 343, suggests that the facial ugliness and expression of the old doctor in Dürer's *Jesus Among the Doctors* was intended to allude to the refusal on the part of the Jews to recognise Christ as the son of God. On the overt anti-Semitism that is reflected in Dürer's picture, see Price 2003.

44 Ilsink *et al.*, 2016, pp. 442–449, cat. no. 29 (c. 1530/40).

45 Meijer in Lugano 1998, p. 71.

46 Ilsink *et al.*, 2016, pp. 224–235, no. 11 (*Ecce Homo*); pp. 248–259, no. 13 (*Christ Carrying the Cross*); and pp. 260–266, no. 14 (*The Crowning with Thorns*).

47 For example, Silver 2014, p. 13: "From grotesque drawings by Leonardo, Massys borrowed male faces with ugly features for use in his religious works as well as his early experiments with genre, where they stood for moral turpitude, folly, stupidity, or evil." See also Clayton in London 2023, pp. 39–40.

48 See Capron in London 2023, pp. 11–31; and Clayton in London 2023, pp. 37–38.

49 Capron in London 2023, p. 15. It is instructive to compare the paired figures in Massys's paintings with Leonardo's drawing, illustrating the half-length figures of a grinning old man and a woman with a monstrous face (Kwakkelstein in Haarlem 2018, pp. 177–178, cat. no. 56). The old man, whose face is not deformed, has his head tilted to one side as he looks attentively at the woman with an expression that is difficult to read. Similar to 'The Ugly Duchess', the woman wears an outsized headdress of a type that had been out of fashion for decades and a low-cut dress revealing her cleavage. Both depictions include the motif of a flower as a token of love and represent the woman and the man gesturing with their right hand. These characteristics suggest that Leonardo's drawing represents "a satire on aged lovers". See Clayton in London 2002, p. 94, cat. no. 40.

50 Some of these sheets with copies are discussed in Haarlem 2018, pp. 135–140, cat. nos. 28–33.

51 Kwakkelstein in Haarlem 2018, pp. 177–179, cat. nos. 56, 57.

52 Capron in London 2023, pp. 15, 20–21. On the portrayal of ugly old women in mediaeval and Renaissance poetry, see Bettella 2005.

53 Kemp and Barone 2010, pp. 84–86, no. 34 (with previous bibliography).

54 *Ibid.,* p. 85. See also Bambach 2019, vol. II, p. 430.

55 Kemp and Barone 2010, p. 85 point to Bernardino Luini's *Christ Among the Doctors* (National Gallery, London) in support of the idea that this work derived from a composition, now lost, that Leonardo may have begun at the request of Isabella d'Este. On the other hand, these authors consider that the figure could also be related to a composition depicting Christ carrying the Cross on which Leonardo appears to have been working, as suggested by his drawing of Christ in Venice and some works by his Lombard followers. See also Kwakkelstein in Haarlem 2018, pp. 181–184, cat. nos. 59–61.

56 On Leonardo's sense of humour and his interest in painting comical themes, see De Klerck in Haarlem 2018, pp. 76–87.

Vicki Bruce & Andy Young

THE FASCINATION OF FACES

As is well demonstrated by the wonderful art presented here, faces have a strong fascination for humans. Our brains are exquisitely tuned and adapted to faces – even newborn babies are interested in faces straight from birth. As adults, we show distinct and fast brain responses to faces, and we see faces in abstract patterns that include any face-like elements. Brain injuries can sometimes have striking effects on a person's ability to perceive and recognise faces.

Part of this fascination stems from the fact that faces are involved in a myriad of different social signals, which are reflected in the many different brain areas involved in their perception. Few of the other things that we look at can carry so many different meanings.

We use faces to decipher emotions from expressive patterns made particularly by the eye and mouth regions – e.g. the characteristic mouth shape of a smile, or eyebrows furrowing in anger or puzzlement. But it is the holistic pattern of these features in combination that matters – brow furrowing alone is ambiguous, as it depends on what is happening lower down the face as to whether this is seen as angry or puzzled. Likewise, a smile can be genuine or insincere, and multiple cues (including the eyes) are needed to interpret which may be the case.

We use faces to help us understand speech, particularly in circumstances where it is hard to hear. Speech sounds which are hard to distinguish by ear are usually easier to tell apart from the shapes made by the mouth. For example, in English the difference between an F and an S is hard to hear but easy to see, as only the F sound has lip closure. Surprisingly, even people with normal hearing make use of this 'lipread' information. This ability is acquired in infancy, when much of language is learnt face-to-face.

We use faces to share or to direct the attention of another person by patterns of head and eye movement. Looking at something tells another that you like or want it, or that it is the thing you are referring to in speech. And faces play a key role in regulating the turns in conversation, which is why interactions may be smoother face-to-face than over the phone. Here too, it is the whole pattern that matters – whether eyes appear to look at you or not depends on the direction in which the head is pointing.

The above are some of the uses we make of the patterns that change in a face from moment to moment. Other meanings derived from faces are based on information that is invariant, or changes only slowly as a person ages.

We use the overall shape properties and other superficial features, such as the skin colour of faces, to judge whether a person seems attractive, intelligent, trustworthy, and to categorise them in other ways, such as their (apparent) sex, ethnicity, and age. These first impressions are formed quickly, often from a single glance. Although they may not be valid, these impressions nevertheless have important consequences for our interactions with people.

Because each face is unique in its conformation, faces are used to identify people. For people we are familiar with, the face is the most important means of identification, though of course we can also recognise other things about people, such as their voices. We do not use particular 'features' to identify faces, but its overall 'holistic' pattern. We are so skilled at doing this that familiar face recognition seems, to most of us, almost effortless and automatic.

The faces presented in this volume are not intended as recognisable portraits – the identities of the people shown are generally not known. It may be that our apparently effortless identification of familiar faces gives rise to a false confidence in situations where we should be more cautious. Unfamiliar faces can play an important role in criminal investigations, for example, but a witness's memory for them is often false.

The pictures in this book show how markedly styles of self-presentation have changed over the centuries, yet the way we interpret the face's age, sex, identity, expression, and so on, have remained largely consistent across this time period. The fundamental meanings conveyed by the faces are much the same as they would have been at the time they were depicted.

Vicki Bruce (1950) and Andy Young (1953) are psychologists who have used diverse scientific methods to research many aspects of face perception. Details can be found in their highly illustrated book for a general audience (Bruce & Young, 1998, In the Eye of the Beholder*, Oxford University Press) and a more comprehensive university-level textbook (Bruce & Young, 2012,* Face Perception*, Taylor & Francis – a revised edition is now in press).*

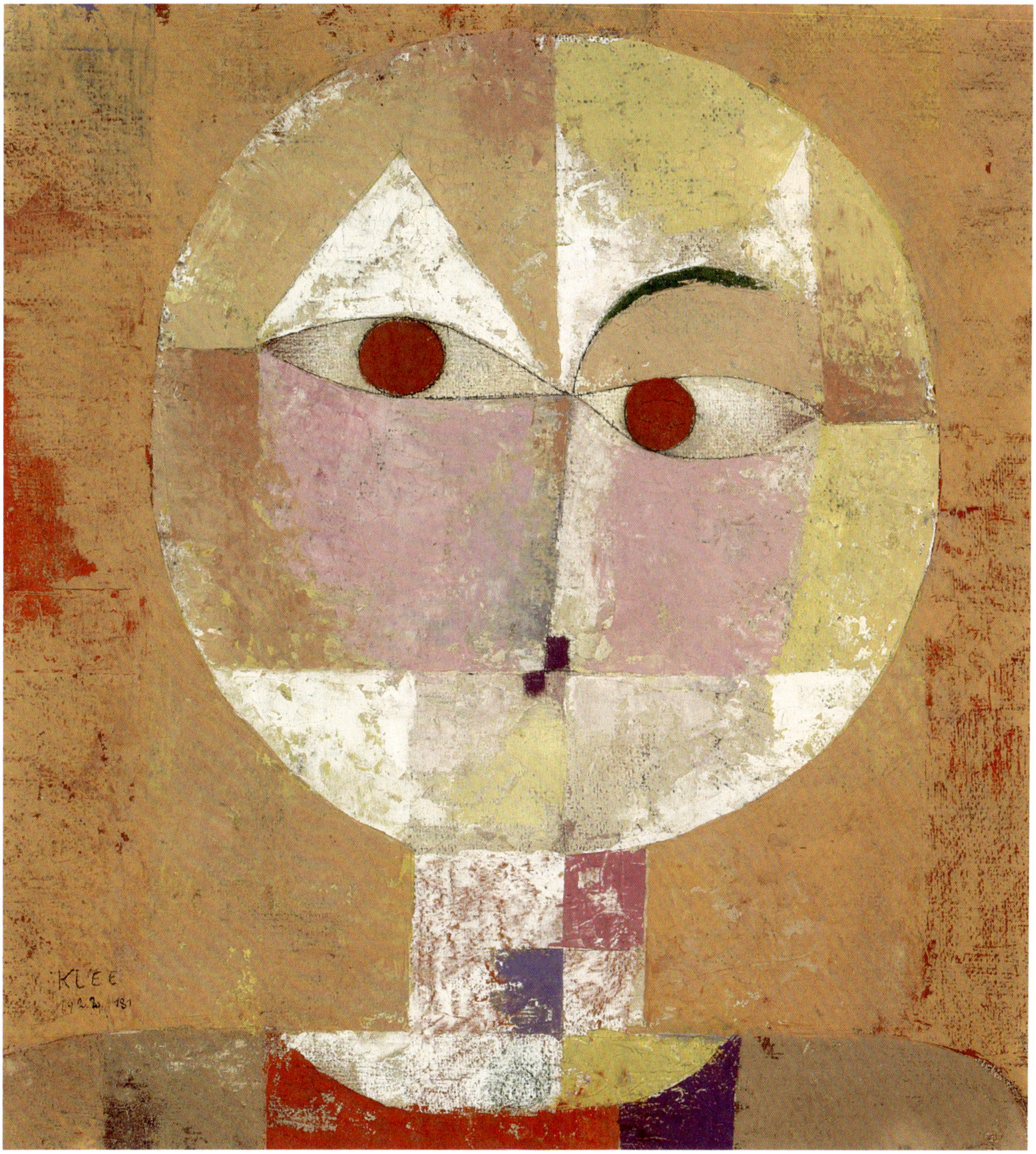

Paul Klee,
Senecio (Baldgreis),
1922, oil on chalk
base on gauze on
cardboard, Kunst-
museum Basel, 1569

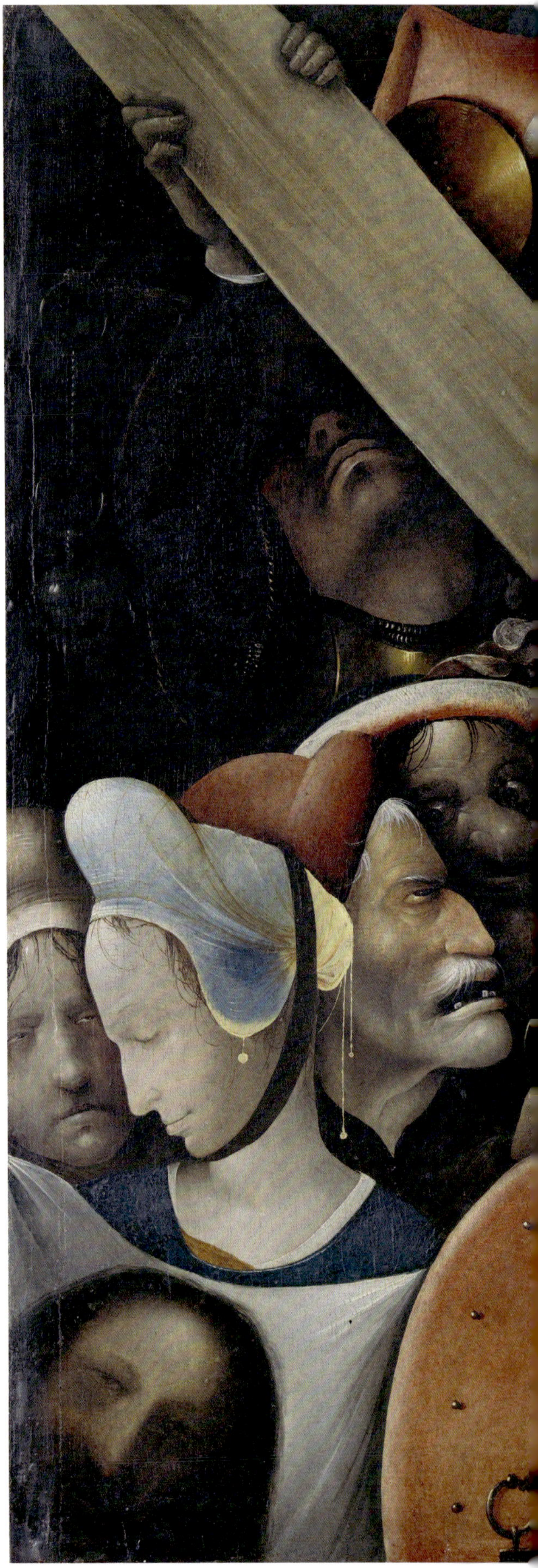

FIG. 30
Circle of Hieronymus Bosch, *Christ Carrying the Cross*, c. 1510, oil on panel, Museum voor Schone Kunsten, Ghent, 1902-H

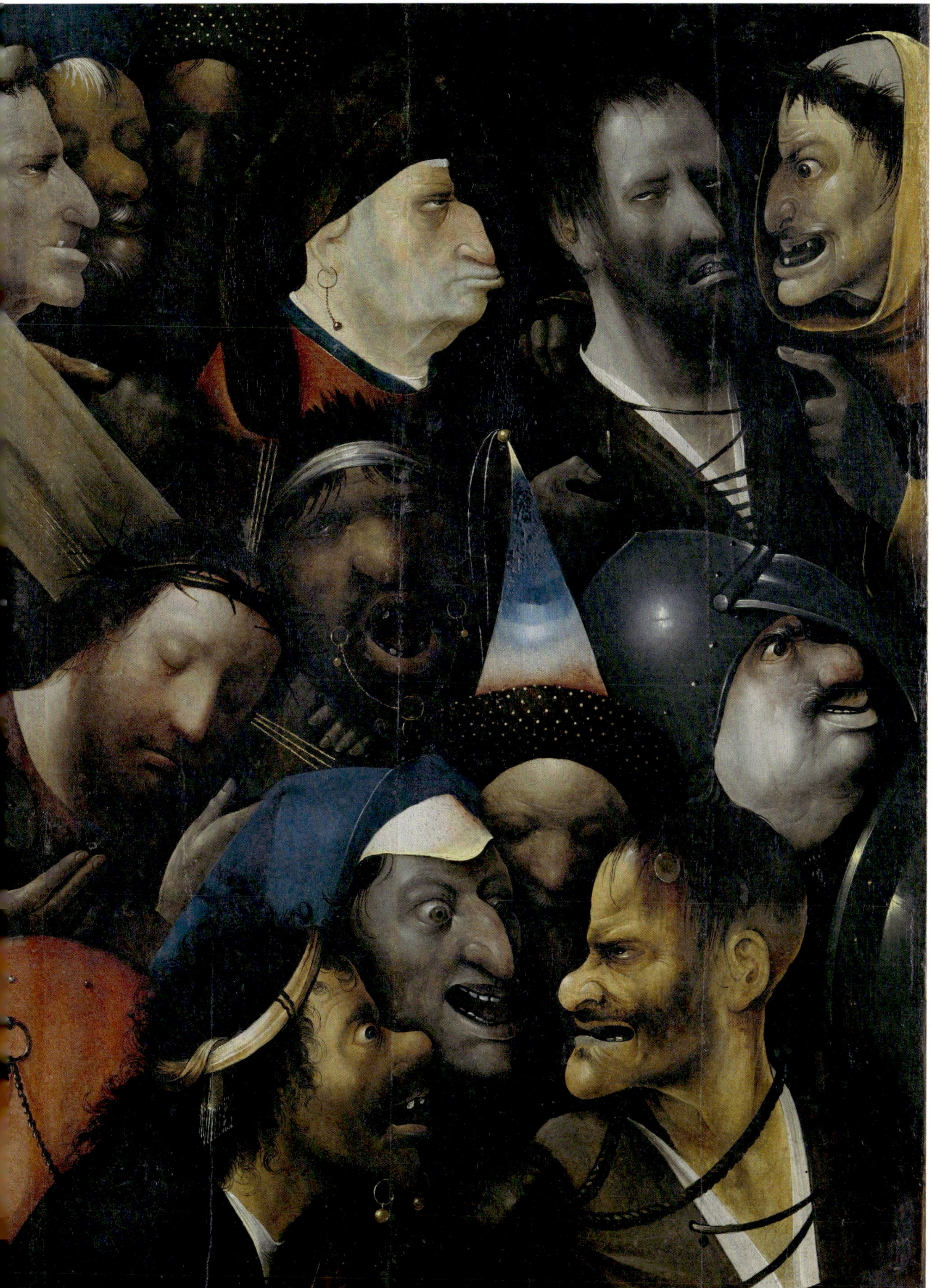

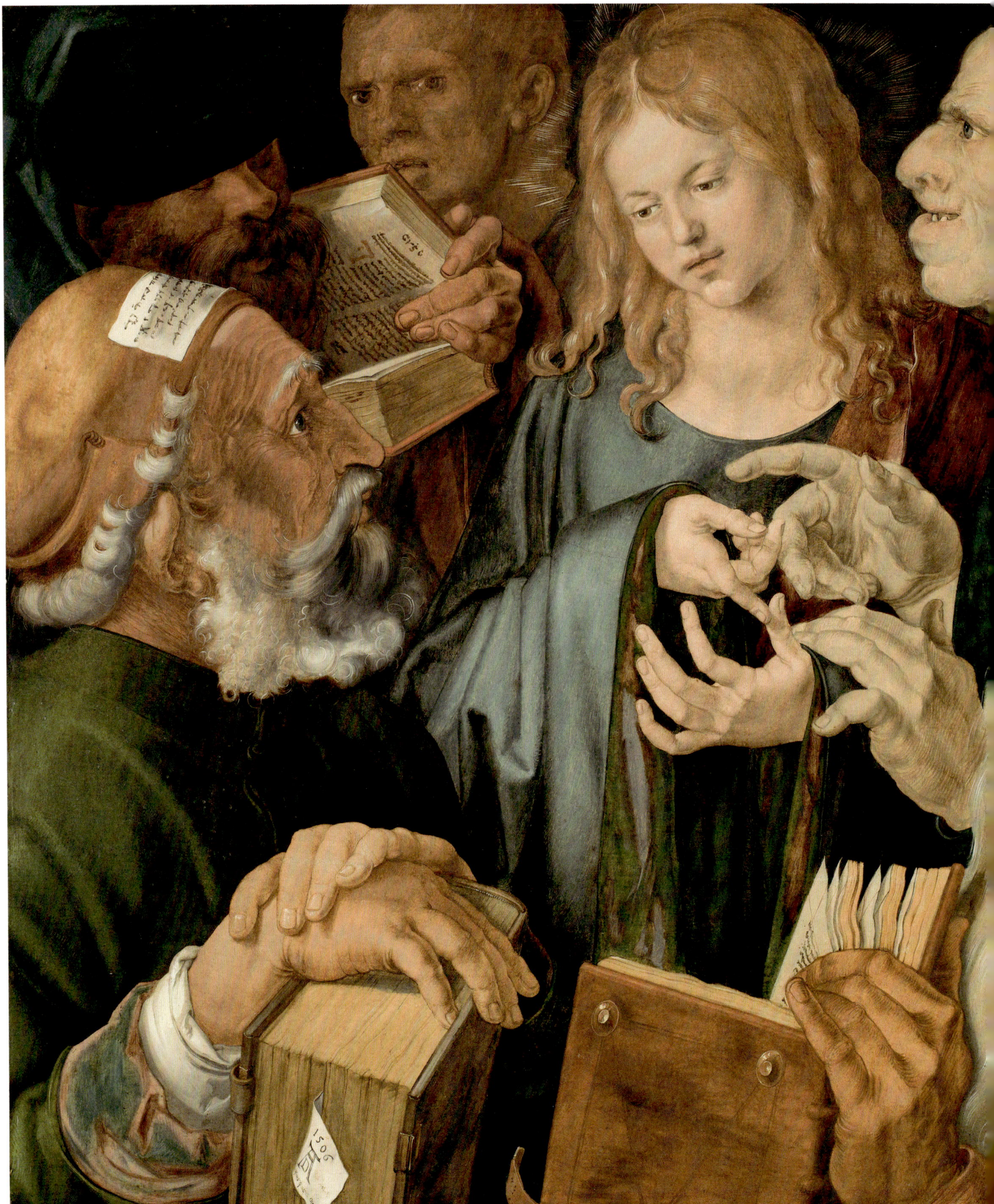

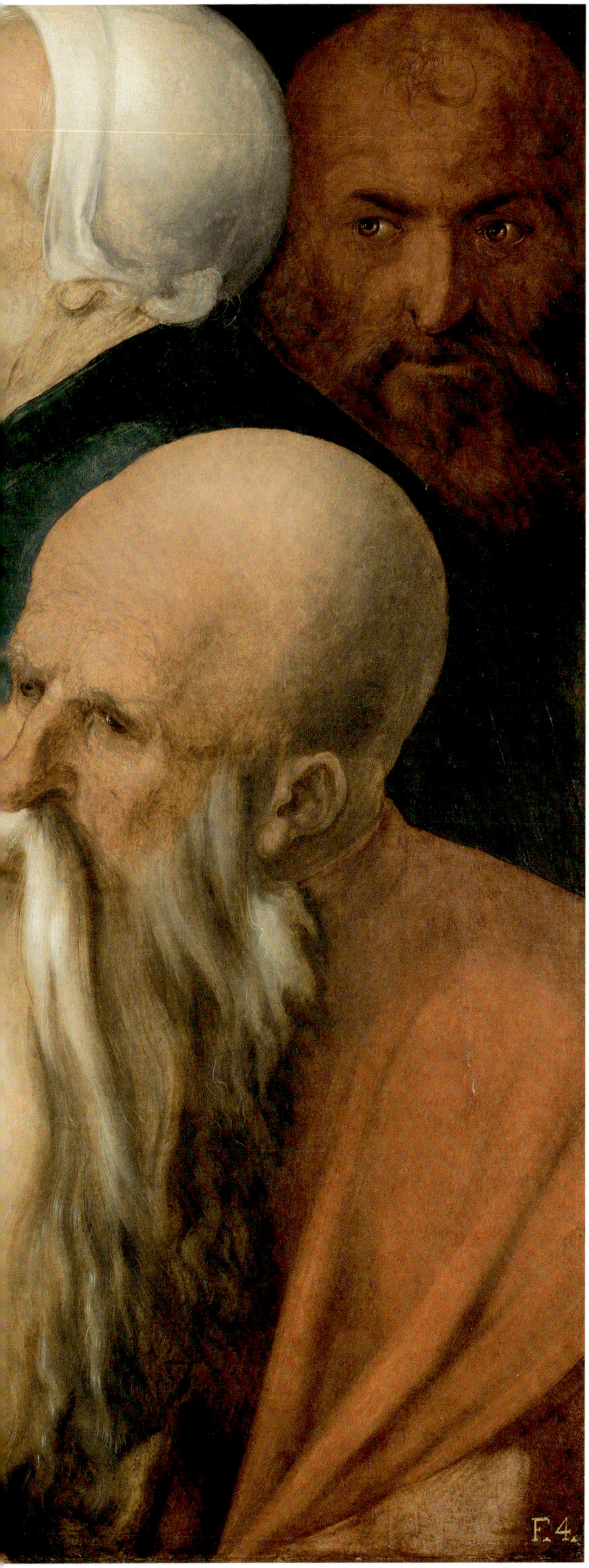

FIG. 31
Albrecht Dürer,
Jesus among the Doctors, 1506,
oil on panel, Museo Thyssen-Bornemisza,
Madrid, 134 (1934.38)

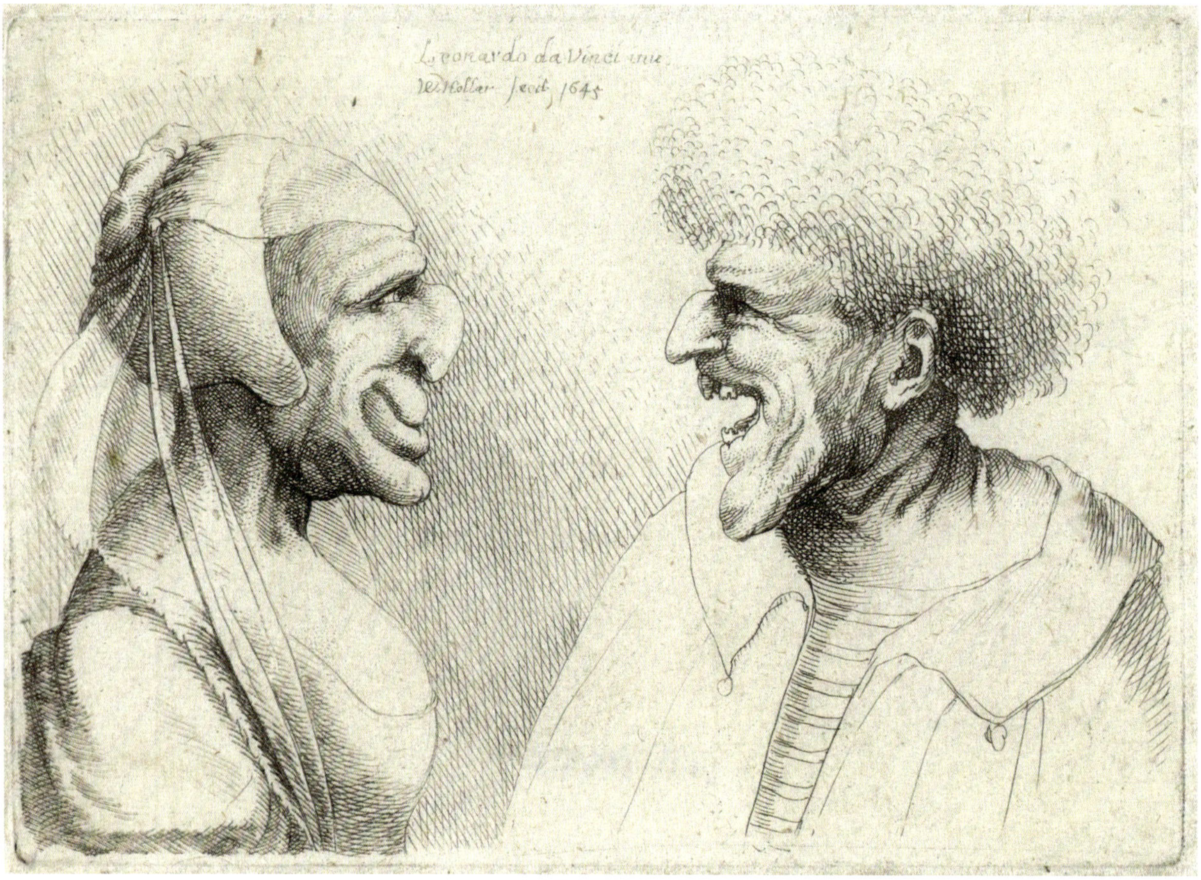
Leonardo da Vinci inv.
W. Hollar fecit, 1645

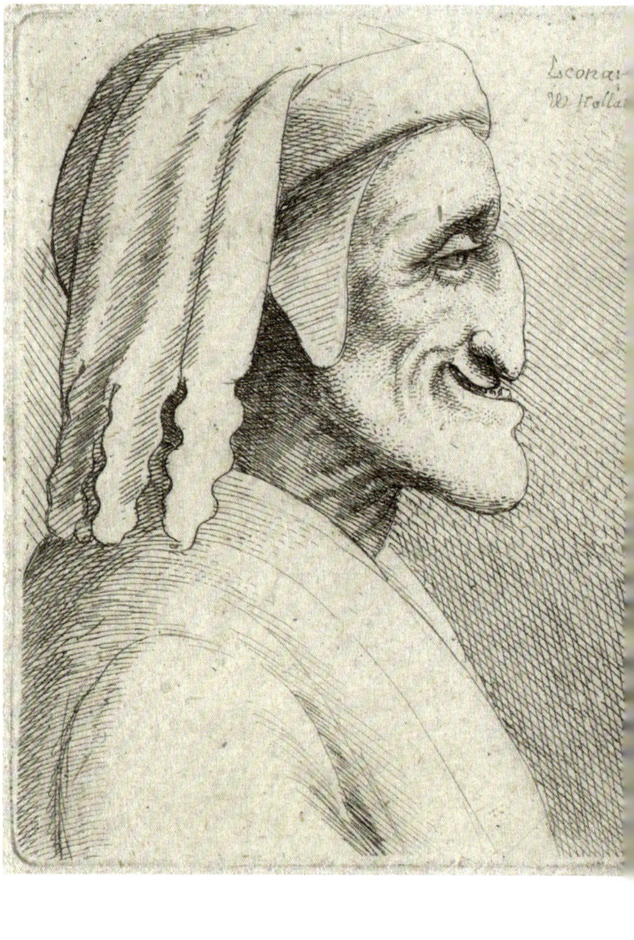

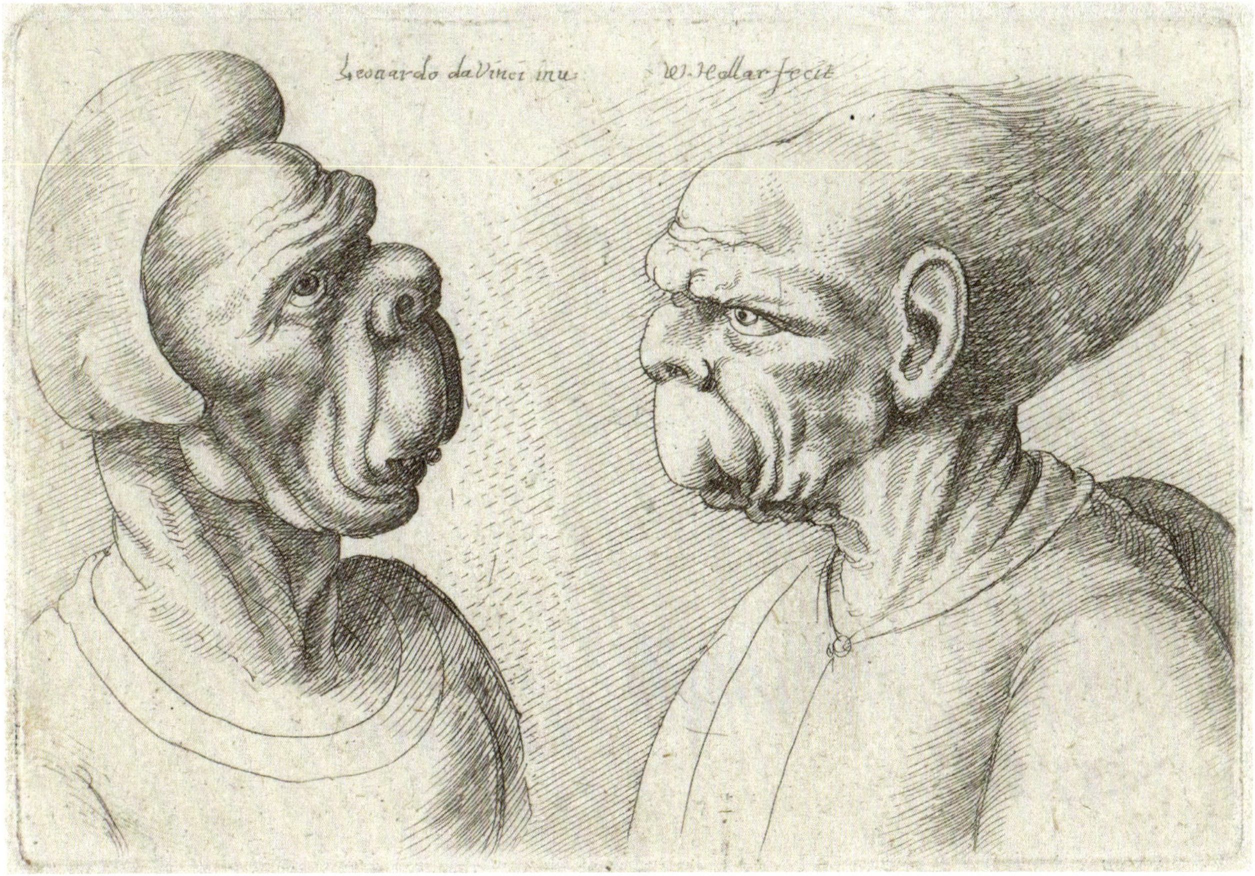

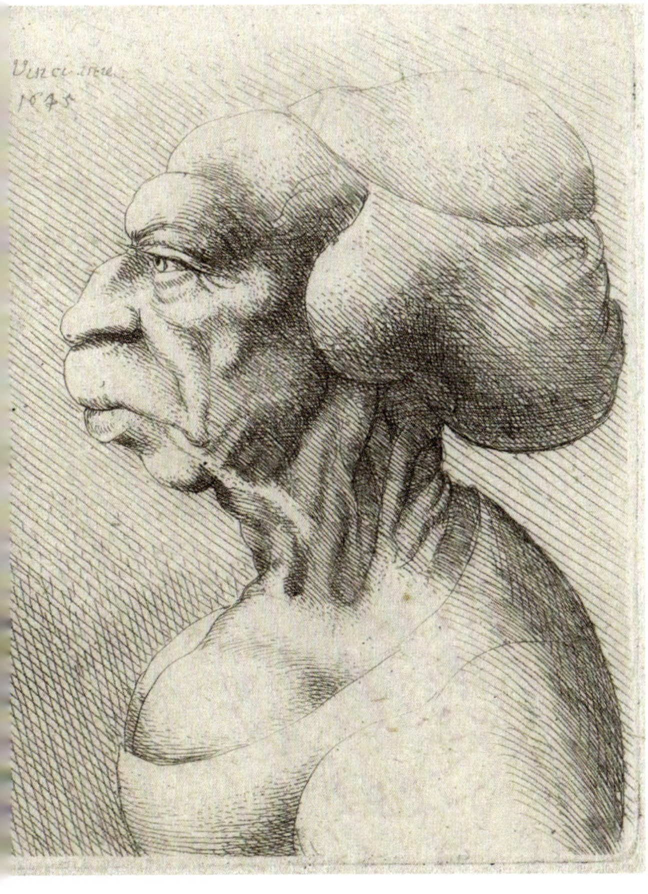

FIG. 32
Wenzel Hollar,
Deformed Heads of a Laughing Man and a Woman with a Cap, 1645, etching, Rijksmuseum, Amsterdam, RP-P-OB-II.453

FIG. 33
Wenzel Hollar,
Deformed Heads of a Man with a Cap (Dante?) and a Woman, 1645, etching, Rijksmuseum, Amsterdam, RP-P-OB-II.451

FIG. 34
Wenzel Hollar,
Two Deformed Heads, 1645, etching, Rijksmuseum, Amsterdam, RP-P-OB-II.454

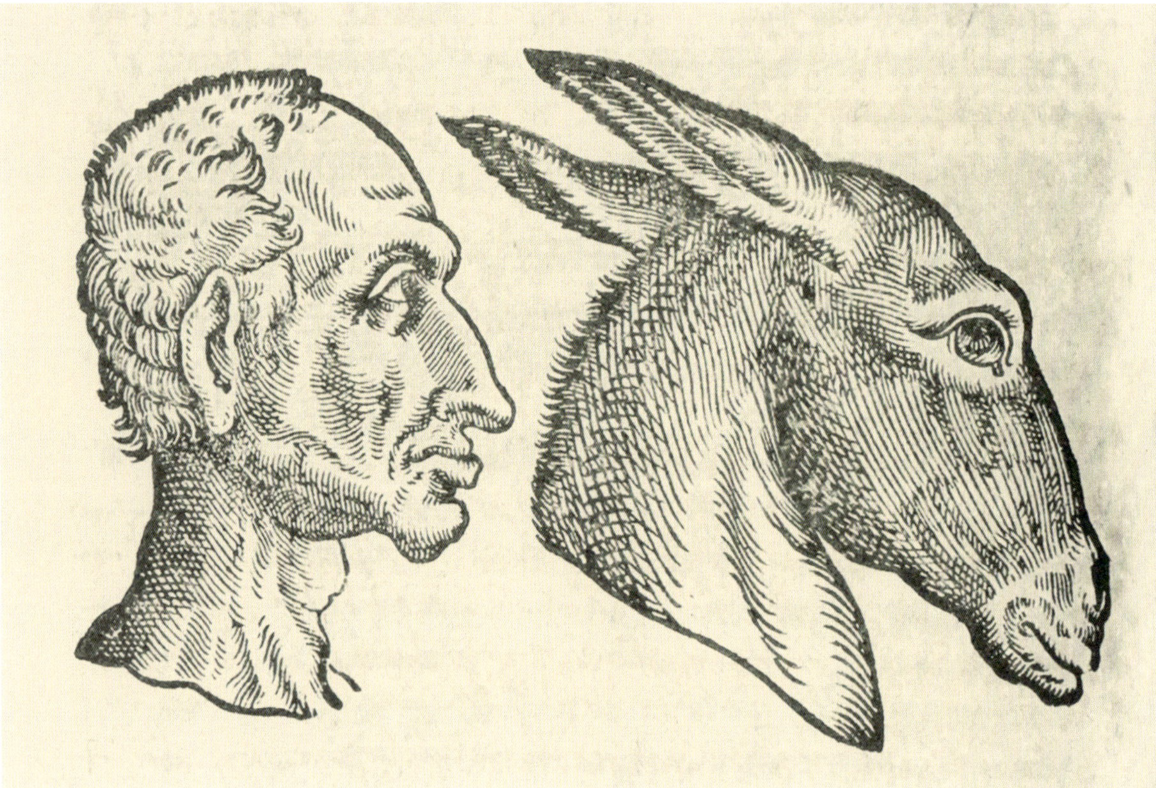

FIG. 35
Giambattista della Porta, *De Humana Physiognomonia*, 1586, letterpress text with engraved illustrations, Royal Library of Belgium, Brussels, VH8.728 A

FIG. 36
Albrecht Dürer, *Hierin sind begriffen vier Bücher von Menschlicher Proportion*, 1528, Erfgoedbibliotheek Hendrik Conscience, Antwerpen, H 11777:a [C2–516 b]

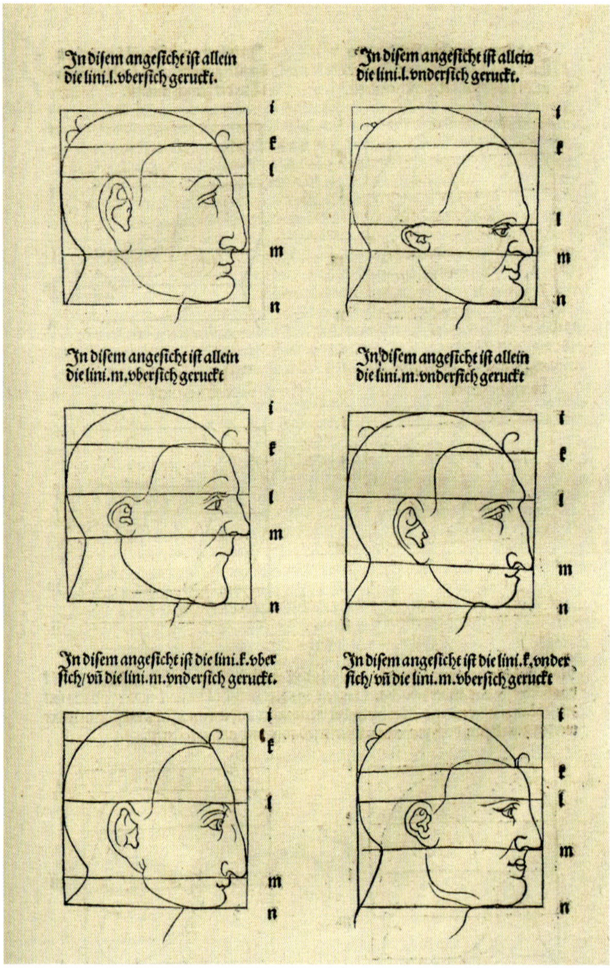

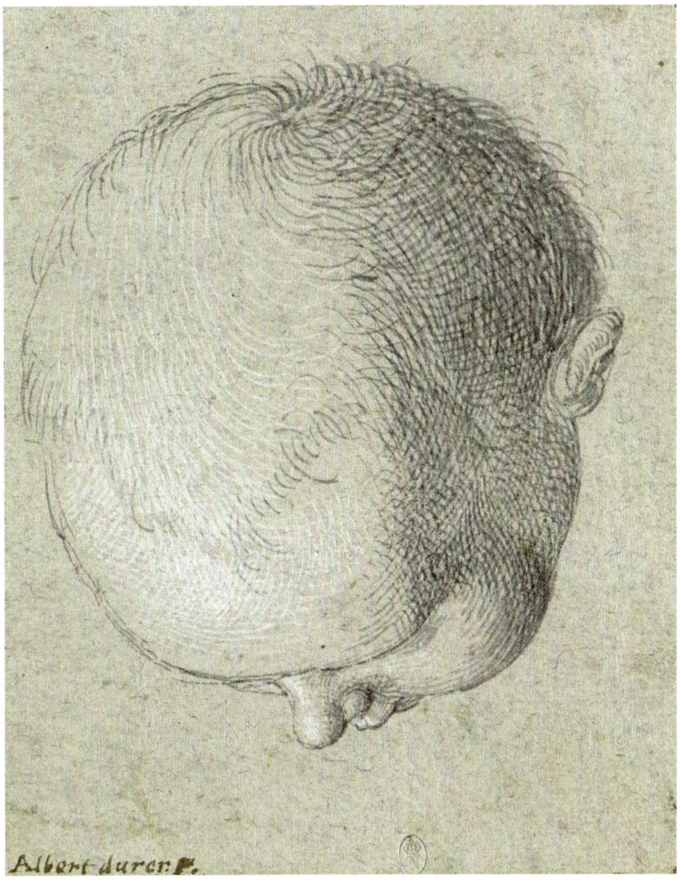

FIG. 37
Albrecht Dürer,
Child's Head in Profile, View from Above, 1506, black ink and white highlights on blue paper, Musée du Louvre – Collections du département des arts graphiques, Paris, 18607.B (recto)

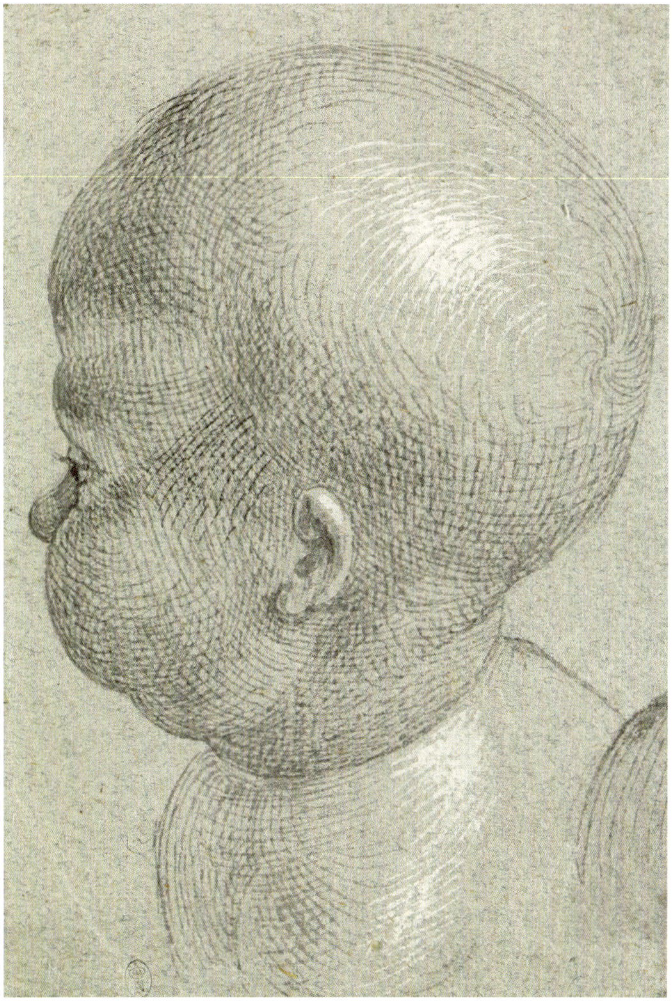

FIG. 38
Albrecht Dürer,
Child's Head in Profile from Behind, 1506, black ink and white highlights on blue paper, Musée du Louvre – Collections du département des arts graphiques, Paris, 18607.A (recto)

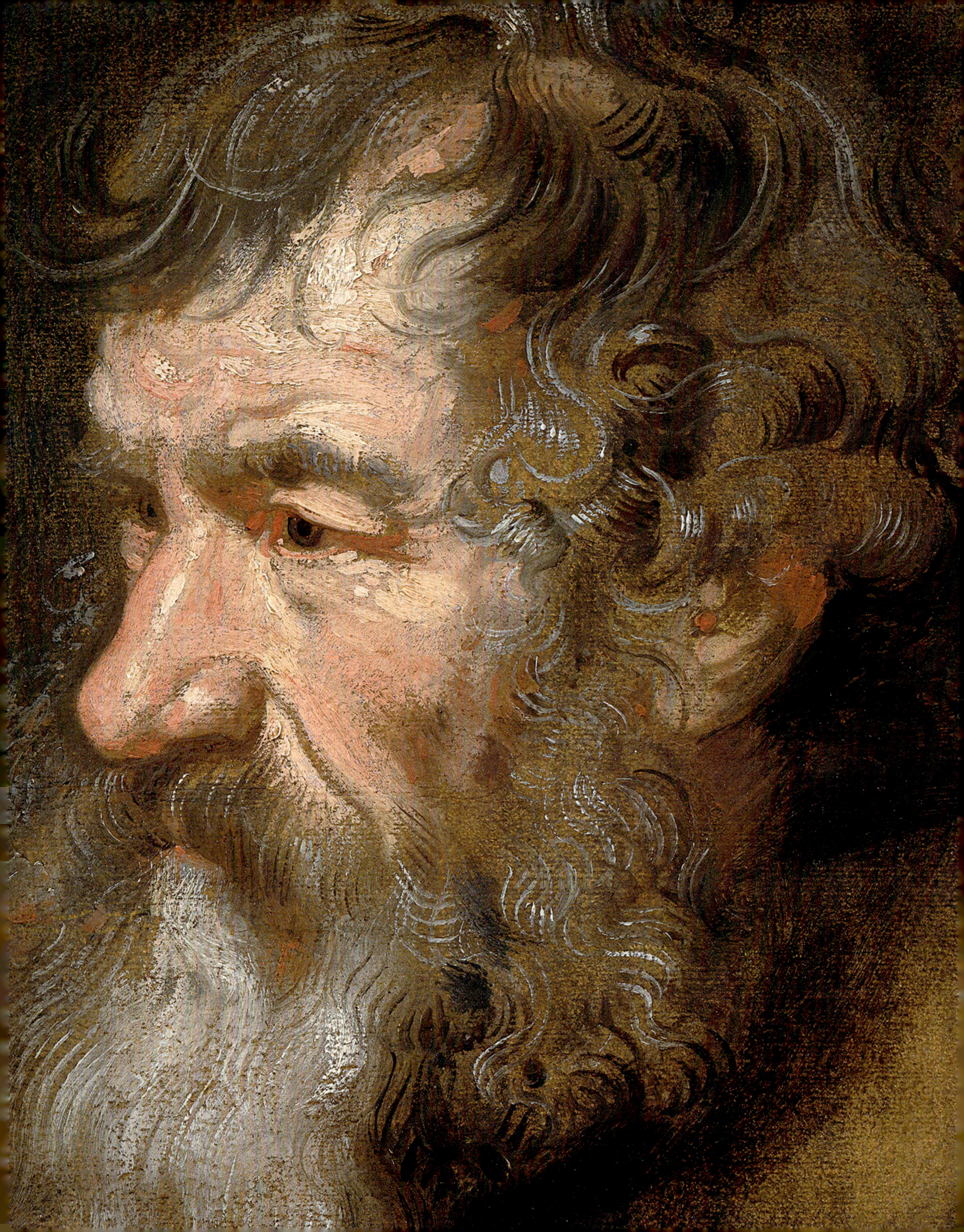

STUDYING FACES

Heads in Northern Histories

Nico Van Hout

For centuries, history painters pursued a similar approach when it came to persuasively depicting biblical, mythological and historical narratives. Given the static aspect of painting, their first task was to select an eloquent moment from the written sources, one that would be recognisable to the viewer and represent the various figures in a clearly legible context. The rendering of individual facial features posed an additional challenge. Prestigious paintings could quickly run to between ten and several dozen characters, each of which the artist needed to provide with an individual appearance, faithful to real life. According to the Roman author Pliny the Elder, the first time this was done was by the Athenian painter Eumarus, who depicted men and women differently, and from life, and by Cimon of Cleonae, who devised the three-quarter profile and represented faces by having figures look backwards, upwards or downwards.[1] Viewers had to be able, moreover, to read a figure's state of mind and supposed character from their face, if they were to understand a story more clearly.

One of the earliest studies of heads in northern Europe is the so-called *Vienna Model Book*,[2] a collection of fifty-six drawings of human and animal heads made in silverpoint on green-tinted paper and glued to small panels that can be folded up like a concertina. The heads were used as models by a book illuminator employed at the court of King Wenceslaus IV of Bohemia (1361–1419) and might also have been employed as a sales tool to persuade potential patrons. Very few drawn or painted preliminary studies by the great Flemish painters of the fifteenth century have survived. Those that have are primarily studies for complete figures or portraits, together with drawn copies: individual heads are much less common.[3] In his discussion of the Van Eyck brothers' *The Lamb of God*, Karel van Mander wrote in his *Schilder-boeck* (1604) that the altarpiece contains some three hundred and thirty faces, none of which resembles another, and that a range of emotions can be identified in them, including divine seriousness, love and devotion. He describes the humble face of the Virgin Mary, for instance, who seems to be murmuring the words in her book.[4] Painters' studios that carried out large-scale and numerous commissions will, in short, have needed a wide variety of drawn or painted studies of heads and limbs that could be used (and reused) in future paintings.

(DETAIL FIG. 50)
Anthony van Dyck, *Two Studies of a Man's Head*, c. 1618, oil on canvas, mounted on panel, Snijders&Rockoxhuis, Antwerp, 77.111

Grotesque heads in Leonardo, Bosch and Dürer

Artists usually chose attractive and symmetrical faces for sacred and noble figures, while grotesque, deformed heads had long been a tried and tested way of depicting morally reprehensible characters. This was entirely in keeping with the philosophy of the ancient Greeks and Romans, who associated the beautiful with the good and the true, and the ugly with the bad and the false. An aristocratic-looking elderly man wearing a laurel wreath, for instance, is depicted in Leonardo da Vinci's pen-and-ink drawing *A Man Tricked by Passers-by* (Fig. 39), surrounded by sinister figures whose grimacing faces signal their wicked intent. There are several similar studies by Leonardo of fancifully deformed couples with strange noses, chins and foreheads, which were turned into prints at an early stage by Wenzel Hollar, among others (Fig. 32, 33 and 34). We find a similar contrast between 'pure' and 'evil' in two crowded compositions executed in close-up to heighten the oppressive atmosphere: *Christ Carrying the Cross*, attributed to a follower of Hieronymus Bosch (c. 1530–1540) (Fig. 31), and *Jesus among the Doctors* (1506) by Albrecht Dürer (Fig. 31). In the first painting, an innocent Christ and a serene Saint Veronica are surrounded by sixteen vicious heads with intimidating noses and conspicuous headgear. The latter are all imaginary and stylised heads which were not drawn from living models, the reality of which has been deliberately distorted. Panofsky rightly likened the evil heads in this surreal image to a scene from a nightmare.[5]

Dürer's painting shows the young Christ surrounded by the heads of six Jewish scribes with pronounced noses, who eye him suspiciously. The gesture of Christ's hands at the centre of the composition seems to express his theological arguments, while the large hands with bent fingers of the scholar shown in profile might suggest that his reasoning is also crooked. The German master completed the painting during his time in Venice, doing so according to the inscription in just five days (*Opus quinque Dierum*). This was possible thanks to his simplified, experimental technique, in which Dürer drew the figures on the panel with finely hatched brushstrokes which he then covered with a thin, transparent layer of paint. He based the Christ figure on a drawing he had made from life of a young man with long hair (Albertina, Vienna).[6] More notably – and not, perhaps without significance – is the absence of preparatory studies for the scribes, who nonetheless define the image to a very large extent. Perhaps the master did not work from life in this instance but was guided instead by his own visual experiences, observations, memories or mental stereotypes because, as Dürer himself wrote, 'a well-practised artist does not need to copy living models for every picture because he sufficiently pours out that which he has been collecting within him for a long time'.[7]

Dürer and human proportion

Like others before and after him, Dürer set out to record the principles and rules of art for future artists. He worked on and off on several ambitious treatises on art theory, which were published posthumously as *Vier Bücher von menschlicher Proportion* [Four Books on Human Proportion] (1528) (Fig. 36). Using these texts, Dürer aimed to teach his readers how to represent a variety of human types based on mathematical figures and pure measurement: to measure, after all, is to know. In the first two books, he distinguished between squat and elongated figures measuring seven to ten times the height of a human head. The human body, the artist believed, could be broken down into geometric figures such as the sphere, cube or cone. We find a neat application of this principle in two drawings on Venetian blue paper of a child's head, observed from above and turned three quarters to the left (Fig. 38).[8] Unlike the Roman Vitruvius or the Italian Alberti, however, Dürer does not seem to have believed in absolute, ideal human proportions, even if he did mention the famous story about the Ancient Greek painter Zeuxis, who supposedly composed an ideal human figure from the most beautiful parts of different models.[9] The artist struggled to define his ideal of beauty, seeking to do so based on vague criteria such as 'function', 'naïve approval' and the 'happy medium'. The third book deals with the alteration of proportions according to mathematical rules applied to both figures and faces. To this end, the artist split the human face into four parts, which he enlarged or reduced to create physiognomies that looked very different – to the point of caricature in some instances (Fig. 35). The fourth and final book deals with the movement of bodies in space.

Head studies and the studio practice of Frans Floris

As well as imaginary heads of their own invention and ones borrowed from the work of others, by the early sixteenth century, artists had already begun to create heads based on living models – often peasants or simple-looking figures.

FIG. 39
Leonardo da Vinci, *A Man Tricked by Passers-by*, s.d., pen and ink on paper, The Royal Collection, Windsor, inv. RCIN 912495

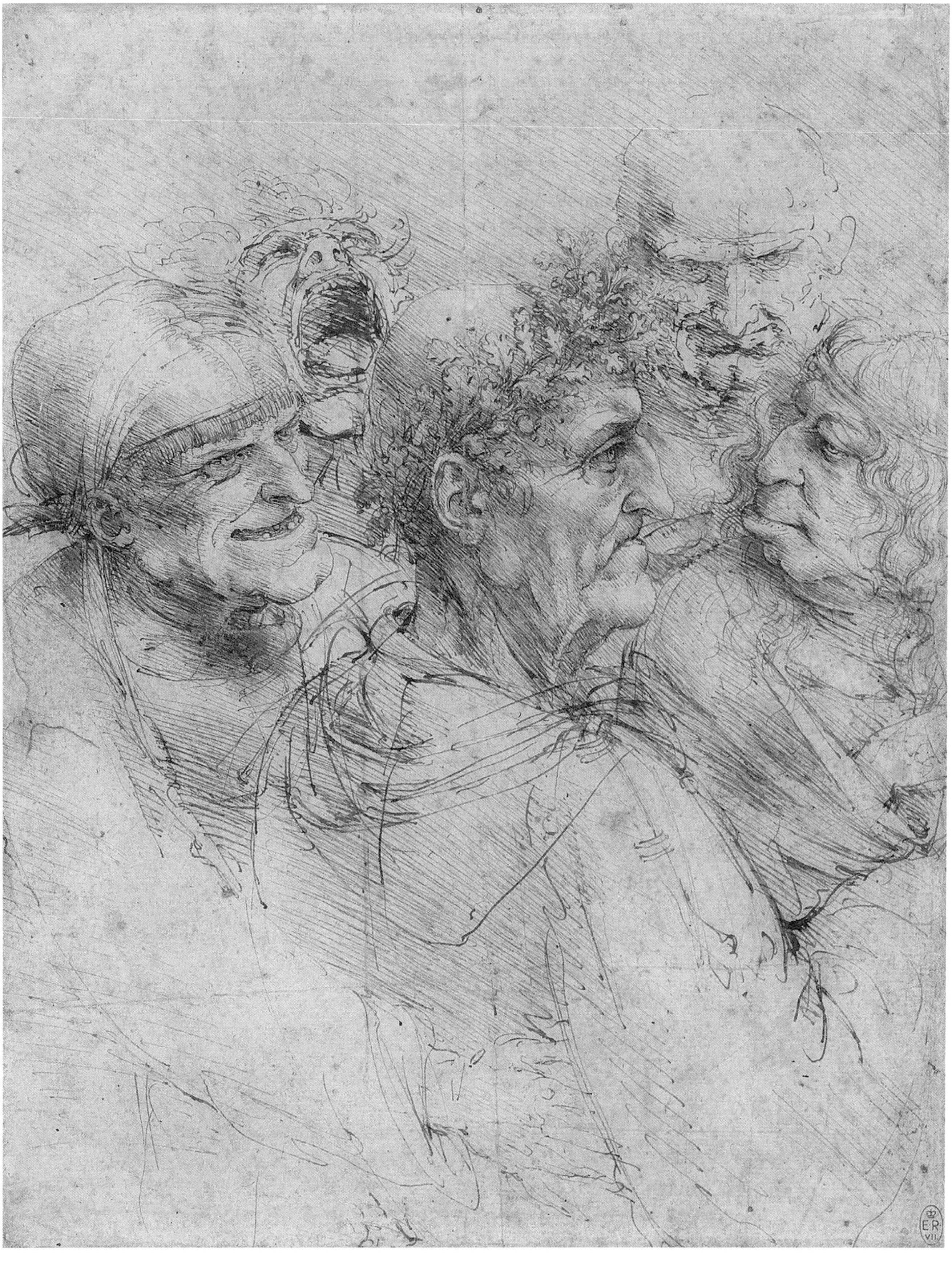

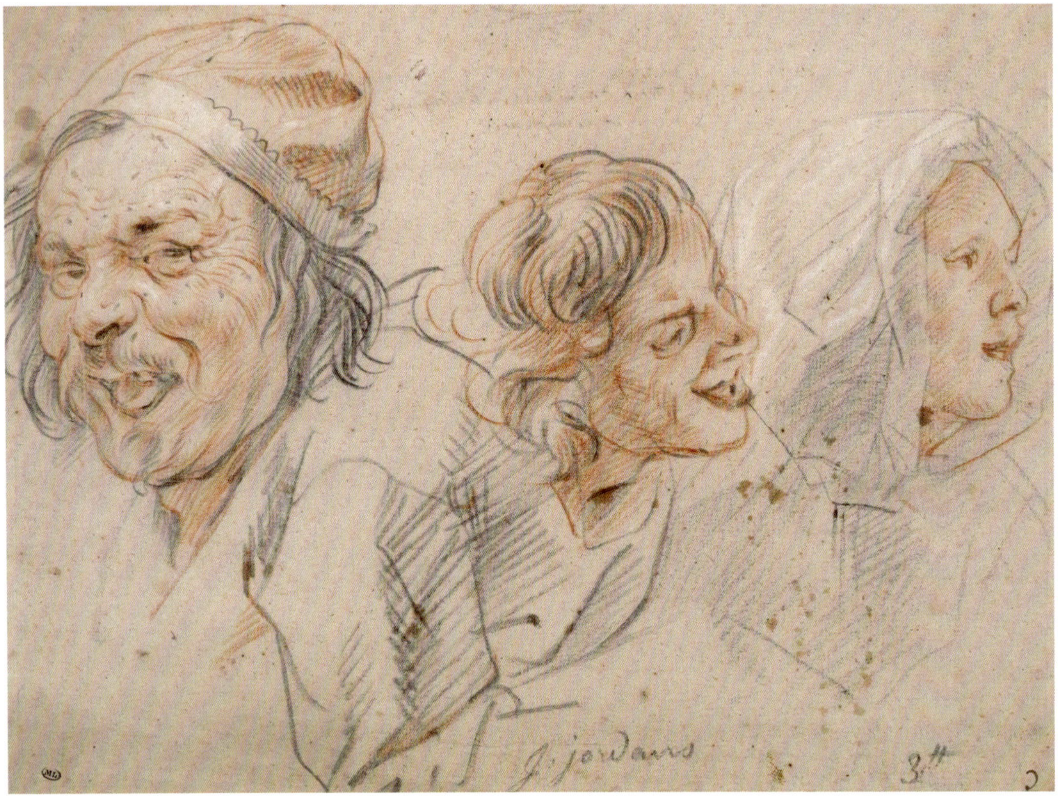

FIG. 40
Jacques Jordaens the Elder, *Three Head Studies,* s.d., black and red chalk, heightened with white, Louvre – Collections du département des arts graphiques, Paris, inv. 20037

Painted studies of this kind have been identified by the likes of Hans Baldung Grien,[10] Quinten Massys,[11] Pieter Bruegel the Elder (Fig. 13), Adriaen Thomaszoon Key and Maerten de Vos.[12] Bruegel's study of a peasant woman has been linked to Van Mander's description of a *Peasant Wedding* in which 'one sees the faces and unclothed parts of the bodies of the peasants in yellow and brown as if tanned by the sun – and their skin is ugly, different from that of town dwellers'.[13]

Various types of head study circulated in Frans Floris's large studio between 1550 and 1570. They included painted heads of bearded men made from life, which can often be found in his religious scenes, and stylised heads of ladies with refined hairstyles, for which the artist drew inspiration from the designs of the Florentine Mannerist Francesco Salviati. Floris used these fashionable prototypes in mythological scenes (Fig. 64).[14] A passage in Van Mander's *Schilder-boeck* offers the reader an insight into how things were done in the master's workshop. The artists' biographer discussed with Frans Menton, a former assistant of Floris, why the best masters of their time had trained up so few pupils. Menton replied 'that it was because of the large works, which Frans frequently had in hand, on which Frans set his journeyman to do the dead-colouring, after he had indicated to them his intention, somewhat with chalk, letting them get on with it, after having said: "Put in these or those heads"; for he always had a good few of those to hand on panels. In this way they gained courage and experience, so that they saw no problem in setting up canvases and designing something themselves and painting from their imagination. Also, those who came to him were mostly the ones with the best talent, who had already learnt for a long time with others, and had practised art, and were well-experienced'.[15]

Head studies and studio practice in Rubens, Jordaens and Van Dyck

When it came to the organisation and practice of his artistic business in the 1610s, Peter Paul Rubens took his cue from the industrious studio of Frans Floris, his predecessor in Antwerp, and from the substantial Venetian and Roman studios of his own time. Rubens and his collaborators, Jacques Jordaens and Anthony van Dyck, received countless ecclesiastical, civil and private commissions in the course of their careers. The European scale on which their Antwerp studios operated created an intense need for head studies as they worked. Research has shown that over a hundred and twenty painted heads continued to circulate on Rubens's premises.[16] It is apparent from one of the artist's letters how carefully he handled his head studies.[17] And he was not the only one: Van Dyck rightly lodged a complaint in 1625 when no fewer than eight such heads were stolen from him in Palermo.[18]

Compilation drawings (Fig. 38 and 48) were used to keep track of the growing variety of heads and available studies. These might have served as a visual reminder when selecting heads and inserting them into compositions, or even as a starting point when designing them, in keeping with what Van Mander had noted regarding Floris's practice. In many cases, they document the original appearance of painted studies containing multiple heads before these were cut down over time into smaller pieces.[19]

It was usually the subject of the painting that determined the choice of models. The faces of gods, biblical kings or heroes needed to radiate power and charisma, characteristics that Rubens found in antique examples. We know from his theoretical notebook, parts of which have survived, that he modelled heads of strong and robust figures from the facial features of famous Roman sculptures, such as the Vatican Nile, the Borghese Gladiator and the Farnese Hercules. Rubens even thought he detected traces of animal in the cuboid facial features of the marble demigod: 'This is evident in Hercules' hair, which perfectly resembles the mane of a lion or a bull, the forehead has something of the bull and the lion, while the neck and the shoulders are fleshy and packed with muscle, like those of the bull.'[20] Physiognomic parallels like this between humans and animals were not uncommon at the time and had already been drawn by the Italian pioneer of facial theory, Giambattista della Porta (Fig. 35). Rubens's notebook is filled, moreover, with metaphysical ideas about the supposed original perfection and subsequent degeneration of the human figure, which drew on antique notions of humanity's decline from a golden to an iron era. Sadly, comparisons of this kind would be lifted out of their artistic context by pseudo-scientists, who wrongly believed they could read a person's character from the shape of their face, thereby laying the foundations for discriminatory racial theories.[21]

For the most part, however, Rubens drew on head studies based on living models. Studies of faces looking up or down were useful for an 'Assumption of the Virgin' or for Christ's miraculous appearance to saints, while the heads of simple folk were desirable when representing the 'Adoration of the Shepherds' following the birth of Christ. A black king was indispensable, in turn, to the iconography of an 'Adoration of the Magi'. As one might expect, artists were keen to depict the facial features and skin colour of an African man faithfully.[22] Several brilliant studies of black models by Rubens are known, but also by Jordaens, as we see in his *Two Head Studies of an African Man* (Fig. 93).[23] The heads in the studies might be coarse, charismatic, pious or sweet in appearance, but above all the faces needed to have a neutral expression if they were to be usable in a variety of contexts. It was only in the final painting that Rubens and his assistants gave them the desired expression, whether attentive, fearful, astonished or laughing. For efficiency's sake, Rubens painted the generally life-size study heads on the same scale as the compositions into which they would be copied.

We do not know whether Rubens found his models in the street and asked them to pose, as Caravaggio and Federico Barocci claimed to do,[24] but he did repeatedly choose monks as models,[25] just as those Italian artists had done (Fig. 53). In all likelihood, he also found suitable models among his household staff.[26] A 1693 inventory, for instance, mentions a head study of Rubens's laundress (*Wasgersse*).[27] Perhaps she was the old woman with the sharp nose, protruding chin and sunken cheeks who is depicted in various studies and from a variety of angles. We recognise the same model in right profile (Fig. 42), from the front, with a somewhat gruff expression (Fig. 43), from below and in profile with a white headscarf (Fig. 46), and turned three quarters to the right with a smaller headscarf (Fig. 45). One of the compilation sketches, incidentally, shows that the first two of these studies were originally linked and probably belonged to the same panel (Fig. 49).

As part of his studio practice, Jordaens painted and drew heads that are laughing, grinning, startled, crying out or yawning (Fig. 40). In contrast to the transparent and subtle way Rubens structured his paint layers, Jordaens executed his oil studies with colourful, visible brushstrokes intended to intensify the expressiveness of his secondary figures. This is what we find, for instance, in the series of heads he painted of an elderly man, including the double oil study in Ghent (Fig. 10). Thanks to a famous portrait by Cornelis de Vos, we can identify the model as the servant of the Antwerp Guild of Saint Luke, Abraham Grapheus (Fig. 9).[28] Another study shows Grapheus looking up and presenting the viewer with the soft, wrinkled skin of his neck (Fig. 51). It is hard to see Jordaens's obsession with the picturesque ugliness of his model in isolation from the earlier tradition of expressive or deformed character heads in Dürer and Massys. The head of the old woman in left profile that we discussed earlier (Fig. 46) can be found in a secondary figure in *Offering to Ceres* in the Prado (Fig. 52). When it came to paintings such as *The Tribute Money* in Copenhagen, Jordaens drew heavily on his stock of heads, which could actually become more of a *raison d'être* for the composition than depicting an interesting story.[29]

Jan Brueghel the Younger once saw his uncle, the engraver Pieter de Jode the Elder, posing in Van Dyck's studio. The young artist promised that 'I will make a fine apostle of him.'[30] Van Dyck had a penchant for wiry, almost gaunt models with wild hair and deep-set eyes, which ensured strong shadows; examples include the imposing *Two Head Studies of a Bearded Man*, in New York (Fig. 117), another *Two Studies of a Man's Head* (Fig. 50) and the *Head Study* (Fig. 54), in Antwerp. He captured the sometimes dark psyche of his models with a palette of earth colours and powerful, confident brushwork. A similar interest in the personality of models characterises the work of Michaelina Wautier, who is known to have produced several studies of young people. This artist had the ability to capture the pose and expression of her model as if in a snapshot (Fig. 55).

As the great Antwerp history painters died and their studios declined in the late seventeenth century, head studies also lost their function. A substantial number of sketched studies of this kind were posthumously 'refined' or 'upgraded' by other artists, who added costumes and attributes to them. In this guise, the works then found their way onto the art market as standalone tronies.[31]

(DETAIL FIG. 117)
Anthony van Dyck, *Two Head Studies of a Bearded Man*, 1618–1620, oil on canvas, private collection

1 Pliny the Elder 1952, Book XXXV, xxxiv, 55–57. Reiterated by Van Mander 1604, 64r.
2 Vienna, Kunsthistorisches Museum, inv. KK 5003. Scheller 1995, 226–232, no. 20. For the transition from patterns to studies from life, see: *From Pattern to Nature in Italian Renaissance Drawing: Pisanello to Leonardo*. Proceedings of the international conference held at the Dutch University for Art History, Florence, 6–7 May 2011.
3 Koreny 2002, 22–25, 64–66, no. 12; 77–81, no. 15.
4 Van Mander, 1604, 200v.
5 Panofsky 1948, I, 114. One of the heads – the man with the hook nose in right profile at the top – is based on a horizontally reversed figure in a drawing by Bosch, the *Disreputable Pair* (c. 1505–1516), Lehman Collection, New York. Koreny 2002, 20, Fig. 23; 188–189, no. 46
6 Dürer made similar sharply observed anatomical studies, studies of drapery and heads looking up on blue paper in preparation for the Heller altarpiece (c. 1507–1509). See Sander and Schulz 2013, 219–233.
7 *Hierin sind begriffen Vier Bücher von menschlicher Proportion*, boek 3, fol. T3v.: 'Das ist die ursach das ein wol geübter künstner nit zu einem yetlichem bild darff lebendige bilder ab machen/dann er geust genugsam herauß was er lang zeyt von aussen hineyn gesamlet hat.' Quoted from Parshall 2013, 399, note 27. The English translation is from *idem.* p. 399.
8 Dürer used these head studies for the putti in the *Feast of the Rose Garlands* (Národní Galerie, Prague) and again for angels in the *Madonna with the Siskin* (Gemäldegalerie, Berlin, both c. 1506) and in the Heller altarpiece (c. 1507/09, disappeared in 1729). See Grollemund 2013, no. 4; Metzger 2019, 458–459, nos. 128–140.
9 Rupprich 1956, vol. 3, 272, lines 19–20 (c. 1512/1513).
10 Hans Baldung Grien, *Head of an Old Man* (Gemäldegalerie, Berlin, cat. 552B, c. 1518/1519), painted on paper and then glued onto a panel.
11 Quentin Massys, *Head of an Old Man* Museu Nacional d'Art de Catalunya, Barcelona, inv. 064998-000, c. 1525).
12 Studies in private hands. Van Hout 2020, 20–21 and text ill. 1–3.
13 Miedema 1994, 193. Sellink 2019, 272–273.
14 Wouk 2018, 216–243.
15 Miedema 1994, 229.
16 Van Hout 2020, 17–70.
17 Rooses-Ruelens 1887–1909, VI, 222–224, doc. DCCCLXI; Magurn 1955, 410–41, no. 244.
18 The artist was robbed of 'Una testa d'un Giovene nominato Baldassaro con I capelli nigri et rizzi una testa di simuni fatta a guise di donna una testa di marinaro una testa di san Petro una testa d'una donna con li capilli sparsi una testa di lucia co lu pettu rigido una testa di lettore alla satiresca et una testa che grida con la bocca aperta,' quoted from Mendola 1999, 61, note 18; and Eaker 2015, 186. Possibly identifiable as Barnes *et al.* 2004), nos. I.4, I.42 and under no. I.41.
19 Van Hout 2020, 59–61.
20 Jombert 1773, 3.
21 By Lavater 1775–1778, among others.
22 McGrath 2008; Van Haute 2015; Kolfin 2017; Esposito 2020.
23 The head on the right from this study can be found in Jordaens's *Apollo and Marsyas*, Belfius Bank Collection (c. 1625).
24 By Barocci's biographer Gian Pietro Bellori. Wohl, Wohl and Monatanari 2005, 171.
25 Van Hout 2020, nos. 47A and B, 52A, 61.
26 Watteeuw 2015, 66–67; Van Hout 2020, 33–34.
27 Inventory of Cornelia van Aken, Antwerp, 4 May 1693. Duverger 2002, 256.
28 Merle du Bourg 2012.
29 *The Tribute Money. Peter Finding the Silver Coin in the Mouth of the Fish* or *'The Ferry Boat to Antwerp'*, c. 1623, (Statens Museum for Kunst, Copenhagen, inv. KMS3198). See Wadum and de la Fuente Pedersen 2008.
30 'Ick sal der wel eenen frayen apostel aff maecken.' See Galesloot 1868, 595. For Van Dyck's apostles, see Roland 1984 and Lammertse 2002.
31 Van Hout 2020, 63–66.

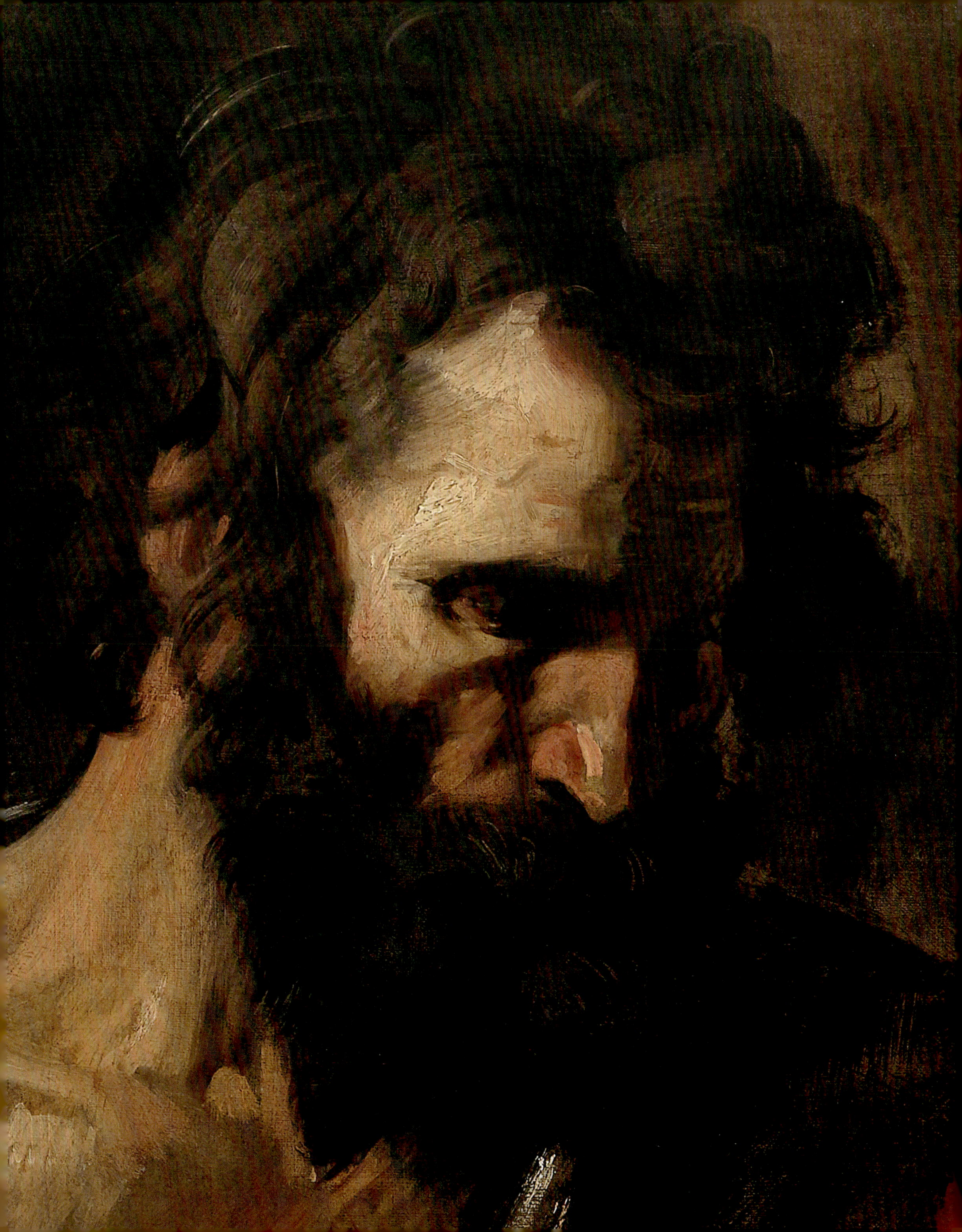

Cian McLoughlin

REFLECTION

CAUGHT IN MID AIR

To look at it is to set it going. Our eyes fizz around the surface as his brush surely must have done as he made it. The trace of his hand is still alive, every brush mark still visible and distinct.

Rembrandt's *The Laughing Man*, painted in around 1629 while he was living in Leiden, is very different from the smoother work he typically made at the time. The face is a slippery network of marks, each sliding one into the next. The whiskers are carved into the wet paint with the back of a brush – the glowing copper and gold leaf of the support transformed into tangled highlights. It feels almost centrifugal in its fluidity. How does it all hold together? The scaffolding of these marks somehow bind themselves into a prismatic unity. Is the laughing man the subject of the painting or is it 'laughter'? Would a conventional portrait have the same inner energy? This painting, to borrow from Robert Frost, is like ice on a stove, riding on its own melting.

I owe a huge personal debt to paintings such as Rembrandt's *The Laughing Man*. I had been making more or less conventional portraits professionally for 15 years before I first heard the term 'tronie'. I knew many of the paintings the term referred to individually but I never realised that they had a collective name and shared a common set of impulses. My research into the subject coincided with a period when I was rapidly losing what interest I had in portraiture's conventions, namely slavish physical likeness of an identifiable sitter mindful of social status, posterity or some sort of narrative. But now I had found 'tronies', a genre of head paintings that had no interest in these conventions in the first place. Reinterpreting these anonymous, expressive heads was about freedom, the same freedom they allowed their original makers. There were times, before tronies, when I'd be right in the work and things would be happening on the canvas that were exciting and unpredictable, but they'd have nothing to do with a 'portrait'. Though I wanted to be able to respond to what was happening in the painting, I would have to remind myself of the goal, the fixed endpoint, and check my instincts to serve the desires of a portrait, often undoing passages of the painting that I was excited by.

A key distinction emerged: the subject of a portrait is the finish line, but in a tronie the subject is the point of departure. This realisation was crucial to what came after. I moved towards un-portrait-like qualities and un-portrait-like ways of making decisions. Precision, yes, but a precision answering to a different logic – the logic of the tronie. Commission portraiture, with its built-in set of requirements, demands a level of precision that, in a world before photography, required stillness. Once, on a visit to the National Portrait Gallery in London, I walked through room after room of royals, merchants and other notables of their time. Were these sitters really all as glum as they were portrayed? Or were their expressions just those of people forced to sit still for hours while an artist laboured over a precise likeness? Was the glumness a posture of gravitas adopted with posterity in mind?

Tronie makers were interested in less-formal images of people – unguarded moments that wouldn't be repeated: a gesture, a fleeting expression done for the simple inspiration the subject provides. They sought out the undisciplined reality of life. They made paintings in the present tense. Less about totems of power and privilege, they framed humanity – alikeness, yes, but one empathetically accessible. These ambitions came with their own challenges. Try to get a sitter to maintain a genuine smile, or a look of shock or, if they've had far too much to drink, any expression at all for more than a minute or two. This book is filled with many such expressions, somehow miraculously captured. Far outweighing those challenges came the freedoms, freedoms that, for me, underscore the appeal of the tronie. The sitter is unknown so the artist is free to paint, say, a portrait of an emotion, a feeling; free to suggest, to ignore, to indulge, to adjust, to insult, play with composition, or experiment with something more elusive again; free to make work undulled by the debilitating gaze of formal portraiture; free from the controlling influence of commissioners and all the expectations that come with that contract. These freedoms carve out an arena for the purest form of an artist's style and technique where the conventional gives way not to the exotic or the comic but to the experience of life caught in mid-air.

Cian McLoughlin (1977) lives and works in Dublin. Having studied architecture and film, he is currently a full-time painter, mainly of portraits and cityscapes.

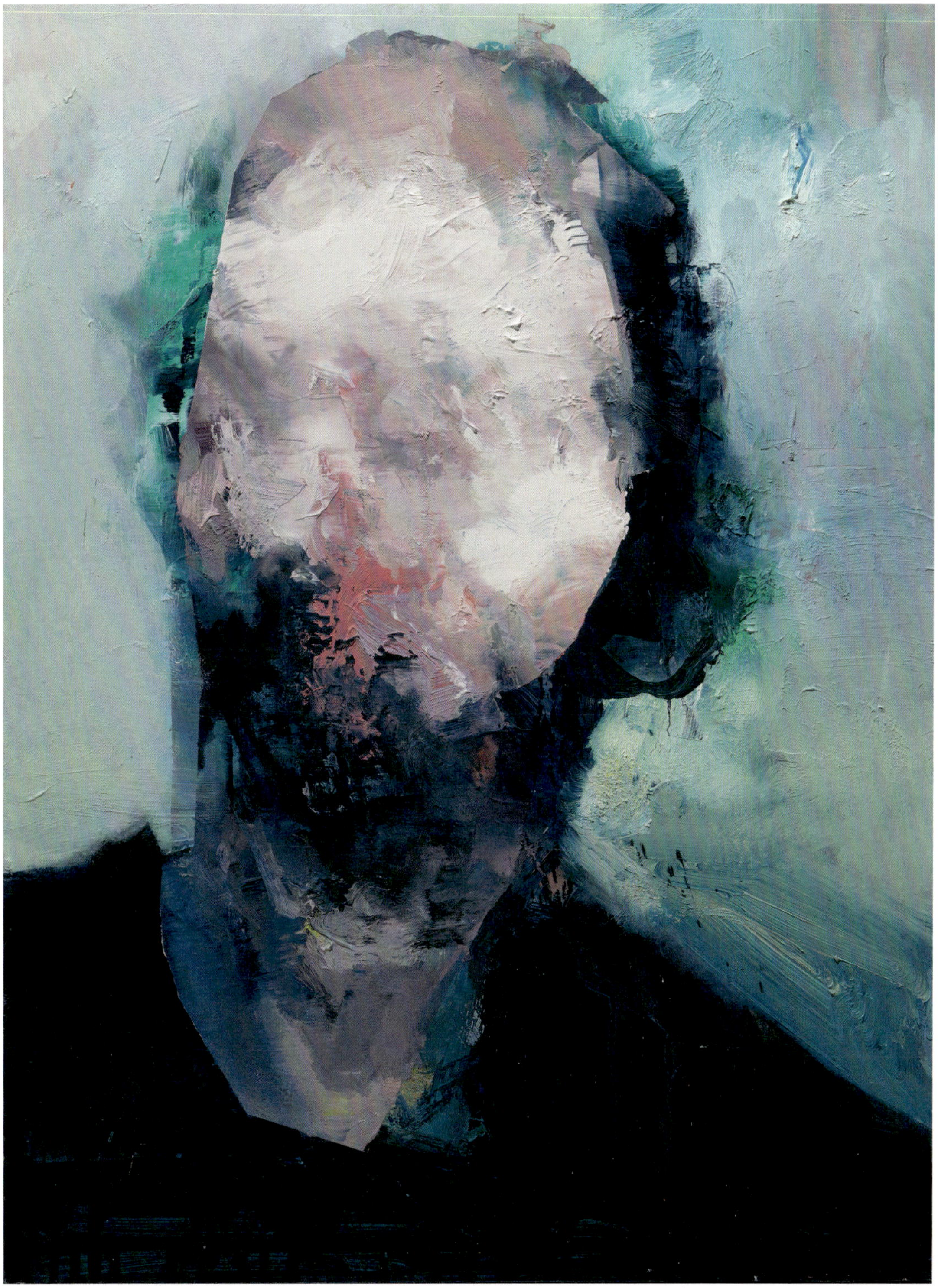

Cian McLoughlin,
Self-portrait, 2018,
oil on board, National
Gallery of Ireland,
NGI.2019.41

FIG. 41
Frans Floris the Elder, *Head Study of a Man with a Beard*, s.d., oil on panel, KMSKA, Antwerp, inv. 5158

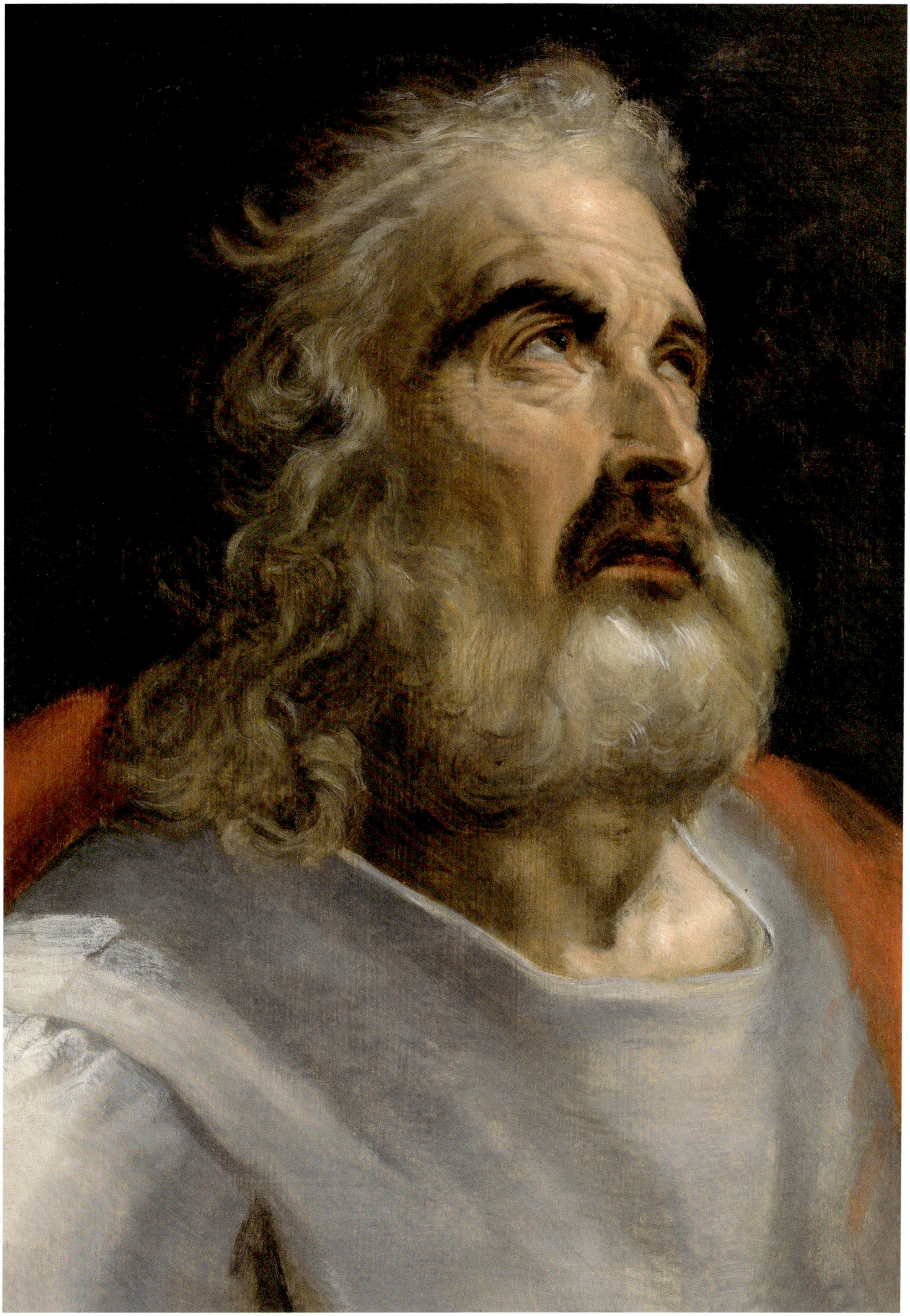

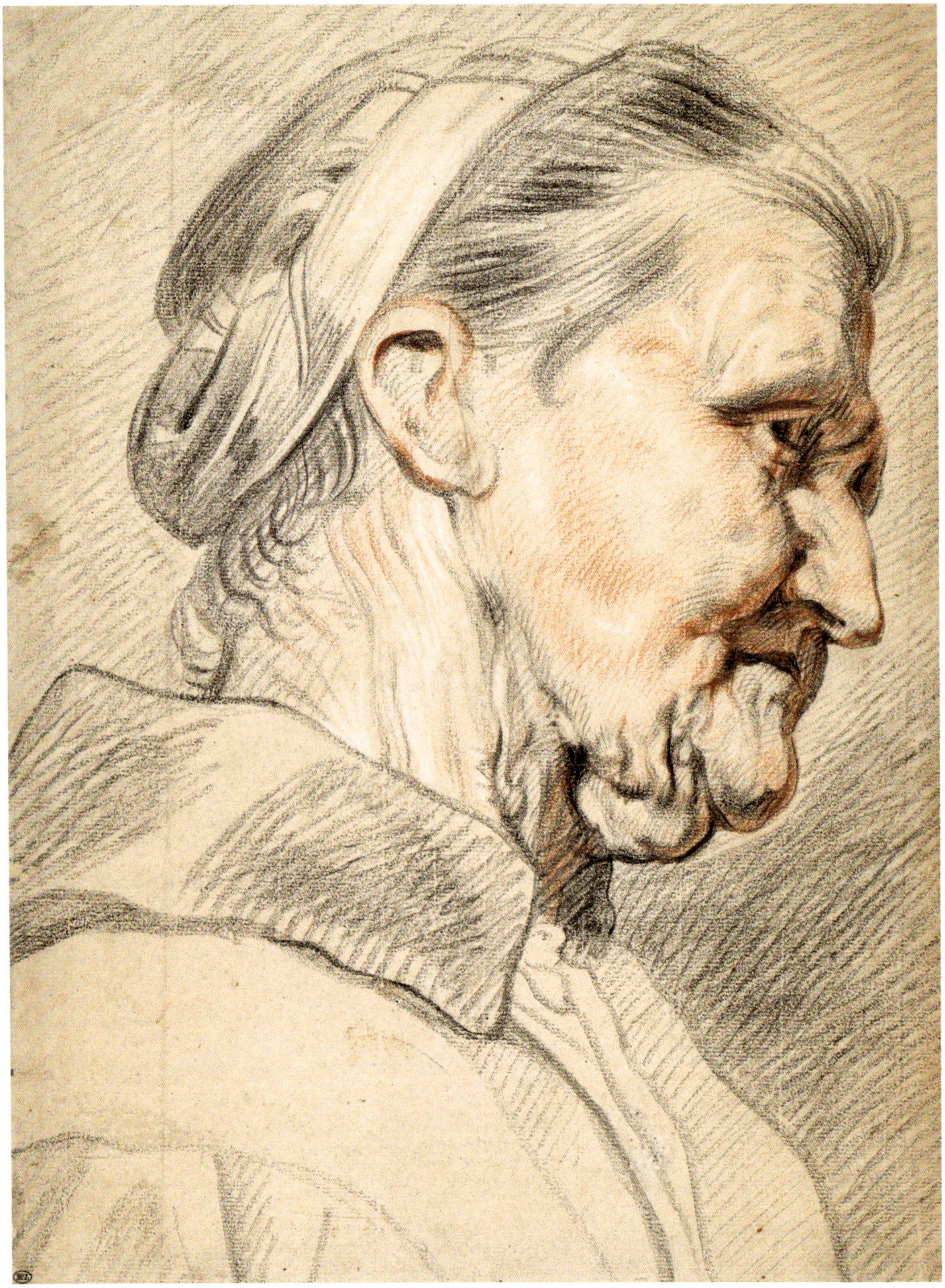

FIG. 42
After Peter Paul Rubens, *Head Study of an Old Woman in Profile to the Right*, s.d., chalk on paper, Musée du Louvre, Paris, 20019, (recto)

FIG. 43
Peter Paul Rubens, *Head Study of an Old Woman Seen from the Front*, c. 1615–1620, oil on panel, The Phoebus Foundation, Antwerp

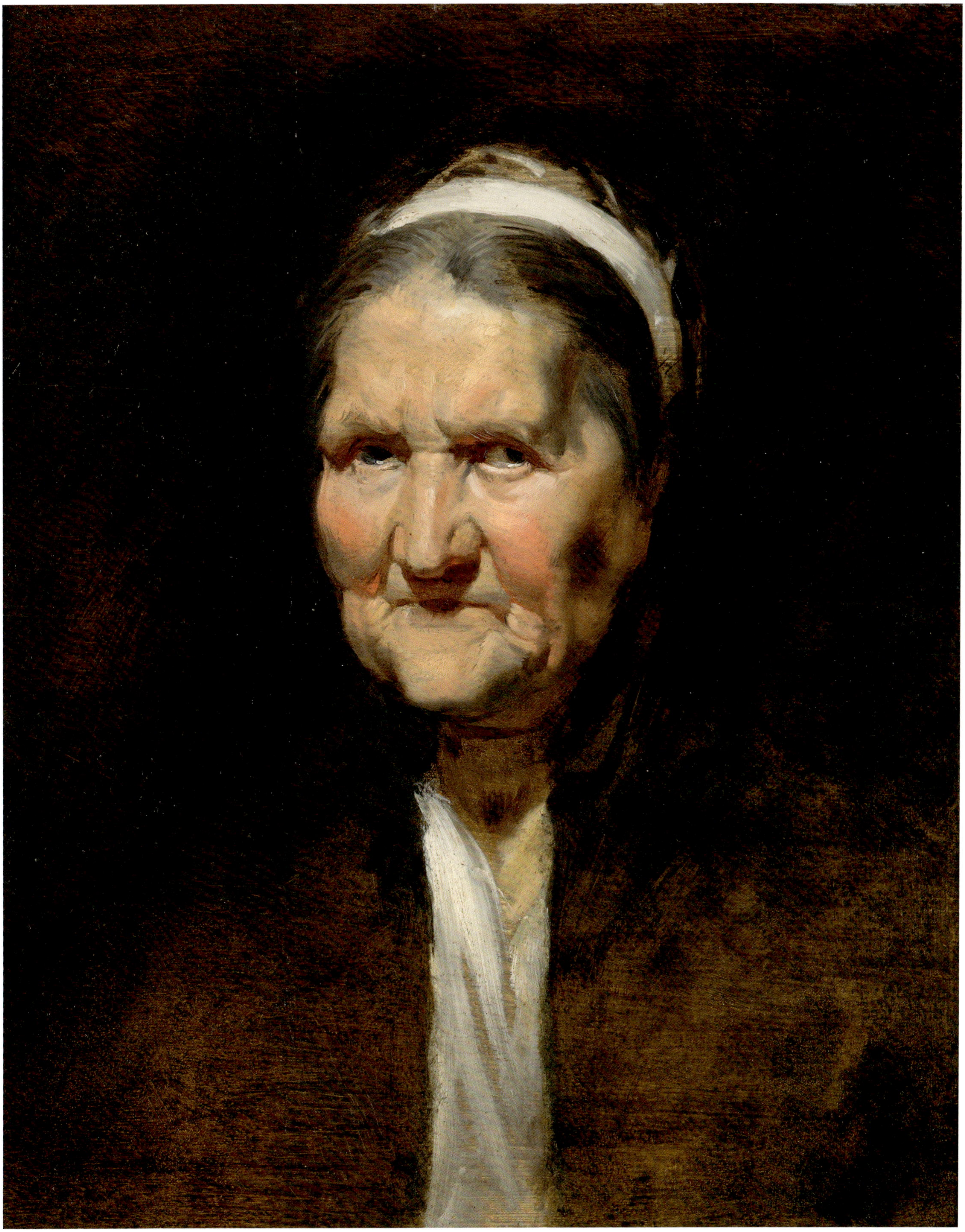

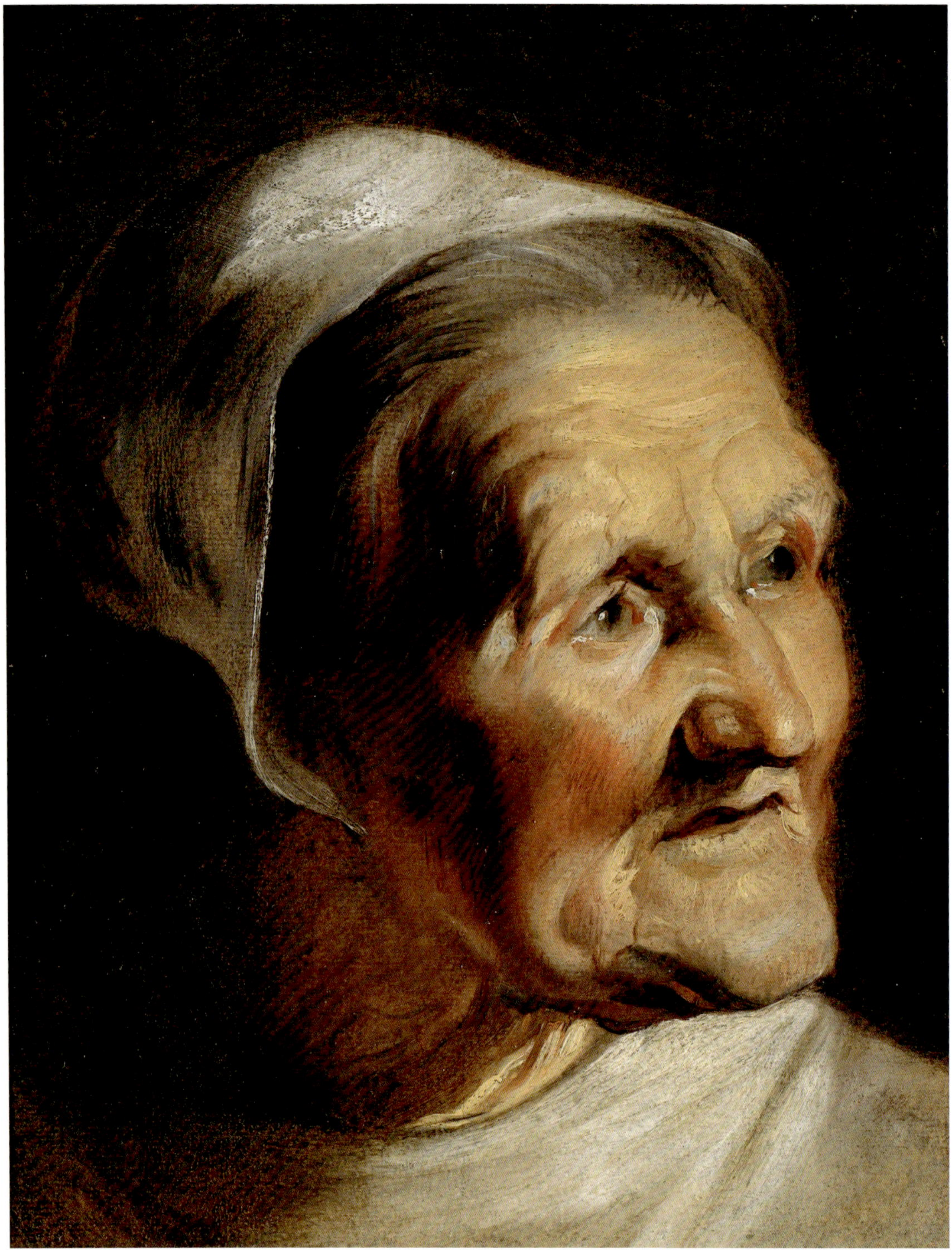

FIG. 44
Jacques Jordaens the Elder, *Head Study of an Old Woman*, s.d., oil on paper, mounted on panel, private collection

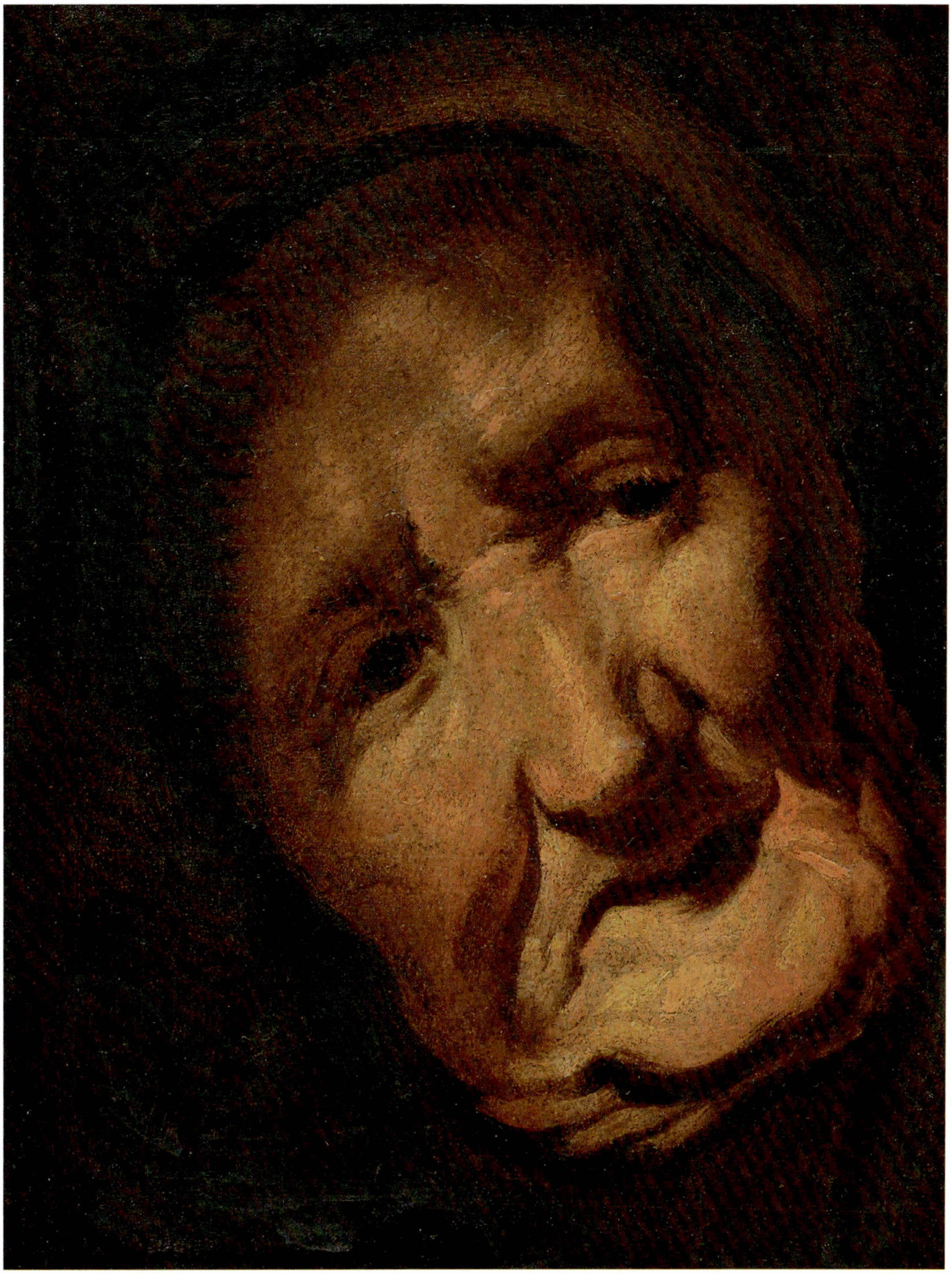

FIG. 45
Jacques Jordaens the Elder, *Head Study of an Old Woman*, c. 1640–1645, oil on paper, mounted on canvas, The Phoebus Foundation, Antwerp

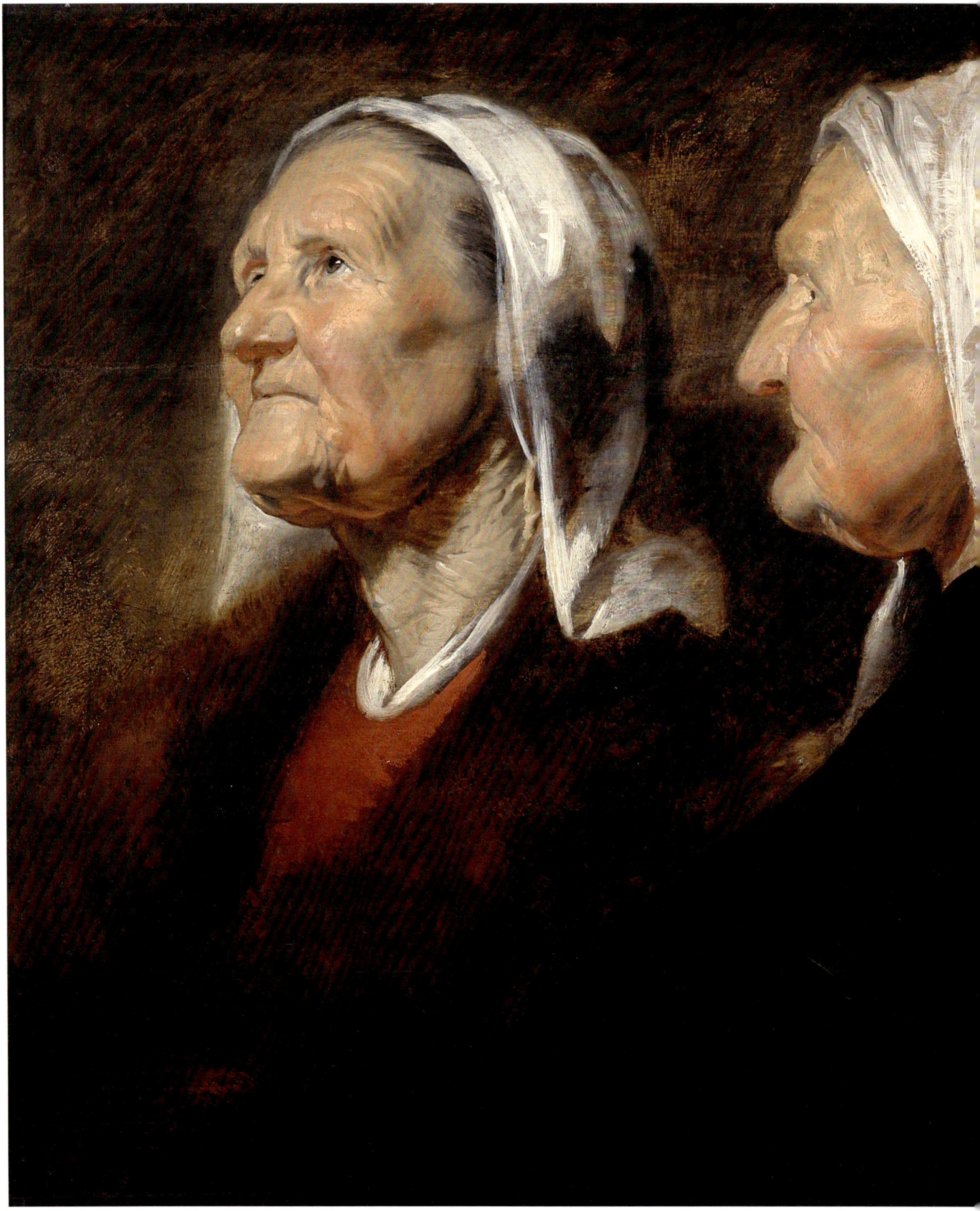

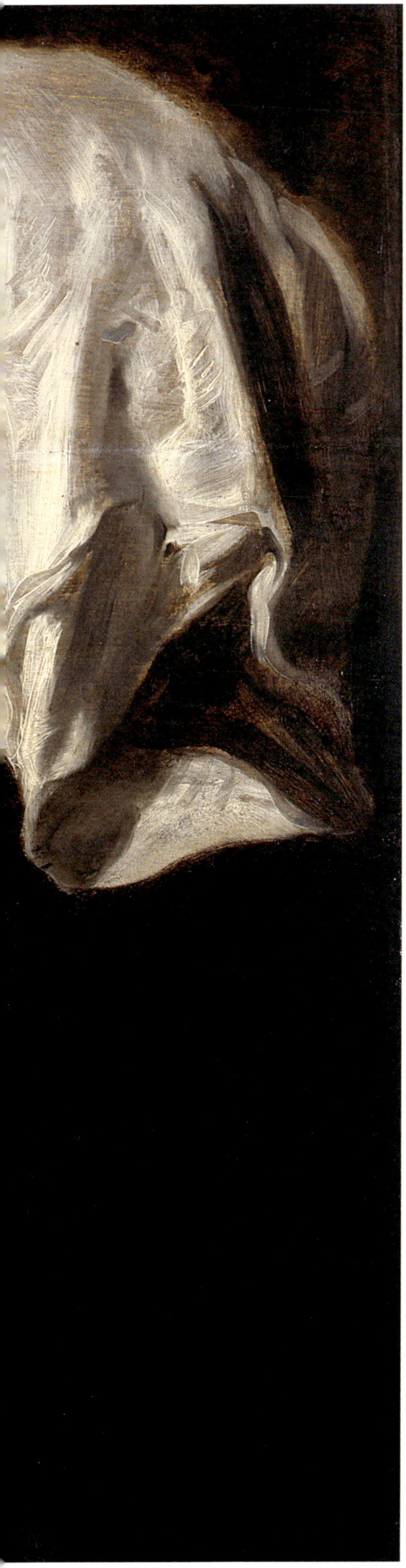

FIG. 46
Jacques Jordaens the Elder, *Two Head Studies of an Old Woman*, c. 1620, oil on panel, Musée des Beaux-Arts, Nancy, 91

FIG. 47
Anthony van Dyck, *Twelve Head Studies of Men*, s.d., pen and brown ink on paper, Musée du Louvre, Paris, 20286, recto

FIG. 48
Peter Paul Rubens, *Eleven Head Studies*, c. 1619, pen and brown ink over black chalk on paper, British Museum, London, Oo,9.36

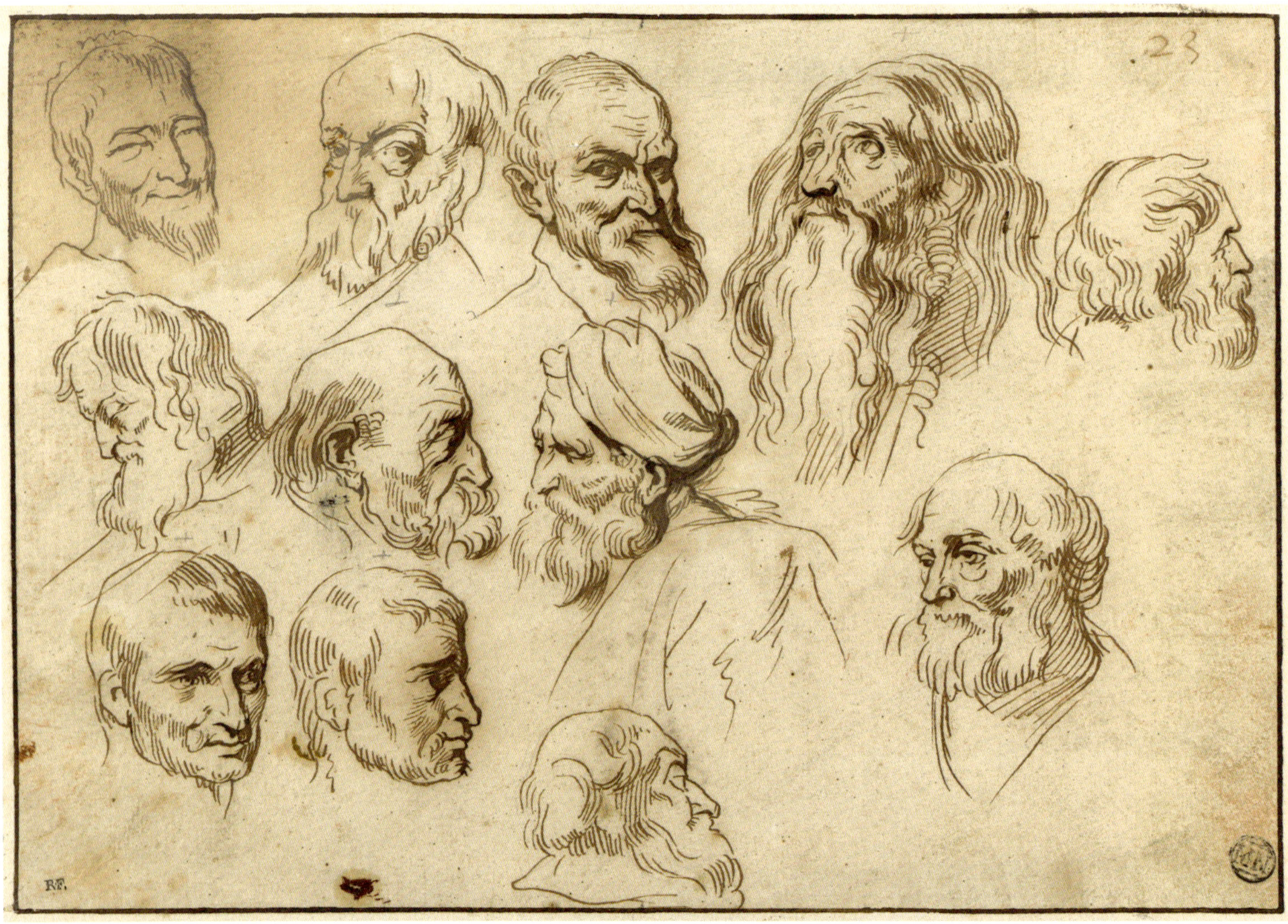

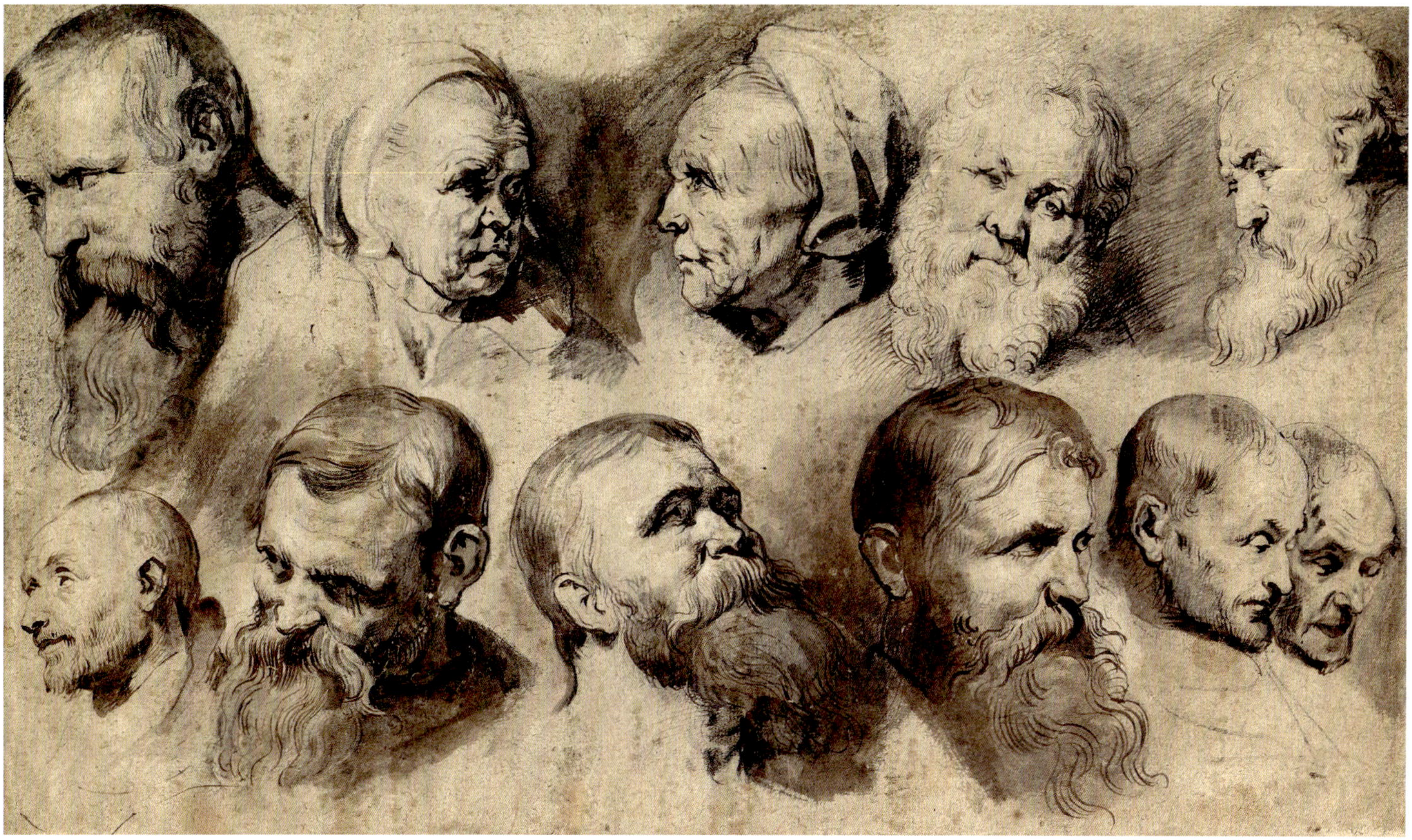

FIG. 49
Peter Paul Rubens, *Head Studies*, s.d., oil on panel, Christie's, London, 9 December 2016, lot 116

FIG. 50
Anthony van Dyck, *Two Studies of a Man's Head*, c. 1618, oil on canvas, mounted on panel, Snijders&Rockoxhuis, Antwerp, 77.111

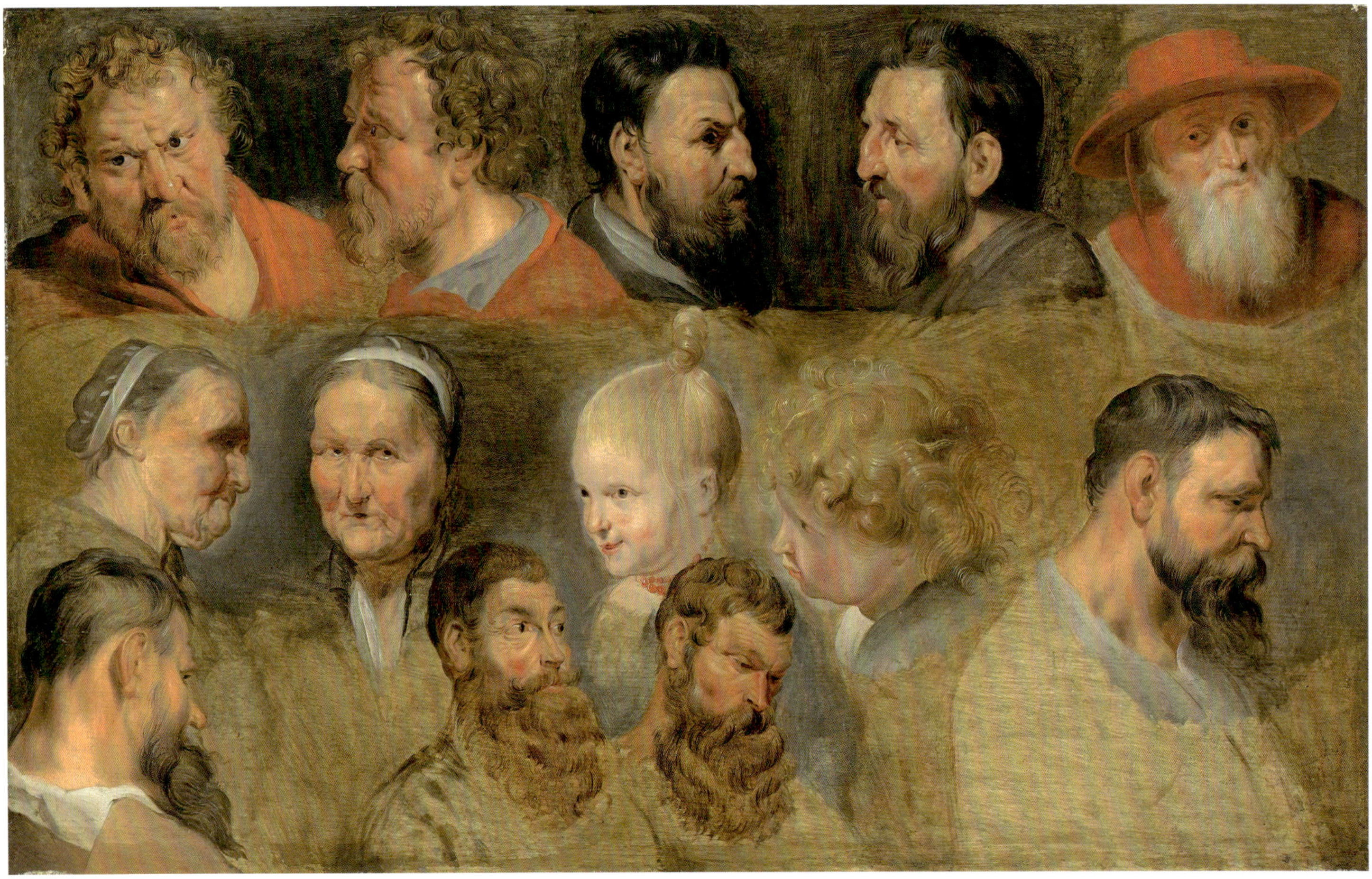

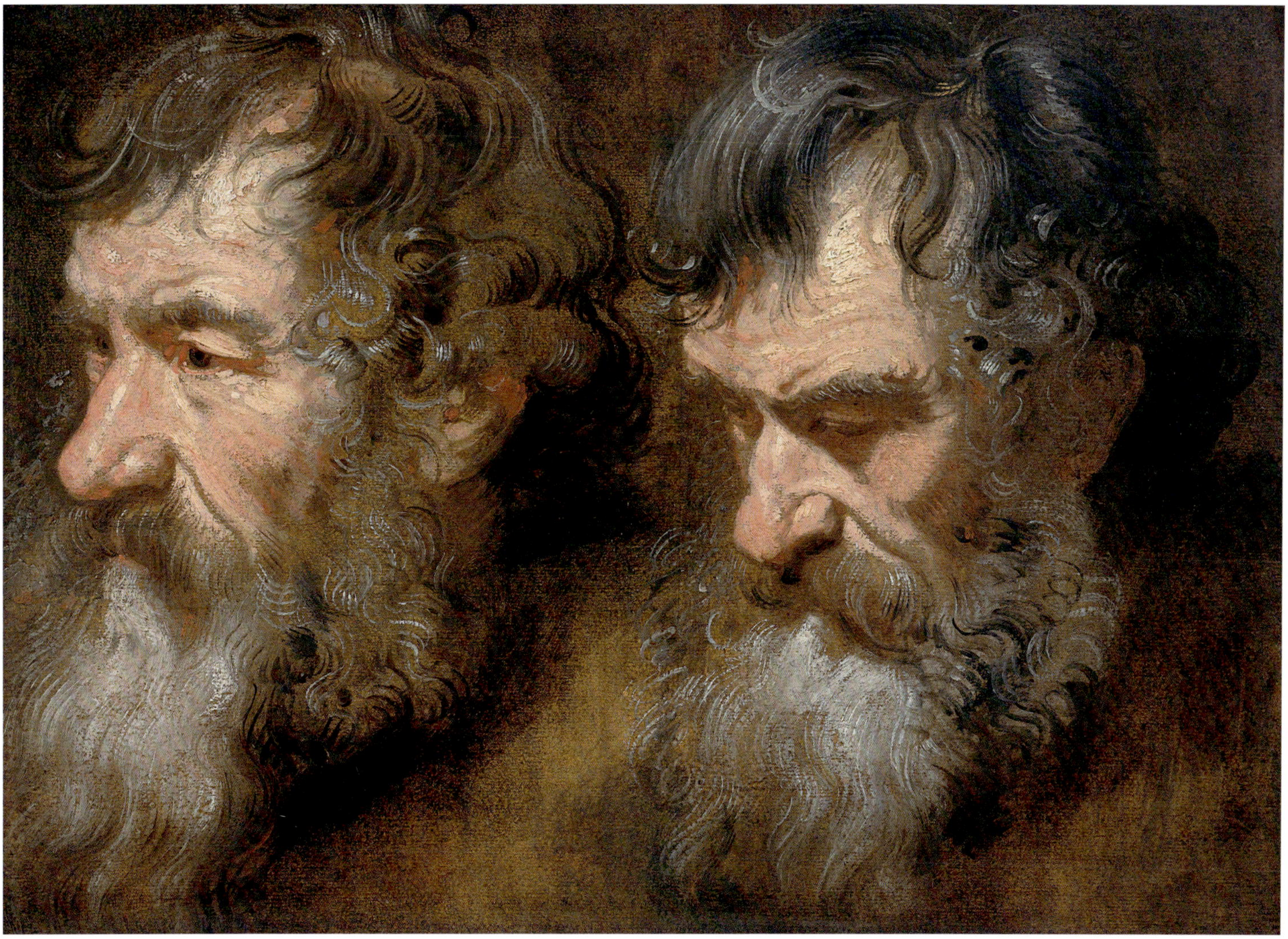

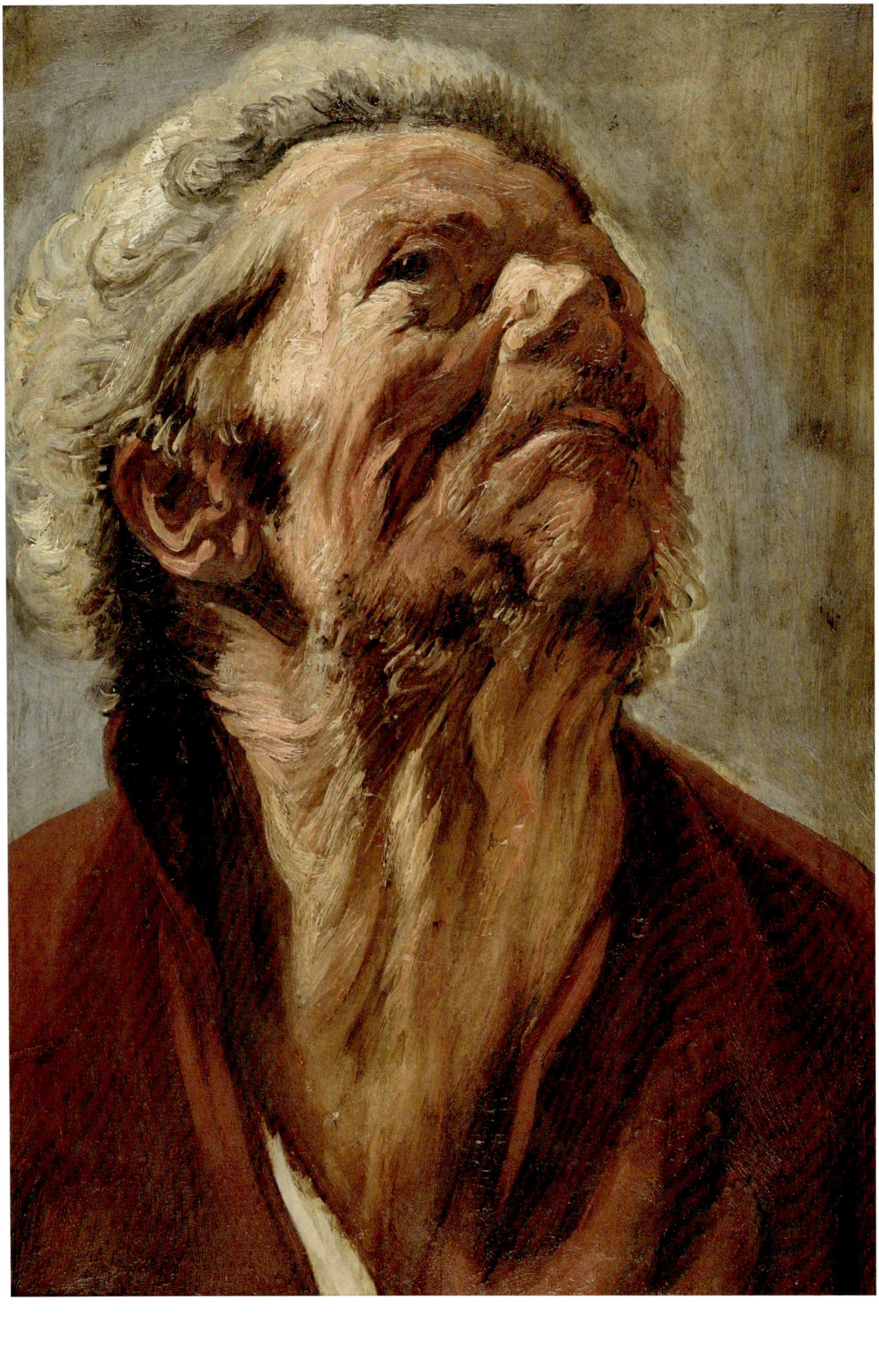

FIG. 51
Jacques Jordaens the Elder, *Head Study of Abraham Grapheus*, c. 1620–1621, oil on panel, Musée de la Chartreuse, Douai, 198

FIG. 52
Jacques Jordaens the Elder, *Offering to Ceres*, c. 1620, oil on canvas, Museo Nacional del Prado, Madrid, P001547

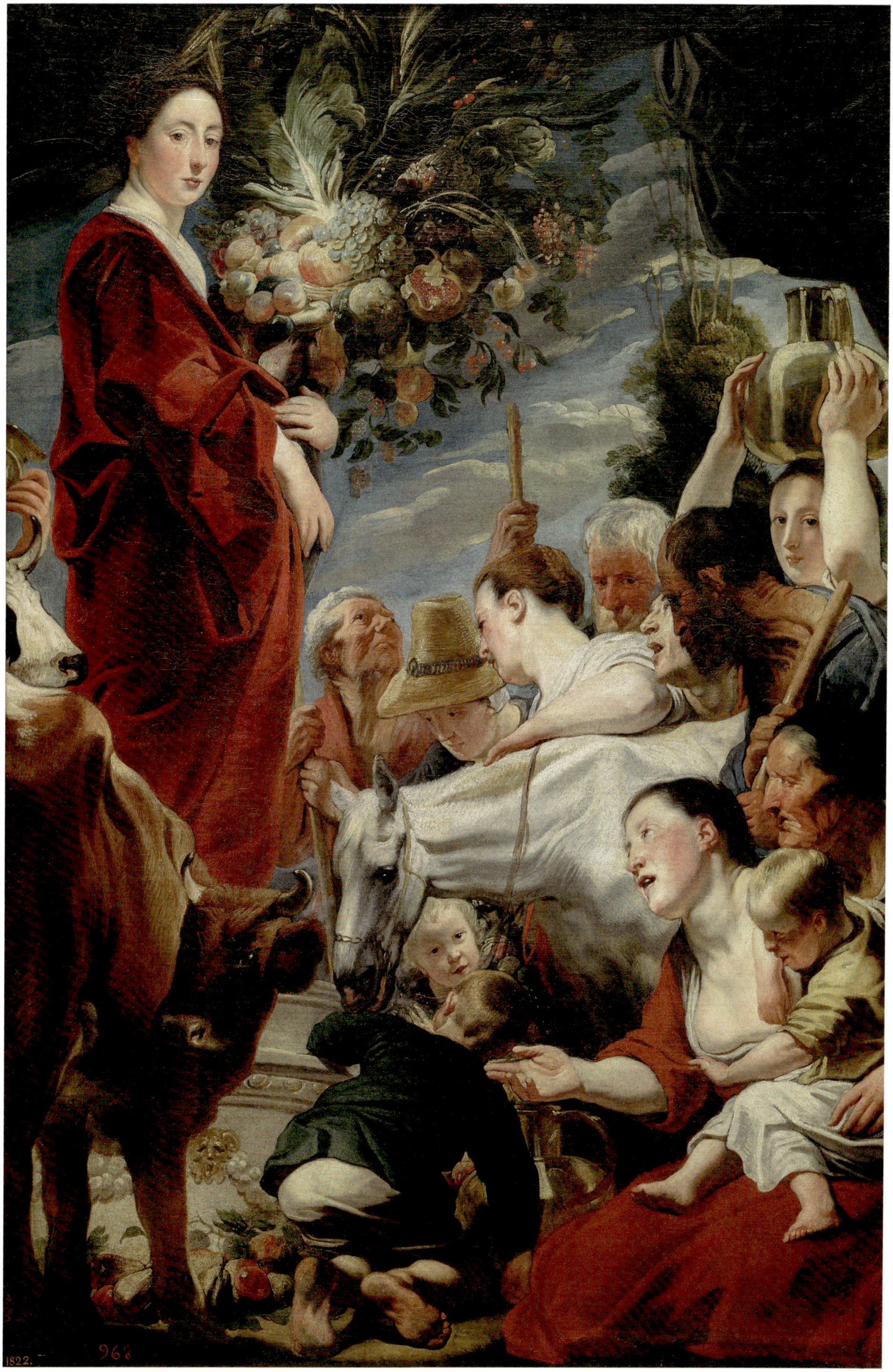
1822.
968

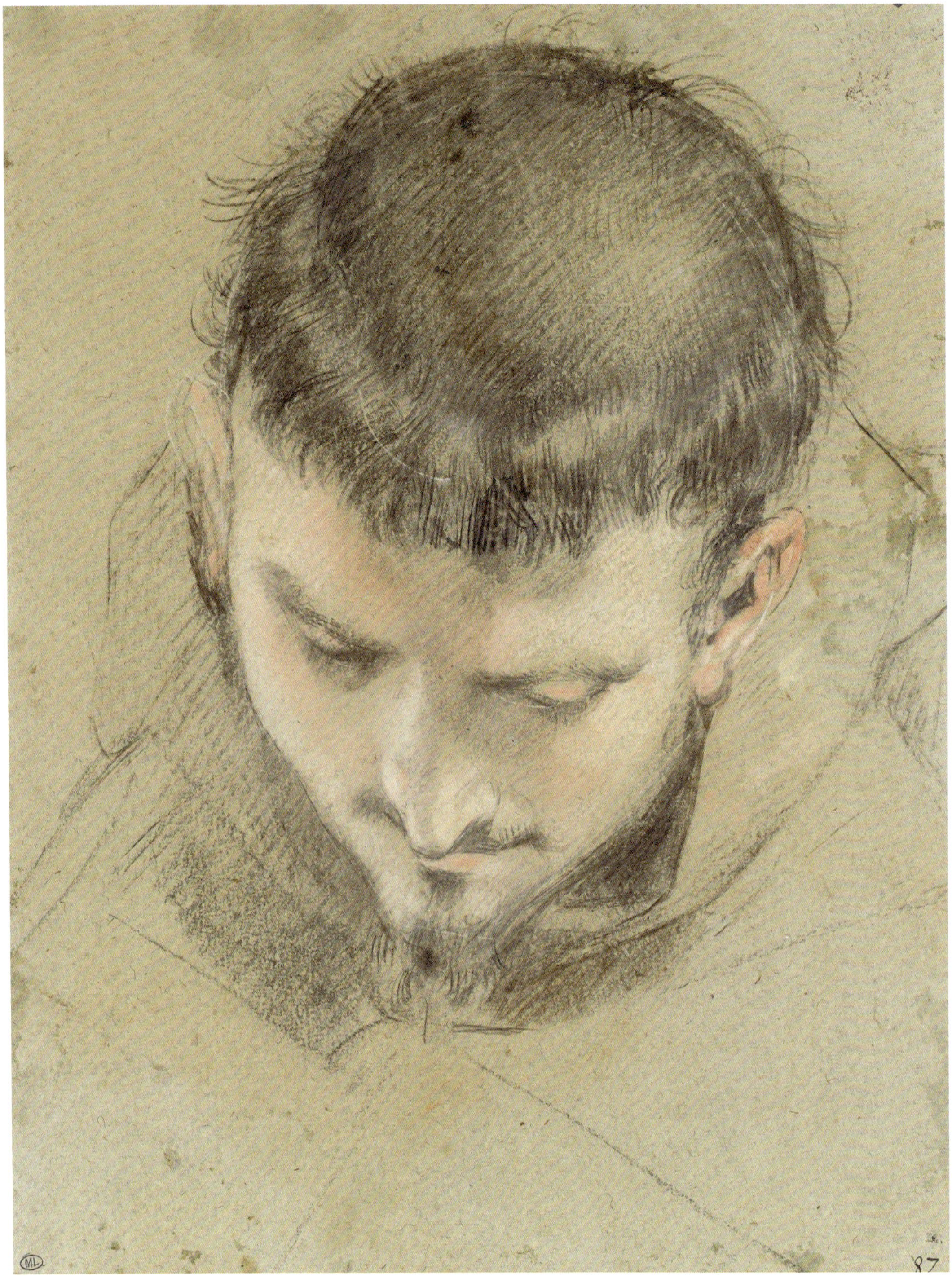

FIG. 53
Federico Barocci,
Head of a Young Monk Bending Over, s.d.,
pencil, chalk and pastel on paper,
Musée du Louvre, Paris, 2874 (recto)

FIG. 54
Anthony van Dyck,
Head Study, s.d.,
oil on panel, KMSKA, Antwerp, inv. 5168

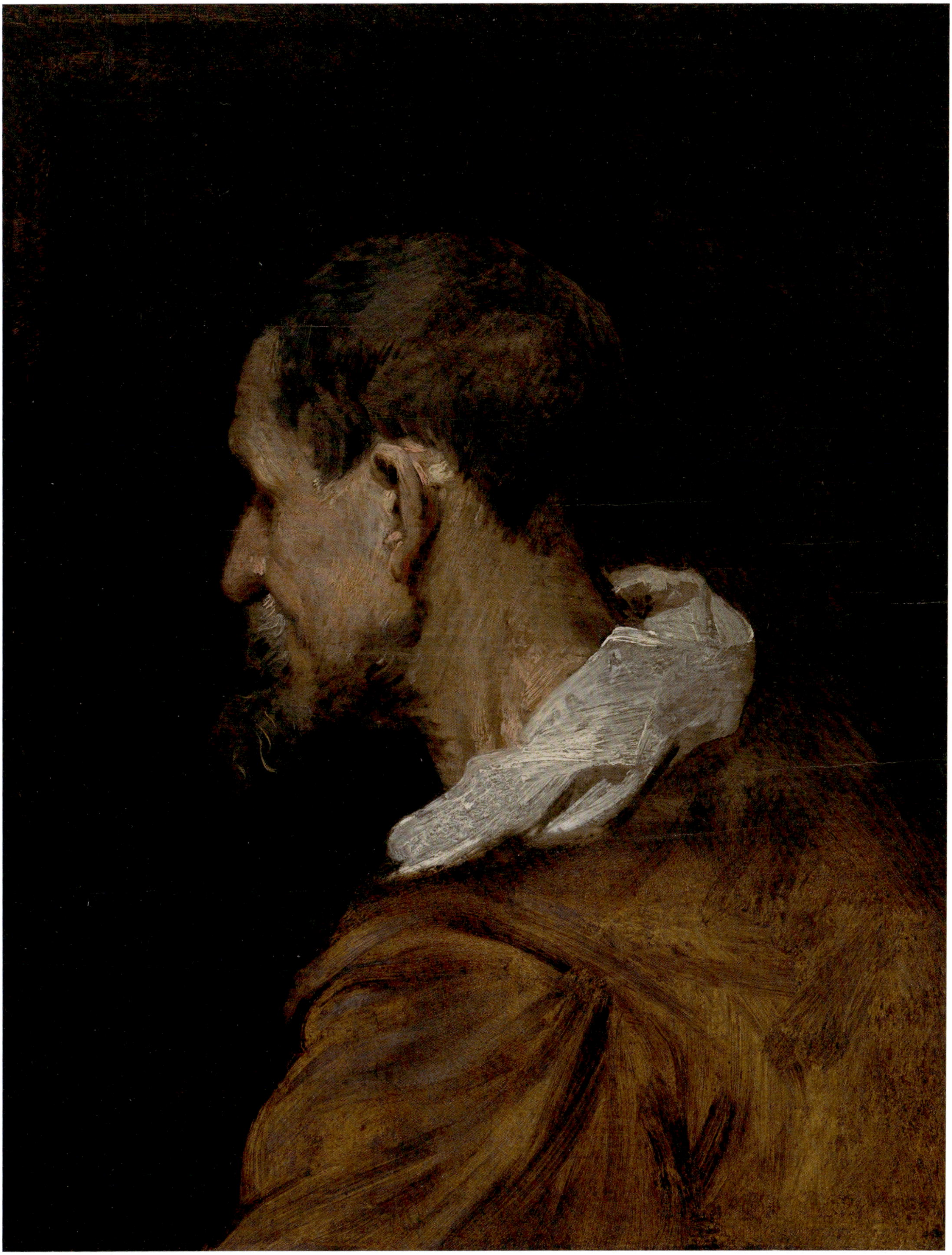

FIG. 55
Michaelina Wautier, *Head Study of a Young Man*, 1655, oil on canvas, KMSKA, Antwerp, inv. 5149

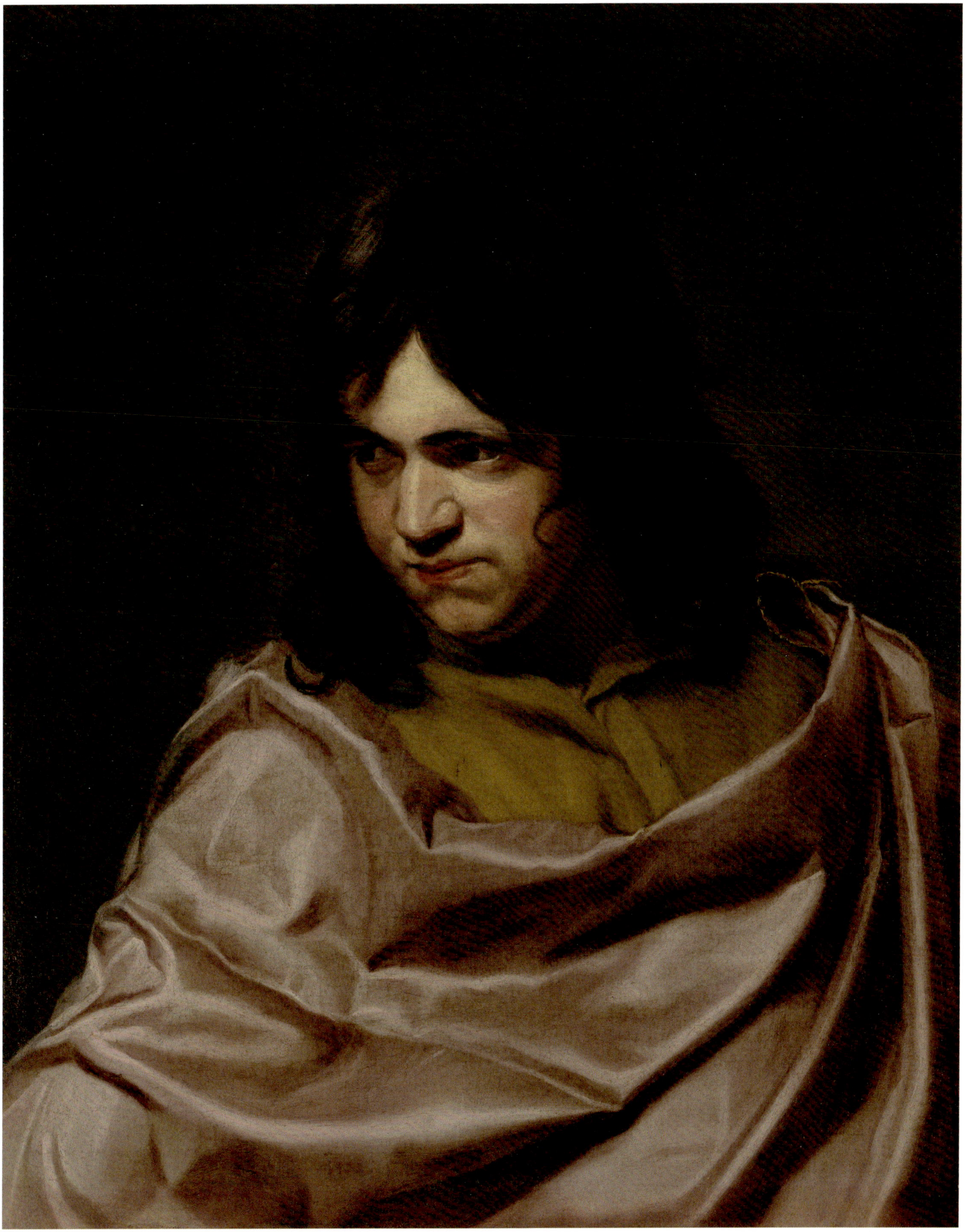

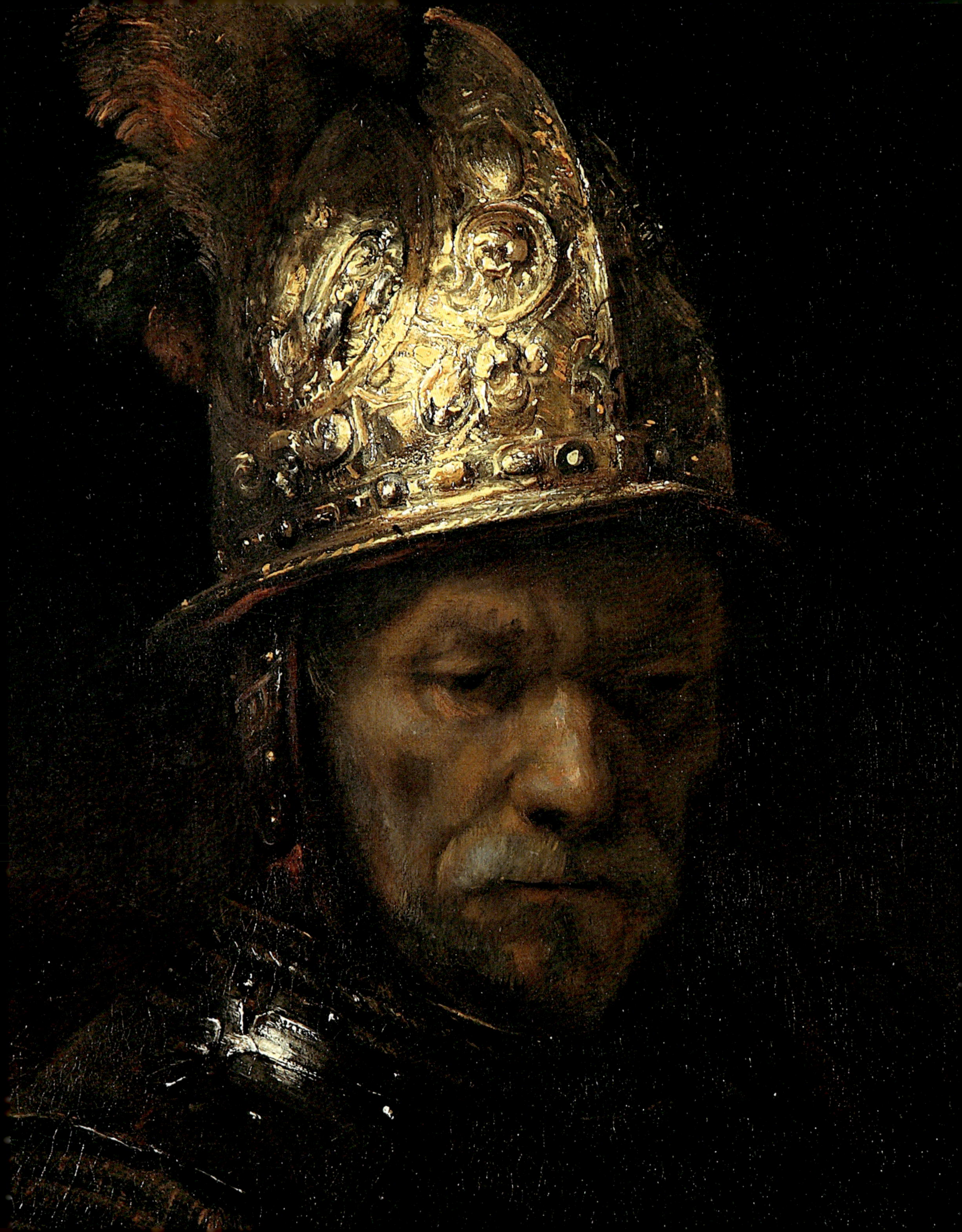

DRESSED UP

'A Thousand Fine Concoctions': Costumed Heads

Lizzie Marx

The taste for textiles

Tronies carefully decorated with a myriad of costumes and accessories represent a subcategory of the genre that captivated artists in the late-sixteenth and seventeenth centuries. Flesh and facial hair converged with feathers, draped pearls, headpieces and swathes of fabric in a costumed tronie. The various trappings that dressed the head placed it into different periods and places, evoking an encounter with a character from a world beyond the viewer's reality.

The artists of the Low Countries were working out of a tradition that valued the qualities of costume, and where particular outfits could hold allegorical significance. The iconographer Cesare Ripa (c. 1555–1622) detailed at great length the role of costume in the identification of allegories where, for instance, "Good Nature" is depicted draped in a robe of golden cloth. Head coverings were also significant, as in the old woman who embodied "Irresolution", shown wearing a black cloth wrapped around her head. The head of the allegory of "Content", meanwhile, is to be lavishly embellished with a plume of feathers and jewels.[1] The artist-biographer Karel van Mander (1548–1606), on the other hand, concentrated his discussion of costume on the fall of drapery, as discussed in the tenth chapter of his *Foundation of the Noble, Free Art of Painting* of 1604.[2] Later, Philips Angel (c. 1618–1664) observed in his *Praise of Painting* from 1642 that knowledge of the varying textures of materials was important, as silk, velvet, wool and linen all responded differently to light.[3]

Costumed head studies were helpful to artists in developing the compositions of the different genres of painting that grew in popularity during the seventeenth century. The genre scene, which was established around the mid-sixteenth century, portrayed the different "types" of characters that made up society in the Low Countries. It required the study of people, where their clothing represented their social background. The taste for history painting called for figures dressed in biblical or antique attire that contrasted with the conventional clothing of the viewers. The head studies lent themselves particularly well as works for reference in the creation of ambitious compositions that recounted stories from distant lands and eras. Studies of elaborately bedecked heads may have also aided working up the fashionable *portrait historié*, or historiated portrait, where the sitter was costumed so as to assume the roles of literary or historical characters.[4]

(DETAIL FIG. 67)
Circle of Rembrandt,
The Man with the Golden Helmet,
c. 1650, oil on canvas,
Gemäldegalerie,
Berlin, 811A

An interest in costumed tronies was further piqued in the Dutch Republic when the expansion of international trade introduced knowledge of new costumes and materials from places further away from Europe than ever before. Feathers, cloths and jewelled embellishments were among the goods imported throughout the seventeenth century. They were brought to the Republic by the Dutch East India Company (VOC) and made available for purchase locally shortly thereafter.[5] The materials that constituted potential costumes for tronies had been transplanted from their original sources and drawn together in an entirely different context in Europe. Artists generated costumed tronies who wore imported wares in new configurations. The resulting paintings had very little to do with the materials' original cultures, and a great deal to do with the artist's imagination. This chapter discusses the sources of inspiration available to the artist in the creation of costumed tronies and head studies. The varying significance that costumed tronies held will also be discussed, by exploring select headpieces and accessories that recur in the paintings spanning the sixteenth and seventeenth centuries.

Grotesques and arcane costumes

The early head studies from the sixteenth century introduced costume to draw out a figure's least flattering features. Leonardo da Vinci's (1452–1519) series of unusual heads burgeoned in prints by artists such as Wenzel Hollar (1607–1677), depicting couples with exaggerated or crooked features and wearing fanciful headpieces. Quinten Massys (1465/1466–1530) must have been inspired by the copies after Leonardo, resulting in highly finished paintings that posed the imagined heads as portraits. *The Ugly Duchess*, as she is unsympathetically known, depicts an elderly woman offering a rosebud to her male counterpart, who is the object of attraction (Fig. 15 and 16).[6] The revealing bodice, which would normally enhance the bust of a younger sitter, here draws attention to her wrinkled skin. The jewel and pearl brooch that fastens the veil alludes to the sitter's vanity. Her headdress, decades out of fashion, suggests a futile attempt to use her outdated clothing to revive her youth. The resulting ensemble compelled Massys' biographer, the Flemish artist Alexander van Fornenbergh (1621–1663), to describe the painted pair in 1658 as "monstrous".[7]

Hendrick Goltzius (1558–1617) also drew on costume to enhance his figures' grotesque features. In *Bust of a Man with Tasselled Cap*, the disembodied head he evocatively depicted has brooding, shaded eyes (Fig. 56).[8] Goltzius brings in idiosyncrasies, such as the mole sprouting hairs on the forehead, to express his individuality, and yet he remains unknown. The uneven surfaces of his forehead, and the rippled flesh on his skin is made further unfamiliar by the very particular hat, recalling the Phrygian cap of Antiquity, whose pointed flaps are pinned back with a button on the left side, and allowed to fall on the other side. The towering hat is finished off with a dangling tassel.[9] Remarkably worked up using pen and ink, the drawing gives an impression of being produced as a print. It is a work that illustrates that the figure came only from the mind of Goltzius.

It was the variability in the ruffs, collars and lappets of garments that Van Mander appealed to artists to invent, turning them into "a thousand fine concoctions".[10] Frans Floris' work perfectly illustrated the inventiveness that Van Mander had called for, by transforming strings of pearls into elegant decorations for headpieces (Fig. 65).[11] The character's elaborately braided hairstyle is embellished with white flowers, and an ample string of pearls winds its way around her head a number of times, passing under her chin and across her chest; a motif that Floris revisited in several of his head studies, which counted in the hundreds. The creativity of the configurations lent themselves particularly well to allegorical scenes.[12] Floris also uses pearls for the goddess Minerva's necklace, earring, breastplate, and to ornament the feathers and helmet (Fig. 64).[13] Combining the costume with a powerful, emphatic expression worked as the point of departure from which the mythological painting would take shape.[14]

Costume books

Arcane costume appealed to Peter Paul Rubens (1577–1640) around a century after the completion of *The Ugly Duchess*. His *Costume Book*, held in the British Museum, London, records around 250 studies, with the fashions of the fifteenth and early sixteenth centuries being of particular interest.[15] While Rubens' other studies focused on the ensemble of costumes, he maintained an interest in headpieces, some of which took direct inspiration from the *Kunstbüchlein* model book devised and printed by Heinrich Vogtherr the Elder (1490–1556) (Fig. 58).[16] The volume was a reference book for craftsmen, with pages outlining the variety of column bases and capitals, hand gestures and headpieces, based on early sixteenth-century Netherlandish models. Vogtherr's handbook was first published in Strasbourg in 1538, followed by further

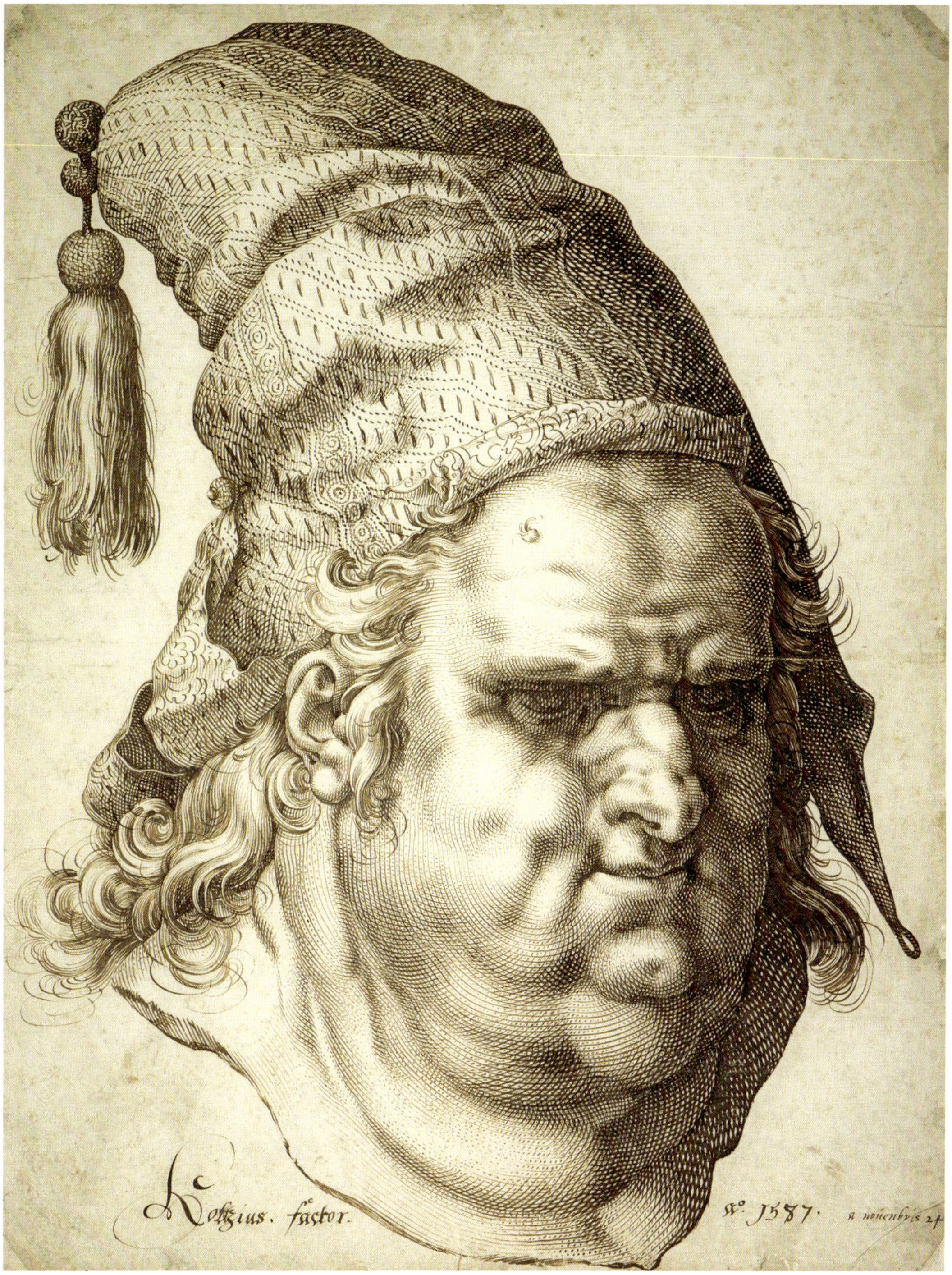

FIG. 56
Hendrick Goltzius, *Bust of a Man with Tasselled Cap*, 1587, pen and brown ink on paper, National Galleries of Scotland, Edinburgh, D 5507

editions up until 1610 when Rubens would have accessed the volume. Rubens makes near-direct copies of select heads illustrated in Vogtherr's book, with each one decked out in an elaborate head covering (Fig. 57).[17] The facial features are economically rendered, giving the headpieces the greatest attention to detail. Among his creations are necklaces braided out of hair, and a study of fluttering fabric. They present formulations of characters that could be considered for Rubens' compositions.

A matter of years before Rubens worked up his *Costume Book*, Van Mander acknowledged the importance of creating variety in painting through costumes. The inspiration for various antique headdresses was to be found in prints by the early sixteenth-century painter and printmaker Lucas van Leyden (1494–1533) as visual borrowings which could then be adapted by the artist.[18] Works by Goltzius, as discussed above, would go on to inspire masters of tronie painting. In February 1638, Rembrandt (1606–1669) bought one of the artist's drawn tronies for a steep 49 guilders.[19] He was also recorded as having a book depicting "Turkish life",[20] and twenty-five Mughal miniatures, also dressed in traditional attire.[21] The costumes recorded by the artist's predecessors were important sources of inspiration for paintings, with headpieces being a subject of interest in their own right.

The bonnet: social difference

In addition to Vogtherr's handbook, the artist's studio could also make use of a printed compendium of tronies believed to be after designs by Pieter Bruegel the Elder (c. 1525–1569), consisting of heads almost entirely portraying rural workers, framed in pairs of oval prints. The thirty-six prints contain seventy-two verses, designating every figure a nickname and humorous rhyming couplets (Fig. 8).[22] They were useful for depicting a particular "type" that would appear in a scene, such as a fool, or a peasant. However the verses reiterated what was believed at the time, that the figure's shortcomings are expressed in their caricatured features.[23] They perpetuate stereotypes by alluding to the figures' sexual promiscuity (*"Bruyntje Springh-in 't-Bed"* [Bruyntje Jump-in-the-Bed]), their criminal behaviour (*"Dief-actighe Tijs"* [Thievish Tijs]), and idleness (*"Leuye Joost"* [Lazy Joost]). The prints could have come from preparatory studies of facial expressions used for the stand-alone paintings of peasants that Bruegel created in 1566–1568 (Fig. 13), like *Head of a Peasant Woman*.[24] The simple white cap that she wears, which was typically donned by women labourers, reaffirms her social background. Although devoid of text beneath the painting, her loosely opened mouth verges on the caricature.

The sardonic sentiment that proliferated in the prints after Bruegel softened in the seventeenth century into more sympathetic portrayals of tronies picturing sitters of a low social status. In Rembrandt's depiction of an elderly maid, she patiently poses with an immaculate white bonnet partially covering her hair (Fig. III).[25] As Rembrandt largely shrouds the woman's eyes, nose and mouth, the painting is less a study of her facial features than a study of her bonnet and accessories pushed into the foreground. She wears an *oorijzer* (literally, "ear-iron"), a metallic headband whose ends press into the recesses below the cheekbones. When ears were hidden behind the bonnet's ear flaps (here upturned), they could embellish the face by displaying jewellery at the ends of the *oorijzer*.[26] In a beautiful study of light, Rembrandt works with a restrained palette to contrast the white bleached linen with the slightly dulled metallic glint of the *oorijzer*'s tip. When it was likely beyond the means of Rembrandt's model to afford a portrait of herself, such a painting can be regarded as the closest representation of portraits of labourers in the Low Countries. Although they remain anonymous, they are portrayed in a comparably dignified manner.[27]

The gorget: light and lustre

Perhaps it was an interest in the contrast between the texture of flesh and metal that encouraged artists to paint tronies in armour. A gorget lined with soft studs armoured the necks of Rembrandt's tronies, including *The Laughing Man*, who displays a row of crooked teeth (Fig. II),[28] and the more formal tronie, *An Old Man in Military Costume* of 1631 (Fig. 68),[29] wearing an illustrious ostrich feather stuck into

FIG. 57
Peter Paul Rubens, *Eleven Studies of Women's Head-Dresses*, 1609–12, pen and brown ink on paper, Herzog Anton Ulrich-Museum, Brunswick, inv. 171

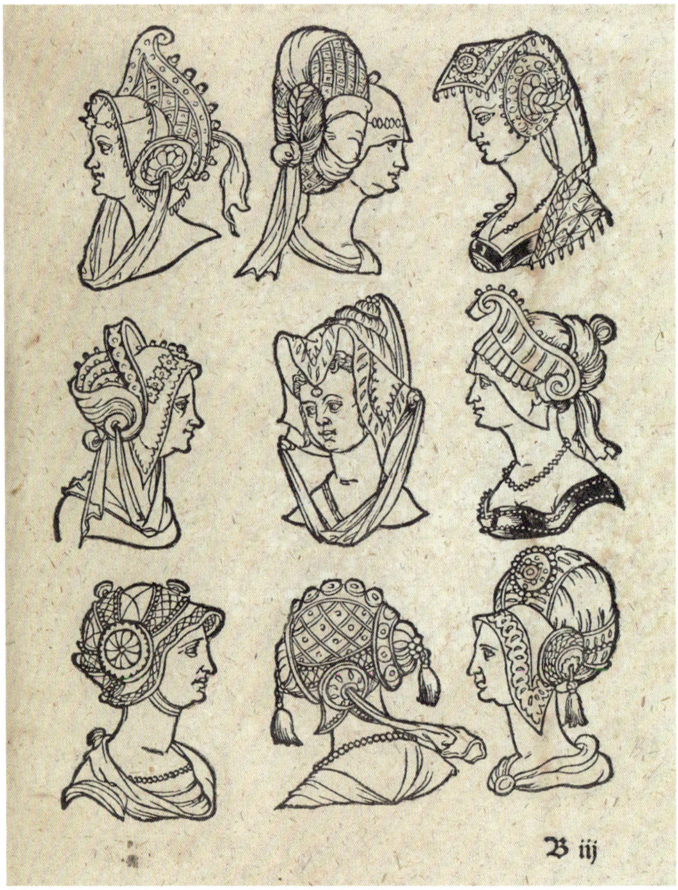

FIG. 58
Heinrich Vogtherr the Elder, *Ein fremdes und wunderbares kunstbüchlein*, 1538, woodcut, The Metropolitan Museum of Art, New York, 19.62.2

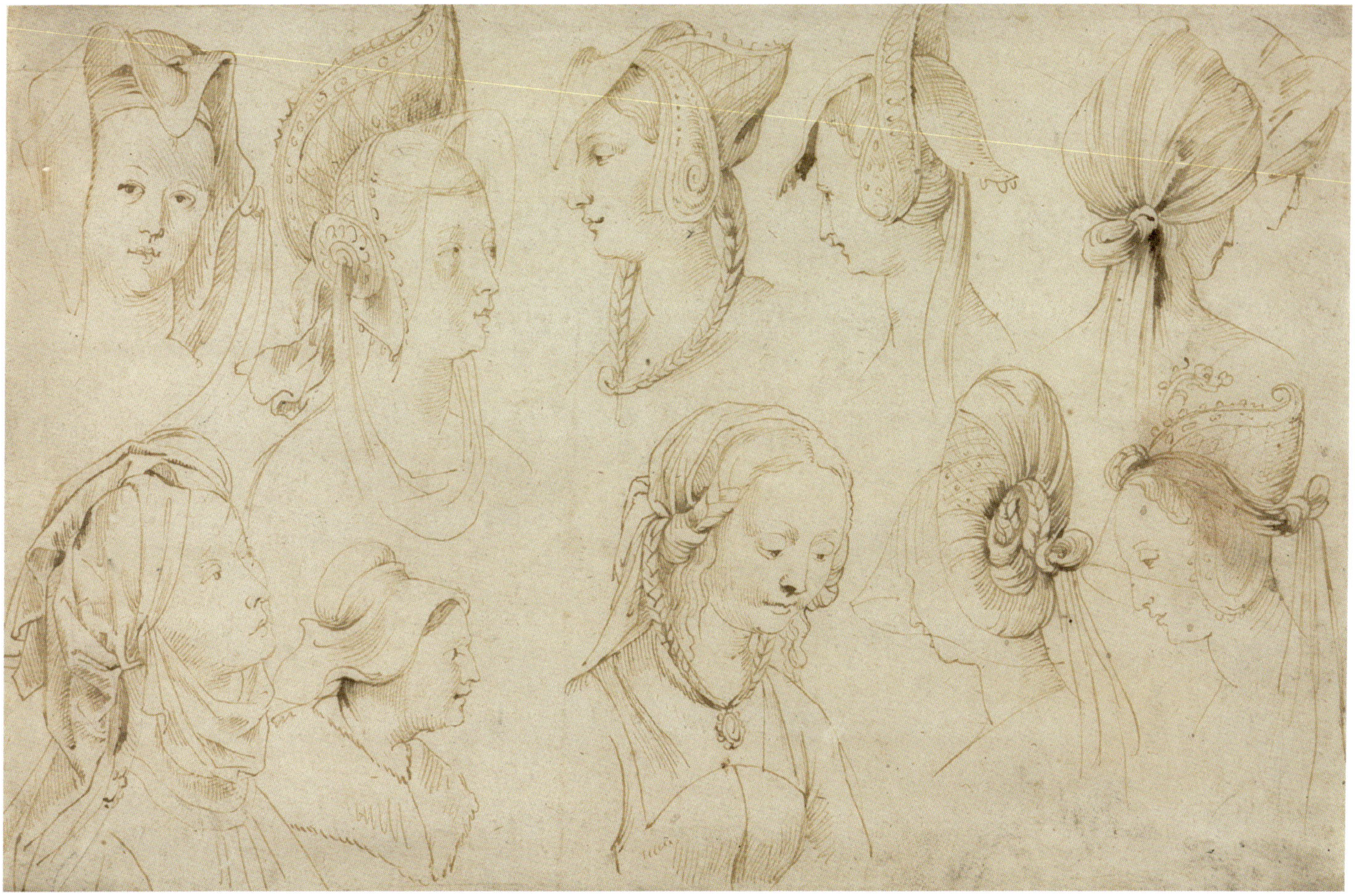

the cap.[30] Both pieces refer to military costumes and grand painted battle scenes of the period. The gorget belonged to a rich collection of military equipment that was recorded in Rembrandt's inventory.[31] Such attire would have been available in the studio, as certain artists belonged to the civic guards where armour constituted a part of their costume.[32]

The artist and art theorist Samuel van Hoogstraten (1627–1678) considered that it was important to evoke the metallic reflections of armour in contrast with the face – a feat that the artist and artist biographer Giorgio Vasari (1511–1574) was unable to achieve when he painted the armoured Duke Alessandro de' Medici. The solution, wrote Van Hoogstraten, was to create more contrast by darkening the surrounds.[33] Van Hoogstraten trained under Rembrandt, and a fellow artist from the master's circle excelled with this effect in *The Man with the Golden Helmet* when painting a deeply introspective tronie, with the sheen of the gorget's metal evoked by the use of lead white paint (Fig. 67).[34] The golden helmet's light behaves quite differently, with yellow paint applied with heavy impasto following the hammered patterns, and then receding into embers of yellow to reflect the surrounding gloom.[35] Through the study of the metals' lustre, the artist is able to expand the spectrum of light in the work, all in oil paint.

The turban: imagining history

The Low Countries' access to the Ottoman Empire increased as it opened up to visitors and traders in the seventeenth century. It likely contributed to the appeal for tronies clothed in Eastern dress to a broad Dutch market.[36] The "*Turckse tronie*" – a generic name for a tronie in non-European costume – was hung in everyday settings. We learn of two such paintings kept in the home of Johannes Vermeer (1632–1675), and a "Turkish tronie" by Rembrandt was part of the well-furnished household of Frederick van Alewijn (1603–1665), who had been appointed Schout in 1658.[37] The tronies' costumes brought flourishes of colour to

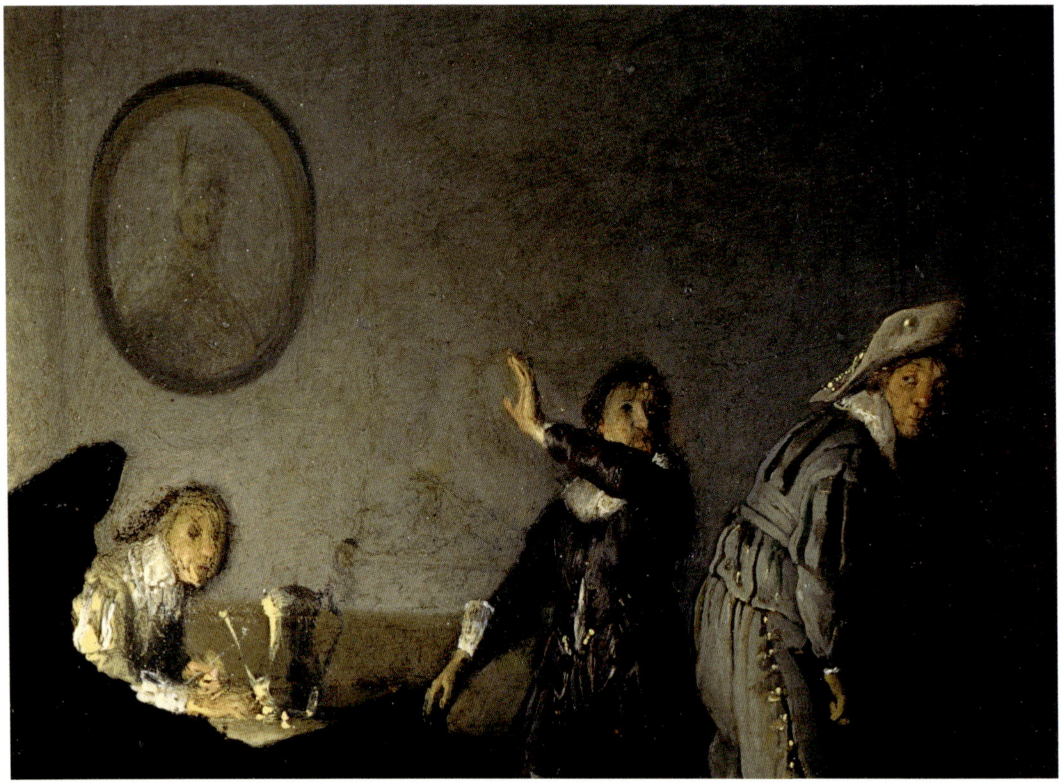

(DETAIL FIG. 66)
Rembrandt, *Interior with Figures ('La Main Chaude')*, c. 1628, oil on panel, National Gallery of Ireland, Dublin, NGI.439

FIG. 59
Peter Paul Rubens, *The Adoration of the Magi*, 1609, oil on canvas, Museo Nacional del Prado, Madrid, P1638

domestic spaces and everyday interiors. The illusion of iridescent silks and sparkling jewels had eye-catching potential.[38] In the gloomy interior of an inn painted by Rembrandt, a tronie with a turban pinned with a feather is part of the interior decoration (Fig. 66).[39]

The popularity of history painting meant that costume took on even more importance, where the accessories that decorated the head distinguished different characters.[40] Van Hoogstraten aspired to an almost encyclopaedic approach to the hairstyles, embellishments and headpieces of different nations and people from Antiquity.[41] At least a generation earlier, Rubens expressed the accuracy that Van Hoogstraten alluded to. Painted on a sheet of paper annotated with bookkeeping entries, Rubens intently studied the head of a man in a white headdress for his *Study for King Balthasar* (Fig. 72).[42] The magus' iconography depicted him as arriving from Africa or Arabia, the native region of myrrh, which he gifted to the Christ Child. The black model who posed for this study assumes the role with a head covering made from a length of white textile that was wound with some skill around his head and neck. The head study was then used for the grand *The Adoration of the Magi* (Fig. 59),[43] painted for Antwerp's city council in 1609, with the addition of a particularly lavish bird of paradise aigrette with a jewel fastening completing the turban.

Rembrandt's interest in the tronie decked out in fantastical, Eastern costume, spans a decade (1626–1636/1637). Preparing the fabric to Rembrandt's satisfaction may have taken as long as executing the painting, as his biographer Arnold Houbraken (1660–1719) commented that the artist "could also spend a day or two setting up a turban to his satisfaction".[44] His friend and competitor Jan Lievens (1607–1674) expressed similar interests when he depicted a *Man in Oriental Dress* (Fig. 71),[45] a tronie not dissimilar to the painting displayed in Rembrandt's *Interior with Figures* (Fig. 66). The tronie extends unconventionally below bust-length, to further describe the costume's splendour, including the glittering veil, known as a *sluyer*, wrapped around the waist.[46] An array of golden hues manifest in the tronie's earring, substantial cape fastening, and the embroidered gold thread of the cape. His turban is completed with a bird of paradise, whose beak functions as a pin. The diplomat and poet Constantijn Huygens (1596–1687) described the cultural mixture in Lievens' painting as "a sort of Turkish king with a Dutch head".[47] In a pair of pendant tronies depicting men of African descent by Lievens' contemporary Jan Adriaensz. van Staveren (1613/14–1669), one of the men wears a turban wrapped in a similar manner to Lievens' depiction, while his pendant wears a European-style feathered beret (Fig. 74 and 73). Lievens and Van Staveren were looking towards the East for inspiration to construct the costumes' ensembles, although they cannot be attributed to specific cultures. Such rich dress would typically find its way into history paintings depicting episodes from the Bible, suggesting the artists' ambitions for larger commissions with many more costumed figures.

The feathered hat: painting fantasy and reality

Costumes served as necessary props for training in the studio where, for example, Rembrandt's inventory records that he held "a stack of antique cloths in diverse colours".[48] Rembrandt's student Willem Drost (1633–1659) likely worked from a fanciful hat belonging to Rembrandt for his study of a man (Fig. 70).[49] The hat's malleable red brim is reminiscent of the headpiece worn in the portrait of his newly wedded Saskia van Uylenburgh, painted in 1633/1634 (Fig. 60),[50] albeit with some variation, such as the absence of a white feather, and the inclusion of a jewelled brooch. The similarities between both hats shed some light on how costume functioned in the tronies of Rembrandt and his circle. Marieke de Winkel has convincingly argued that the cloths in Rembrandt's studio pale in comparison to the sheer variability of costumes in his history painting. It would suggest that the tronies by Rembrandt and his contemporaries are wearing costumes that are based on their collections of fabrics and accessories, however diversified into numerous variations through the artists' fantasy.[51]

Vermeer, on the other hand, likely painted the costumes on his tronies from direct observation.[52] In *Girl with the Red Hat*, his sitter wears a satin patterned gown, draped quite casually over her shoulders (Fig. 120).[53] A white cravat crawls up her neck, and her outfit is completed by a feathered hat. The carmine colour beautifully offsets the blue gown, with the lake glaze outlining the hat evoking the ends of feathers that cover the head-

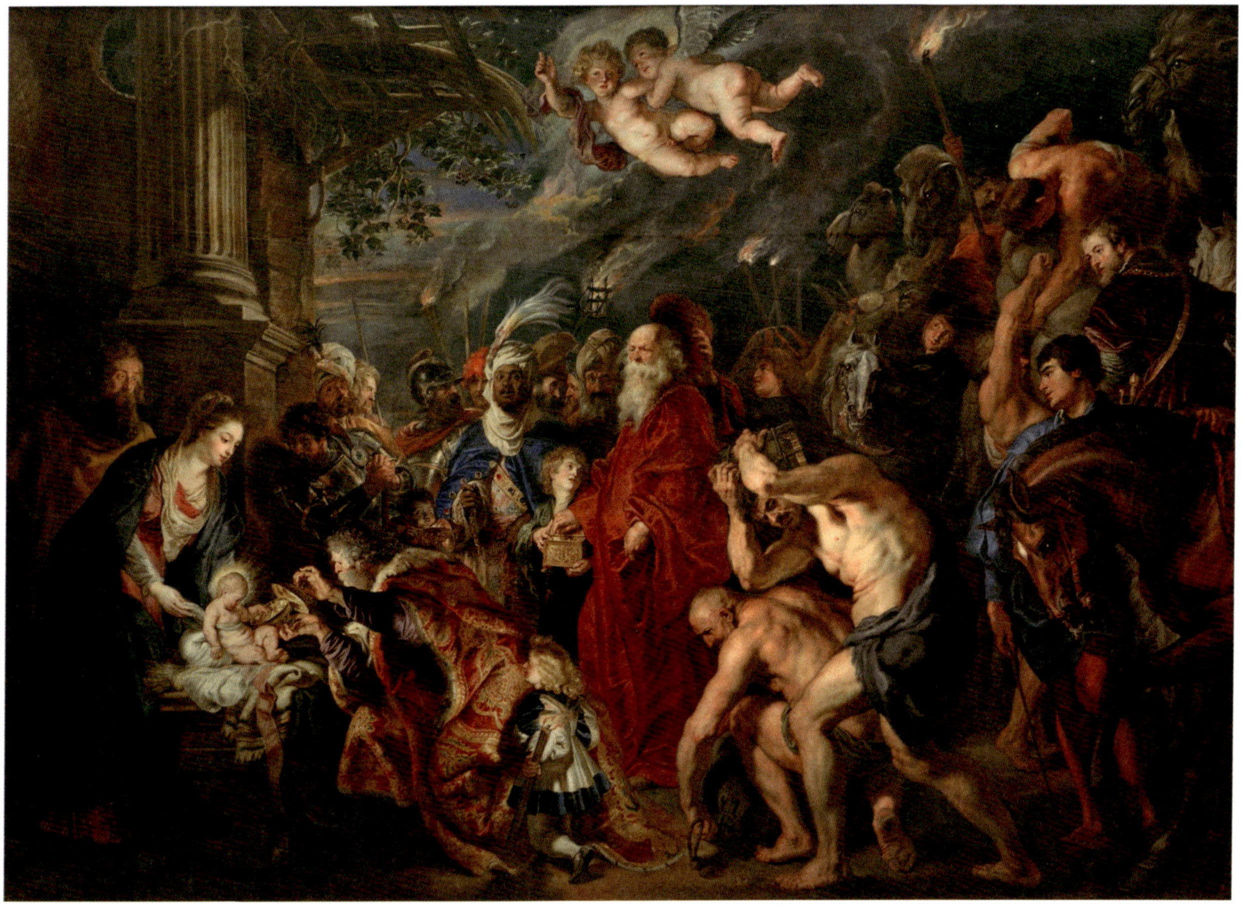

piece. A pair of teardrop earrings are suggested through white glints of light.[54] Perhaps the pearls were contrived from the artist's imagination, as their sheer size would have been valued beyond what an artist could ever afford. Or rather the large pendants were most likely imitation pearls created out of blown glass, an import from the expert glassmakers of Venice.[55] The rest of the costume's ensemble was also probably sourced for his studio, such as the red hat, whose feathers were presumably dyed with cochineal in such a way that the colours could maintain their rich intensity.[56] The headdress sparks the imagination, recounting images of birds plucked from far-flung places.[57] While the tronies by Rubens and Rembrandt wore conjured-up costumes, inspired by prints and collections of cloths, Vermeer, in all likelihood, worked directly from the clothing that he had to hand.

Conclusions

Certain costumed heads served their purpose as focused studies that would eventually culminate in pieces, grander in scale and detail, of the genre scenes and history paintings that proliferated in the seventeenth century. Costumed tronies, however, were a particular subcategory that had their own appeal for the art market. In a period when new materials were being introduced to Europe, the tronies dressed in imported goods spoke to consumers who had an appetite for the eclectic. The artists could deftly depict the costumes' textures, but could not authentically display the materials' original purpose. As was the nature of tronies, the costume alluded to different times and regions, but remained ambiguous enough to connect it to anything more specific. Freed from a precise time, or place, the costumes introduced a character that lived beyond the confines of the quite ordinary rooms in which they were displayed. The "thousand fine concoctions" of costumed characters that the artist was able to create was only limited by the imagination.

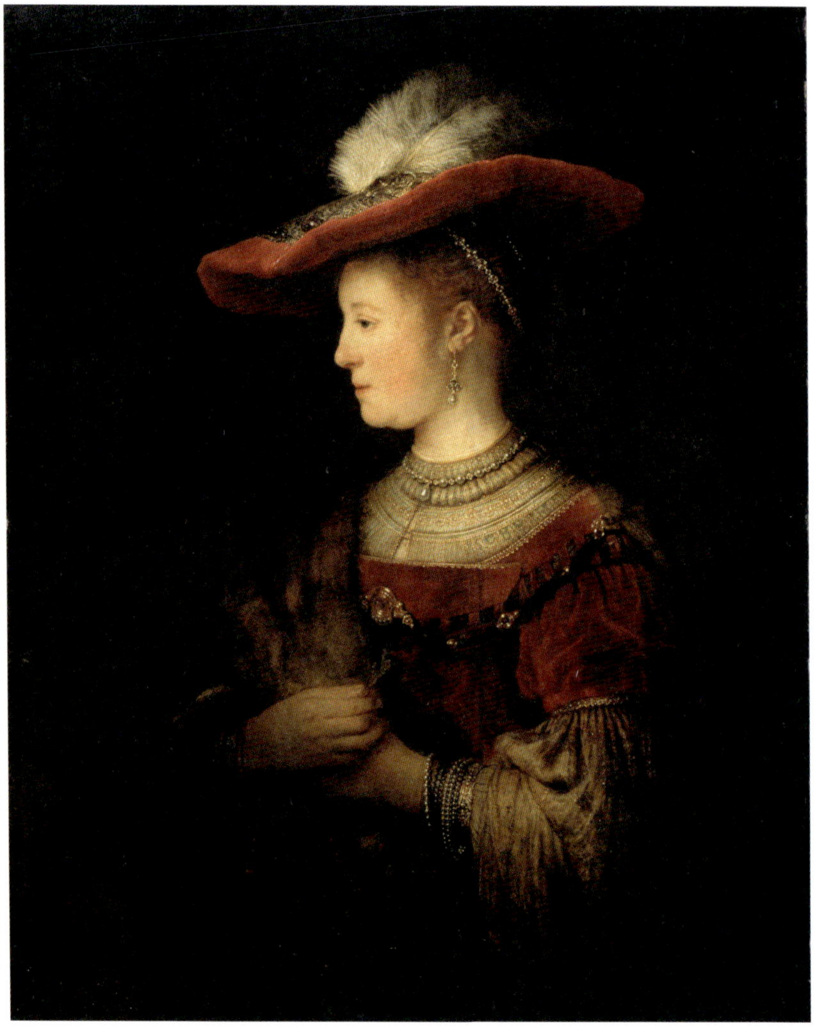

FIG. 60
Rembrandt, *Portrait of Saskia van Uylenburgh*, c. 1633/34–42, oil on panel, Gemäldegalerie Alte Meister, Kassel, GK 236

1 Ripa 1603, 45, 234, 87; Ripa and Tempest 1709, 11, 43, 17.
2 Van Mander 1604) 42r-45r; Melion 2022, 313–320.
3 Angel, Hoyle, and Miedema 1996, 248.
4 Hirschfelder 2008, 93–97. On the artist's particular interest in portraying themself in *portraits historiés*, see Manuth 2016, 191–202.
5 Van den Boogert 1999–2000, 28. For the latest research on the importing of textiles, see Anderson and Kehoe 2023, in *JHNA*'s special issue on the Dutch Textile Trade Project.
6 Silver 1984, 143–144, cat. 32 A; Schütt, 2021, 147. Emma Capron suggests that the duchess may also be regarded as a cross-dressed man (Capron 2023, 24–26).
7 "*ouw-bollighe Monstreuse Tronyen te sien, Mans en Vrouwen, waer-van daer twee waren, by d'Heer Borghermeester Smidts tot Aelst*" ("*... old-fashioned, monstrous heads [were] to be seen, men and women, of which there were two, at Mr Borgher, master smith in Aalst.*") Muylle 2002, 183. Capron 2023, 20–21.
8 Thomson 2001, 19–20, cat. 18.
9 De Winkel 2006, 268–269, 331 n. 358.
10 "*duysent fraey versinsels*". Van Mander 1604, 44r; Melion 2022, 317.
11 Wouk 2018, 219, 231.
12 This painting was a study for an allegory of Spring. *Ibid.*, 232.
13 Huvenne 2020, 300–301.
14 The tronie's headpiece and breastplate are then depicted in Floris' *Minerva Visiting the Muses*, c. 1568, Condé sur l'Escaut, Hôtel de Ville. *Ibid.*, 238–239.
15 Lohse Belkin 1980.
16 Vogtherr 1538, B iii.
17 Belkin, *Costume Book*, 176–179, cat. 45.
18 Van Mander 1604, 43v; Melion 2022, 316. More than six decades after Van Mander's volume, the art theorist Willem Goeree echoed the importance of prints for the study of ancient costume and hairstyles. Goeree 1670, 50–51.
19 Van den Boogert 1999–2000, 38.
20 Here, "Turkish" should be taken as a loose term to describe the habits from the Ottoman and Safavid empires of the time. Vrolijk 2020, 87.
21 Robinson 2018, 43–59.
22 Bruegel 1658. For transcriptions of all verses, see Muylle 2002, 140–148. The works would then be taken up by Adriaen Brouwer in oval-shaped paintings, carrying out various activities and pastimes. See also Brouwer's *Youth Making a Face* (Fig. 90), where the mischievous boy, dressed in a fur hat accessorised with a handy dagger, reflected the behaviour associated with his peers. *Idem*, 121–125.
23 See Michael Kwakkelstein's essay in this volume.
24 Sellink 2007, 257, cat. 168; Muylle 2002, 179.
25 De Witt 2020.
26 Ribeiro 2017, 121.
27 For similar tronies, see also sitters dressed in white bonnets in Jacques Jordaens' *Two Head Studies of an Old Woman* (Fig. 46), *Head Study of an Old Woman* (Fig. 45), and Michael Sweerts' *Head of a Girl* (Leicester, Fig. 118), and *Head of a Woman* (Los Angeles, Fig. 14).
28 Van der Wetering 2015, cat. 35.
29 *Ibid.*, cat. 56.
30 A figure with a fur collar or gorget (perhaps another tronie) has been identified beneath the painting's surface. Trentelman 2014, 801–811.
31 They were also integral to the artist's own regard of their studio practice. In a work attributed to Gerard Dou, a helmet foregrounds the painting, alongside a swathe of fabric and a breastplate, probably referring to the role of military costume as part of larger history paintings. Surh 2023.
32 Van den Boogert 1999–2000, 45, 49–50; De Winkel 2006, 140.
33 Van Hoogstraten 1678, 229–230; Brusati 2021, 265.
34 Kelch 1986.
35 See *The Laughing Man*, which is painted on copper ground with gold leaf. Rembrandt evokes the sheen of the metal through a different technique, where the gorget is depicted using a thin layer of paint. It allows for the metallic ground to be partially visible and to reflect light.
36 Breukink-Peeze 1989, esp. 132.
37 Vermeer's "*twee tronijen geschildert op sijn Turx*" [two tronies painted in a Turkish fashion] were displayed in the interior kitchen. Perhaps one of them was *Girl with the Red Hat*, discussed below. The "*turcxe tronij*" [Turkish tronie] was recorded in the 1665 inventory of Van Alewijn. Roelofs 2023a, 64–74, 293; Van Alewijn 2023.
38 Schwartz 2010, 62. On the "Turckse tronie" see Swan 2021, 129–137.
39 Potterton 1986, 127–129, cat. 439.
40 Goeree 1670, 75–76.
41 Van Hoogstraten 1678, 147–153; Brusati 2021, 192–197.
42 Van Hout 2020, 88–89, cat. 9; Van Haute 2015.
43 Devisscher and Vlieghe 2014, 110–123, cat. 23. See also Marcaida 2014.
44 "*ook wel een dag of twee konde doorbrengen om een Tulleband naar zyn zinlikheit op te tuigen*". Houbraken 1718, 261. Horn and Van Leeuwen 2021, 261.
45 Lievens' painting is believed to have been displayed in a more lavish interior than the turbaned tronie in Rembrandt's painting discussed above. It likely belonged in the collection of Stadtholder Frederik Hendrik. Treanor 2008-2009, 118–119, cat. 19.
46 On the *sluyer* see De Winkel 2006, 255.
47 "*een soort Turkse vorst met een Hollands hoofd*". Huygens 1987, 88.
48 "*een pertije antieckse lappen van diversche coleuren*". Van den Boogert 1999–2000, 147. See also Rembrandt's pupil Arent de Gelder and his "rag shop" in his studio. *Idem*, 50.
49 Potterton 1986, 35–36, cat. 107.
50 Van der Wetering 2015, cat. 95.
51 De Winkel 2006, 170. Rubens also applied artistic licence to non-European costume. See Young-Jae 2013.
52 Vermeer's interest in tronies may have been sparked by his former neighbour, the artist Cornelis Dame Rietwijk, who was renowned for his painted tronies. Roelofs 2023b, 208.
53 On Vermeer's use of the *japonsche rok*, a Japanese silk robe, see Hollander 2011.
54 Incidentally, beneath the painting's surface is a portrait of a man in a wide-brimmed hat. The man's identity and the work's author – tentatively attributed to Vermeer – remain inconclusive. The work is considered to be a portrait rather than a tronie (see Rembrandt's habit of painting over tronies in this volume's *Introduction* and note 30 above). Libby 2022.
55 Roelofs 2023a, 212.
56 See Rublack 2021.
57 See fanciful and arcane hats depicted in works by Ferdinand Bol and Rembrandt van Rijn. Roelofs 2023a, 211.

THE HAT MAKES THE PERSON

The career of the celebrated hat designer Elvis Pompilio began in 1987 with a simple showroom. These days he is known all over the world. This is a story of the milliner's profession and what it does to both the maker and the wearer of the headgear we call 'hats'.

'I started making hats when I was very young and have been doing it for forty years now. We didn't wear hats ourselves back then, but I loved accessories. I studied art and learnt to paint and sculpt. At the end of the day, a hat is a piece of sculpture. That's also what prompted me to start designing fashion.'

'Lots of designers buy their wooden forms ready-made. That's not creation as far as I'm concerned. I make them myself and choose my own materials. I'm involved in the design and execution from the beginning to the end. As Accessories teacher at La Cambre in Brussels, I ask my students at the beginning of each academic year to make a volume in paper or other material, and then reproduce it in a wooden model. Models like that don't follow the shape of the skull, they change it. You can use round, pointed or very high or low shapes to change the way someone looks. It's my job, after all, to improve my customers' appearance, to make them look good. If you have a long face, a high hat won't work. A beret or a low-cut shape is better in that case.'

'The right hat can balance a face. It's a bit like the way Dürer plays with the proportions of facial features in his treatise. If you put on a hat very low or very high, it changes the dynamic, the intention to please or to repel. Depending on the hat you wear, you can feel more welcoming, more dominant, or more aloof. Even when I have a shape that looks good, I still have to trim it sometimes to achieve the ideal proportions. That's very labour intensive. A difference of two centimetres in a hat changes everything.'

'The invasion of cheap hats means that everyone these days is wearing the same imported headgear. It's making the millinery profession increasingly rare. Once upon a time, I was one milliner among many. Nowadays, I'm steadily turning into an artist. The more time that goes by, the stronger the artistic idea is within me. It has turned into *haute couture*. Materials are important to this. I take account, for instance, of how fabrics reflect. In a photograph, a hat can catch the light or cancel it out. You see the face or you see less of it. You can really transform people with a hat.'
'You almost never see the writer Amélie Nothomb without the hat I made for her. The accessory creates her character, even in cartoons of her. I like to create characters with my collections. Without the hats, they would be almost unrecognisable. Which means they can go incognito, while wearing my hats lets them reshape their personality. There's something very strange about it.'
'Conversely, the character of the models inspires me too. That's important. Before I choose a hat, I talk to people to see whether they are more of an extrovert or an introvert. After we've talked, we can decide what to choose. Outgoing people could use a little compensation and a little respite. In that case, I won't suggest overly extravagant, overly flashy hats. Shy people, on the other hand, need to be pushed a bit. So for them I recommend extravagant and colourful hats.'

'There are also people who wear hats to protect themselves and make themselves less accessible, to create distance or look different. In those cases, the hat becomes a mask. Some people who attend weddings want to conceal something. The same goes for funerals, with black veils to disguise the pain and emotion. Big hats cast deep shadows and create mystery. In the famous painting, *The Man with the Golden Helmet*, the artist emphasises the helmet, which tells us more about the model. The military accessory defines the figure. Without the helmet, he could be anything, he might be a farmer. Now we see that he is a warrior. It is more the idea of the helmet that counts and more the reflection of the light than the face of the sad old man, who seems to have lost all his sparkle.

Hollywood stars understand the potential of hats to seduce or to accentuate their femininity or masculinity. It's linked to wearing a uniform. Without a hat, the uniform doesn't exist. Think of police officers and their caps, the fezzes worn by Greek Evzones in their skirts and pompom shoes, and the wide-brimmed feathered hats of the Italian Bersaglieri, which my father used to wear, and which showed which regiment you belonged to and what rank you were. Things like that might not mean much these days, but they used to signal your status in society.'

Elvis Pompilio (1961) is a Belgian hat designer. He works for leading fashion brands like Dior, Chanel, Valentino and Demeulemeester. His creations are owned and admired by celebrities including Madonna, Sharon Stone, Axelle Red, Harrison Ford and members of several royal families. Some of Elvis Pompilio's designs are now on display in major museums, such as the Musée des Arts Décoratifs in Paris.

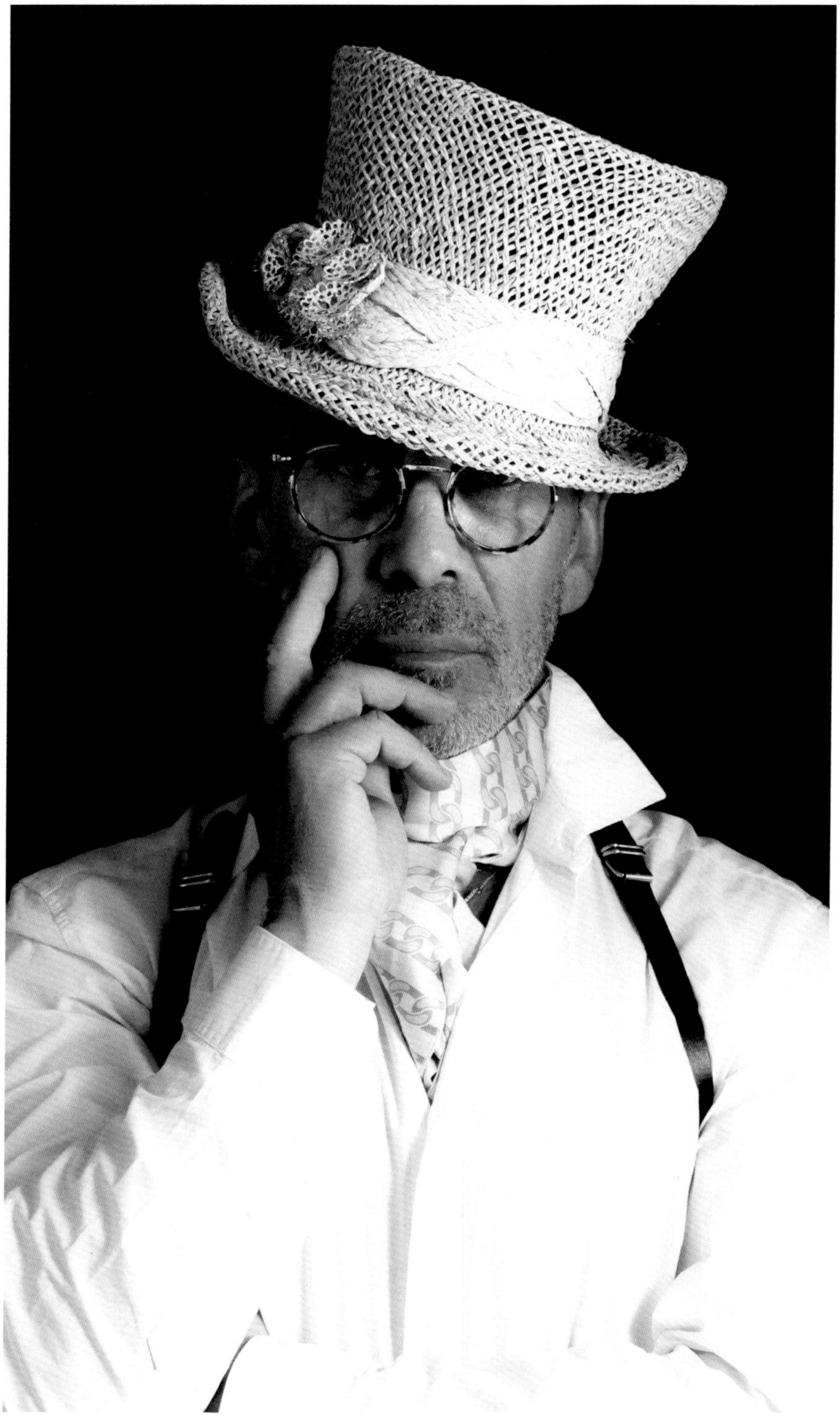

Stephane Boudin,
Elvis Pompilio,
2022, photograph

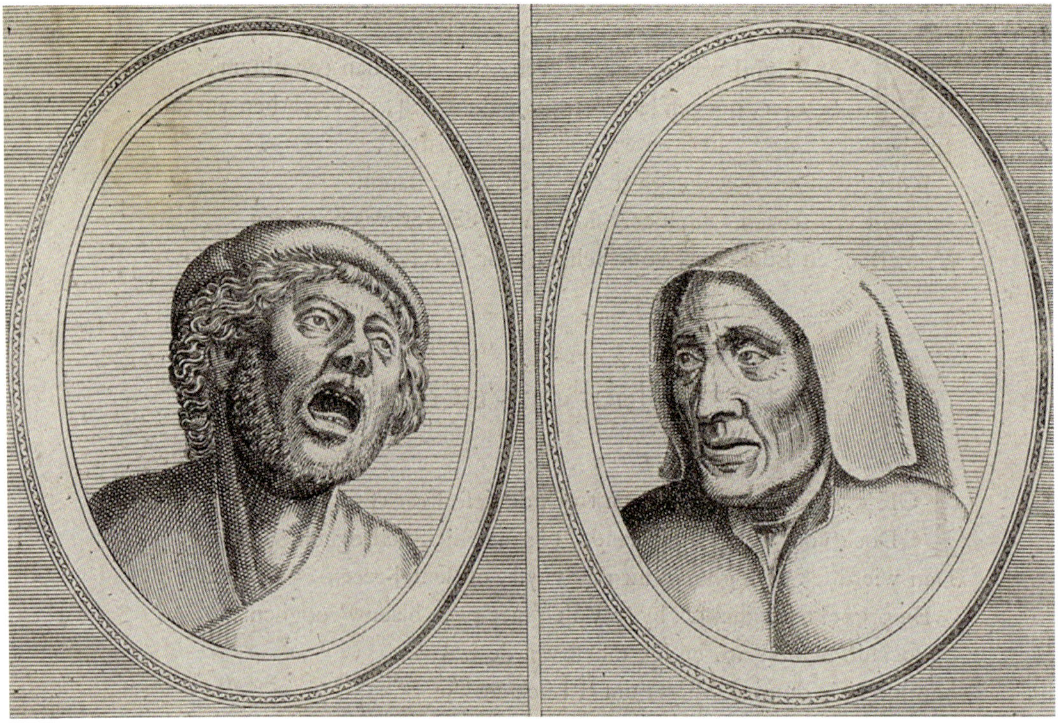

FIG. 61
Pieter Bruegel the Elder, Engravings from '*Toonneel des wereldts: Ontdeckende de ongestuymigheden en ydelheden in woorden ende wercken deser verdorvene eeuwe*', 1658, Royal Library of Belgium, Brussels

FIG. 62
Hendrick Goltzius, *Laughing Jester with Needle and Thread*, 1590–1610, gravure, Rijksmuseum, Amsterdam,

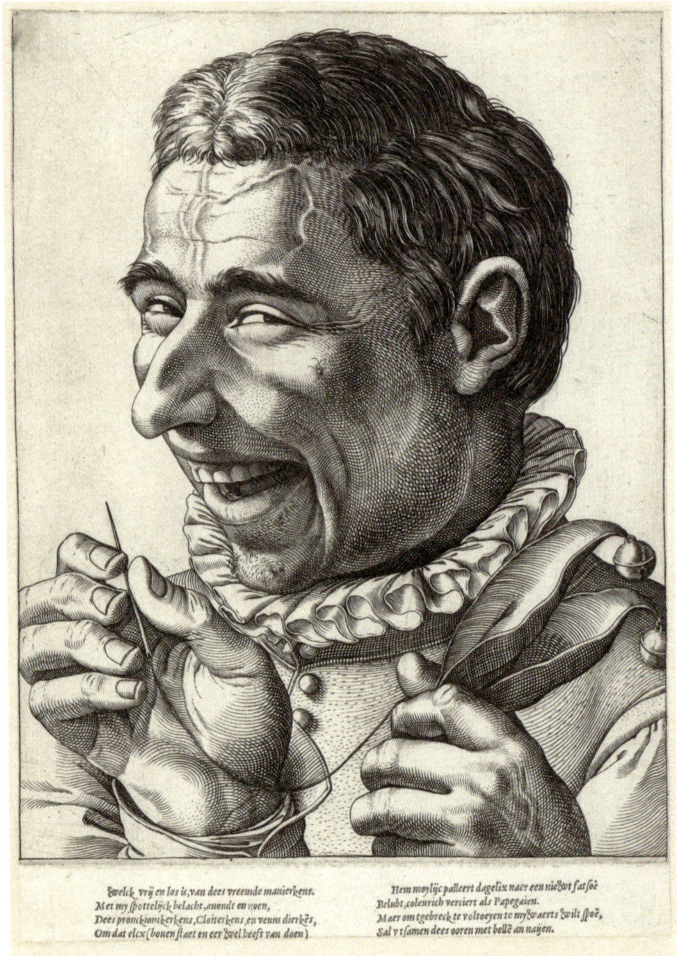

FIG. 63
Philips Galle, *Head of a Jester*, c. 1560, ink on paper, Noord-Hollands Archief, Haarlem, NL-hlmNHA_1477_53008458

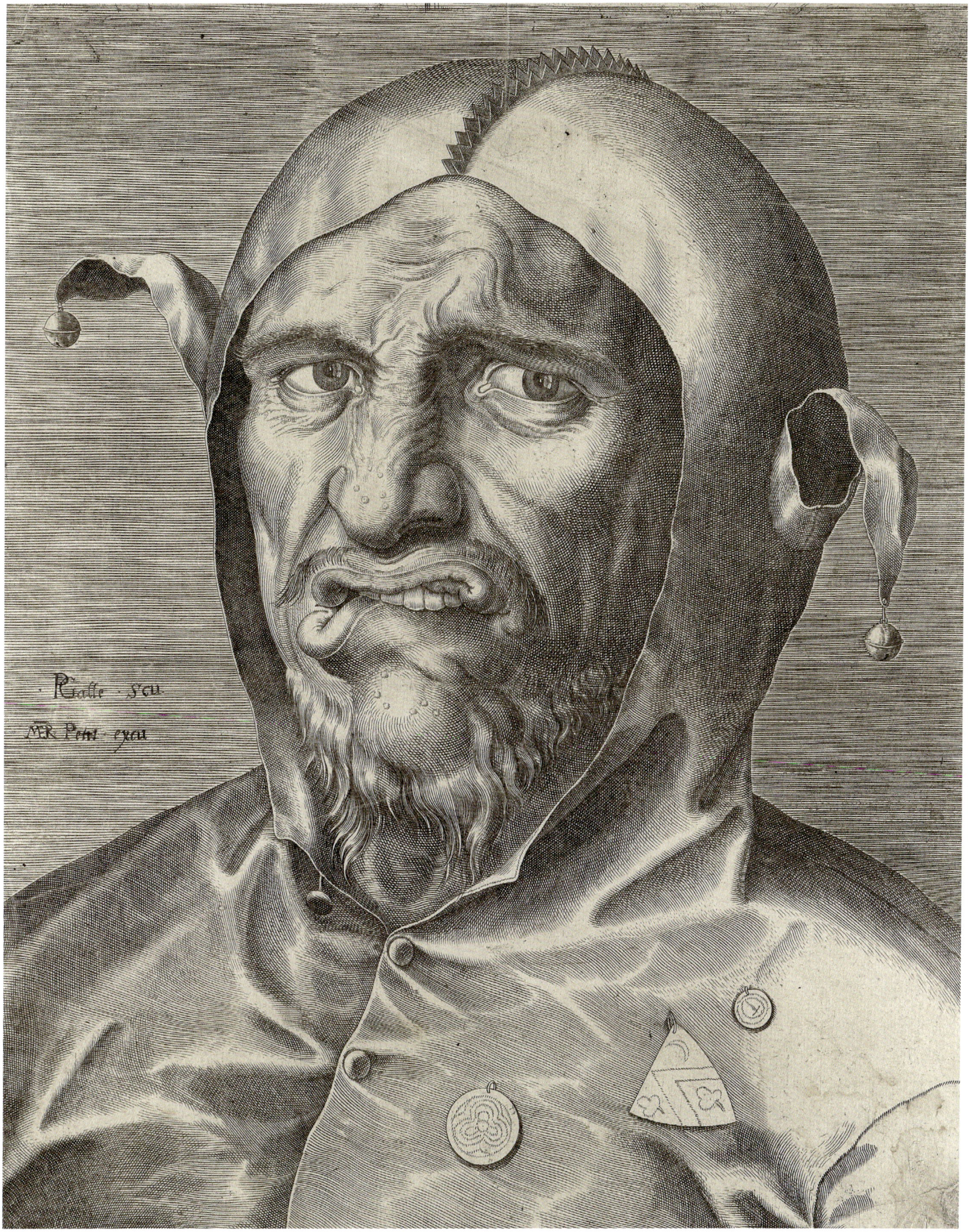
PGalle scu
MR Petri excu

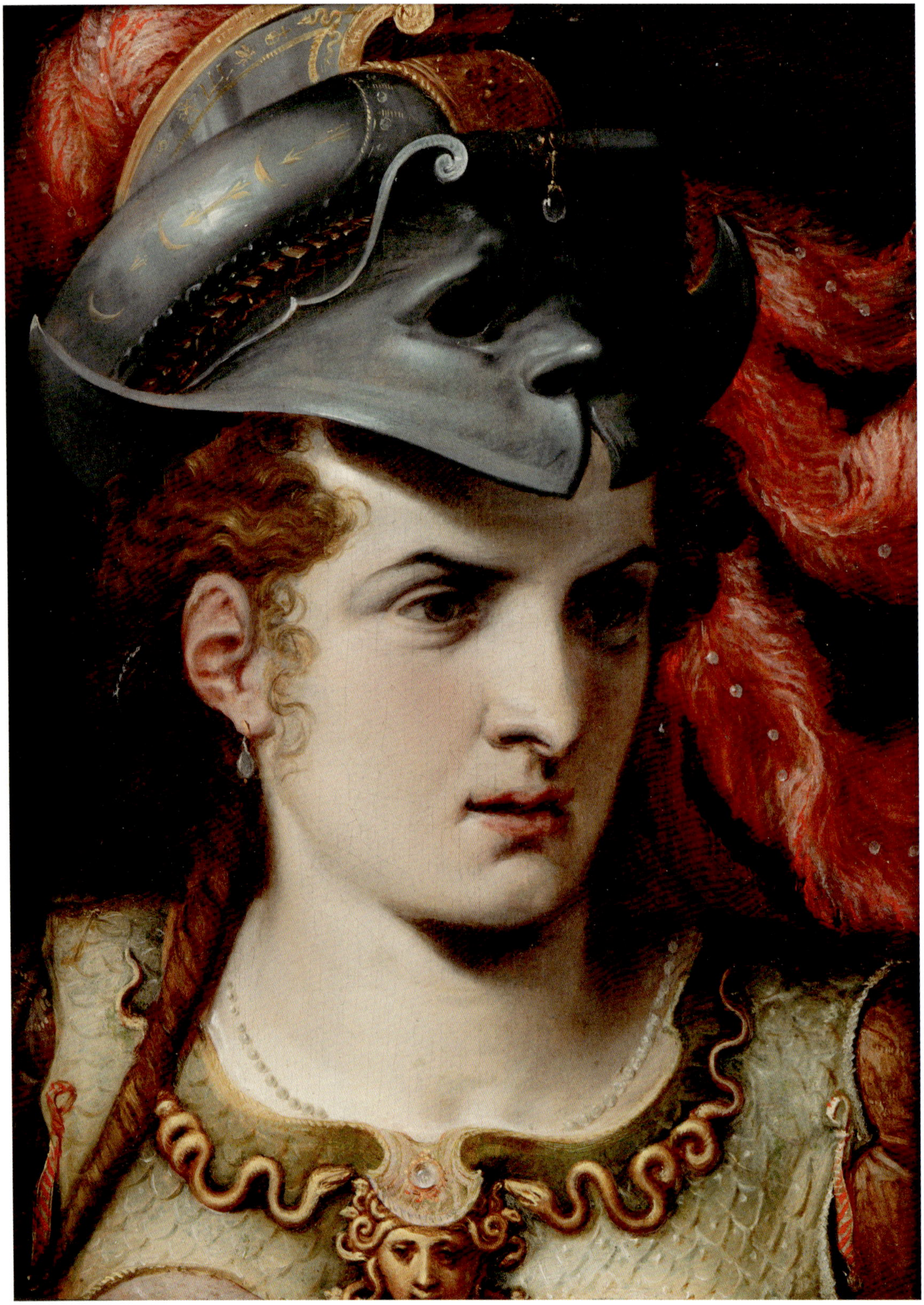

FIG. 64
Frans Floris the Elder, *Minerva*, c. 1567, oil on panel, The Phoebus Foundation, Antwerp

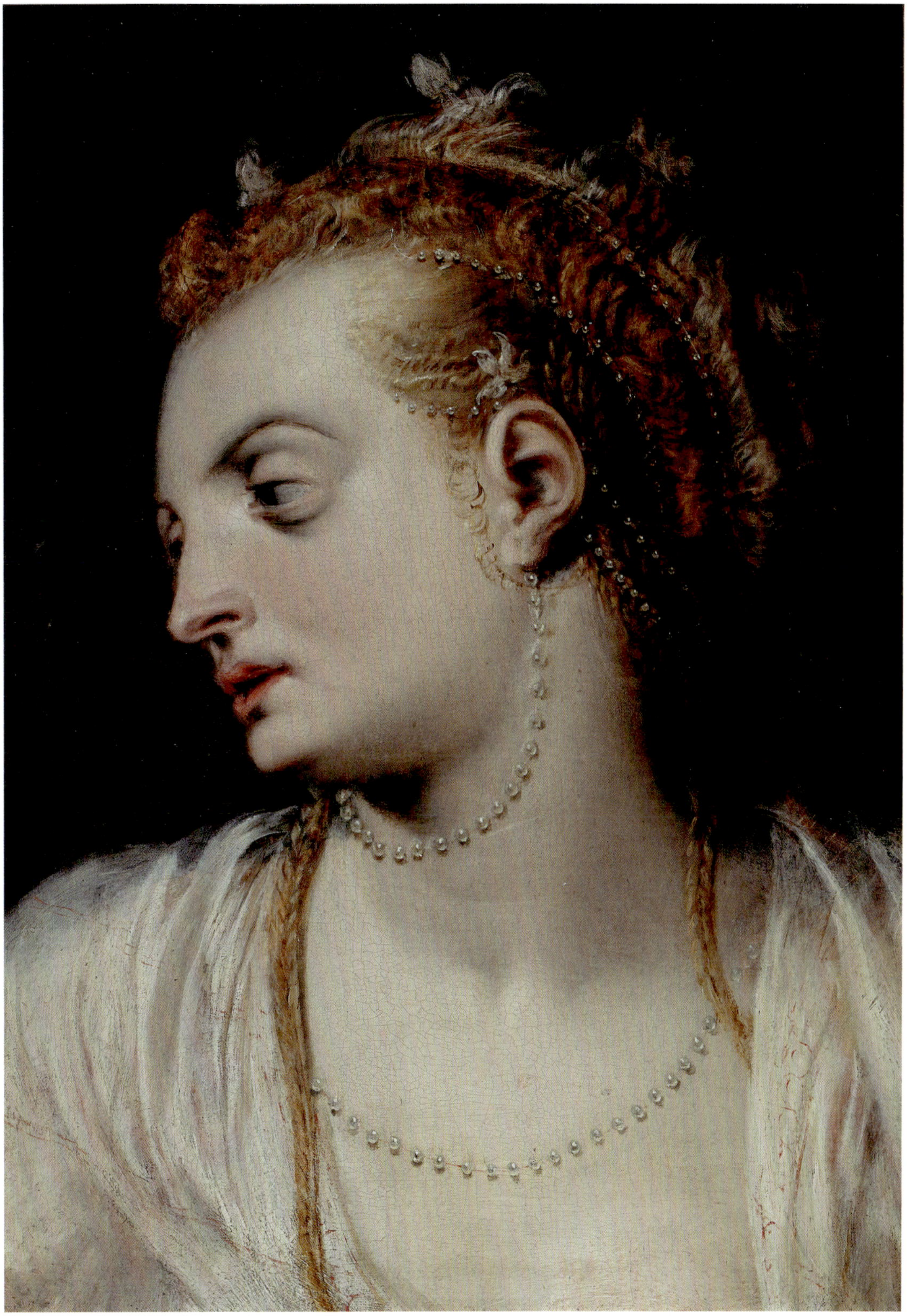

FIG. 65
Frans Floris the Elder, *Head Study of a Young Woman*, s.d., oil on wood, National Gallery, Prague, DO 4300

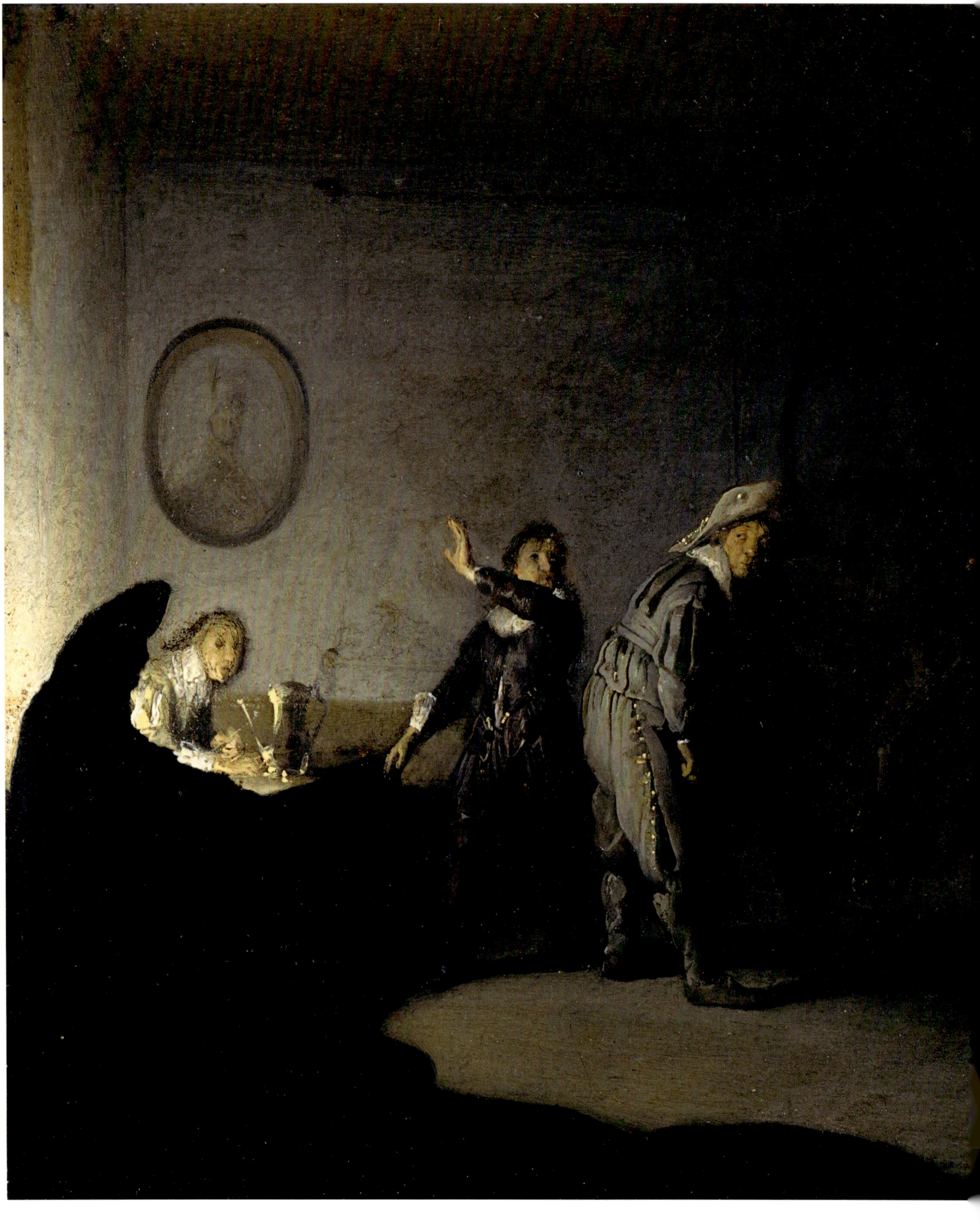

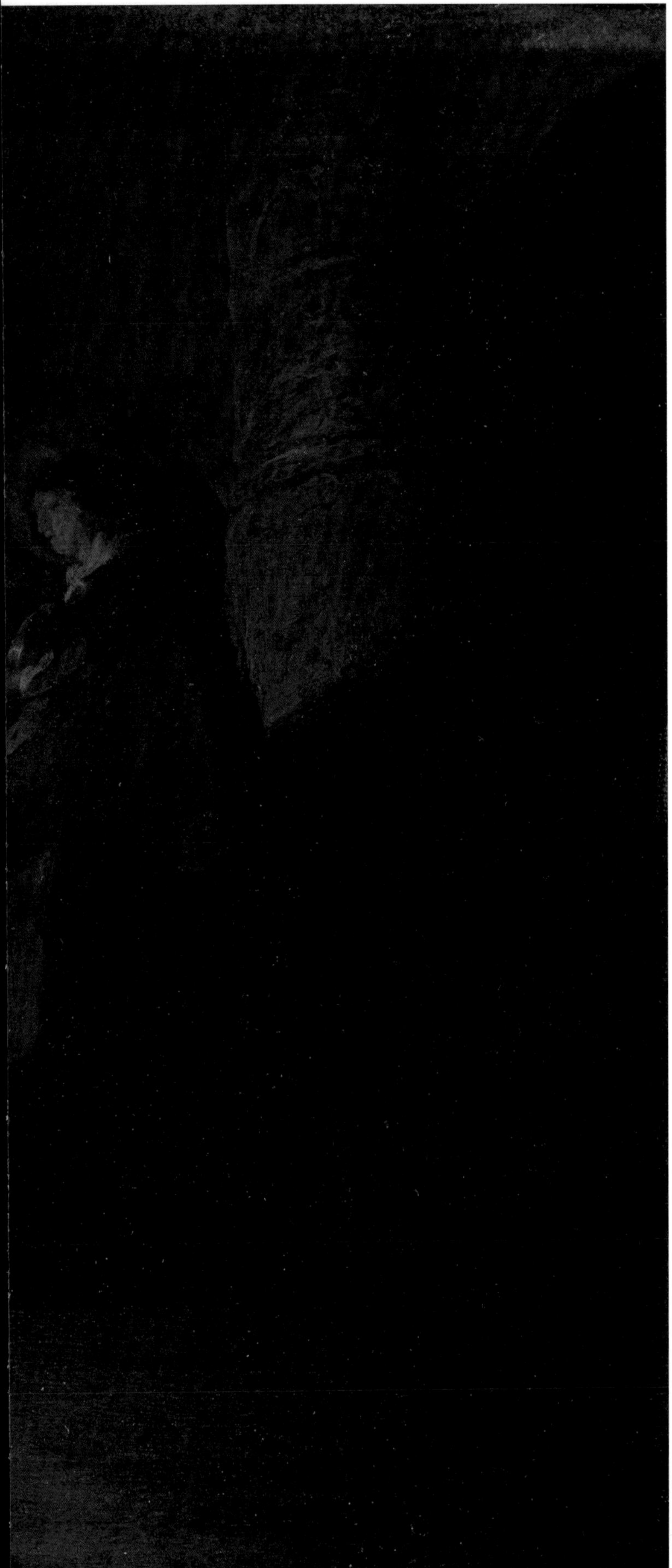

FIG. 66
Rembrandt, *Interior with Figures ('La Main Chaude')*, c. 1628, oil on panel, National Gallery of Ireland, Dublin, NGI.439

FIG. 67
Circle of Rembrandt,
The Man with the Golden Helmet,
c. 1650, oil on canvas,
Gemäldegalerie,
Berlin, 811A

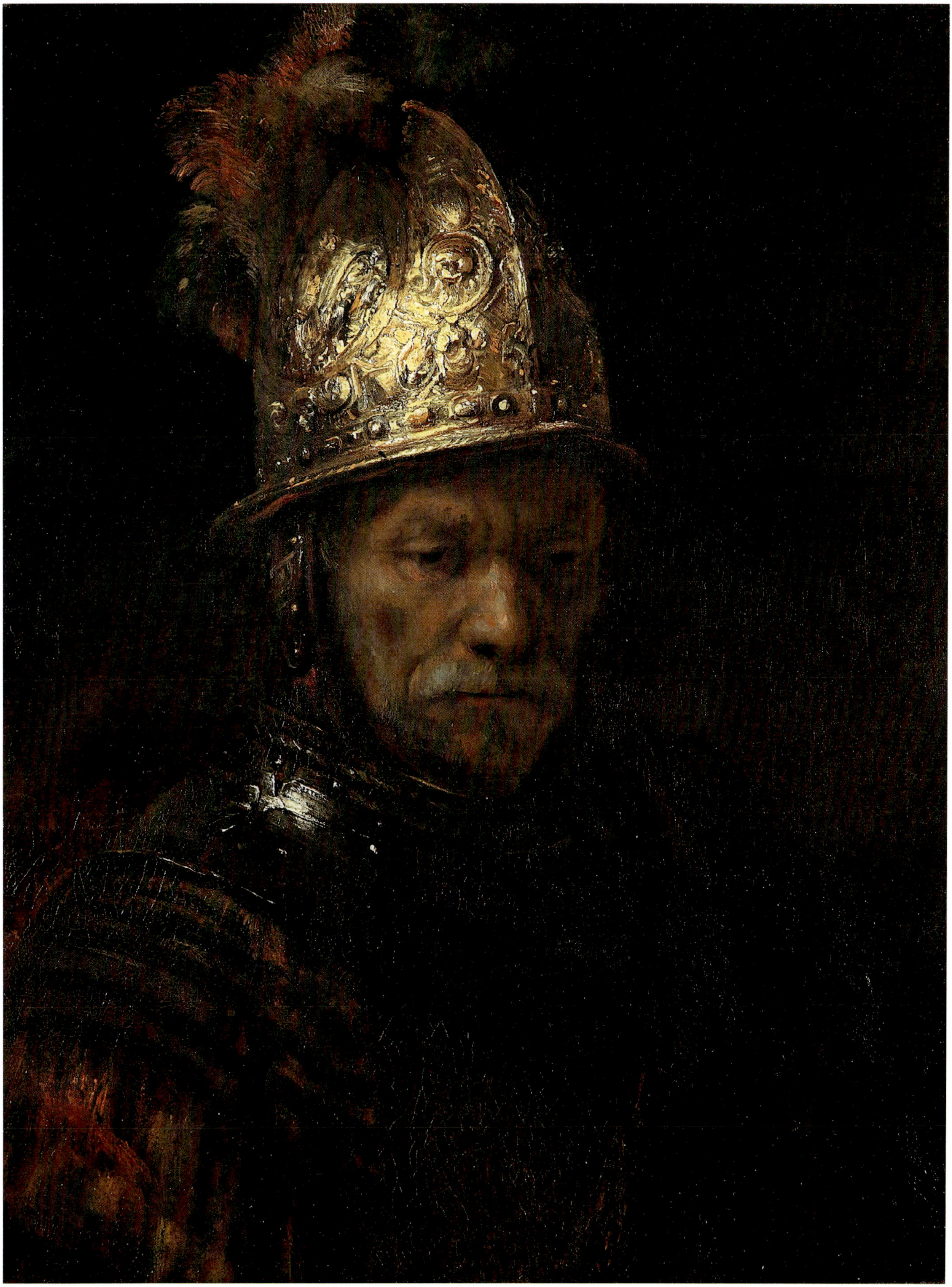

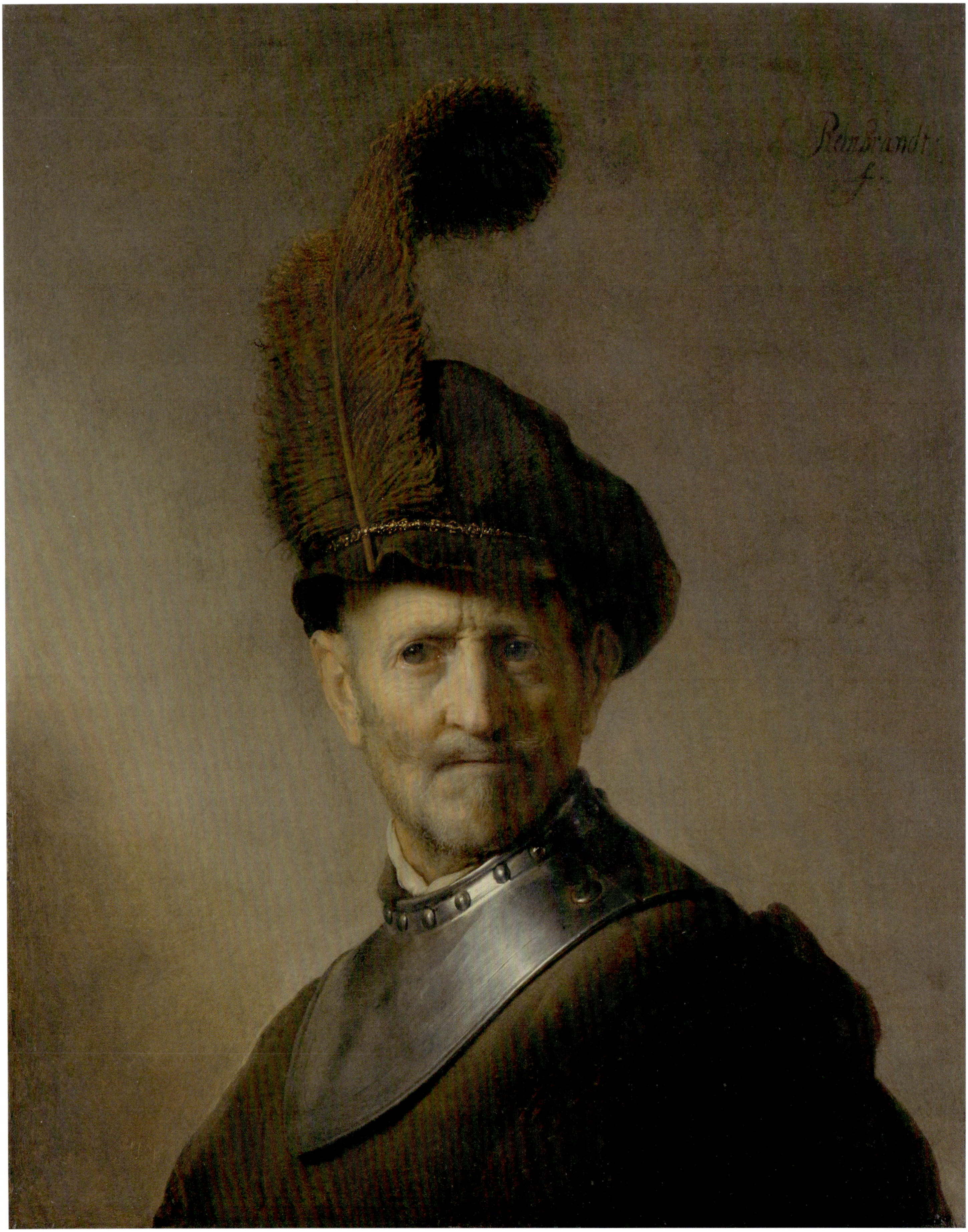
Rembrandt
f.

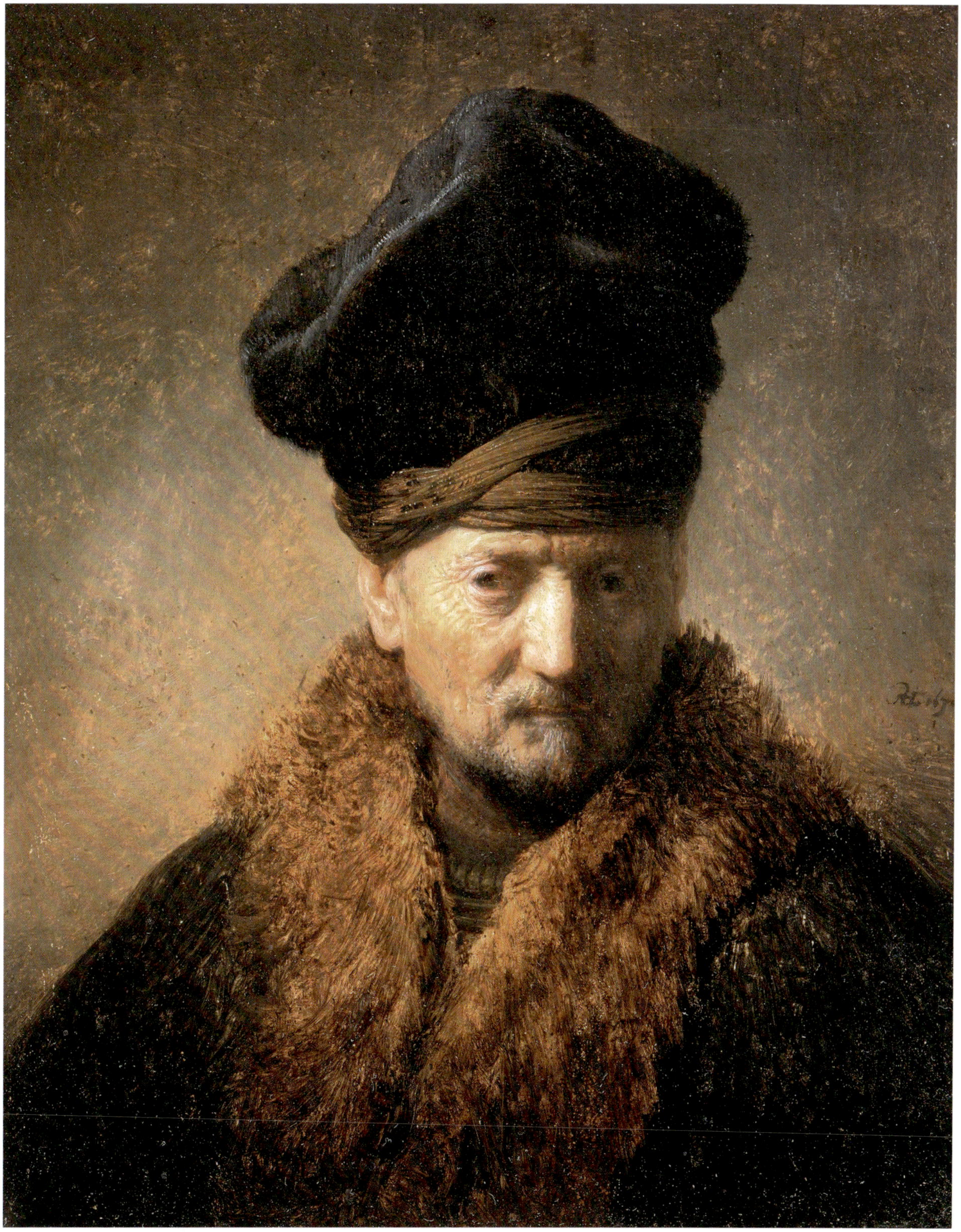

FIG. 68
Rembrandt, *An Old Man in Military Costume*, 1631, oil on panel, The J. Paul Getty Museum, Malibu, 78.PB.246

FIG. 69
Rembrandt, *Bust of an Old Man Wearing a Fur Cap*, 1630, oil on panel, Tiroler Landesmuseum Ferdinandeum, Innsbruck, Gem 599

FIG. 70
Willem Drost,
Bust of a Man Wearing a Large-brimmed Hat,
c. 1654, oil on canvas,
National Gallery of Ireland, Dublin,
NGI.2016.21

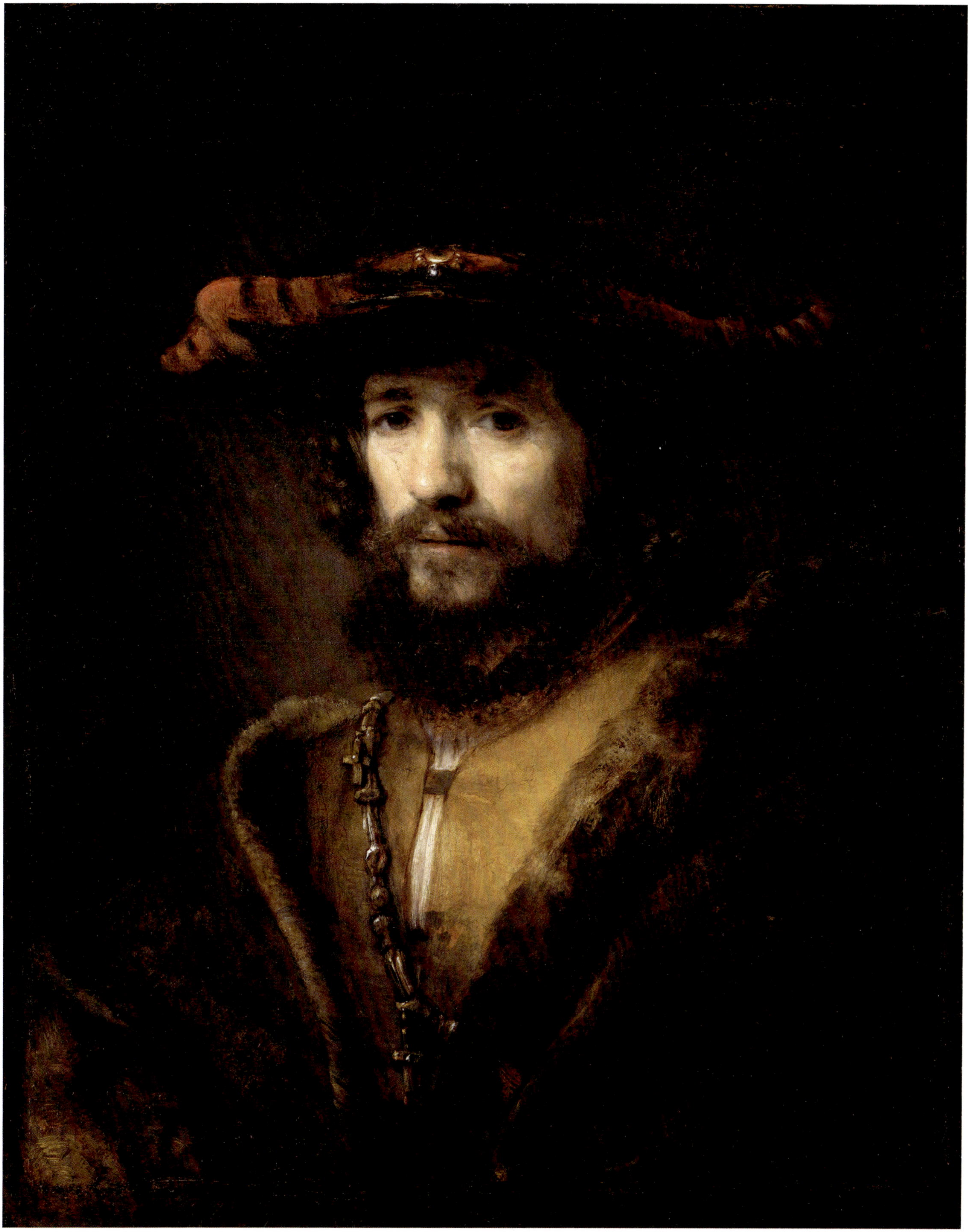

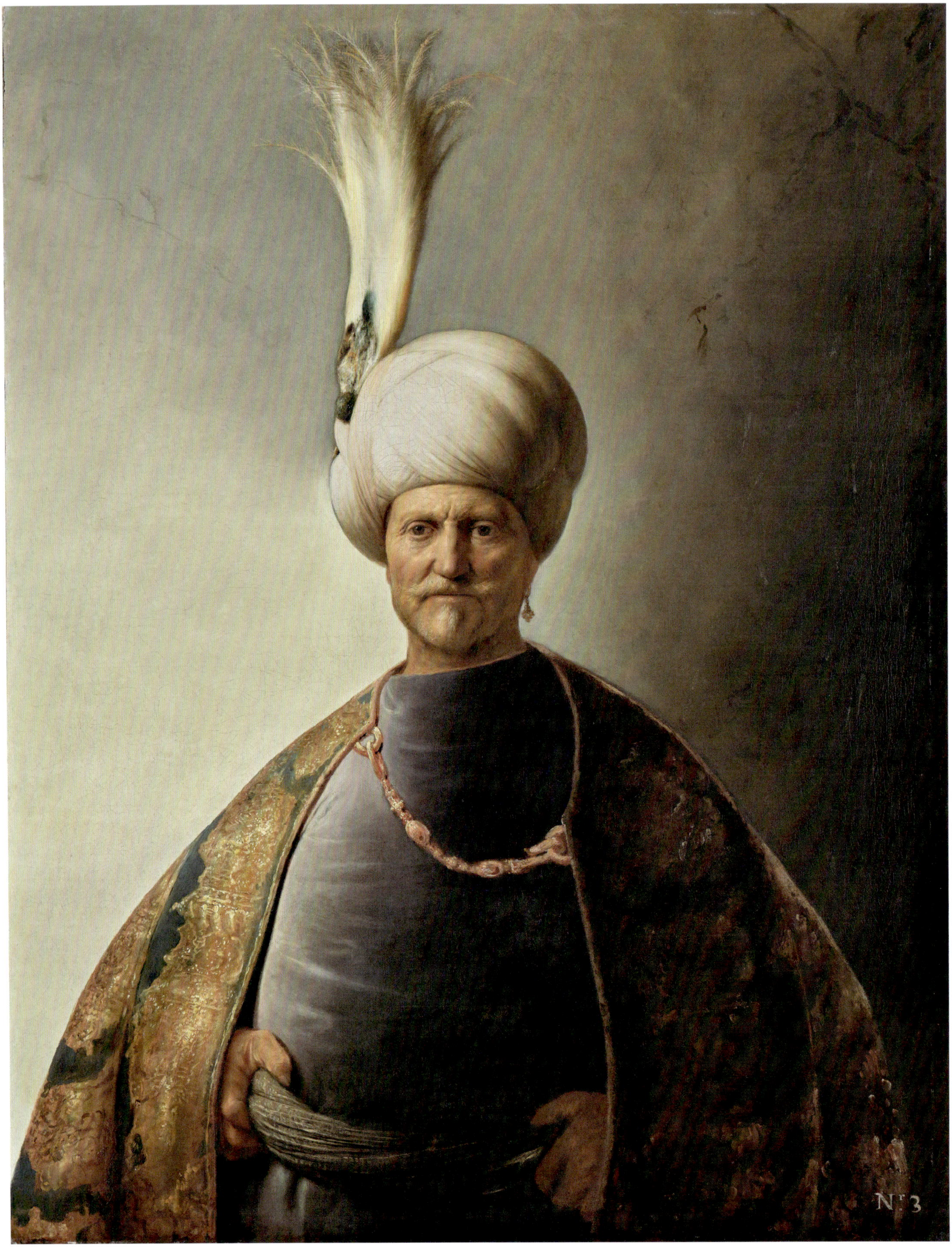
N°3

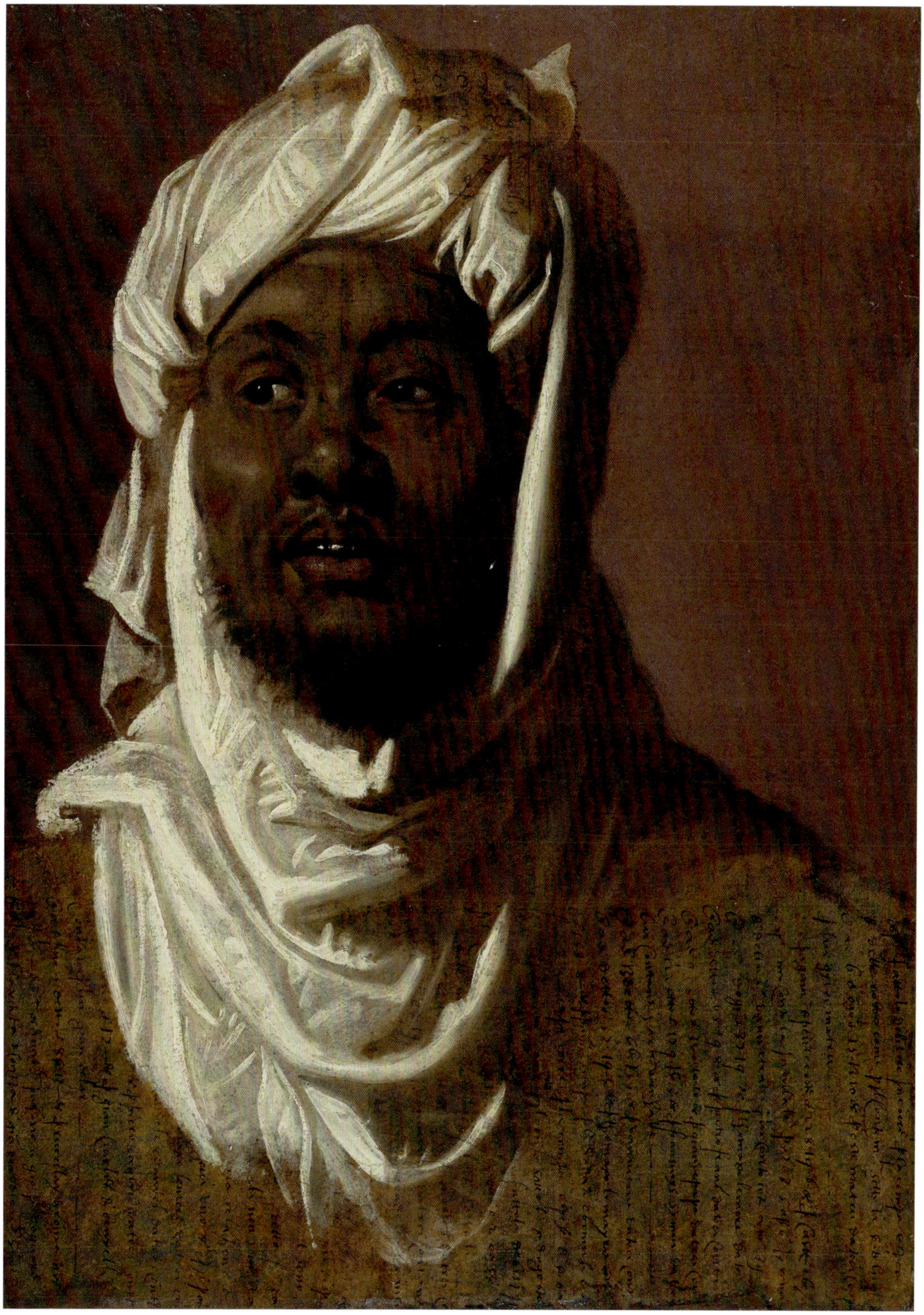

FIG. 71
Jan Lievens,
Man in Oriental Dress,
c. 1629–1931, oil on
canvas, Bildergalerie
Sanssouci, Potsdam,
GK I 884

FIG. 72
Peter Paul Rubens,
Study for King Balthasar,
1608, oil on paper
laid down on panel,
The J. Paul Getty Museum,
Malibu, 2018.48

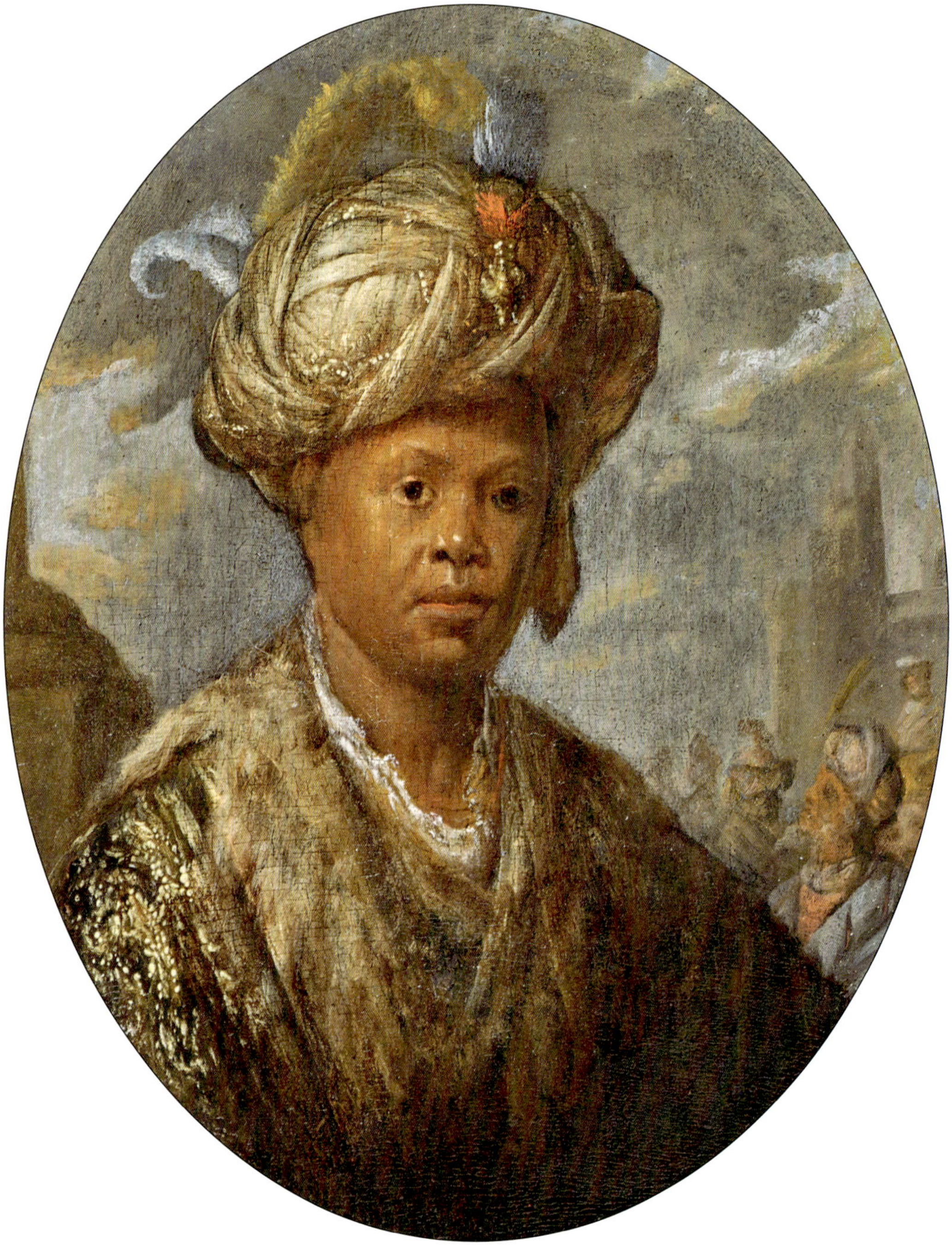

FIG. 73
Jan Adriaensz. van Staveren, *Tronie of a Young Man of African Origin in Oriental Costume,* (1640–1643), oil on panel, FENIX

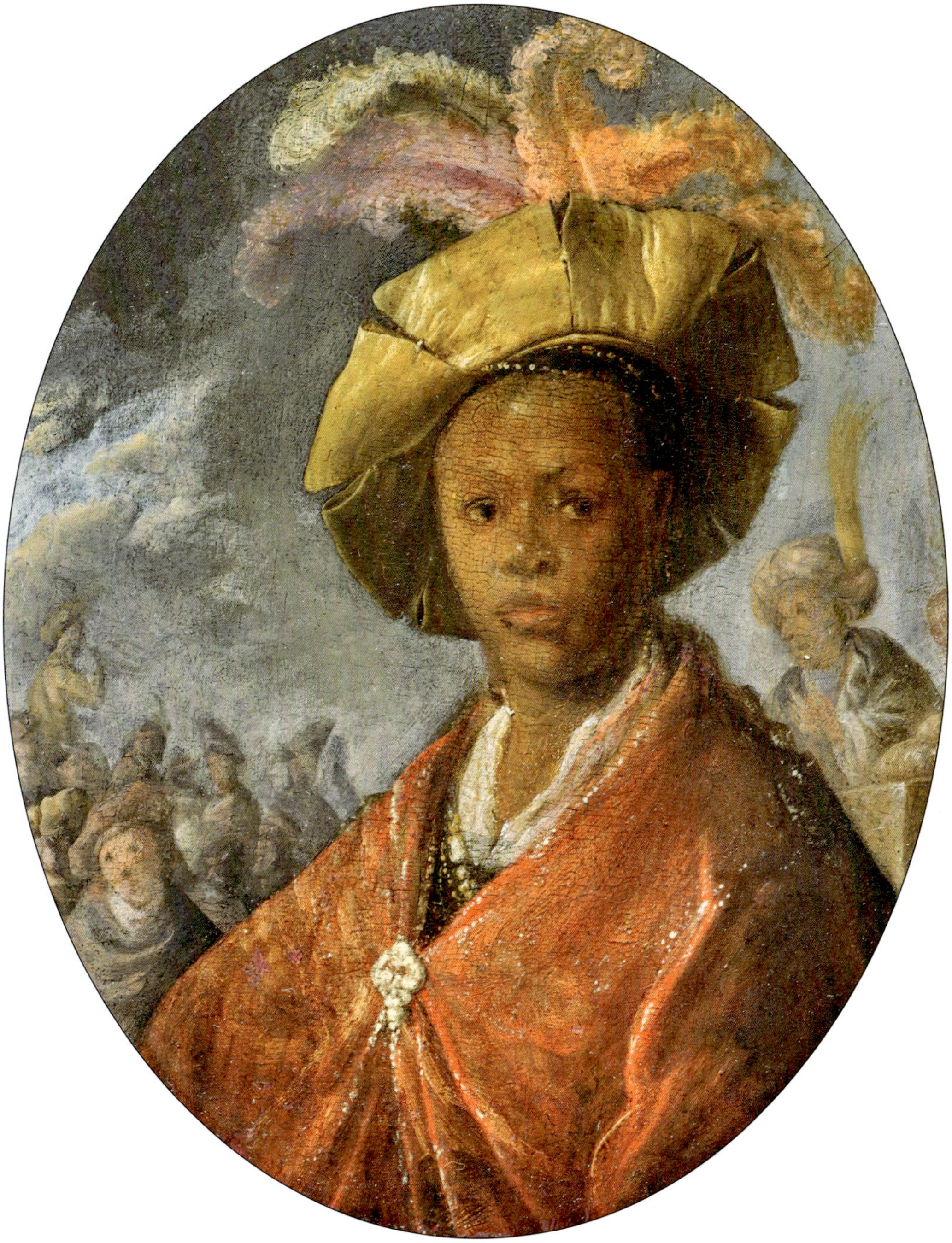

FIG. 74
Jan Adriaensz. van Staveren, *Tronie of a Young Man of African Origin Wearing a Yellow Feathered Beret*, (1640–1643), oil on panel, FENIX

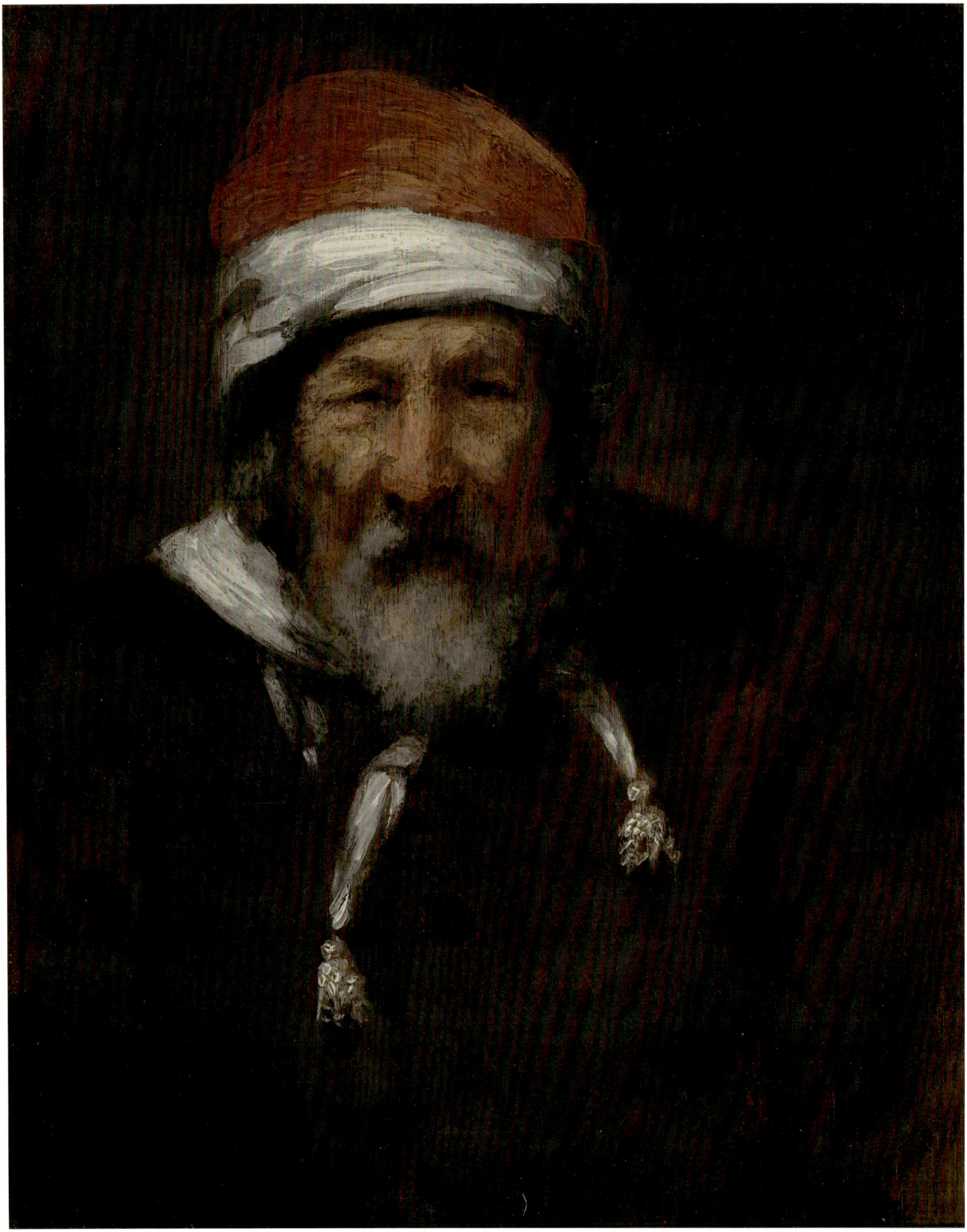

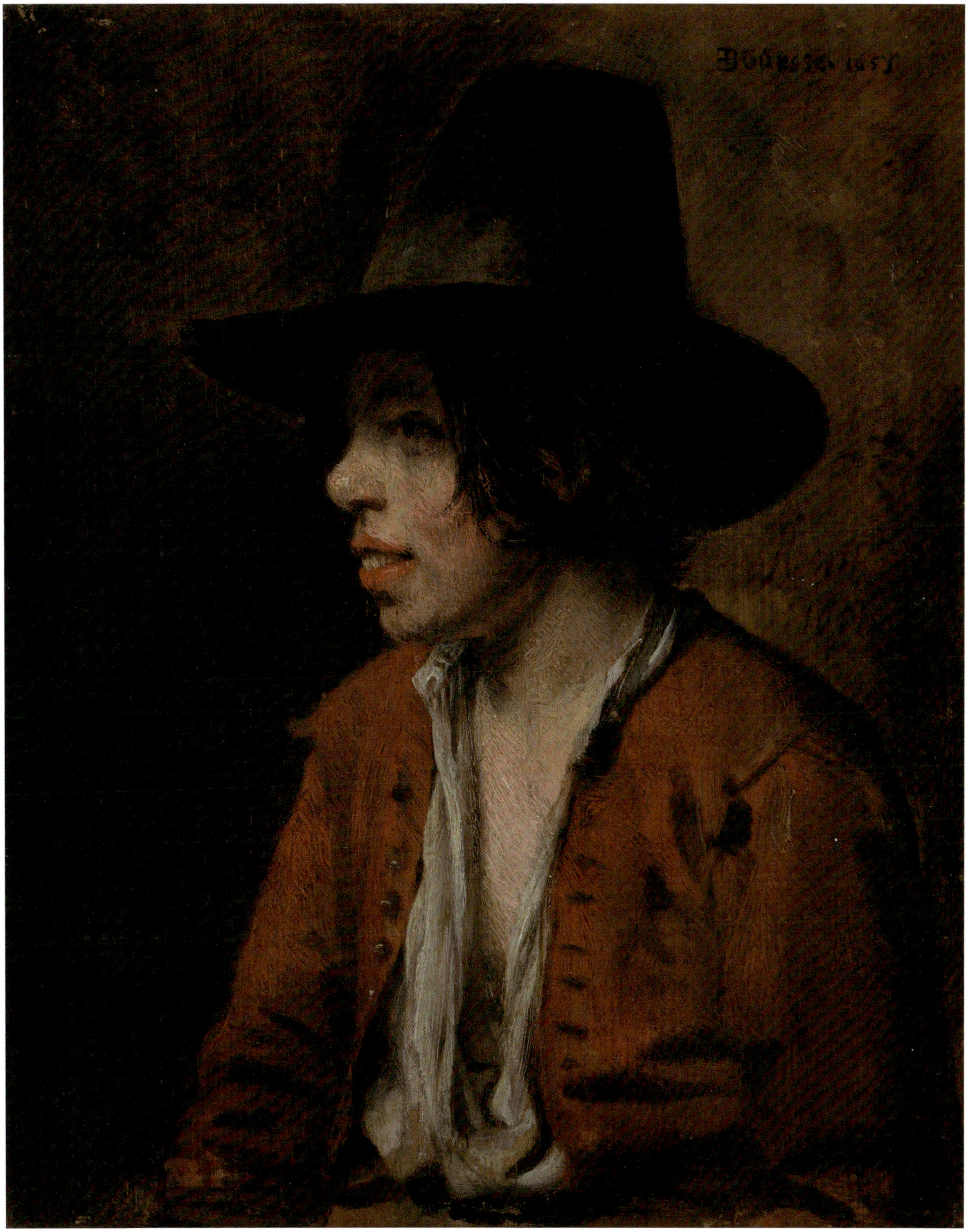

FIG. 75
Abraham van Dijck,
Old Man, s.d.,
oil on panel, KMSKA,
Antwerp, inv. 295

FIG. 76
Esaias Boursse,
Fisher Boy, 1655,
oil on panel, KMSKA,
Antwerp, inv. 294

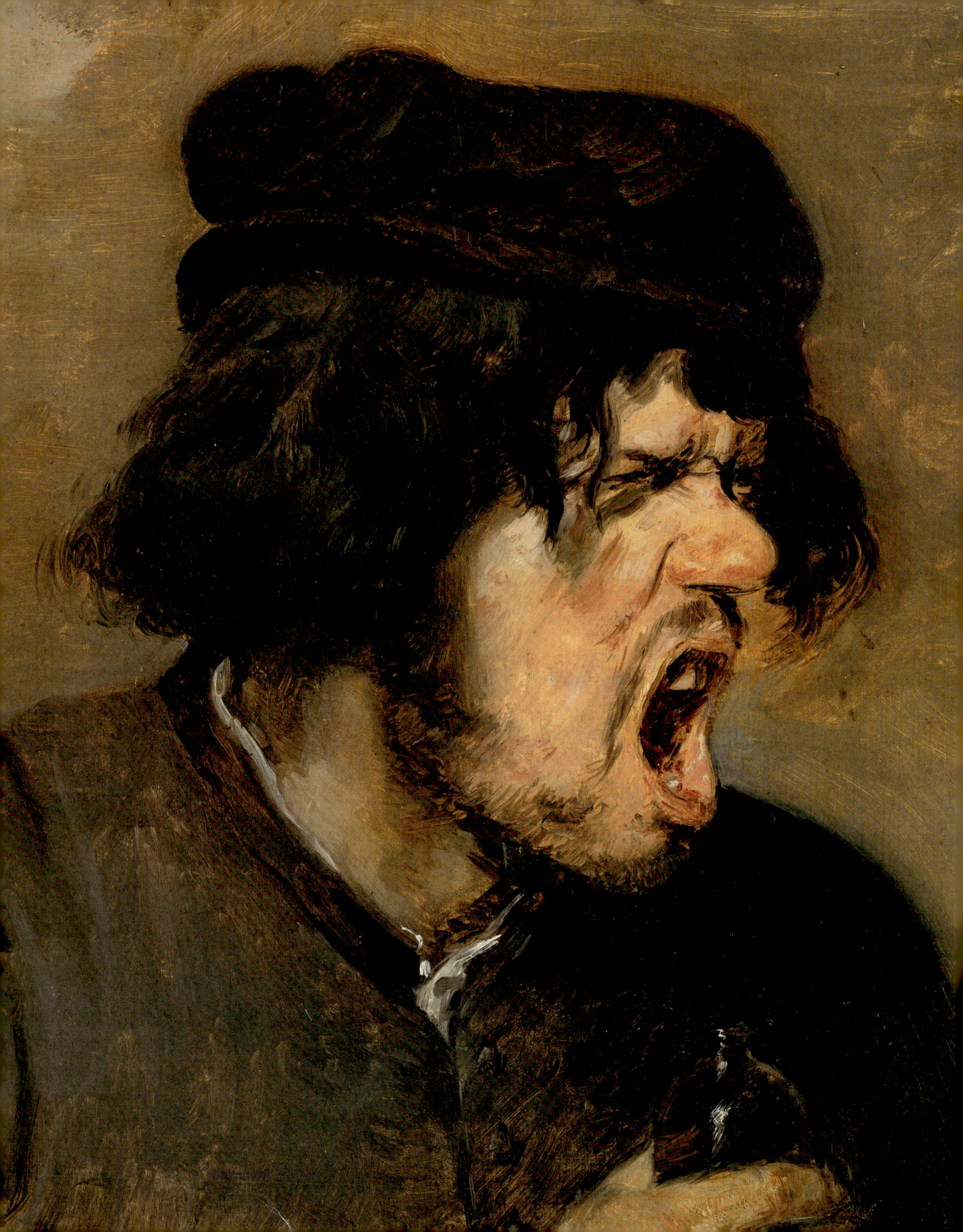

EXPRESSION

Faces as a Vehicle of Expression and Emotion

Friederike Schütt

Radiant joy, childlike pride and a touch of mischief are all expressed in the face of the *Laughing Boy* (Fig. 85), which Frans Hals captured in a tondo around 1625. The boy's spontaneous lack of inhibition instantly makes the viewer smile. Hals's brilliant rendering of the facial expression enables him to convey the child's emotions extremely persuasively. The snapshot character of the face fits seamlessly with the strikingly loose brushwork: the unruly hair, the pink cheeks and the light reflections on the skin communicate the touching and fleeting nature of joy. The Haarlem artist placed his initials to the left of the head, indicating that this is a fully-fledged work of art. His exceptionally fine observational skills enabled him to achieve a quintessential tronie – in a restricted space and in front of a neutral background – focusing entirely on the facial expression.[1]

This focus and distillation link the work with the *Study of a Child's Head* (Fig. 87), which Anthony van Dyck probably created between 1627 and 1632, and in which the Flemish artist has only roughly set down the details, other than those of the face itself.[2] Van Dyck used the deliberately unfinished oil sketch on paper purely for the artistic development of an expression as he prepared the head of a putto for his painting the *Lamentation of Christ*.[3] With a small number of brushstrokes in different tones of red, he explored an expression around the dark eyes that is far removed emotionally from Hals's *Laughing Boy*. The child's bowed head speaks of sorrow, anger and wilfulness. Hals and Van Dyck created their tronies around the same time, but independently of each other. It is highly likely, nevertheless, that both artists drew on the example of the studies of children's heads that Peter Paul Rubens had been painting and drawing since 1614.[4]

Appearance = inner character

This comparison of expressive children's heads leads us to a selection of seventeenth-century Dutch tronies, which are especially noteworthy for the different manners in which the facial expressions and the emotions they contain were elaborated. The way artists depicted them was closely bound up with the discourse conducted at the time in art-theoretical, physiognomic and philosophical treatises concerning the face's ability to convey expression. We can safely assume that artists were familiar with the basic tenets of such texts. The belief that people's inner character could be read from their outward appearance dates back to Antiquity.

(DETAIL FIG. 89)
Adriaen Brouwer,
The Bitter Potion,
1636–1638, oil on panel,
Städelsches Kunstinstitut und Städtische Galerie, Städel Museum, Frankfurt am Main, 1076

According to this view, the soul – the seat of the emotions – was reflected not only in the movements of the body, but also in the shape of the face and its expressions.[5]

Where innermost feelings had chiefly been conveyed in Renaissance art through physical movements, in the seventeenth century the face grew increasingly relevant as the site where emotions were expressed.[6] Representing affect was considered one of the most difficult and at the same time most highly valued artistic challenges. The quality of an artwork was decisive to its impact and persuasive power when it came to reaching the public in accordance with the rules of rhetoric applying to art at the time.[7]

Karel van Mander offered a guide to the artistic representation of facial emotions in the didactic poem *Den Grondt der Edel vry Schilderconst* [Foundation of the Noble, Free Art of Painting] (1604), which he published as part of his *Schilder-boeck* in Amsterdam. According to the artist-author, the following emotions belonged to the canon: 'Love, desire, joy, sorrow and anger, anxiety and sadness that seize the heart, cowardice, fear, that is hard to suppress, as well as self-importance, irate feuding, these and others are all called affects.'[8]

These manifested themselves externally through movements in the face, which Van Mander describes in detail. To depict joy, he advised painters as follows: 'We should make the eyes nicely half-closed, the mouth slightly open, pleasant and smiling cheerfully.'[9] Representing a happy mood required a smooth forehead: 'A happy forehead, which is smooth and honest, and not lined with many wrinkles.' He goes on to explain that this makes the cheeks wider and creates wrinkles around the ears. At the same time, Van Mander stresses how hard it is to depict a laughing person.[10]

Studying one's own face

It was the very difficulty of making tronies that meant artists could use them to show off their skills. This must have been what the young Rembrandt van Rijn was seeking to achieve when he painted his *The Laughing Man* (Fig. 11) on a small copper plate in 1629/1630. Amid a fine head of curls and contrasting strongly with the dark background, we see the bright face, laid down in layers of opaque paint and broad brushstrokes, which Rembrandt sketched in the 'rough manner' he had used only rarely up until then.[11] The open and dynamic style, the lively turn of the head and the facial expression make the laughter seem even more animated. This tronie is a fine example both of the pleasure Rembrandt took in his experiments and of his exceptional talent in conveying expressions.[12]

To adhere to nature as closely as possible and to create the greatest possible diversity of expressions in his painted and graphic tronie designs, Rembrandt – who would later be praised as the 'master of the passions' – explored his own face as well as those of models.[13] He had already depicted himself smiling with his head tilted backwards on a similar copper plate around 1628 (Fig. 77).[14] While that tronie from the Getty Museum, based on a self-portrait, shows a larger part of the body in a more refined painting style, Rembrandt made his *The Laughing Man* in the Mauritshuis a bust, so he could render the facial expression in close-up.

Researching expressions using one's own face was highly recommended in art-historical

FIG. 77
Rembrandt Harmensz. van Rijn, *Rembrandt, Laughing*, c. 1628, oil on copper, The J. Paul Getty Museum, Malibu, 2013.60

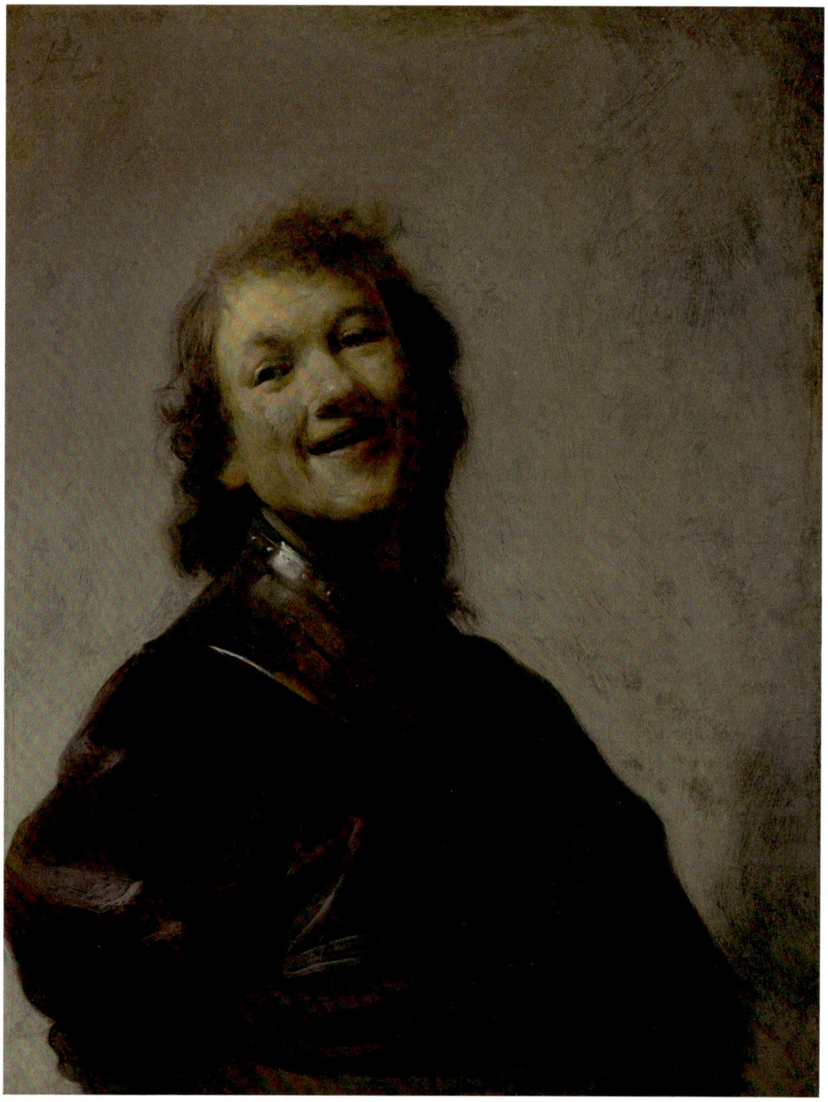

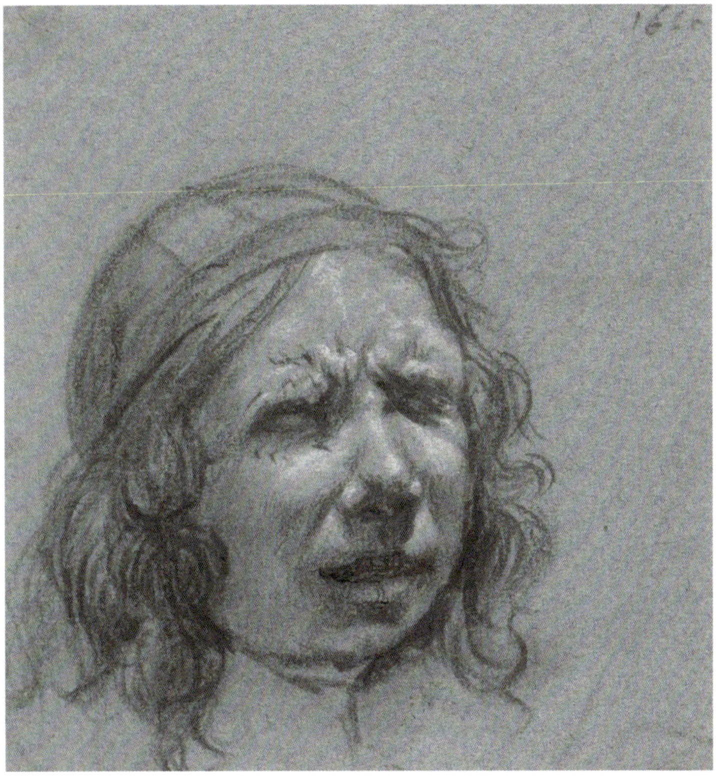

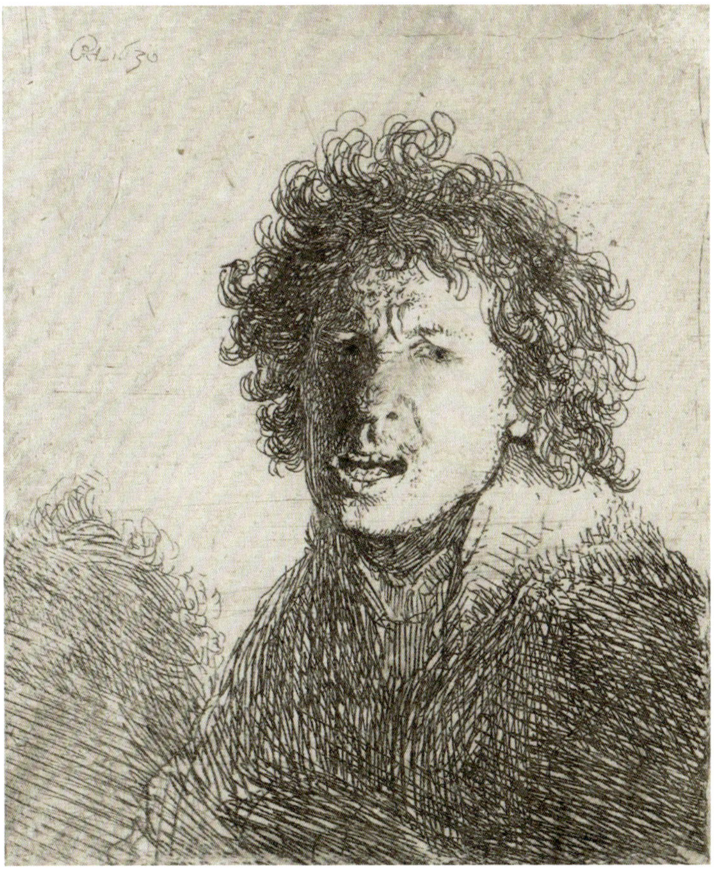

literature, from Karel van Mander to Franciscus Junius (1641), Samuel van Hoogstraten (1678) and Gerard de Lairesse (1707). The more effectively the artist could identify with his own state of mind and develop his powers of observation, the better able he would be to depict specific emotions.[15] The painter Moses ter Borch, born in Zwolle in 1645, used this method to explore his different facial expressions in drawings (Fig. 78) and in a *Self-portrait, so called 'Portrait of Jan Fabus'*, smaller than a postcard, in oil paint (Fig. 91). The downward gaze in this work reveals that the artist painted it from his reflection in the mirror. Ter Borch's search for a successful expression tells us that the talented fifteen-year-old, who grew up in a family of artists, liked to experiment. It is entirely possible that he took Rembrandt's similar studies of small-scale affects, including the etched *Self-portrait Open Mouthed, as if Shouting* (Fig. 79), as the model for the study of his own face.[16] Where Ter Borch's efforts in this regard were primarily intended as an exercise, from the 1630s onwards Rembrandt increasingly offered his expressive heads, which fall somewhere between tronie and self-portrait, as standalone works on the art market, where they enjoyed considerable success.[17]

A head by Rubens

Rembrandt's interaction in Leiden with his fellow artist and rival Jan Lievens – with whom he shared a studio – were important to his development of the tronie as an image type.[18] Lievens had already begun to paint tronies around 1625/1626, drawing on Flemish examples, just as Frans Hals did in that same period. Evidence of this is provided by a drawing from the years in question with the *Bust of an Old Bearded Man* (Fig. 81), which he derived directly from Rubens's original (Fig. 86) or from a work based on it in

FIG. 78
Moses ter Borch, *Self-portrait with a Furrowed Brow*, 1660, chalk on grey-blue paper, Rijksmuseum, Amsterdam, BI-1887-1463-129A

FIG. 79
Rembrandt, *Self-portrait Open Mouthed, as if Shouting*, 1630, etching, Rijksmuseum Amsterdam, RP-P-OB-25

Rubens's studio. If Lievens's copy is compared closely with Rubens's painting in oil from around 1612, it becomes clear how artistically difficult it must have been to capture the specific emotional expression on the man's face, which gazes out of the picture at once piercingly and mischievously.[19]

The life-size bearded man bows his head slightly so that his forehead is positioned prominently in the foreground. Rubens worked out the right half of the face, above the narrow nose and flushed cheeks, with bright, glossy tints, while rendering the left side with shadows around the eyes and temple. The interplay between the frontal presentation and the effect of the light gives the man features that are simultaneously striking and playful. Even though the mouth is almost completely covered by the flowing beard, Rubens succeeds in conveying the man's physiognomy in a nuanced way. On the other hand, we do not detect a clearly and unambiguously legible affect here. This accurate head study of a model in a largely neutral perspective served the Flemish master and his assistants primarily as the basis for a varied series of characters in religious and secular history paintings. Rubens used this model's face in around 1615, for instance, in his painting *Satyr and Girl with a Basket of Fruit* (Fig. 80).[20] In the 1612 tronie, the artist had already carefully worked out the features that mark the satyr's facial expression as lustful: the slightly lowered head, one half of the face in shadow, the cheeks raised and flushed by the smile, the frank gaze, the wrinkles on the forehead and the arched eyebrows. By intensifying the expression, Rubens made the face a vehicle of affect – lust in this instance – within the narrative of the painting. For its part, the tronie belonged to the preparatory process. It was only after Rubens's death in 1640 that his head studies left his studio and became sought-after by collectors. Up until then, his assistants had been able to use them to create other studies and designs.[21]

Head of an African man

It was also not unusual during this process to produce studies that depict the same model from different angles. This allowed the physiognomy and expression to be explored and alternative designs to be developed.[22] Jacques Jordaens did this, for instance, in his *Two Head Studies of an African Man* (Fig. 93) from the late 1620s.[23] These heads are similar in physiognomy to Rubens's *Four Studies of a Black Man* (Fig. 82) from around 1615. Jordaens – who, like Rubens, was active as an independent master in Antwerp at the time – probably painted the same model. 'Sharing' in this way does not necessarily indicate that black models were in short supply at the time. A great many black people from different African countries had been living in the commercial metropolis of Antwerp since the sixteenth century, and their portraits and tronies formed an integral part of the visual culture of the time.[24]

Jordaens depicted the man's head in three-quarter profile, with a sideways glance full of humour and a loving, joyful smile. He displays an immense artistic fascination with the interplay of light and shade, and – just as Rubens did – applied refined nuances in the dark brown and red tones, so as to capture every facet of the man's skin colour and to represent it realistically. This naturalistic precision is chiefly expressed in the working out of the wrinkles, which determine the expression of the face. Jordaens's detailed rendering means the skin also becomes a support for the expression, which further enhances the authenticity of the good-humoured gaze and smile. To focus even more on the expression, Jordaens surrounded the face with contrasting elements such as the white headscarf, a stereotypical garment which points at the same time to a possible role played by this character.

FIG. 80
Peter Paul Rubens, *Satyr and Girl with a Basket of Fruit*, c. 1615, oil on canvas, private collection, long-term loan to Liechtenstein, The Princely Collections Vaduz–Vienna

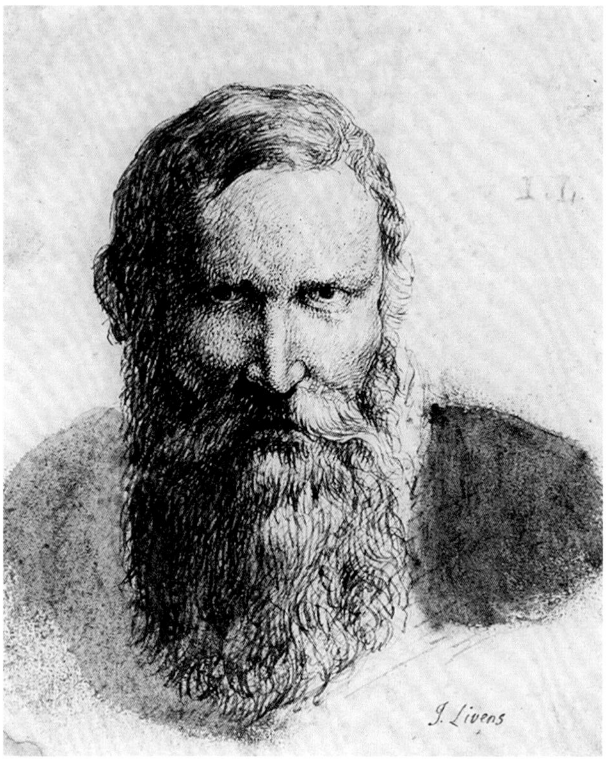

FIG. 81
Jan Lievens after Peter Paul Rubens, *Bust of an Old Bearded Man*, s.d., drawing, private collection

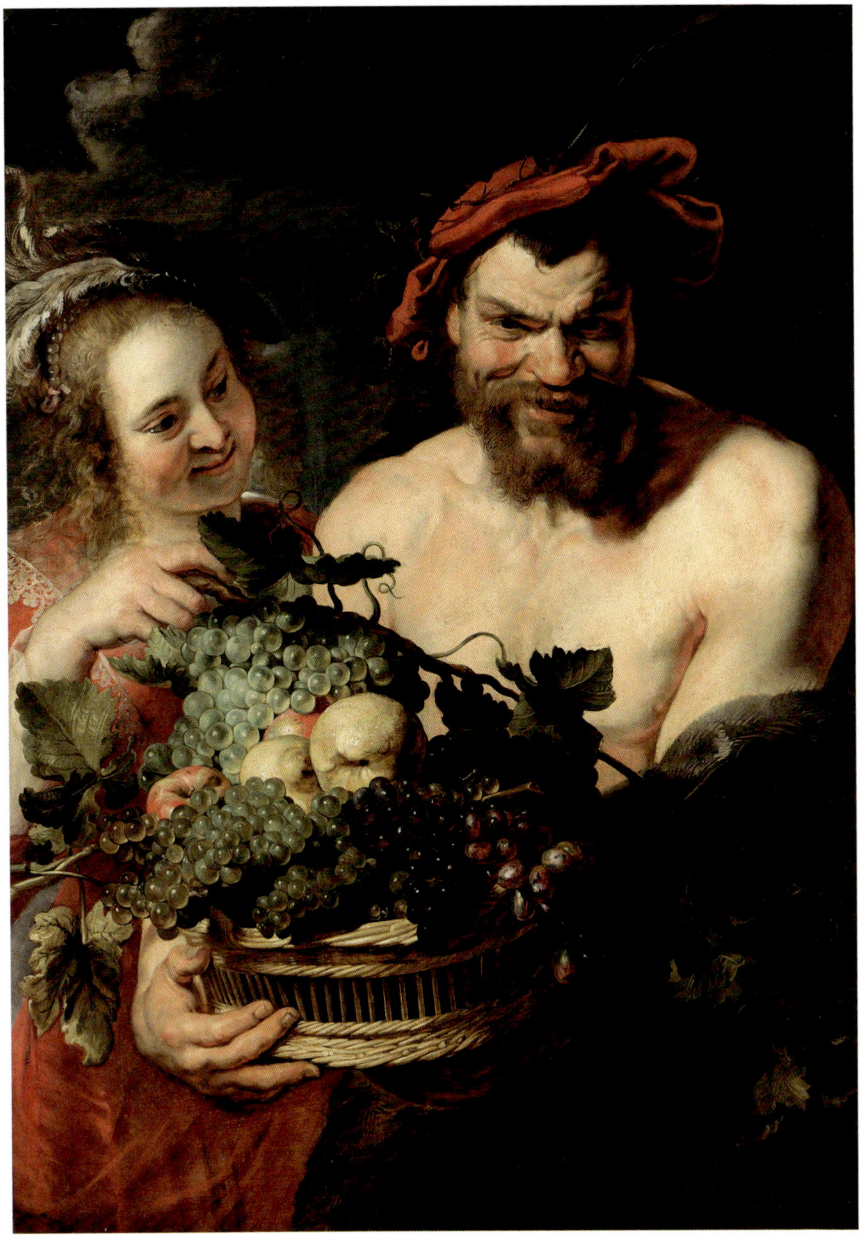

Other subtle tronies

Wallerant Vaillant also rendered the nuances of dark skin in an extremely refined way in a mezzotint (Fig. 107) he made between 1664 and 1675. The artist, who was active in Amsterdam at the time, was one of the first to use the technique to depict a black man.[25] Mezzotint, which had only recently been developed, involves polishing or roughening the copper plate in certain places so that the ink is taken up unevenly. This allows even tonal areas to be printed and soft transitions between light and dark zones to be created.[26] Vaillant instilled such nuance in the play of light and shadow on the skin and in its different shades that full justice is done to the man, shown here smiling in three-quarter profile.[27]

The expressive rendering of flesh tones was, of course, not only applicable to models with dark skin. It was a long-established element of the theoretical and artistic tradition in the seventeenth century that the skin, whether pale or rosy, wrinkled or smooth, played an essential role in the representation of character, frame of mind and expression.[28] The effect can also be found in Hals and Van Dyck, for instance, who reddened the cheeks of the children in their tronies to intensify their expressions in a similar manner.

The layered nature of the expression is also reflected in the skin tones in Michael Sweerts's *Head of a Woman* (Fig. 14), made in around 1654, which range from ash-grey to reddish colours.[29] The female model's face is shown frontally before a dark background. Sweerts visibly deviated from the prevailing portrait conventions and aesthetic ideals of the time by painting a wart below the right corner of the mouth. The woman gazes at us blurrily, with traces of tears in her eyes. All the same, the Brussels painter seemingly did not intend to show sadness here, as a smile plays about her lips. The subtly rendered expression conveys several emotions at once. The philosopher René Descartes, whose 1649 study *Les Passions de l'âme* exerted a powerful influence on artists, described the more complex inner emotions as 'composite affects', that is to say emotional experiences in which, for example, joy is accompanied by pain. Such emotions are expressed in a combined facial expression and can also be artistically represented in this manner.[30] The gentle and sensitive facial expression with which Sweerts depicted the woman enables her to maintain her dignity, even as her simple clothes allude to a rustic context. Because of its lucid simplicity, Sweerts's tronie contrasts sharply with the heads borrowed from frivolous genre scenes and coarse peasant satires of the kind that featured prominently in the work of the Flemish painter Adriaen Brouwer in the 1630s.

Direct and familiar: Brouwer

Brouwer's *Youth Making a Face* (Fig. 90) is a product of that visual language. While the focus is on the facial expression and the communication of emotion, the objects on the table add narrative elements to the seated figure.[31] The jug and the glass, presumably filled with beer, situate the youth, who wears a knife in his hat, in an inn. With his two index fingers, he firmly pulls the corners of his mouth apart to surprise the viewer with a grimace. Brouwer was aiming

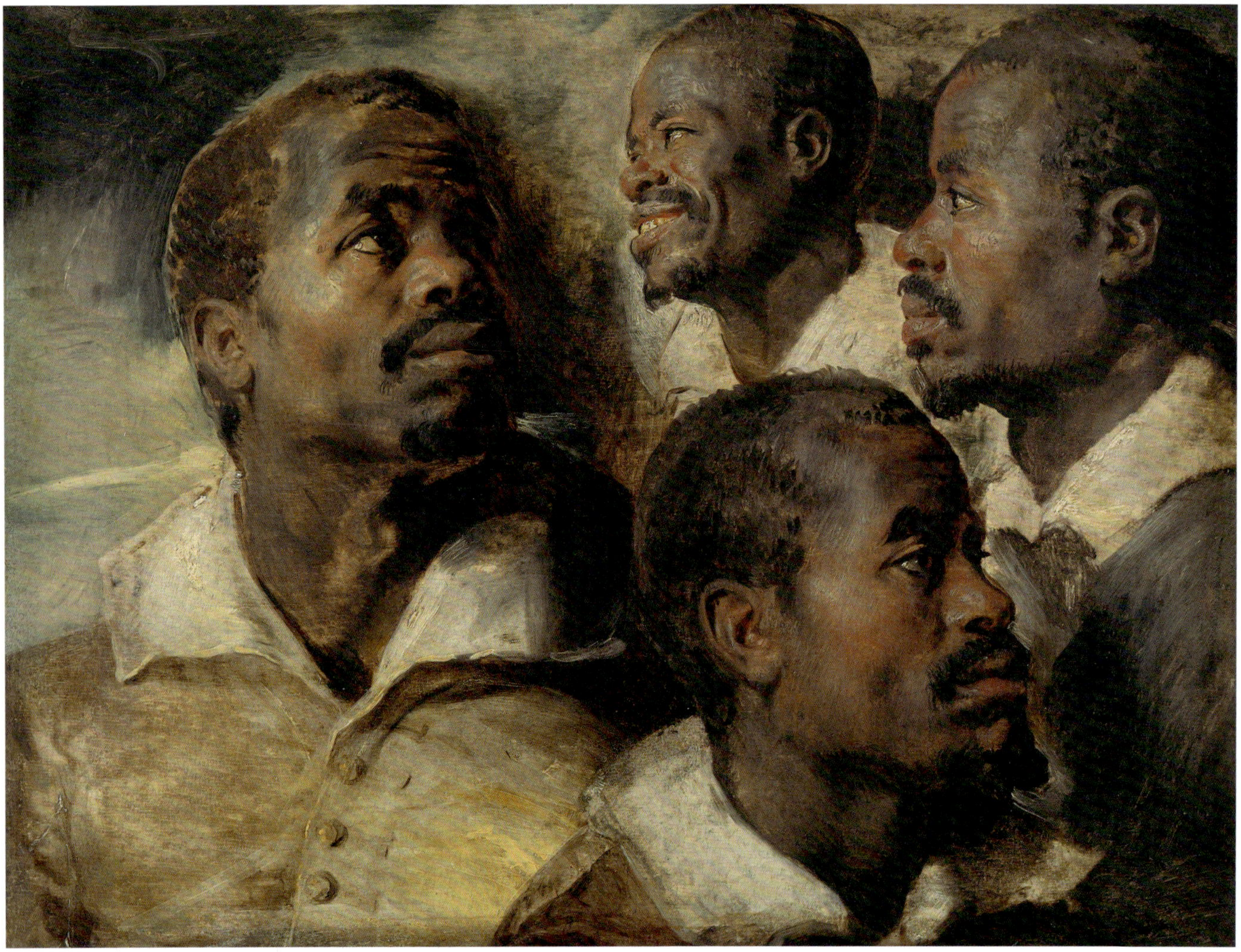

here to entertain his more upper-class viewers. The scene was meant to mock the coarse peasant boy, while also encouraging self-reflection on the viewer's part. The painter wanted to trigger a process in which he could explore his own moods and moral convictions from a safe distance.[32]

Brouwer's painting *The Bitter Potion* (Fig. 89) is geared even more towards expression. For a while, scholarly studies interpreted this motif as the personification of taste. It was thus said to belong to a series devoted to the five senses, in which it served as a counterpart to *The Smoker* (Fig. 88), symbolising the sense of smell.[33] *The Smoker* is now attributed, however, to Joos van Craesbeeck, one of Brouwer's pupils.[34] Where the facial expression in Van Craesbeeck's painting results in the first instance from excessive tobacco consumption and – combined with the wide-open eyes – creates more of a comic effect, the reaction of the peasant in *The Bitter Potion* is seemingly triggered by an extremely tart, presumably alcoholic liquid. Whether, with his eyes tightly closed and his mouth wide open, he is exhaling sharply or even crying out, remains an open question. Brouwer's real motif is the man's impulsive reaction, captured in close-up, which he depicts with an intensity not previously seen in the visual art of the time.[35] With his sketchy and rough style, he skilfully emphasises the immediacy of this recognisable reaction to a sip of bitter liquid, while at the same time deftly characterising the man as a peasant.[36] Unlike the tronies of Rubens and Sweerts, the expression in Brouwer is not achieved through refined differentiation but by drastic exaggeration. In this way, the painter has created a generic type that will have been interpreted as a negative moral and aesthetic example.

The exuberance of this affect, which Brouwer conveys brilliantly, is directly at odds with the code of social conduct of the time. As far as

FIG. 82
Peter Paul Rubens, *Four Studies of a Black Man*, s.d., oil sketch, Royal Museums of Fine Arts of Belgium, Brussels, inv. 3176

FIG. 83
Pieter Huys, *Woman Enraged*, c. 1558, oil on wood, private collection on loan to Worcester Art Museum

contemporary Neo-Stoicism was concerned, the ideal to be pursued was that of equanimity (*tranquilitas*). Emotions were to be curbed, and self-control and a restrained expression were the order of the day. Maintaining one's *decorum* was important to the middle class. Demonstrative expressions of emotion were the preserve of the lower classes and, to a certain extent (laughter, for instance), children.[37]

Wide-open mouth

Like the laughter in the tronies by Rembrandt and Hals, the first reactions elicited by the wide-open mouth in Brouwer's *The Bitter Potion* are fellow feeling and an imitation of the affect. Something similar can be detected in Jan Asselijn's anthropomorphising *Bellowing Ox* (Fig. 95), pictured in the manner of a tronie, albeit on a large scale, and reflecting human feelings.[38] All the same, contemporaries were not allowed to succumb entirely to their immediate reaction when confronted with expressive depictions like this. They were supposed to learn how to appreciate the artistic quality of an expression while also interpreting the affect, to distinguish positive and negative examples, and to maintain their own emotional balance.[39] As a side-effect, there was a growing fascination for the impulsive and the deviant as presented in genre-like peasant tronies.[40]

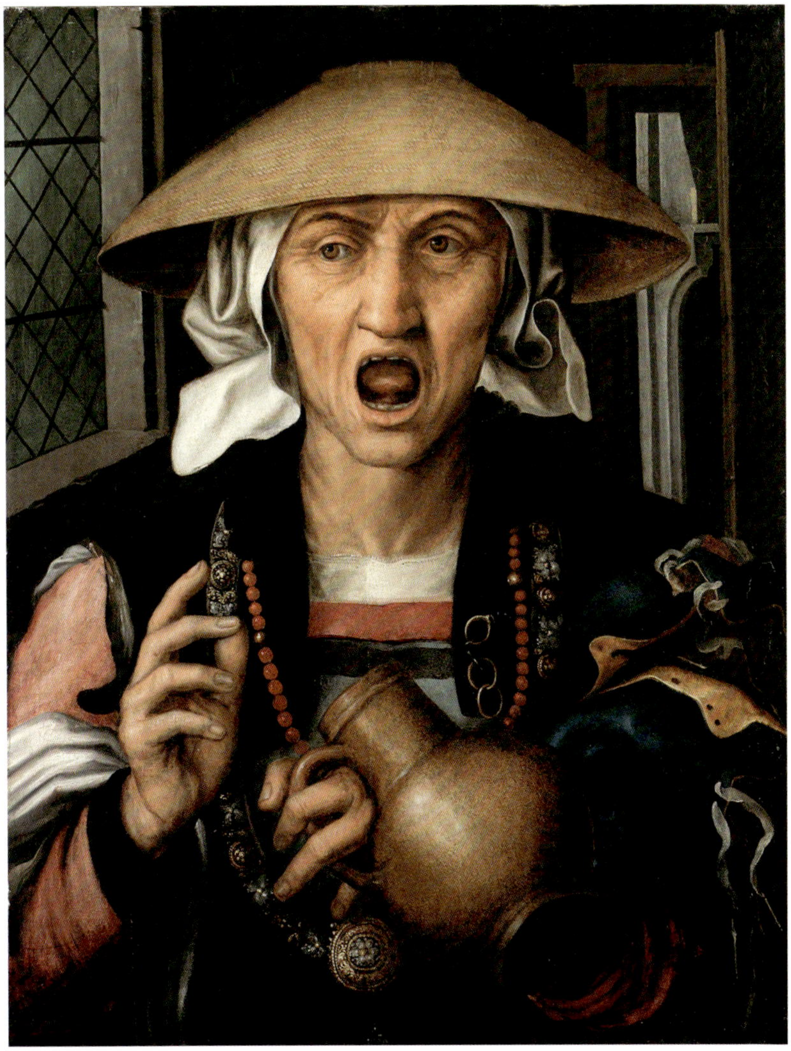

In *The Bitter Potion*, Brouwer uses the mouth as a formal element much more so than we find in other artists. The wide-open, exaggerated, yet still naturalistic lips convey disgust and momentary pain. Through this form of overstatement, Brouwer also inspired other artists, including Rubens and Rembrandt, both of whom collected a large number of his works.[41]

Over a century later, the same facial feature also caught the attention of Franz Xaver Messerschmidt. The Austrian sculptor might well have made effective use of several inventive Netherlandish tronies, as well as single-character genre scenes, when he cast *The Yawner* (Fig. 94) in tin for the *Character Heads* series in the 1770s.[42] Pieter Bruegel the Elder's *The Yawner* (Fig. 6), which was owned by Rubens and probably inspired Brouwer too, is a good example in this regard.[43] A wide-open mouth can also be found as an expression of rage in paintings such as Pieter Huys's *Woman Enraged* (Fig. 83). All the same, Messerschmidt stripped his head sculpture of any details that might suggest a particular age or social status, drawing inspiration for the almost medical purity of his piece from the sculpture in the *Méthode pour apprendre à dessiner les passions* [Method for Learning How to Draw the Passions] developed by Charles Le Brun in 1668 and published for the first time in 1698. Like Descartes before him, Le Brun based himself on simple and composite affects, which can be represented with different degrees of complexity. The system he presented in his book is illustrated with drawings. As well as open mouths, it contains depictions of pain, surprise and fear (Fig. 84).[44]

The tongue in Messerschmidt's sculpture is not placed up against the palate, as it would be when yawning, but he does depict the stretched tongue web in the same way that Pieter Huys did in his painting of the angry peasant woman. It therefore also seems likely that Messerschmidt is depicting a scream and referring to conventional images of pain and anger.[45] For all its extreme form, the expression remains vague and artificial due to the tightly-closed eyes, the way the crow's feet extend ornamentally to the temple and cheeks, and how the lines around the mouth continue into the neck. *The Yawner* cannot be compared with nature. Messerschmidt was exploring instead the artistic intensification of an expression, which he compiled from an amalgam of theoretical and artistic examples and from studies of his own face.[46]

In so doing, the sculptor was putting into practice a form of expression that was taught in a similar way at French academies in the eighteenth century. The *tête d'expression* became an important element in that period of an artist's training. As in the case of the Netherlandish tronies, the challenge was to convey expression simply through the face, with no additional accessories.[47]

Anchored in tradition

Roughly half a century after Messerschmidt, the French painter Louis-Léopold Boilly set about a similar task. His *Thirty Five Character Heads* (Fig. 96) consists of a large variety of deformed and twisted faces. The non-narrative arrangement is reminiscent, in a sense, of the multiple head studies on a single sheet (Fig. 47, 48, 49), such as we know from followers of Rubens.

Boilly's grimaces, stretched out or squashed up in every conceivable direction, do indeed resemble imaginary heads at first sight. Only on closer inspection does it become clear that even the most deformed faces might have been derived from observation.[48] Perhaps Boilly was inspired by the *grimaciers* who won considerable admiration and prizes for their gurning abilities.[49] The degree of exaggeration and characterisation also brings this compilation close to the realm of caricature. The heads nonetheless remain true to their goal – the artistic exploration of expression – without assuming a critical stance.[50] Like Messerschmidt, Boilly pushed realism to an extreme.

The ambivalence of both *The Yawner* and Boilly's *têtes d'expression*, which fall somewhere between exaggeration and naturalism, anchors

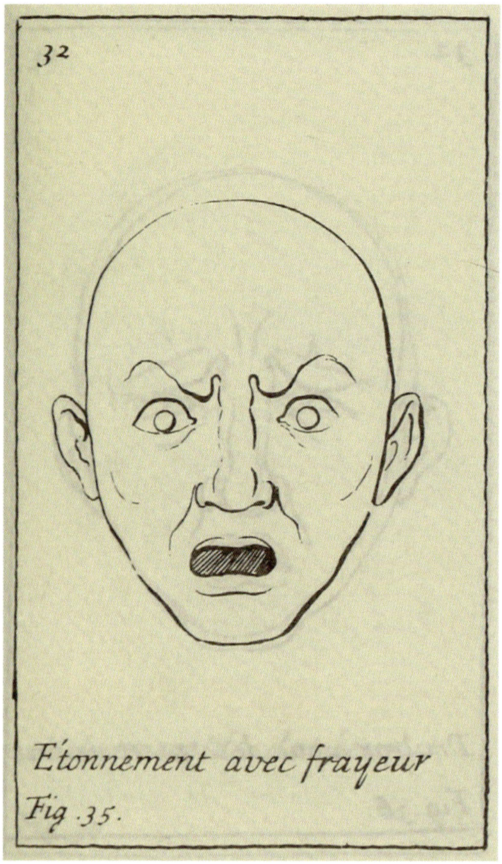

FIG. 84
Charles Le Brun, *Etonnement avec frayeur – mouvement composé*, c. 1667, pen drawing, Musée du Louvre, Paris, 28346, recto

them in traditions that are also relevant to seventeenth-century Netherlandish studies of facial expressions. Their strict focus on the face, their reference to contemporary theories of affect and art and their artistic experimentation link them with the head studies made by artists such as Rubens, Rembrandt, Hals and Brouwer. Depending on the medium and function of the work, each artist tackled the demanding task of heightening the expressiveness of these tronies in his own way. They continue to move us to this day and have lost none of their emotional power.

1 See Hirschfelder 2008, 72–73; Van der Vinde 2007, 44–45.
2 For a discussion of the dating, see Hirschfelder 2008, 80, note 293; Barnes *et al.* 2004, 389, cat. III.198.
3 The work was in the Kaiser-Friedrich-Museum in Berlin, where it was destroyed in 1945. Cf. Barnes *et al.* 2004, 272–273, cat. III.34 with Fig.
4 Hals probably got to know Rubens's work when he visited Antwerp in 1616. Van Dyck, meanwhile, collaborated with Rubens on various occasions between 1615 and 1620. Cf. Hirschfelder 2008, 80; Van Haute 2015, 28. For Rubens's children's tronies, see Van Hout 2020, vol. 1, 134–138, no. 42 and also 140–141, no. 44b.
5 See also in this regard the essays by Michael Kwakkelstein and Nico Van Hout in this book, as well as Hirschfelder 2008, 321–334, Dickey/Roodenburg 2010 and Schwartz 2014, esp. 10–25.
6 See Gottwald 2011, 20–22; Hirschfelder 2008, 322.
7 See Hirschfelder 2008, 329–330.
8 Van Mander 1604 [Hoecker 1916], 135, English translation by Gary Schwartz.
9 Van Mander 1604 [Hoecker 1916], 147.
10 See *ibid.*, 149. Van Mander was following Leon Battista Alberti in this respect. See Gottwald 2011, 20; Kirchner 2014, 11.
11 See Hirschfelder 2008, 47.
12 The fact that Rembrandt's *The Laughing Man* was re-engraved by Jan van Vliet and later given the name of the smiling philosopher Democritus is proof of how his tronie was received as a model; cf. Muylle 2014, 87.
13 See Schwartz 2014, 22 for this praise, with a reference to Samuel van Hoogstraten's *Inleyding tot de hooge schoole der schilderkonst* (1678).
14 See Chapman 2010, 253–257.
15 See *ibid.*, 250–252; Kirchner 2014, 21–24; Schwartz 2014, 19. For the details of representational types that fall between likenesses of the artist himself and tronies, see Hirschfelder 2008, 109–113 and also Chapman 2010 (with Rembrandt as an example).
16 See Moes, 163–164. The fact that Ter Borch was familiar with the art of his famous contemporary, and clearly showed an interest in the way he staged images of himself, is evident from at least three drawings, including one from an early etched self-portrait by Rembrandt, see inv. RP-T-1887-A-1077 in the Rijksmuseum in Amsterdam.
17 See Hirschfelder 2008, 166–167.
18 See *ibid.*, 130.
19 Regarding Rubens's tronie, see *ibid.*, 64–66; Gottwald 2011, 95; Van Hout 2020, vol. 1, 167-169, no. 55.
20 See Van Hout 2020, vol. 1, 168.
21 See Van Hout 2020, vol. 1, 54–59. For the variations on this tronie in Rubens's studio, see *ibid.*, nos. 56 and 59.
22 Van Hout 2020, vol 1, 36–38.
23 Regarding the attribution, see Held 1965, 112–114, and also Held 1982, 152–153. Larsen 1988, 64–65 attributed the oil sketch to Van Dyck's studio and dated it to around 1618.
24 See Van Haute 2015, 18–20, 30–32, which argues against the proposition that it is the same model. Kolfin 2008, 78 and Van Hout, 2020, vol. 1, 161 present the counter-arguments.
25 See Kolfin 2008, 84–85 and Kolfin 2020, 34.
26 Kolfin 2008, 84.
27 See *ibid.*
28 One point of departure for interpreting the skin in terms of the visualisation of affect can be found in the theory of the temperaments, according to which a person's frame of mind is reflected in the different colours of the skin. Wrinkles and other signs of ageing were already viewed in the Renaissance as pathognomonic indicators of a person's character and emotions. See in this regard Schütt 2021, 118–121.
29 See Hirschfelder 2008, 150–152.
30 Kirchner 2008, 269–270. See Schwartz 2014, 14, regarding the significance of Descartes's treatise on art.
31 See Hirschfelder 2008, 177–178 regarding single-character genre scenes and their relationship to the tronie genre.
32 Brouwer's grotesque realism drew on mechanisms that contemporaries knew from plays and performances by the Antwerp chamber of rhetoric, see Lichtert 2018, 91–93.
33 See Tieze 2009, 105–108; Lichtert 2018, 84.
34 Craesbeeck's head is based on a portrait of the artist that Adriaen Brouwer incorporated in his work *The Smokers* (The Metropolitan Museum, New York, inv. 32.100.21). See Lichtert 2018, 188–189.
35 See Tieze, 2009, 109.
36 Regarding the example set by Brouwer for so-called 'peasant tronies', see Hirschfelder 2008, 158–163.
37 See Hirschfelder 2008, 102–105.
38 It was common at the time to draw parallels between human and animal emotions. For a comparison of man and ox, for instance, see Giambattista della Porta, *De humana physiognomonia libri IIII*, 1586, 76; see Schwartz 2014, 15–16.
39 See Dickey/Roodenburg 2010, 13. Hirschfelder 2008, 330–333.
40 Dickey/Roodenburg 2010, 10–12.
41 See Atkins 2018, 117. Rubens owned seventeen works attributed to Brouwer, while Rembrandt acquired seven for his collection.
42 See Bückling 2006, 158.
43 Tieze 2009, 1078–108.
44 See Weissert 2016, 251–256; Kirchner 2006, 269–272. Just as Messerschmidt was making his *Character Heads*, moreover, the physiognomic studies by Johann Caspar Lavater were published. These studies, which proved controversial, were certainly known to the artist: see Kirchner 2006, 267.
45 See Bückling 2006, 158–159.
46 See Kirchner 2006, 271–276.
47 See Weissert 2016, 265–271.
48 Siegfried 1995, 123.
49 See *ibid.*, 126–127.
50 See Kirchner 2006, 278, 280; Siegfried 1995, 121–122.

'LOOKING AT THE FACE OF THE OTHER'

The artist in Albert Camus' *L'Homme révolté* tries to resist the passage of time. For an actor, though, the passage of time is precisely what we work with. I am engaged in the most ephemeral form of art there could be. There is no real time in a play, there is only mythical time. You are never in a frozen moment, in a representation of a smile, or in a film about anger. We might show as many as twenty emotions – expressions – in a play. Unlike a visual artist, who observes a model from the outside, my expression has to come from within.

The position of your head does all manner of things to your expression. With my students I focus on speech directions. You turn away or you turn your gaze toward someone. You raise your face when you ask existential questions, and direct your speech downwards to internalise things. This is something young actors gradually become aware of. I find it interesting that as an actor – just like a painter – you have technical tools like this at your disposal. Light is important too, because what it means to a theatre actor is attention.

You know that the play isn't real, yet it still has to be authentic. That's the dilemma. In general, I rely on the combination of thoughts and feelings leading to an engaging and appropriate expression. This genuine interest in your profession is a prerequisite for creating pleasure in it and for continuing to evolve. Creation is always a combination of analysis and intuition, or of analysing why that intuition led you to that expression. In this way, a form of sincerity is generated within what is an artificial art form.

When you act, you think about empathy and about communication, about what it is to be human. Just as a painter tries to show from the outside how an individual's head looks and how it experiences a particular emotion, I want to understand someone's pain – to look at the face of the Other, as Emmanuel Levinas put it. By thinking of a loved one's pain I can play grief. *Voir un ami pleurer* – to see a friend in tears – as Jacques Brel sang, is perhaps one of the strongest emotions you can have. I can evoke that feeling in myself, and I assume that the audience can read the expression of it in my face. I can't imagine achieving the same result if I deliberately tried to move my facial muscles in a particular way. I'm definitely not the kind of person who stands in front of a mirror and thinks, 'this is how that affect works'.

I'm currently appearing in the play *Antigone in the Amazon*. My character, Creon, makes every bad choice imaginable. He's guilty across the board and ends up wishing he could just die. I try to evoke that sense of tragedy in every performance and to convey it as accurately as possible. There are scenes of my head in close-up on a giant screen. In the end, I reproduce on stage the grief of witnessing my child's suicide. Such extreme emotions are incredibly difficult to represent. Much harder than a little joy, a little anger, or growing indignation. Yet you still have the presumption, the ambition and even the heaven-storming will to pull it off. It is formal experiments like this, after all, that keep the profession interesting.

There is a big difference between theatre and film or television. In film, the camera often comes very close, and there is editing. The actor's expression is more minimal than in theatre. A glance is often enough, an intense thought is sufficient to evoke an emotion. Film is a medium in which strong facial expressions can often be too extreme, almost ugly. When you're in front of a camera, you have to imagine you're being watched by a loved one. The bond of trust automatically softens expressions. Figures of saints in old paintings were also beautifully depicted, which is understandable. It is simply the case that an angelically lovely appearance arouses more empathy in the audience. Perhaps that's why, in our visual culture today, people want faces that are as polished and as marketable as possible. That can be quite confronting for an actor. I personally like to look at people with a characterful face.

In *Regarding the Pain of Others*, Susan Sontag explored the effect on us of all the images of war and injustice to which we are exposed every day. Expressions and emotions lead you back to the people behind these abstractions. She ends up with Goya's etchings *Los desastres de la guerra*, one of the most affecting pictorial accounts of horror. Since these works of art are preceded by reflection, they go a step further than the snapshot offered by a photograph. The design already entails a processing of anger, of emotion. The same is true of theatre.

Sara De Bosschere (1972) is a Flemish actor and screenwriter. She is a theatremaker and has appeared in feature films, series and short films.

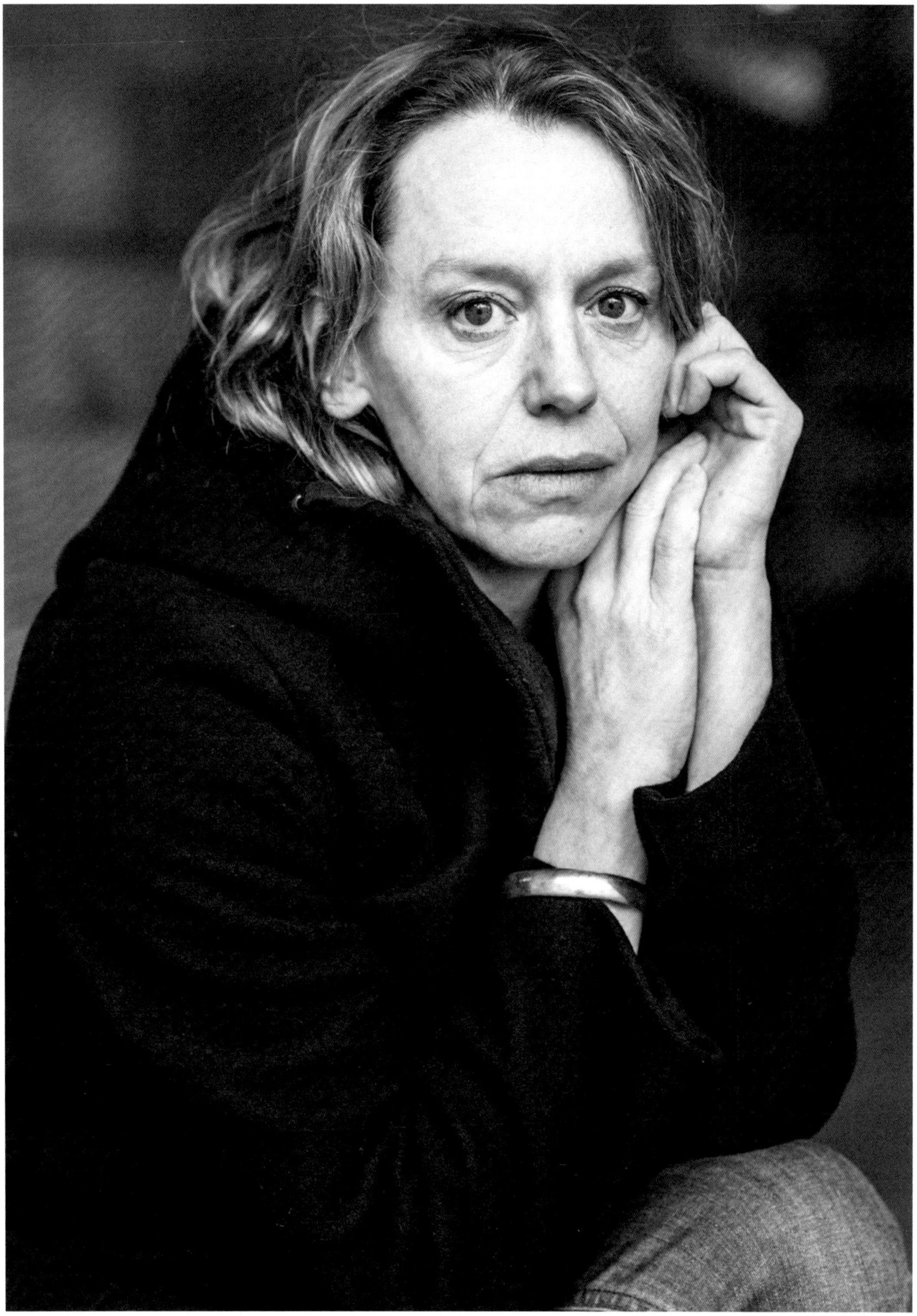

Liza François,
Sara De Bosschere,
2023, photograph

FIG. 85
Frans Hals the Elder, *Laughing Boy*, c. 1625, oil on panel, Mauritshuis, The Hague, 1032

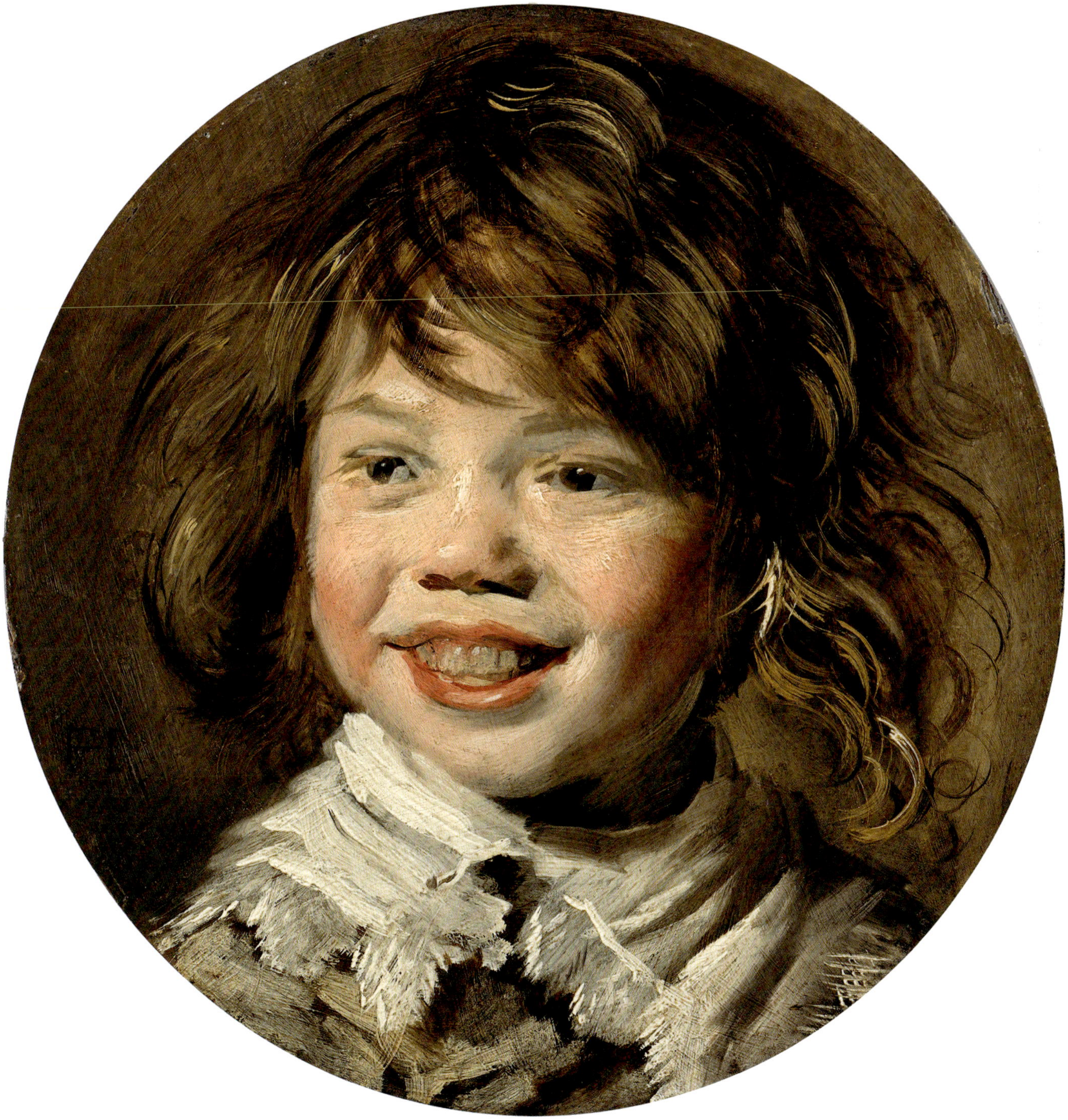

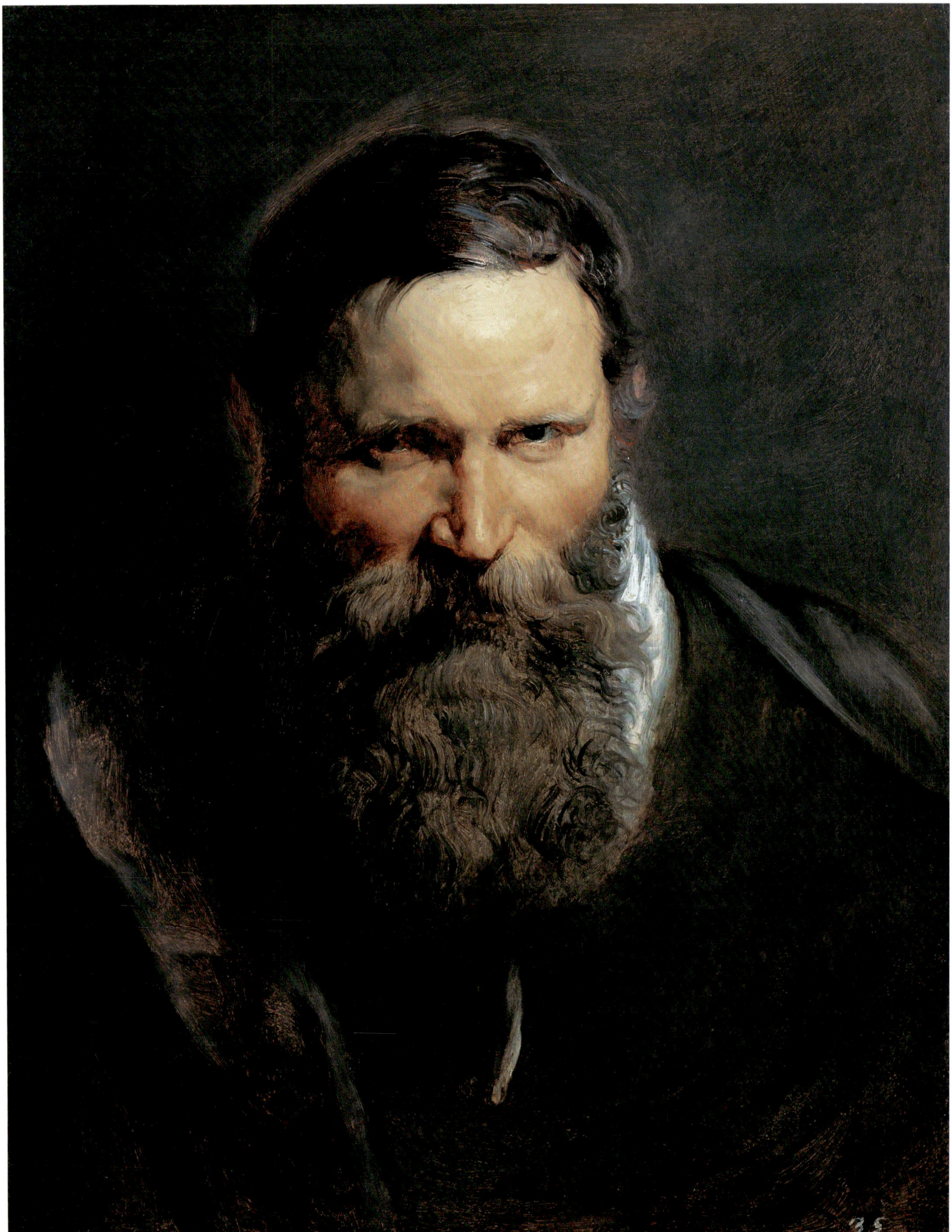

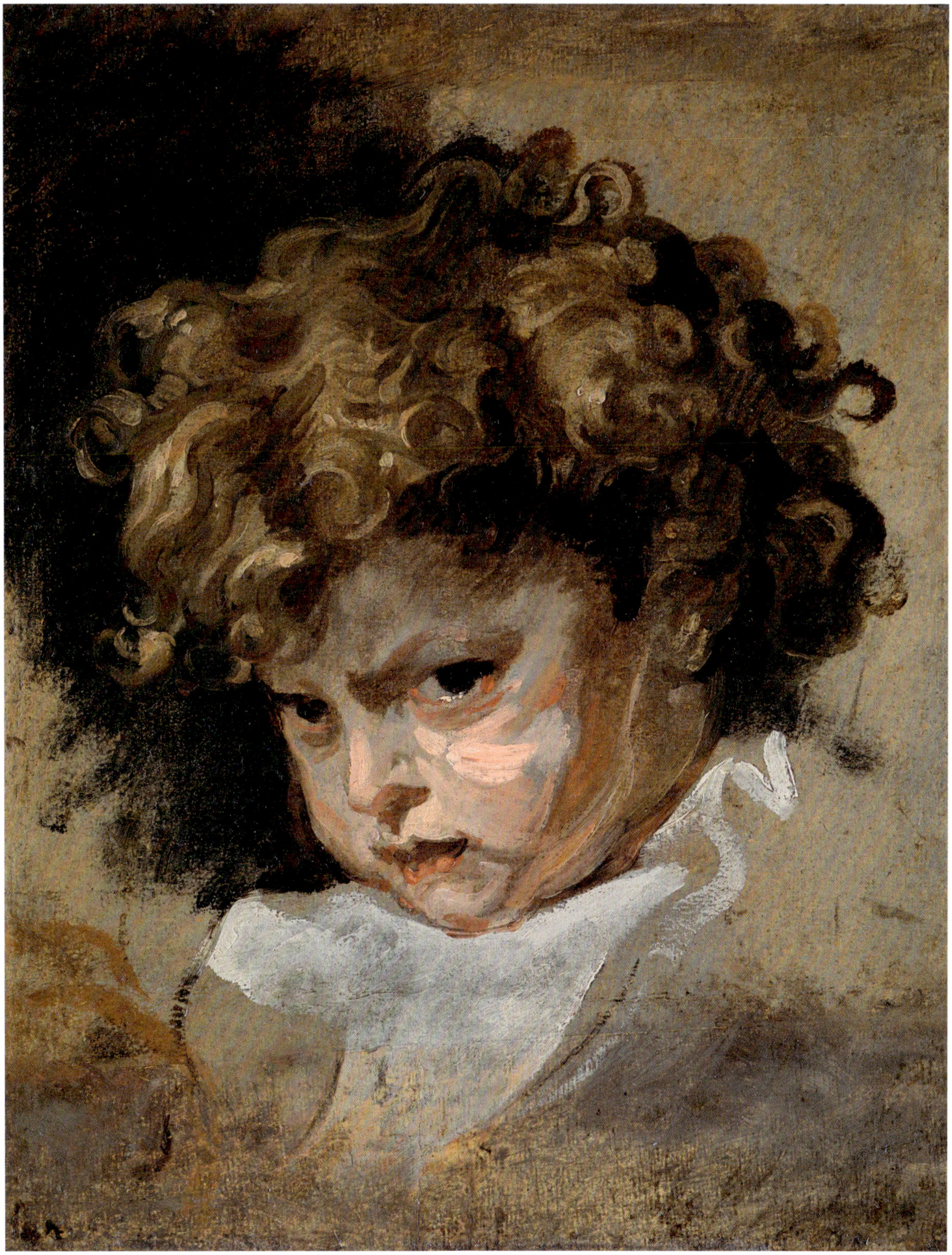

FIG. 86
Peter Paul Rubens,
Head Study of a Man,
s.d., oil on panel,
Liechtenstein Museum
Vienna, GE 113

FIG. 87
Anthony van Dyck,
Study of a Child's Head,
s.d., oil on paper on
panel, Hohenbuchau
Collection

FIG. 88
Joos van Craesbeeck, *The Smoker*, 1630–1640, oil on canvas, Musée du Louvre, Paris, M.I.906

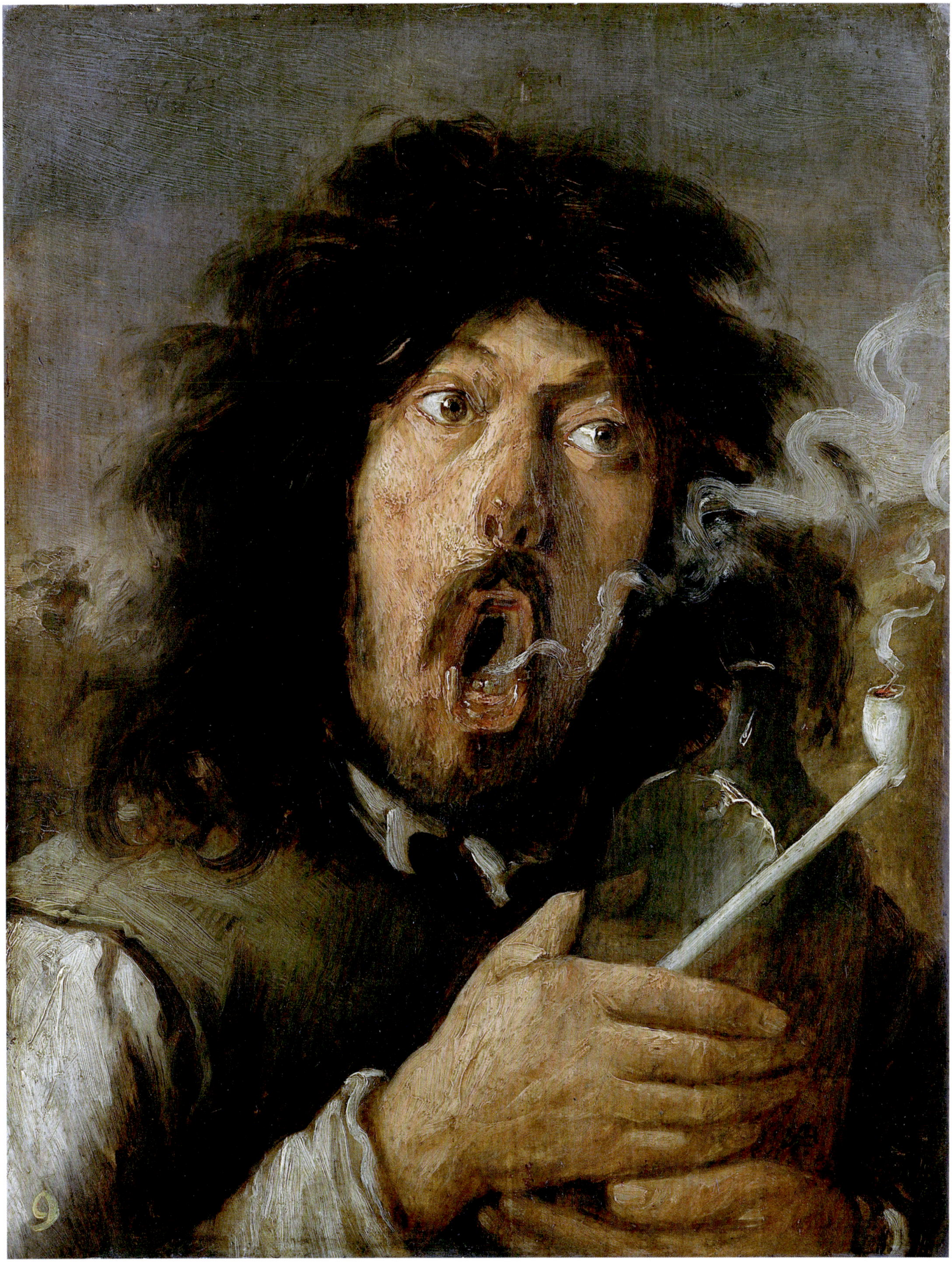

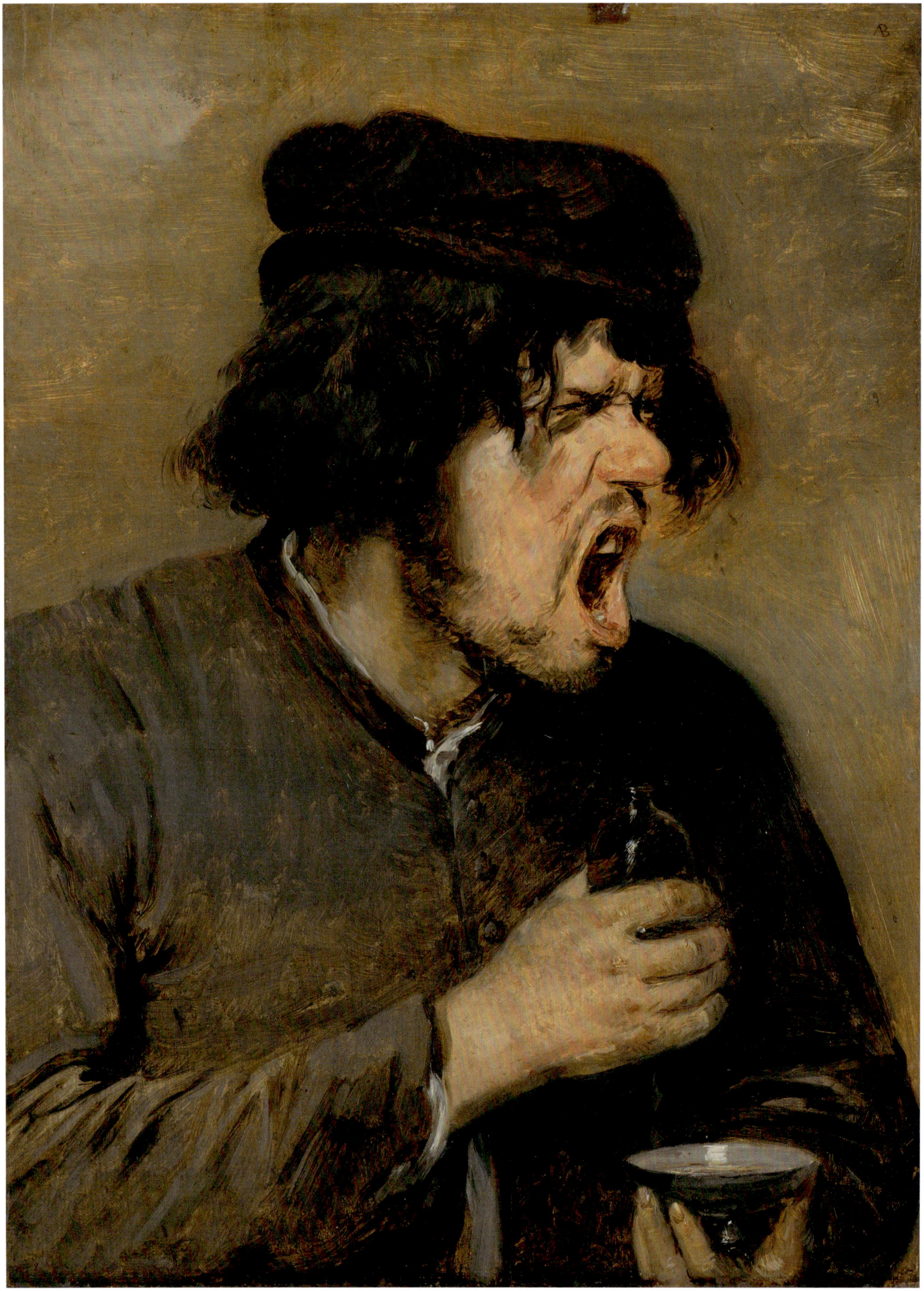

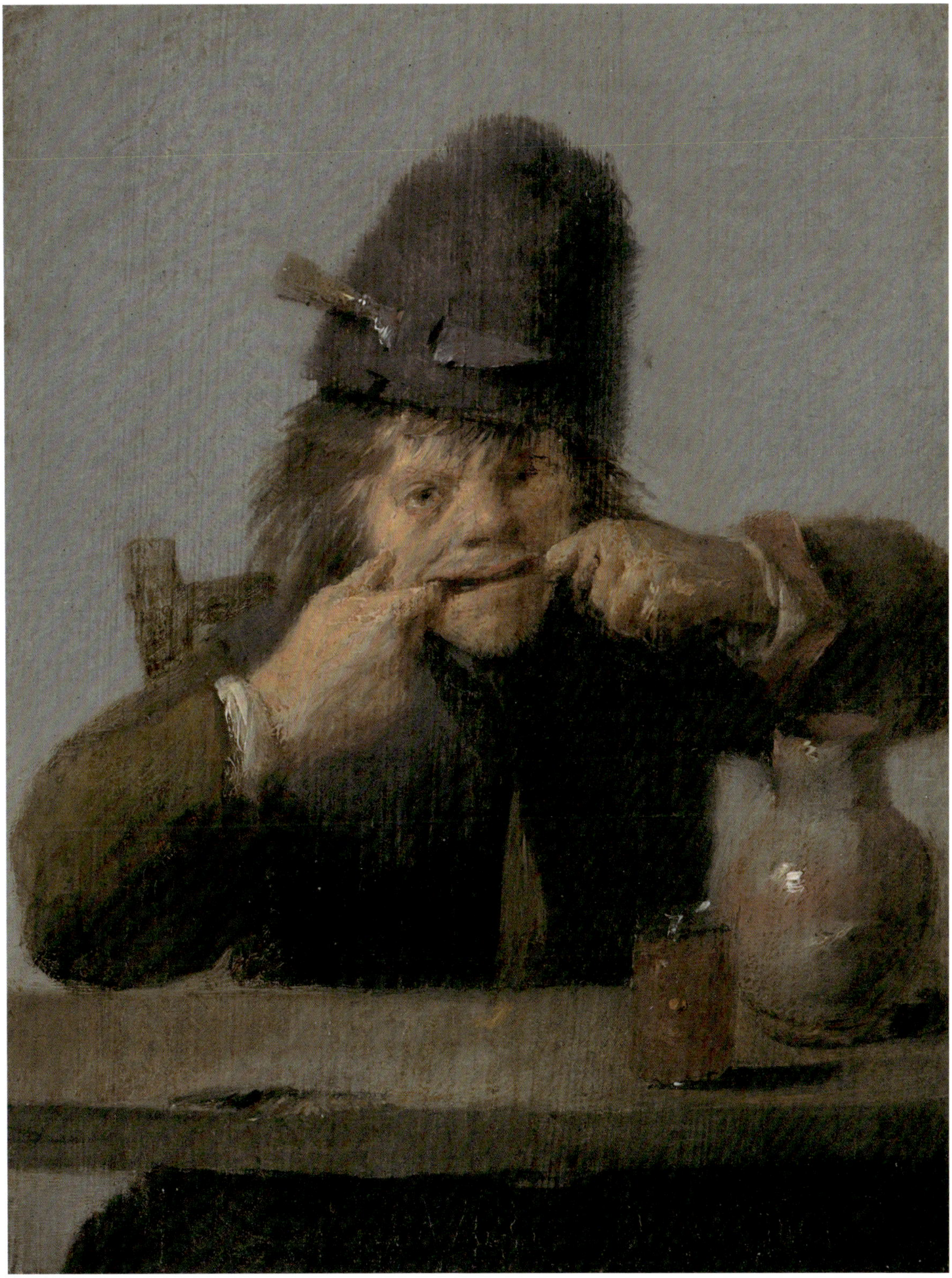

FIG. 89
Adriaen Brouwer,
The Bitter Potion,
1636–1638, oil on panel,
Städelsches Kunst-
institut und Städtische
Galerie, Städel Museum,
Frankfurt am Main, 1076

FIG. 90
Adriaen Brouwer,
Youth Making a Face,
1632–1635, oil on
panel, National Gallery
of Art, Washington DC,
1994.46.1

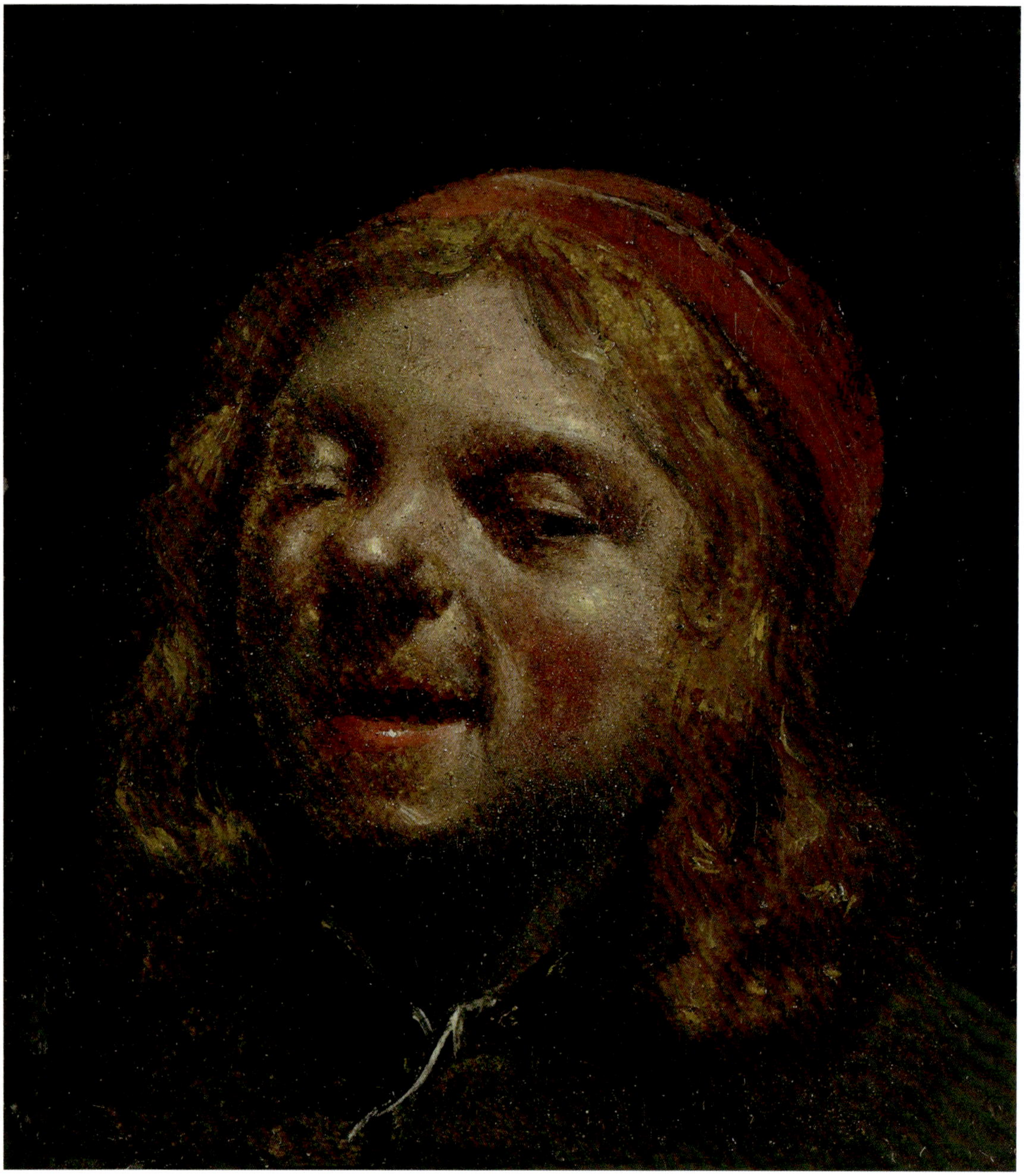

FIG. 91
Moses ter Borch,
Self-portrait, so called 'Portrait of Jan Fabus',
1660–1661, oil on paper, Rijksmuseum, Amsterdam, SK-A-2118

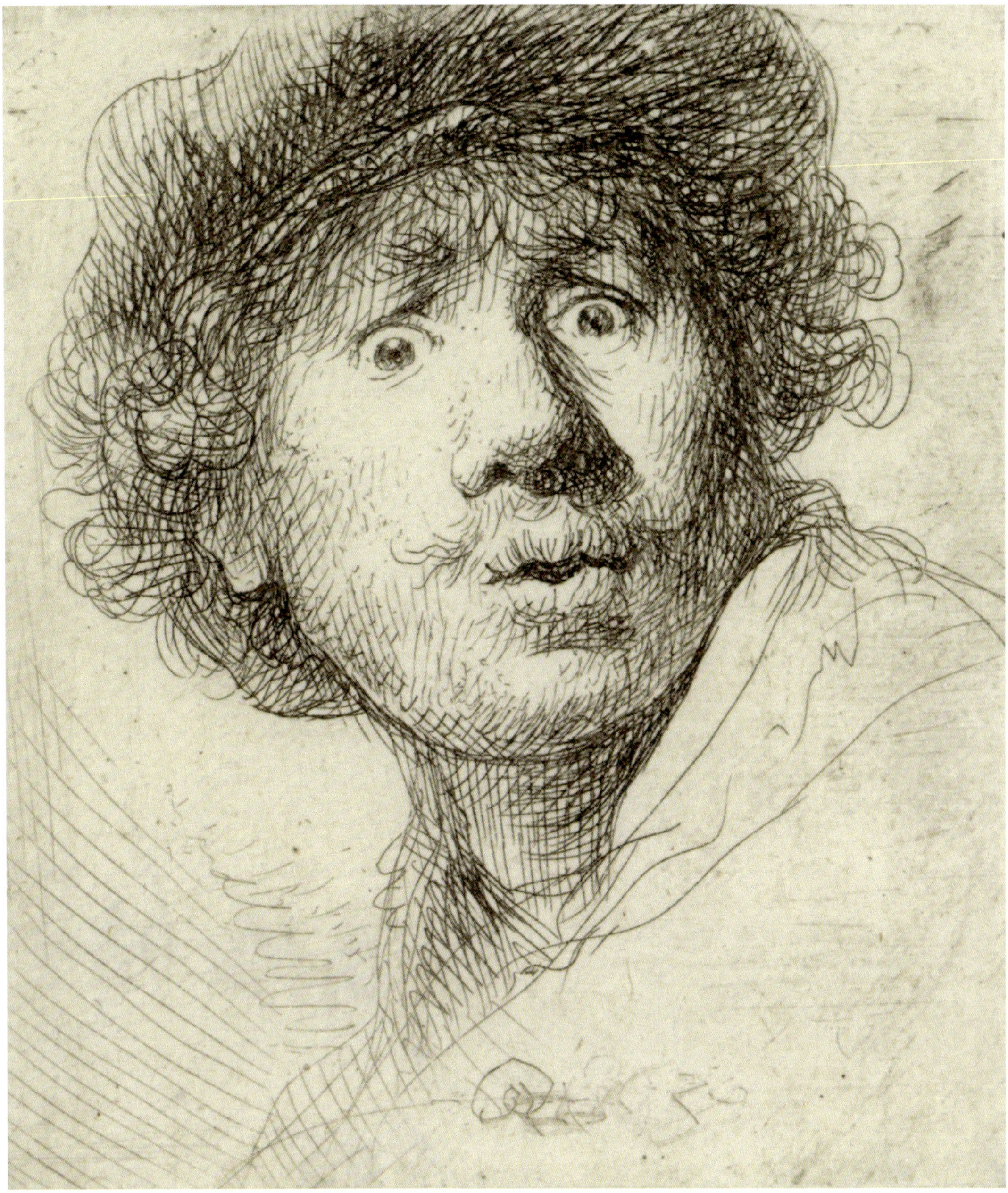

FIG. 92
Rembrandt, *Self-portrait in a Cap, Wide-eyed and Open-mouthed*, s.d., Royal Library of Belgium, Brussels, Brussel, inv. S. II 135

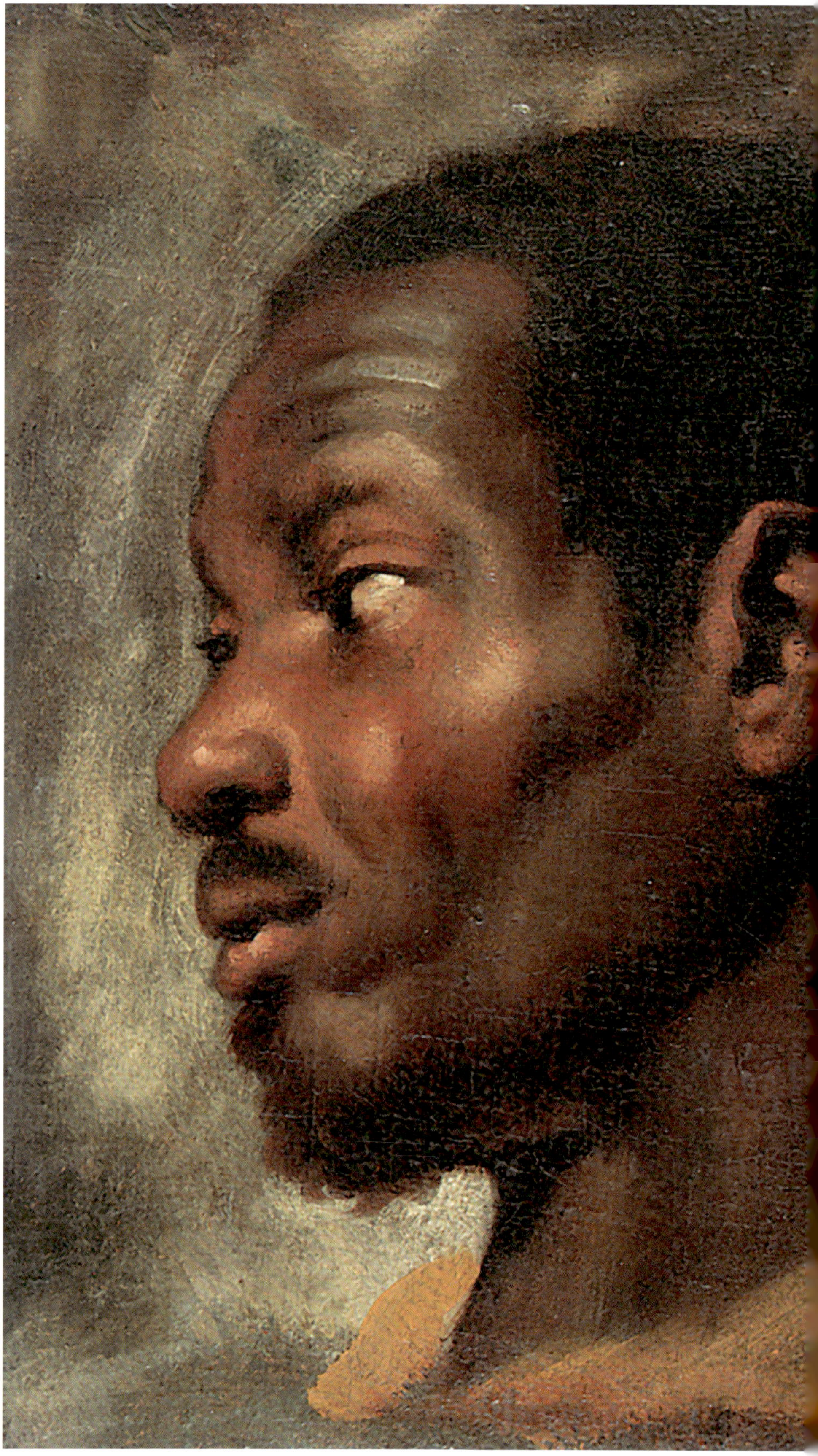

FIG. 93
Jacques Jordaens the Elder, *Two Head Studies of an African Man*, after 1620, oil on canvas, private collection

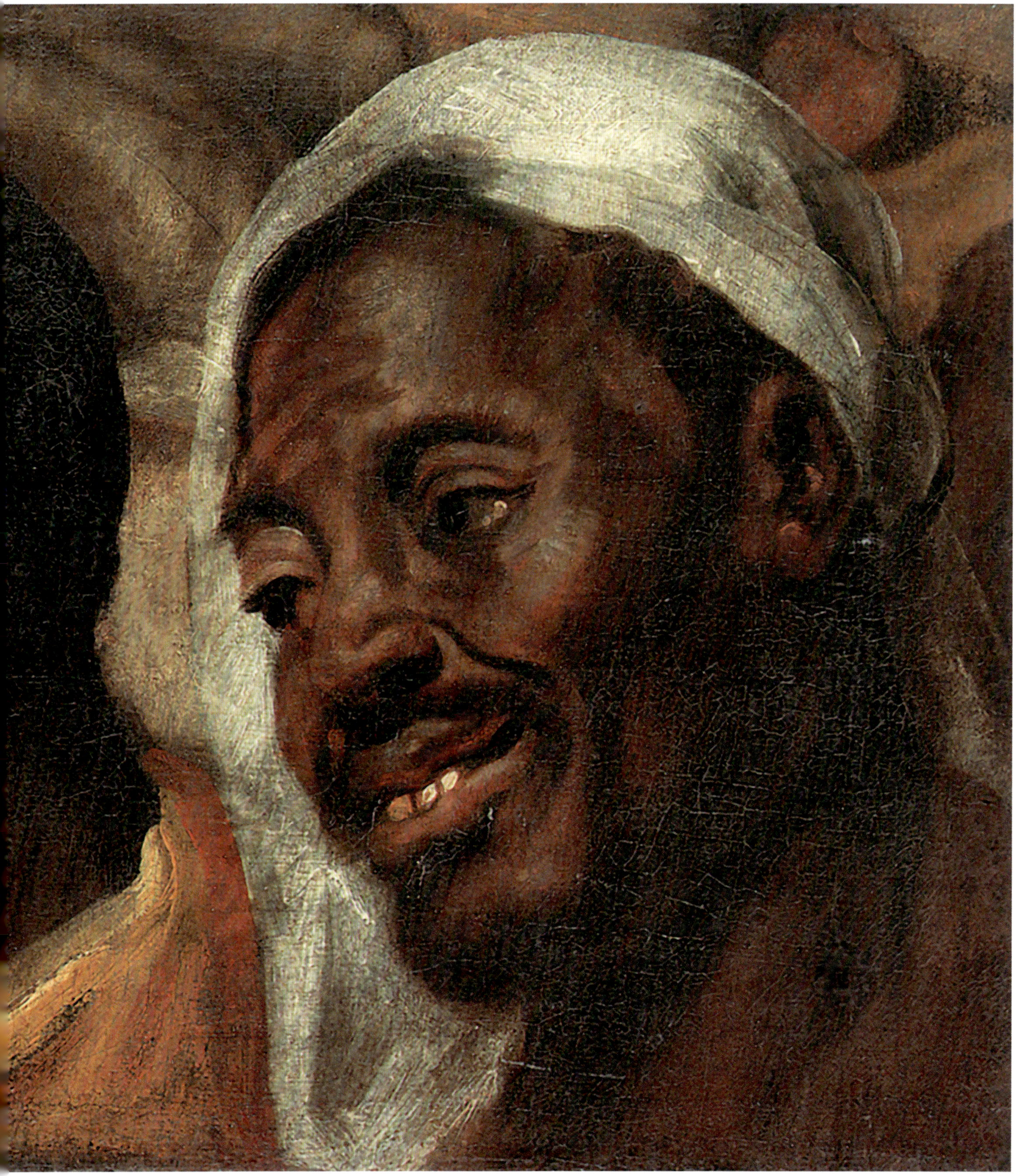

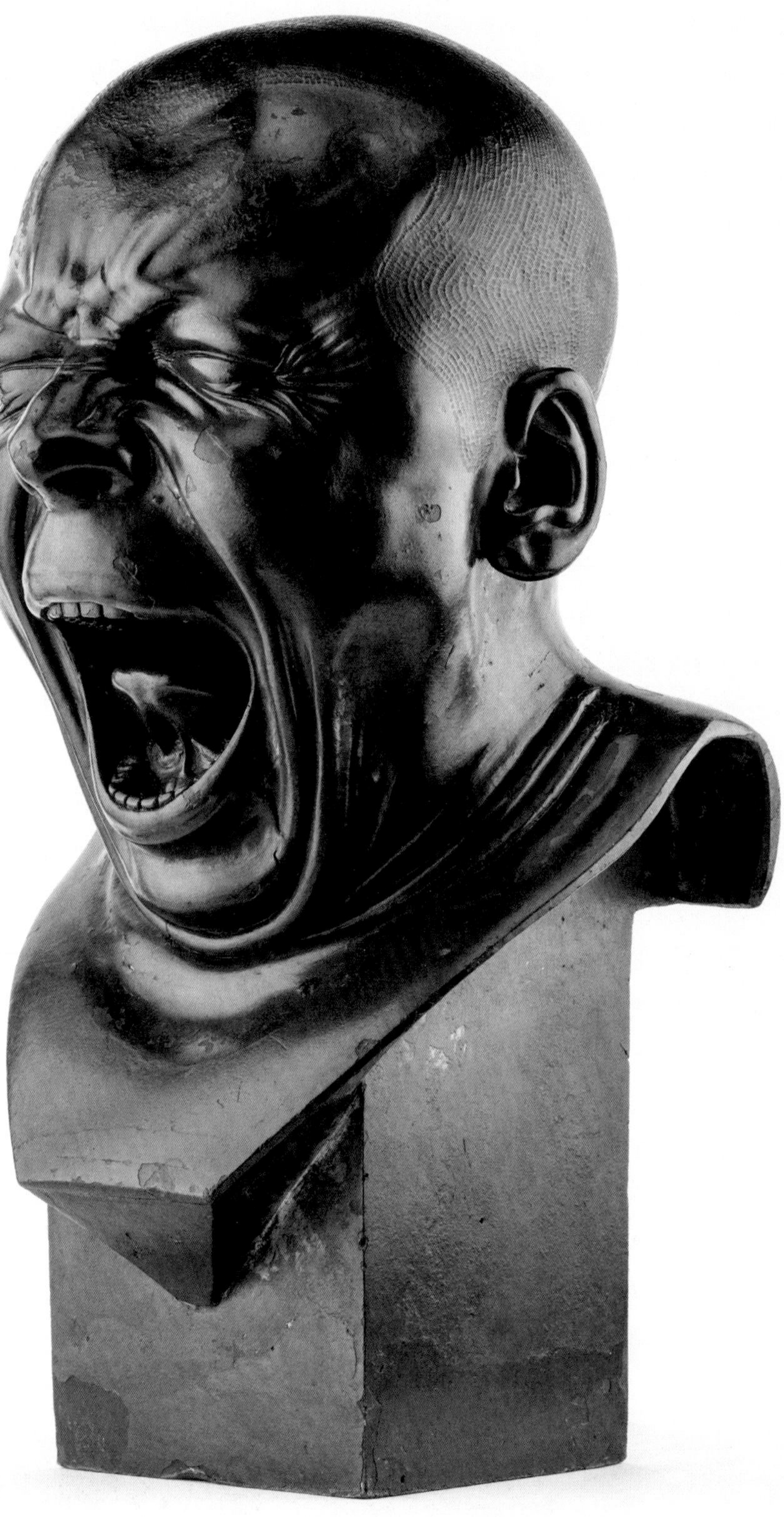

FIG. 94
Franz Xaver Messerschmidt, *The Yawner*, 1771–1783, tin, Museum of Fine Arts, Budapest, 53.655

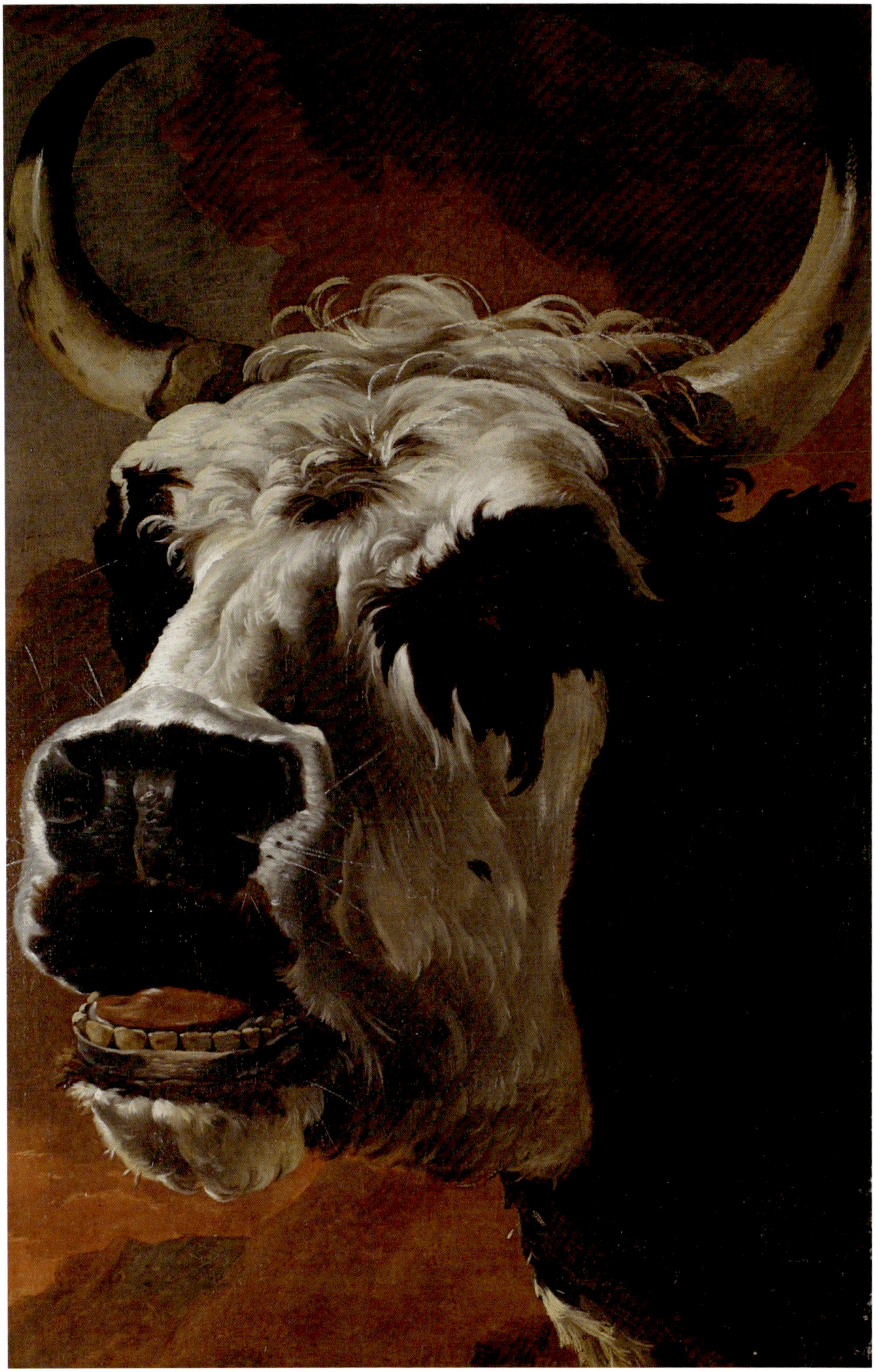

FIG. 95
Jan Asselijn,
Bellowing Ox, c. 1647,
oil on panel, Musée
des Beaux-Arts,
Nîmes, IP 317

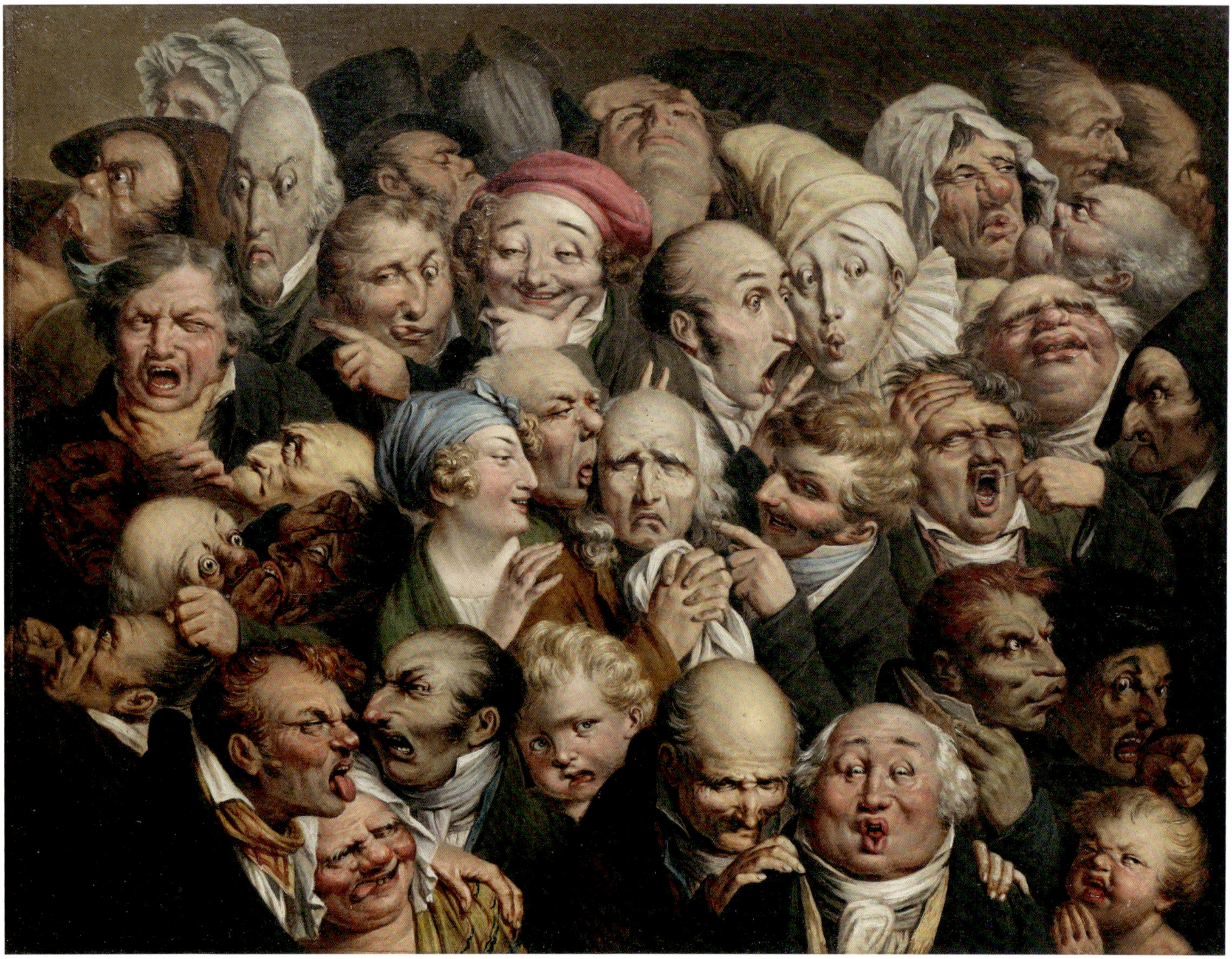

FIG. 96
Louis-Léopold Boilly, *Thirty Five Character Heads*, c. 1825, oil on panel, MUba Eugène Leroy

FIG. 97
Anonymous Master, second half of the sixteenth century, *Eight Head Studies of Men and Women,* s.d., ink on paper, Musée du Louvre, Paris, 20924 (recto)

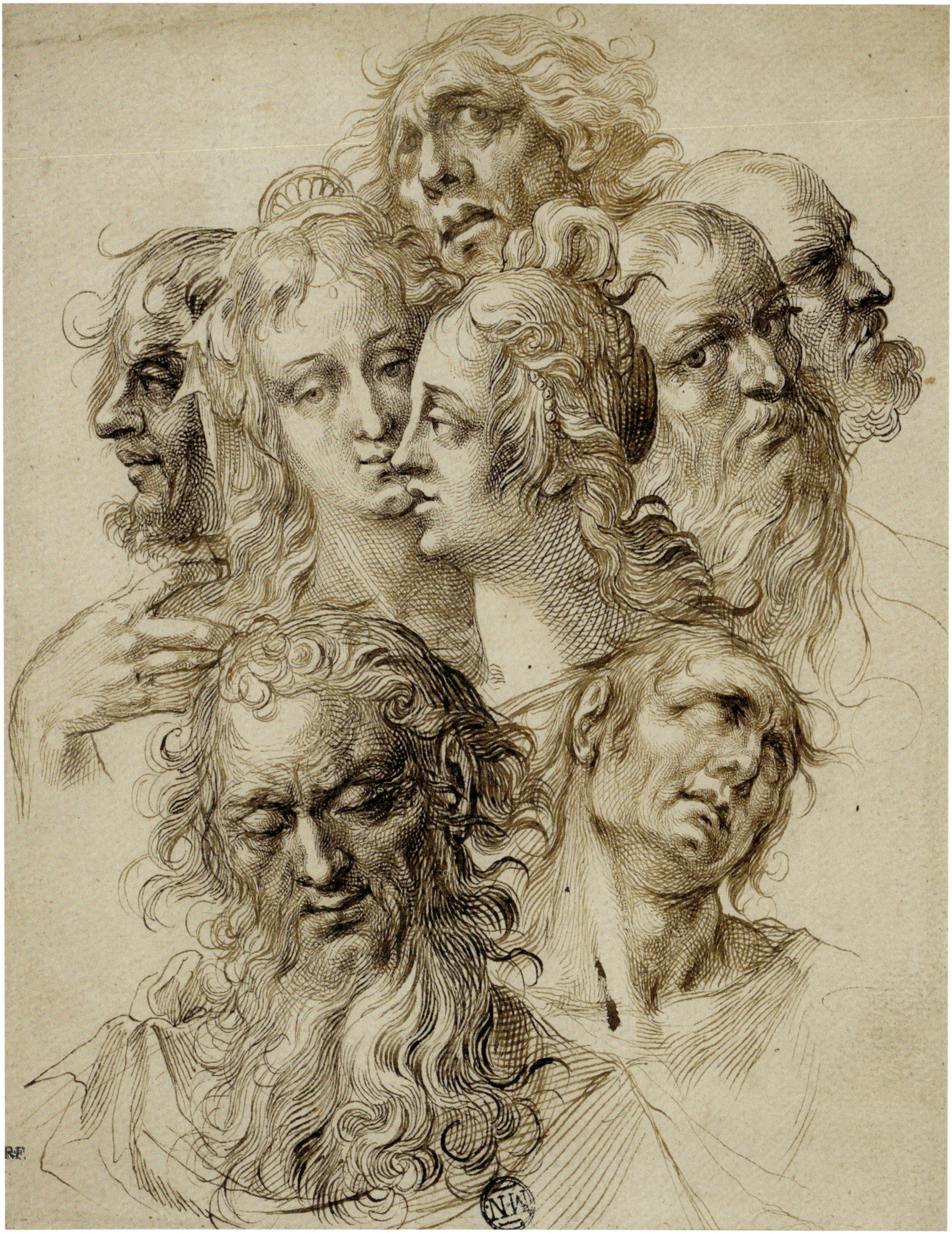

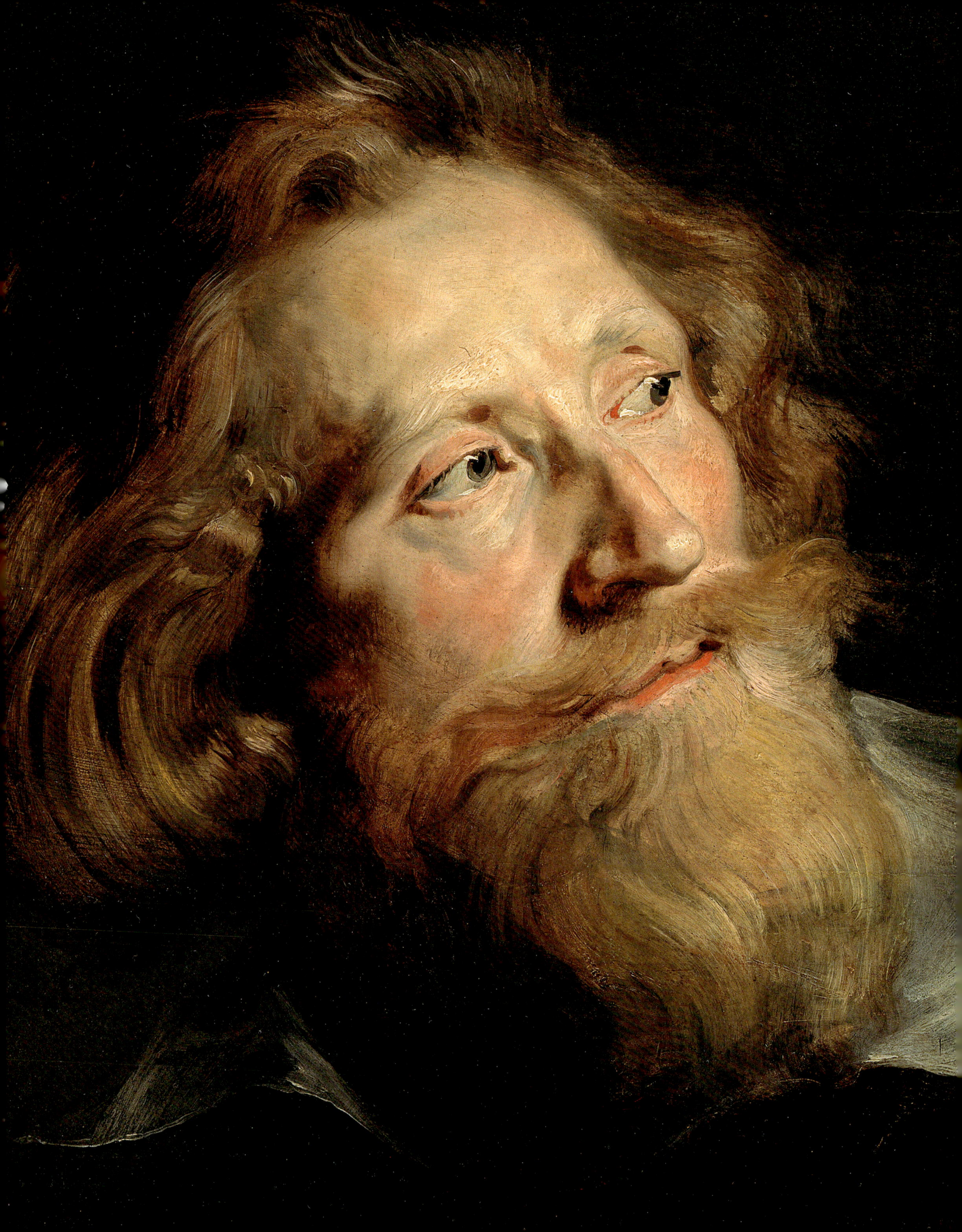

LIGHT AND SHADOW

'According to the Demands of the Composition' On Light, Tronies, and Head Studies

Koen Bulckens

Jeremiah Lamenting the Destruction of Jerusalem (Fig. 102) displays Rembrandt's brilliant mastery of light as an artist. The prophet is seated in a cave, alongside items he managed to save from the temple of Jerusalem before it was destroyed.[2] Colours and tones create a delicate atmospheric perspective, blending into a convincing illusion of depth. There is an attention to light effects created by particular elements. The brocade fabric and precious metalware shimmer. A fire devouring the city in the background colours the night sky golden. Lastly, the artist directs our attention to the face at the centre with a dramatic spotlight, giving extra force to its wrinkled expression of melancholy.

Rembrandt (1606/7–1669) has long held a reputation as a painter of light, yet he was but one of many artists who studied this phenomenon with great intensity in his day.[3] Evidence of an increasing engagement with light is found in works of art of the period as well as in contemporary writings on them. North of the Alps, lighting became the focal point of changing preferences in art theory.[4] This tradition was inaugurated in the Dutch city of Haarlem in 1604, where Karel van Mander (1548–1606) published the first Dutch-language book on painting. Van Mander developed new concepts to describe the novel effects of light which he saw in paintings by his contemporaries.[5] Importantly, the interest in light was not confined to the realm of art. Natural philosophers and mathematicians studying optics, understood to be the science of sight, devoted increasing attention to it. This culminated in Isaac Newton's (1643–1727) radically new understanding of the nature of light and colour.

The painterly fascination with light will here be studied in conjunction with the artistic interest in faces. Painters studied heads from life in particular lighting conditions, noting how light and shade defined their features in different settings. This interplay of light and faces is the topic of this essay. After a brief word about light in tronies painted in the Northern Netherlands – in Rembrandt's circle – focus then shifts to head studies produced in the Southern Netherlands – Rubens's circle. The lighting of these pictures has received little attention in art-historical literature, while the artists who painted them were clearly very concerned with it. I will discuss several of their works and notes on light in order to make this clear.

(DETAIL FIG. 116)
Peter Paul Rubens, *Head Study of a Bearded Man*, 1622–1624, oil on panel, National Gallery of Ireland, Dublin, NGI.2016.21

Light in tronies in the northern tradition

In the 1620s, Rembrandt and his colleague Jan Lievens (1607–1674) began producing tronies in their Leiden workshop. These playful paintings of faces soon became a major success on the art market. They were generally small in scale and were executed with virtuoso brushwork. Art historians have often called attention to the lighting in these works.[6] This painterly quality apparently engaged their makers.

Rembrandt's *Bust of an Old Man with Turban* (Fig. 109)[7] illustrates this. The picture shows a figure facing right in three-quarter profile. As the sitter's face is brightly lit from the left, his features remain largely shaded. Rembrandt constructed the nose and eye sockets using refined tonal nuances in the dark area. The jewel and feather in the man's turban have minor reflections at the side, giving the head a sense of volume. A similar engagement with light and faces is evident in works by Jan Lievens. In his *Head of a Young Girl in Profile* (Fig. 112),[8] for example, the face and blonde locks appear to glow.

Tronies also appeared in the north in prints, where lighting effects were also explored. Rembrandt made several etchings of an expressive old man's face using the same model who posed for his *Jeremiah* painting. (Fig. 103–106).[9] He needed no story about a destroyed temple here. The sitter's head, defined through fields of light and shade, is the sole subject. Rembrandt created darkness using overlapping hatchings, which he scratched into his etching plate with a needle. An alternative was to use a special tool with teeth, making little indentations in the plate to create shading. This later technique is known as 'mezzotint' and allows for greater nuance. One of its pioneers was the portraitist Wallerant Vaillant (1623–1677), who was born in Lille but later set up shop in Amsterdam. His *Bust of a Black Man* (Fig. 107) shows an astounding array of tonal values in the sitter's skin, achieved using this novel process.

Head studies and light in the Southern Netherlands

There were similar explorations of light and faces in the Southern Netherlands, in head studies produced in the circle of Peter Paul Rubens (1577–1640). Rubens ran a large workshop which employed many artists, and as such the enterprise was a hub for new artistic ideas and practices relating to light. Rubens's attention to light has been studied by art historians, but not with the same zeal as was the case for his Dutch colleagues Rembrandt or Vermeer.[10] What few publications on Rubens and light do exist do not pay any attention to head studies.

Rubens used head studies painted from life in his workshop. These served as models for faces in large-scale history paintings, and as didactical examples for apprentices who copied them.[11] They were sometimes made for one specific work, and sometimes without a composition in mind. Some head studies show an interest in lighting akin to that seen in tronies by Rembrandt and Lievens. The radiating illumination of Rubens's *Head Study of a Bearded Man* in Dublin (Fig. 116),[12] to which a costume was added later when it was sold, is an excellent illustration. The artist's dealings with light are even more apparent when we examine its variations. A panel with three head studies shows the same model in three different positions, but also in three distinct lighting conditions (Fig. 113). From left to right: strongly lighted, strongly shaded, and somewhere in between, worked out mostly in half-lights and half-shades.[13]

Such a study would have been a valuable educational tool for young artists who could copy the panel rather than having to return to the live model. Learning from art was considered the first step in mastering the depiction of nature. Still, some artists in Rubens's circle

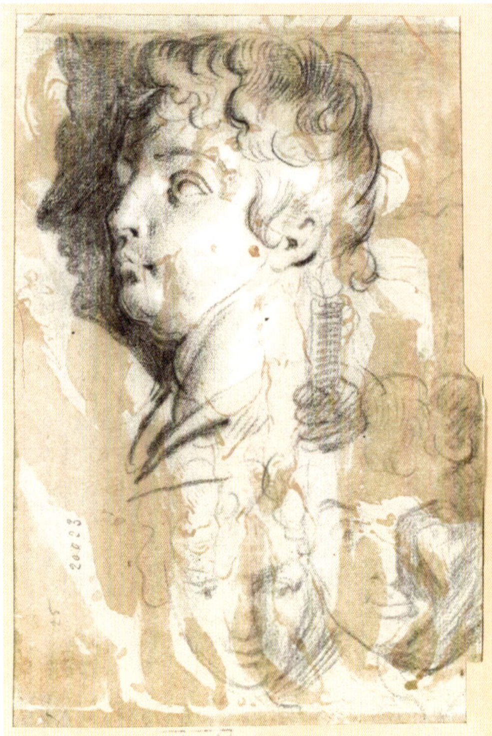

FIG. 98
Peter Paul Rubens, *The Descent from the Cross*, 1611–1614, oil on panel, Onze-Lieve-Vrouwe-kathedraal, Antwerp

FIG. 99
Jacques Jordaens, *Three Head Studies of a Man*, c. 1616–1617, black chalk on paper, Louvre – Collections du département des arts graphiques, Paris, 20023 (verso)

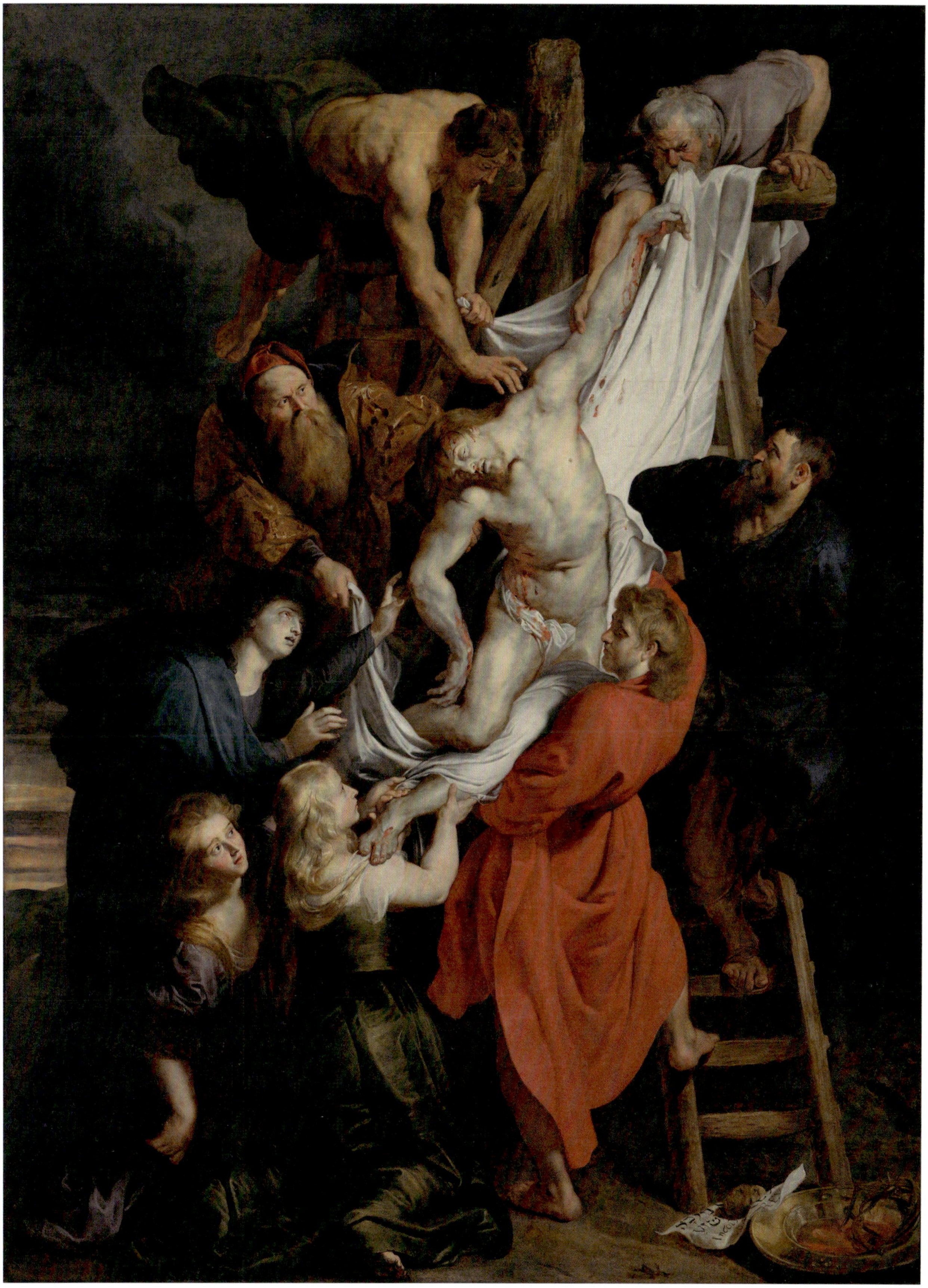

also did their own work from life. *Two Studies of a Man's Head* (Fig. 50) by Anthony van Dyck (1599–1641), for example, could be considered an exercise in painting light and shade.[14]

Head studies were also painted in artificial light, such as candlelight. This practice was described in contemporary treatises and is particularly inferred for Rubens's circle from the various sources which discuss his former collaborators.[15] The 1685 inventory of the engraver Alexander Voet records a head study by Van Dyck as 'painted by candlelight'.[16] A study drawing by Jacques Jordaens (1593–1678) of circa 1616 shows the head of a sitter with a cast shadow. Curiously, Jordaens also included the candle lighting the figure (Fig. 99).[17]

Anticipating the lighting of large compositions

The above-discussed head studies appear to have originated from a desire to capture light in its many forms. In other examples, the effort was more directed. This was the case when the lighting of a head study anticipated that of the final composition in which a head would figure. This phenomenon can be observed in the studies Rubens used for *The Descent from the Cross* (Fig. 98), his altarpiece for the Harquebusiers Guild, which were made especially in preparation for that work.

Early modern European paintings were conventionally lit from the upper left, which was described as the 'proper light' (*reghten dach*) in contemporary writings on art.[18] One notable motivation for deviating from the norm was the desire to conform pictorial light to architectural light. If a picture would receive light from a window on its right, artists would paint the light in their composition as if it were coming from that side. Rubens did so on several occasions, including in *The Descent from the Cross*.[19] The work was positioned on the Harquebusiers' altar at the south transept in the Cathedral of Our Lady in Antwerp, meaning it would be lighted from the right-hand side. Anticipating this, Rubens conceived his composition with 'inversed light' (*verkeerden dach*), coming from the upper right.

Importantly, two surviving head studies made for this project show the same inversed light. The first (Fig. 114)[20] is for the man in richly ornate dress on the ladder above Mary, leaning in to support Christ's shoulder, who has been identified as Joseph of Arimathea.[21] The head study was copied exactly in the final painting, though the red cap was a later addition. The second study (Fig. 115)[22] was for the man dressed in black on the opposing ladder, behind the red-cloaked John. He probably represents Nicodemus. Since this figure is facing left, his face is in the shade. This distinct lighting might strike us as odd when viewing the head study in isolation. The choice is perfectly sensible, however, if we consider the system in which it partakes. Interestingly, Rembrandt's *Study of a Woman in a White Cap* (Fig. 111) shows a lighting much akin to that of the head study for Nicodemus, which has been explained in similar terms.[23]

During the seventeenth century, the practice of attuning real to painted light became increasingly complex. A testimony to this evolution is the Oranjezaal, the central hall in the Huis ten Bosch palace in the Northern Netherlands, which was decorated with 39 canvasses by twelve painters. Jacob van Campen (1596–1657) supervised the project, keeping track of which paintings received which type of light, and providing the artists with cues accordingly.[24] Jordaens contributed a colossal canvas with *the Triumph of Frederick Henry, Prince of Orange* to the Oranjezaal, installed in 1652.[25] Sources relating to this work express a concern with lighting heads.

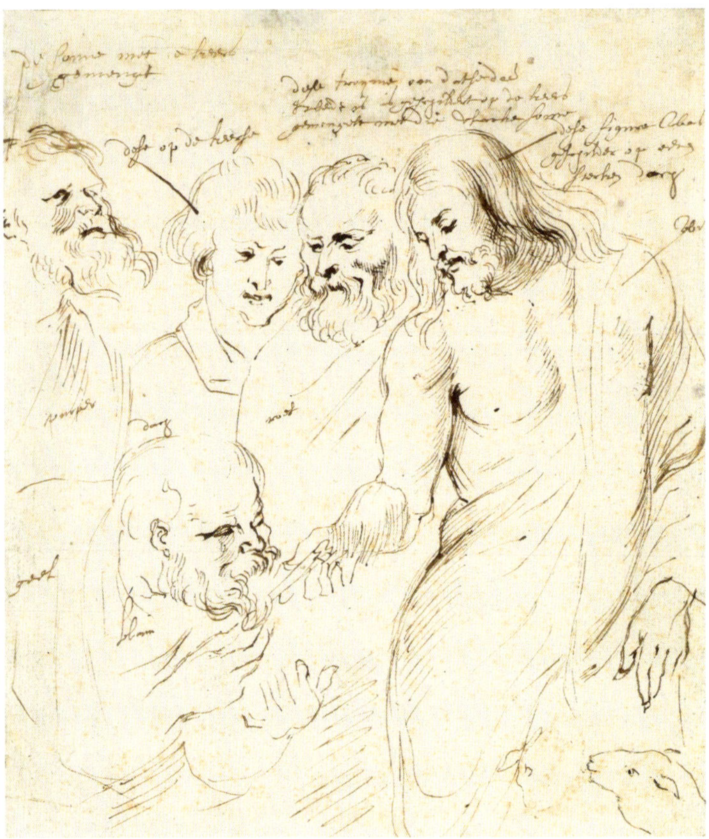

FIG. 100
Workshop of Peter Paul Rubens, *Christ Delivers the Keys to Peter*, c. 1616, oil on panel, Wallace Collection, London, P93

FIG. 101
Anonymous workshop collaborator of Peter Paul Rubens, *Christ Delivers the Keys to Peter*, c. 1616, pen in brown ink, Museum Boijmans van Beuningen, Rotterdam, MB 5017 (PK)

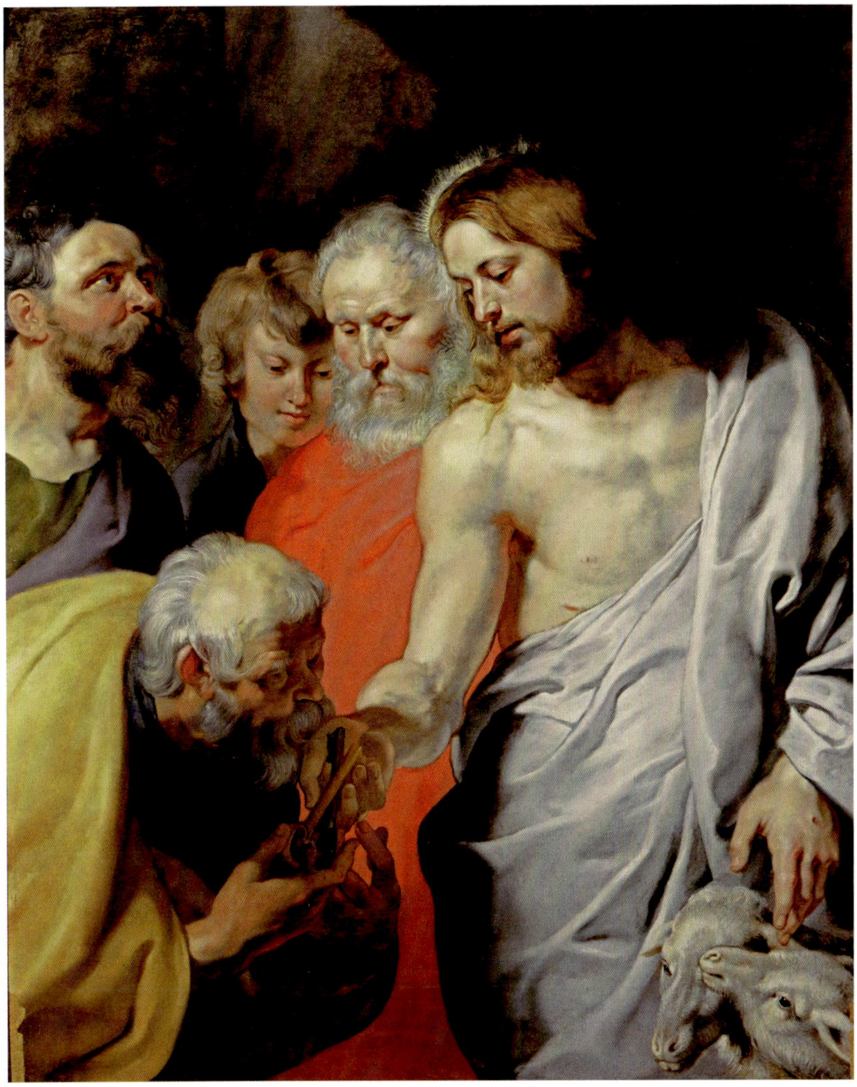

Jordaens wanted to include the likenesses of Stadtholder Frederick Henry (1584–1647) and his son William II (1626–1650) in his composition. Since both men were deceased, however, the artist could not have them pose in specific lighting conditions, as Rubens did with his models for *The Descent from the Cross*. Jordaens therefore requested portraits of both men made by Gerard van Honthorst (1592–1656). He specified that he needed these examples for two reasons. Firstly, they would allow him 'to take over the pose' in his own work. Secondly, he needed them to 'install the faces in their proper light'.[26] He added that he wanted the head of William II 'on a double light, according to the demands of the composition', which he could 'not express well in writing'.[27] It is hard to tell from the Oranjezaal canvas whether Jordaens ever achieved the effect he wanted but could not describe in detail.[28] Nonetheless, the letter illustrates that light was on the artist's mind when planning to insert the head of the prince in his massive tableau.

Categories of light

A last case takes us back to the Rubens workshop. This drawing (Fig. 101) by a workshop collaborator copies *Christ Delivers the Keys to Peter* (Fig. 100), Nicholas Damant's epitaph from circa 1616.[29] With each of the five heads in the composition, the draughtsman noted in what type of light it was painted. This ranged from 'a strong light' (*eenen stercken dach*) with Christ in the foreground to 'candlelight' (*op de keerse*) with the youth at the back. The two heads on the middle ground had a combination of daylight and candlelight, according to the inscription: 'sunlight mixed with candlelight' (*die sonne met die keers gemengt*) and 'candlelight mixed with flat sunlight' (*de keers gemengelt met die vlacke sonne*). Taken together, these notes suggest a hierarchy in which light gradually decreases toward the background, which can indeed be discerned in the picture.[30] The phrasing with the man in red at Christ's left is especially interesting from this perspective. The full text explains that 'this head is painted with candlelight mixed with flat sunlight *because* it is praying *there*' [my italics], conclusively linking the lighting of the head to its position in the pictorial space.[31] This is evidence of a logic similar to that which underpinned *The Descent from the Cross* and *The Triumph of Frederick Henry*.

The inscriptions are interesting also because they make us attentive to the great nuances of light in the painting. Indeed, the shadings of the faces in *Christ Delivers the Keys to Peter* show differences in their intensity and edges, and the tone and colours of the lighted areas likewise differ. These nuances require some focus in order to be noticed.[32] They are less evident than strong contrasts, like those in the above-mentioned *Bust of an Old Man* by Rembrandt, which immediately catch our attention. Nonetheless, the artist devoted great care to systematically differentiating light from shade in a subtle register, as in *Christ Delivers the Keys to Peter* or *Head of a Girl* by Michael Sweerts (1618–1664) (Fig. 118), with its trademark diffuse lighting.[33] Some painters even developed a specialised vocabulary in this process, as the inscriptions in the Rubens workshop drawing and Jordaens' notion of 'double light' testify. The precise meaning of these words cannot be reconstructed, but their very existence is noteworthy.[34]

As noted above, the inscription with the man in red states that 'this head' (*dese tronyie*) was painted in sun and candlelight. This wording implies that there was a head study for this figure, made under the lighting conditions described. However, I believe that we should not take the draughtsman's words at face value. I have found no reference to the combined use of day and candlelight in contemporary texts, which do expand on studying natural and artificial lights individually.[35] Moreover, experiments confirm that the combination of candlelight and daylight produces few desirable effects in nature.[36] On both cloudy and sunny days, the candlelight becomes discernible only as the candle is about to touch the face. Moreover, it generates brightness at that point. This means that the mixed light would actually be stronger than daylight alone, which does not match the system observed in the painting, darkening toward the background. Also, the shaded parts of the face, a crucial means for an artist to create volume, are evened out because of the candle. It is difficult to imagine how this could add up to the effects seen in the painting.

Considering the practical experiment as well as the lack of references in treatises, it is more likely that the mixture described in the drawing reflects an artistic middle ground between daylight and candlelight, rather than an effect observed in real life. Having acquainted the properties of distinct types of lighting in different head studies from nature, one painted by candlelight and another by daylight, Rubens or his collaborators could create a combined light in art. This implies that there was no exact prototype for the heads in question, as there was for those in *The Descent from the Cross*.[37]

Conclusion

The most well-known artist engaging with light north of the Alps in the generations after Rembrandt was undoubtedly Johannes Vermeer. The range of effects which can be observed in a panel such as *Girl with the Red Hat* (Fig. 120), one of the artist's smallest works, is baffling.[38] The light dances over the sitter's blue cloak and mysteriously fluffy red hat. Vermeer often adds dotted highlights with the tip of the brush, as can be seen on the arm of the chair in the foreground. The highlight in the woman's right eye is especially intriguing. An artist following tradition would have painted this highlight in white. Vermeer, through his diligent examination of light and colour, did it in light green. This unusual choice nonetheless creates a perfect tonal harmony.

It has often been suggested, in specific reference to *Girl with the Red Hat*, that Vermeer used a camera obscura to study light effects. The painter may have become acquainted with the apparatus via the Jesuit community in Delft.[39] However, Vermeer also refined strategies studied and passed on in the workshops of previous generations of artists. The head studies discussed in this essay testify to a significant though under-acknowledged tradition of studying light in the Southern Netherlands. Artists in Rubens's circle painted models in different lighting conditions, occasionally anticipating the light of the composition in which they would figure, and devised categories of light for heads. These artists, I have argued, were also painters of light.

1 Letter from Jacques Jordaens to Constantijn Huygens, 8 November 1651. Worp 1916, doc. 1590. This essay elaborates on ideas first developed in a chapter on light in my dissertation on the workshop of Peter Paul Rubens (Brown University, 2023). I thank Jeffrey Muller, Bert Watteeuw, and Nico Van Hout for their helpful thoughts and suggestions. "[…] *volge ns den eijsch van de compositie* […]".

2 Josua Bruyn *et al.* 1982, no. A28; Van de Wetering 2015, no. 39.

3 A recent overview of sources and literature on Rembrandt and light can be found in Scott and Hillyard 2019.

4 The essential study of ideas on light in northern art theory is Kern 2014. The author discusses the writings of Karel van Mander (1604), Philips Angel (1642), William Goeree (1668), Samuel van Hoogstraten (1678) and Gerard De Lairesse (1707).

5 See especially Paul Taylor 1998, 159–178, an analysis of the concept of 'glow' in the writings of Karel Van Mander. As Taylor observes, the artistic impetus to study light came from Italy (p. 169), however, this study in turn gave way to local traditions in the north. The later term *'houding'*, also studied by Taylor, is indicative thereof. Taylor 1992, 159–78.

6 Examples citing earlier references are Hischfelder 2008, 47, 53; Gottwald 2011, 117.

7 Van de Wetering 2015, no. 21.

8 Duparc, Diercks and Neff 2011, no. 35.

9 Hinterding and Rutgers 2013, nos. 63–65. Several other tronie prints by Rembrandt are included in the volume.

10 One particularly famous example is Julius Held's study of Rubens's inscription on an optical effect in the drawing of trees at sunset, which he linked to the work of the Jesuit scholar Franciscus Aguilonius. Held 1979, 257–64.

11 On Rubens's head studies, see the introduction to Nico Van Hout 2020, as well as the author's contribution to the present volume.

12 Van Hout 2020, no. 16.

13 Van Hout 2020, no. 108.

14 Van Hout 2020, no. 100.

15 For example, Leonardo da Vinci advised artists to mount a sheet of oiled paper between the light and the model when working by lamp- or candlelight, so as to soften its shade. Da Vinci 1989, 216.
Ulrike Kern notes that Leonardo's suggestion was taken up in Willem Goeree's treatise (p. 104). See also her overview of comments by Karel van Mander, Joachim Sandrart and Samuel van Hoogstraten on the 'edgy' nature of shadows cast by candles (pp. 123–6). Jordaens apparently did not bother with Leonardo's advice in the drawing discussed below. Kern 2014.
For comments on the practicality of artificial light in studios, see Kleinert 2006, 37–38.

16 *"een Tronie profiel op de keers geschildert, van van Dijck"* ("a painted head in profile on the back, by Van Dyck"). Duverger 2001, 352.

17 The sheet is securely attributed to Jordaens by way of the *Ecce Homo* composition on the recto. The dark light brown areas on the verso are not washes but ink from the recto shimmering through. D'Hulst 1974, no. A27. The author points out that the composition on the recto also shows an interest in light effects.

18 Van Eikema Hommes 2013, 183.

19 However, Justin Underhill's thought-provoking hypothesis that Rubens conceived the composition of the *Descent* so that certain pictorial features would be spotlighted at specific times of the year, goes too far for the present author. Underhill 2018, 1–22.

20 Van Hout 2020, no. 27.

21 Judson 2000, nos. 43–46.

22 Van Hout 2020, no. 28.

23 Van de Wetering 2015, no. 182.

24 Van Eikema Hommes 2013, passim.

25 Van Eikema Hommes and Speleers, 'no. 32', in Ekkart *et al* (eds.), *De Oranjezaal. Catalogus en Documentatie*, online: <htttp:// oranjezaal.rkdmonographs.nl/>, accessed July 1, 2018.

26 "[…] *dat ick maer de posture en hadde in te stellen ende het stuck syn volcomenheit hadde, en de tronien op haeren behoorlycken dach ingesteldt waeren*, […]" Letter from Jacques Jordaens to Constantijn Huygens, 8 November 1651. Worp 1916, doc. 1590.

27 "[…] *moet Insonderheydt dat van den jongen Prins op een dobbel licht gemaeckt werden, volgens den eijsch van de compositie, die ick niet wel met schrijven en can wtdrucken.*" Letter from Jacques Jordaens to Constantijn Huygens, 8 November 1651. Ibid.

28 The main reason for this is that we lack a clear understanding of what Jordaens meant by 'dobbel licht'. Moreover, Margriet van Eikema Hommes writes that Jordaens, having requested Honthorst's portraits of Frederick Henry and William as a prototype, also asked for the Dutch artist's assistance in completing these faces in *The Triumph*. During conservation of the large canvas, it was observed that these portions have a different technique. Since the brushwork is rather coarse, they have been attributed to an anonymous workshop collaborator of Honthorst. Van Eikema Hommes 2013, 203.

29 For the painting, see Freedberg 1984, no. 24. For the drawing, see Meij and De Haan 2001, no. 52, and Müller Hofstede 1965, 312ff, who first published the sheet. Both the drawing and the painting are reviewed at length in Bulckens 2023, Chapter IV.

30 Compare this to the hypothetical situation described by Giovanni Paulo Lomazzo in his *Trattato Dell' Arte Della Pittura, Scultura et Architetettura*. Milan: Paolo Gottardo Pontio, 1584, 216–217: "If you ask me what a painter ought to do when he would paint two or three or four men standing behind one another, all of them illuminated with equal clarity, I answer according to the following teaching: even though they be equally lighted, it is nonetheless necessary to paint the second, who is further from the eye, darker, and the third more, and the fourth most of all, until the eye can see no more."

31 *"dese tronyie om datse daer / gebede is is geschildert op de keers / gemengelt met die vlacke sonne"* This is an early instance of the use of the word 'flat' (*vlack*), which became key in northern art theory in the second half of the seventeenth century. In his drawing manual of 1662, William Goeree defined 'flat shadows', which enjoyed his preference, as having clear edges and a uniform darkness. In so doing, he established the use of flat shadows as the opposite to the sfumato style. See Taylor 2008, 153–84; Kern 2014, Chapter 3. At the time of the drawing after Rubens was made, *'vlack'* was not yet clearly defined. Karel van Mander used the word in the context of light, without explaining it properly. Jacques De Ville used the word in an apparent reference to Caravaggism, as noted by Miedema 2017, 184.

32 Rubens's work of 1612–1618 can serve as an example. Critics have often described 'even lighting' as one of its key characteristics, however, Rubens was in effect actively expanding his vocabulary of light at this point. Bulckens 2023, Chapter IV.

33 Kultzen 1996, no. 101.

34 Paul Taylor and Ulrike Kern (see note 5) have done exceptionally useful work in elucidating the meaning of art-theoretical concepts regarding light. For the isolated workshop language passed down to us by the Rubens collaborator and Jordaens, however, we lack the context or comparative material necessary for further definition.

35 For the individual study of artificial light, see the references cited in note 15. Giovanni Paulo Lomazzo observed that a candle's coloured glow could still be discerned during daytime. However, this comment related to history paintings with varied light sources rather than studying composite lights in nature. Lomazzo 1584, 220.

36 Experiment by the present author in the summer of 2020.

37 One head study used in the work survives. The modelling of the head in the painting follows that of the study quite closely. Unfortunately, however, the yellow varnish over the head study makes it difficult critically to compare its colouring to that of the painting. Because of this, it is therefore impossible to test whether the lighting of the head study was copied exactly in *Christ Delivers the Keys to Peter*. See Van Hout 2020, no. 56.

38 Roelofs and Weber 2022, 209–10.

39 The topic was most recently reviewed from the perspective of Vermeer's Catholicism. Weber 202, 97 ff.

Stephan Vanfleteren

TRONIES

Heads. You see them everywhere. In shopping streets, on the tram, in cafés, on screens, between the sheets and even in the mirror. It is nothing more than a fleshy egg with skin. Often the head – as well as our hands – is the only uncovered part of our body. The rest keeps secrets from strangers. A face is unguarded. Stark naked, despite a range of camouflaging techniques such as moustaches, beards, sunglasses, hats. The head is where looking, hearing, kissing, cursing, smelling and speaking all happen. The most important little factory of small humanity. Heads are the incubators of loves, ideas and decisions.

I have a weakness for remarkable heads. When I see one on the street, I become enraptured and the world stands still for a moment. You know a striking head when you see it, before you even know why.

It could be the big nose, unusual eyes or ears; or atypical proportions that only become apparent later. Or sometimes not even then. Sometimes you just can't explain why one person's head stands out from thousands of other more average ones. Why is it that certain faces "work" in the two-dimensional world of a photograph or painting? It's a riddle that after all these years of watching, observing and studying I still can't solve. Some heads don't "speak", even if they have a voice. The code of the face defies all efforts to crack it.

Humans evolve slowly, that's what wise old Darwin taught us. The question of whether faces today are different from faces in the Middle Ages often crosses my mind. There probably shouldn't be much difference but, just like our planet, people themselves are currently caught up in a whirl of accelerated change brought about by artificial influences. The big changes can't be explained by the slow theory of evolution, but the answer may lie in the habits and customs of modern humans. It used to be normal for teeth to fall out and for jaws to collapse because of a lack of hygiene. Forward-jutting chins weren't corrected in the past either. A used-up body fell apart more quickly in olden times. I saw it with my own eyes in the very old people I encountered in my earlier days. Sometimes I fool myself I'm one of the last to have captured that in photography. I came across these extraordinary heads amongst the solitary farmers living in remote and derelict houses, and amongst the fishermen who still sailed distant seas without the use of modern technology. Hard labour occupations, at one with the elements of nature. Signposts from a time when there was no dentist in every village and no creams against the sun's glare.

That has certainly had its impact on the appearance of the face. Fisherman Julien is a typical model, his skin well tanned by the salt of many decades at sea, his pores fairly sand-blasted. With his chin sticking out like the prow of a ship and a nose so curved that you could cast it as an anchor, he would fit right into *Christ Carrying the Cross* painted by Hieronymus Bosch. You can spot at least five Juliens in the crowd populating that masterpiece.

Today, children are sent to orthodontists, everyone goes to the dentist for an annual check-up, little ones are lathered in sunscreen before playing on the beach, and most people work in offices instead of outdoors. The *tronie* is gradually fading from view in our society and is being replaced by the *face*.

The word *tronie* has taken on a negative connotation in modern Dutch, associated with ugly criminals, outlaws and bad guys, like *beak* or *mug* in English. It used to be a more innocent word, with a specific meaning in the art-historical context. Julien had a *tronie* but no trace of malignancy. His face is an iconic picture of an old fisherman. It's not really about him personally, but about what his face expresses: tanned by the hard life of another time.

In recent years, the modern face is presenting an even greater transformation. Botox, hair implants and other cosmetic procedures are becoming more and more common. The face is not the barometer of age that it used to be. What's worse, emotions sometimes disappear from the face that sports lip injections, fillers, or eyelid corrections. If the current wizardry continues on its careening path, it will become impossible to guess whether somebody is happy or sad, angry or excited, distraught, apathetic or turned on. Out-of-control aestheticisation of the human body and face comes at the price of a frozen facial expression.
A wrinkle is no longer seen as time's badge of honour; one prefers the fool's gold of a face plumped with silicone. The tauter the skin, the less interesting the physiognomy. Due to an obsession with eternal youthfulness, the face is losing its vitality and is becoming increasingly difficult to read. Bereft of its essence, the face is becoming a metaphorical orphan.

Stephan Vanfleteren (1969) is a multiple-award winning Belgian photographer. Internationally he is best known for his piercing portraits and documentary work.

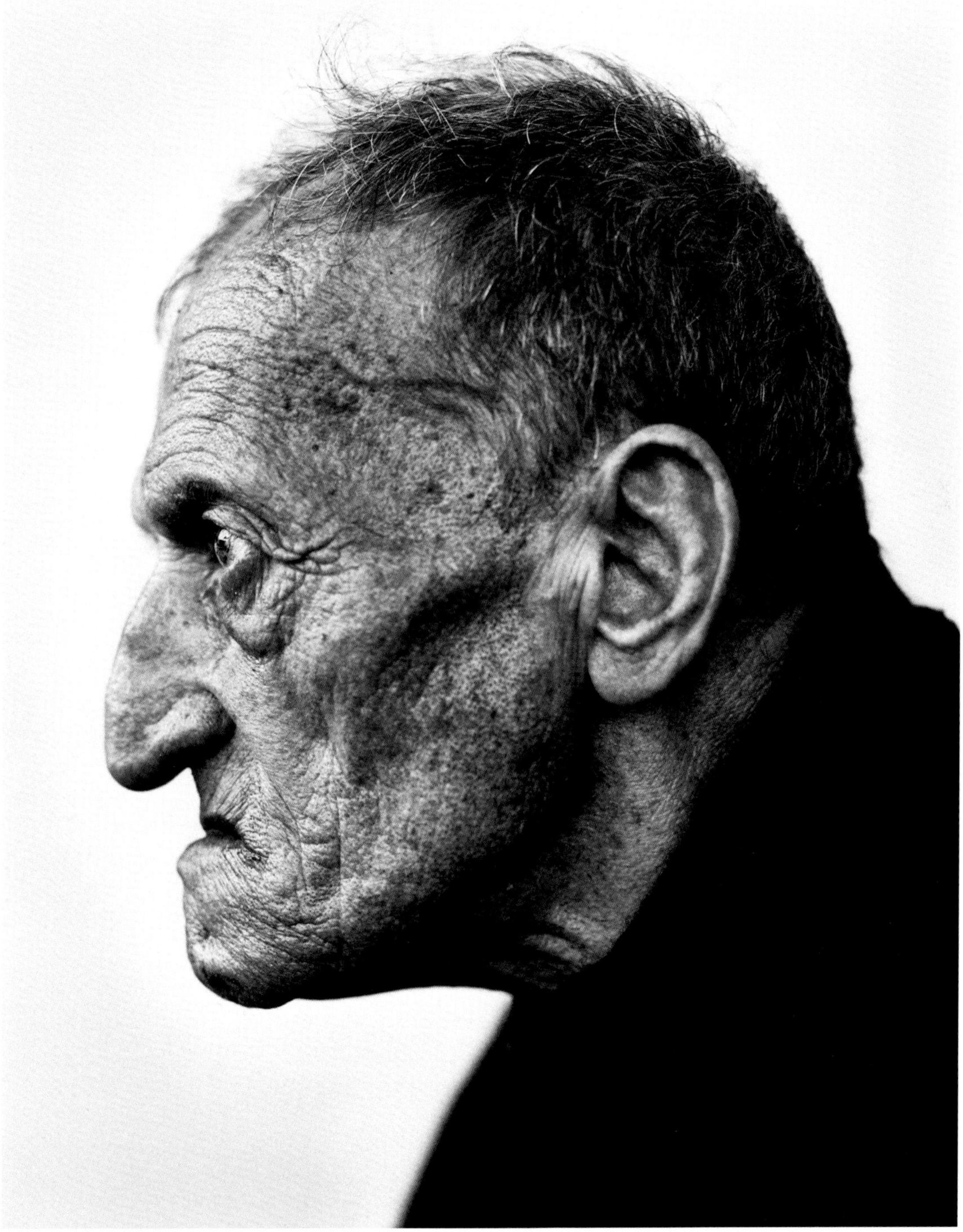

Stephan Vanfleteren,
Julien, 2003, photograph

FIG. 102
Rembrandt,
Jeremiah Lamenting the Destruction of Jerusalem, 1630, oil on panel, Rijksmuseum, Amsterdam, SK-A-3276

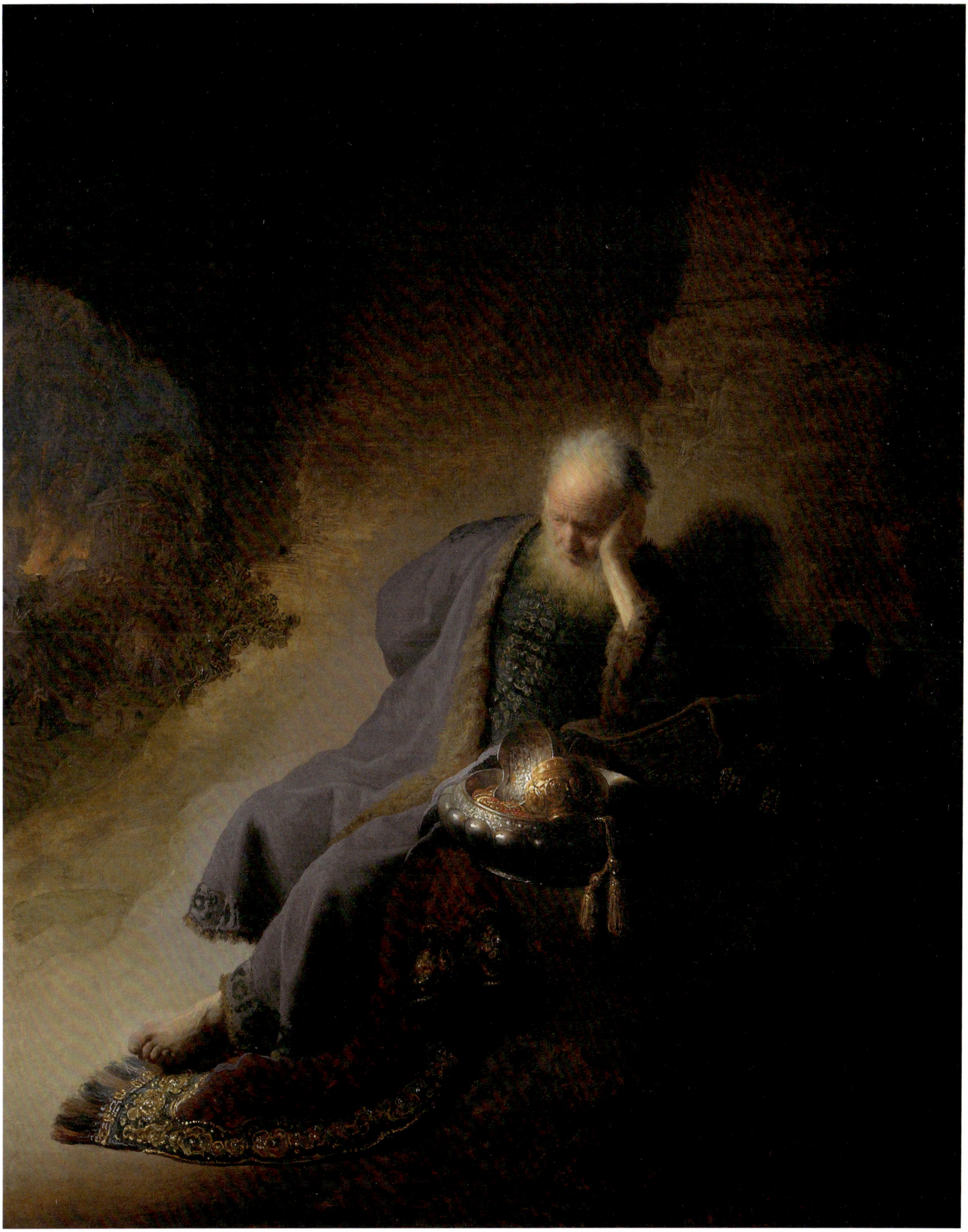

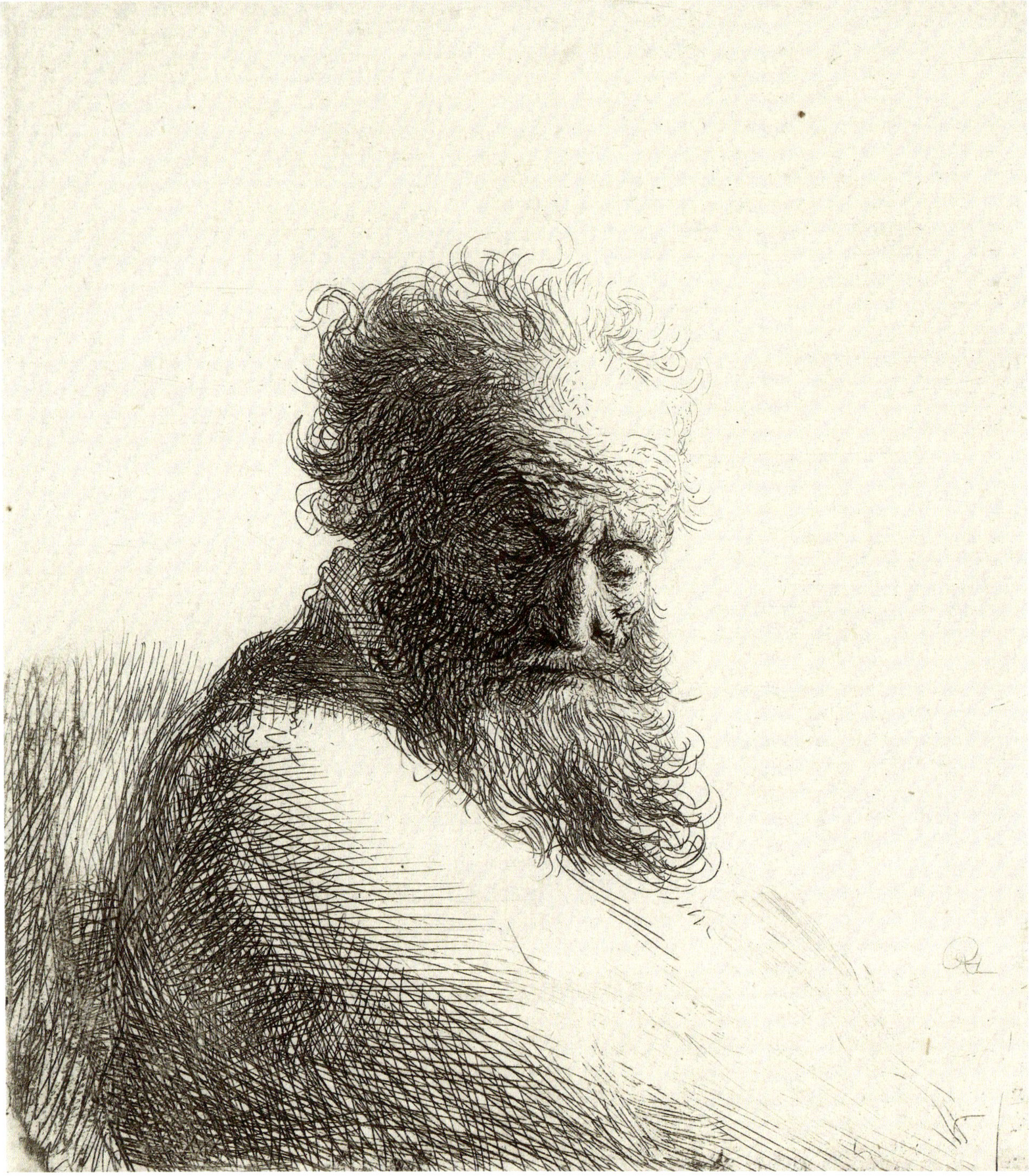

FIG. 103
Rembrandt,
Old Man Looking Down,
1631, etching, Museum
Het Rembrandthuis,
Amsterdam, 177

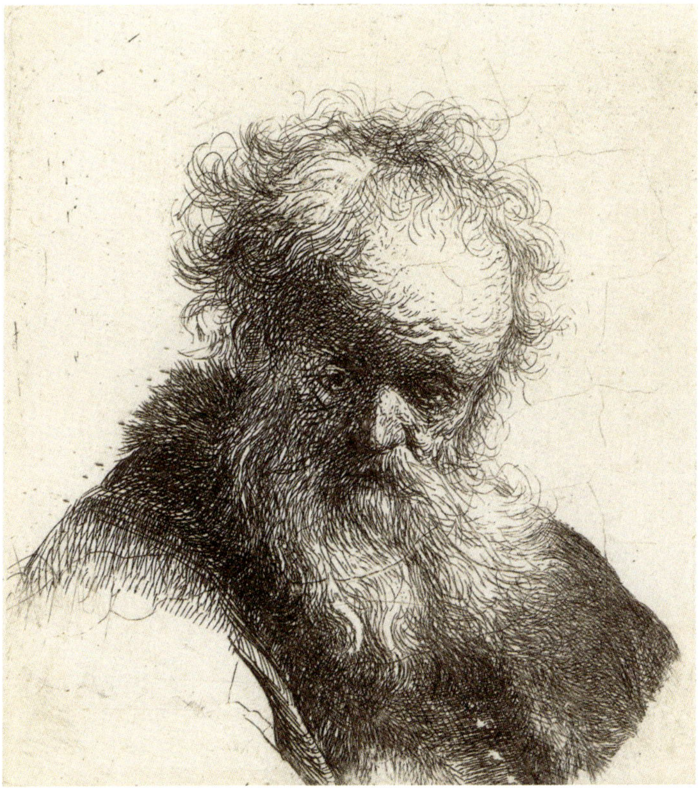

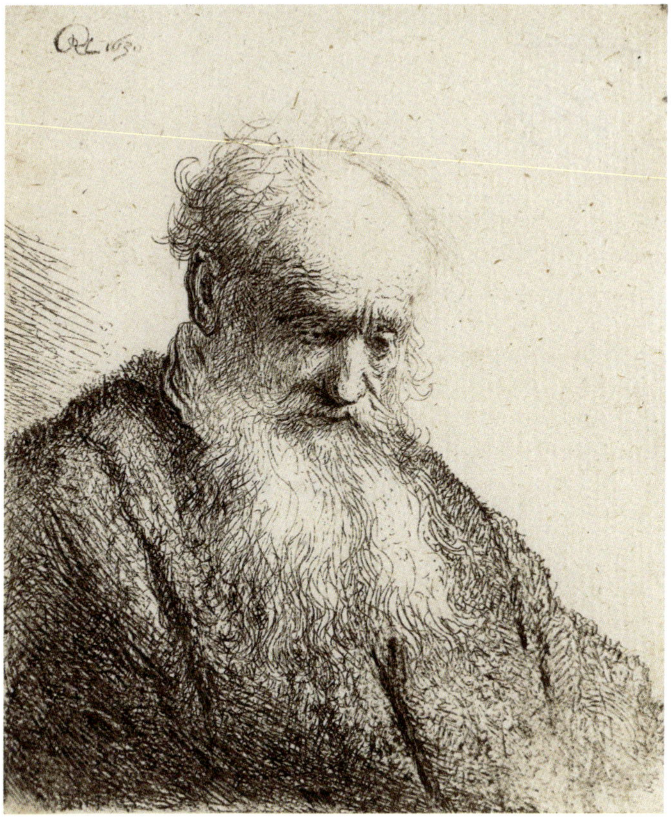

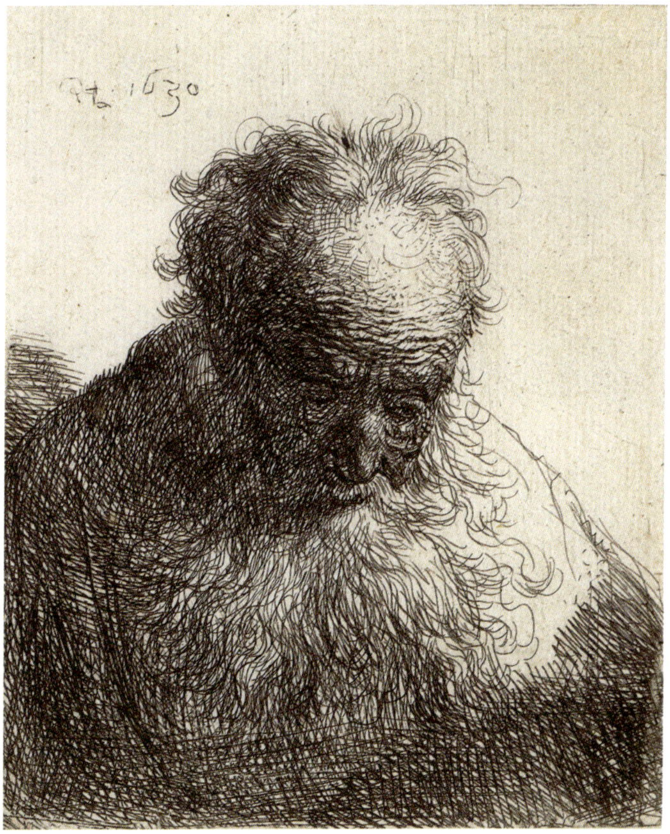

FIG. 104
Rembrandt,
Old Man with a Beard and White Sleeve,
s.d., etching, Museum
Het Rembrandthuis,
Amsterdam, 204

FIG. 105
Rembrandt,
Old Man with a Long Beard, c. 1630,
etching, Museum
Het Rembrandthuis
Amsterdam, 208

FIG. 106
Rembrandt, *Old Man with Long Beard Looking Down*, 1630,
etching, Museum
Het Rembrandthuis,
Amsterdam, 216

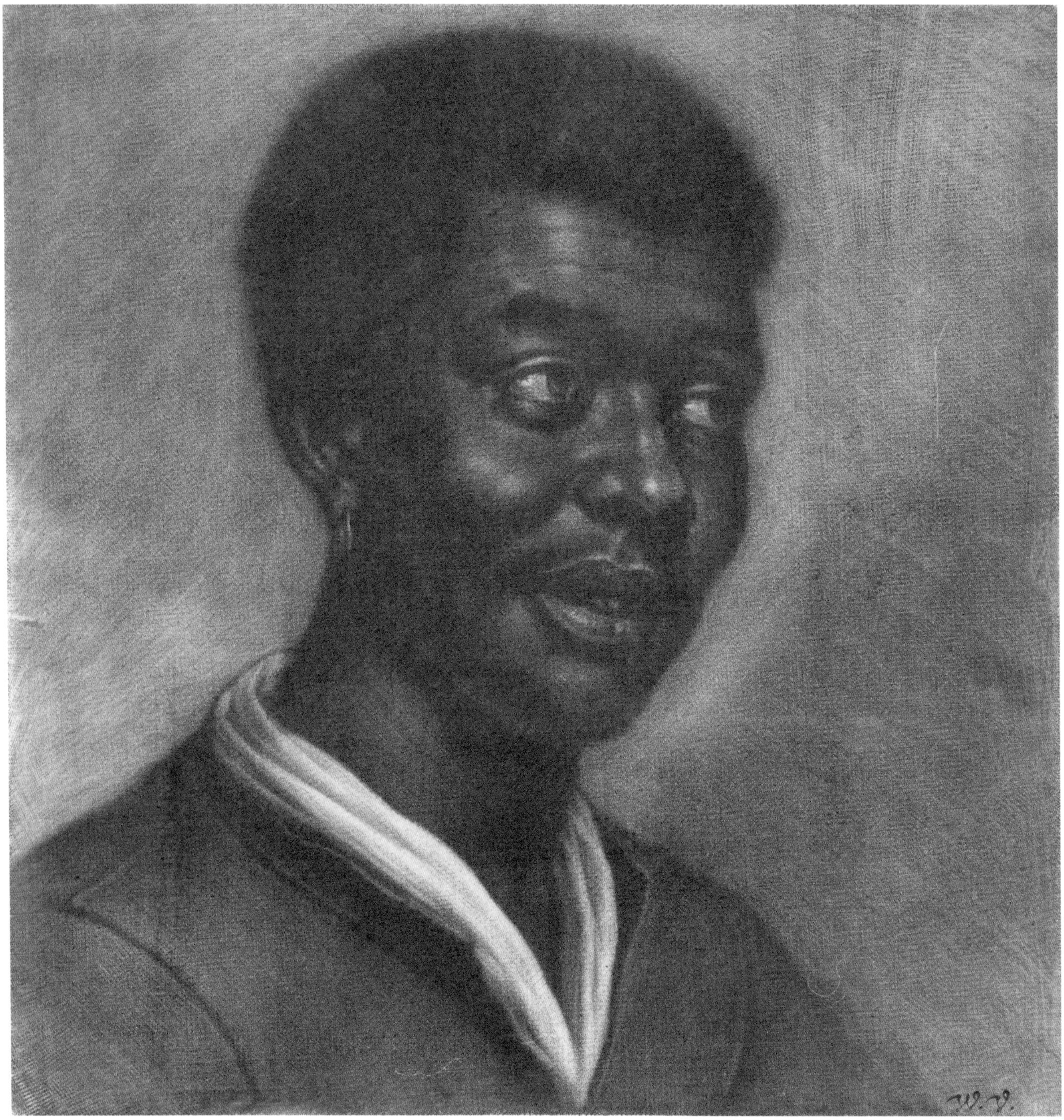

FIG. 107
Wallerant Vaillant,
Bust of a Black Man,
c. 1658–1677, mezzotint,
Rijksmuseum Amsterdam, RP-P-1911-66

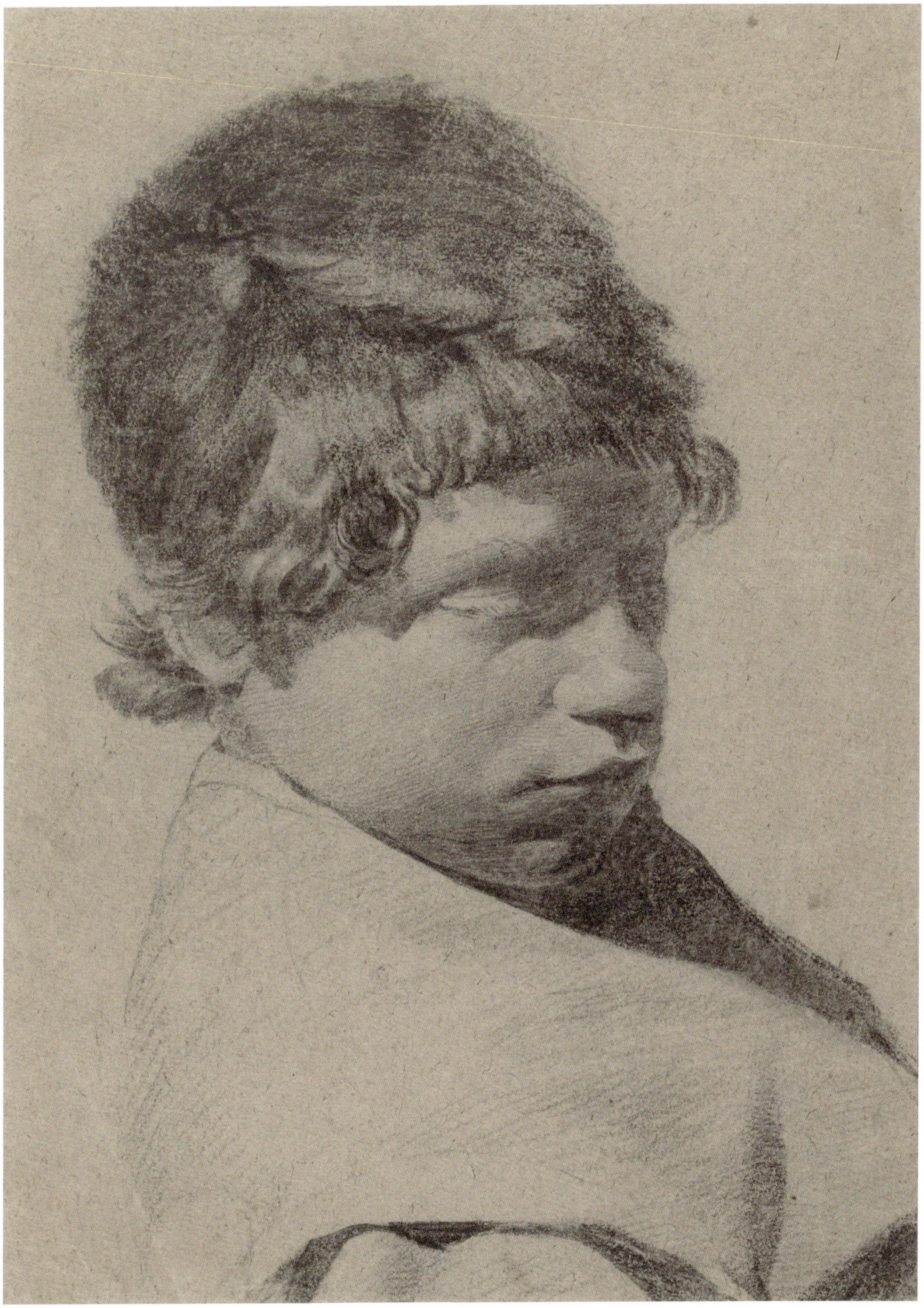

FIG. 108
Leendert van der Cooghen, *Bust of a Boy*, 1642–1681, black chalk on brown paper, Rijksmuseum, Amsterdam, RP-T-1889-A-2136

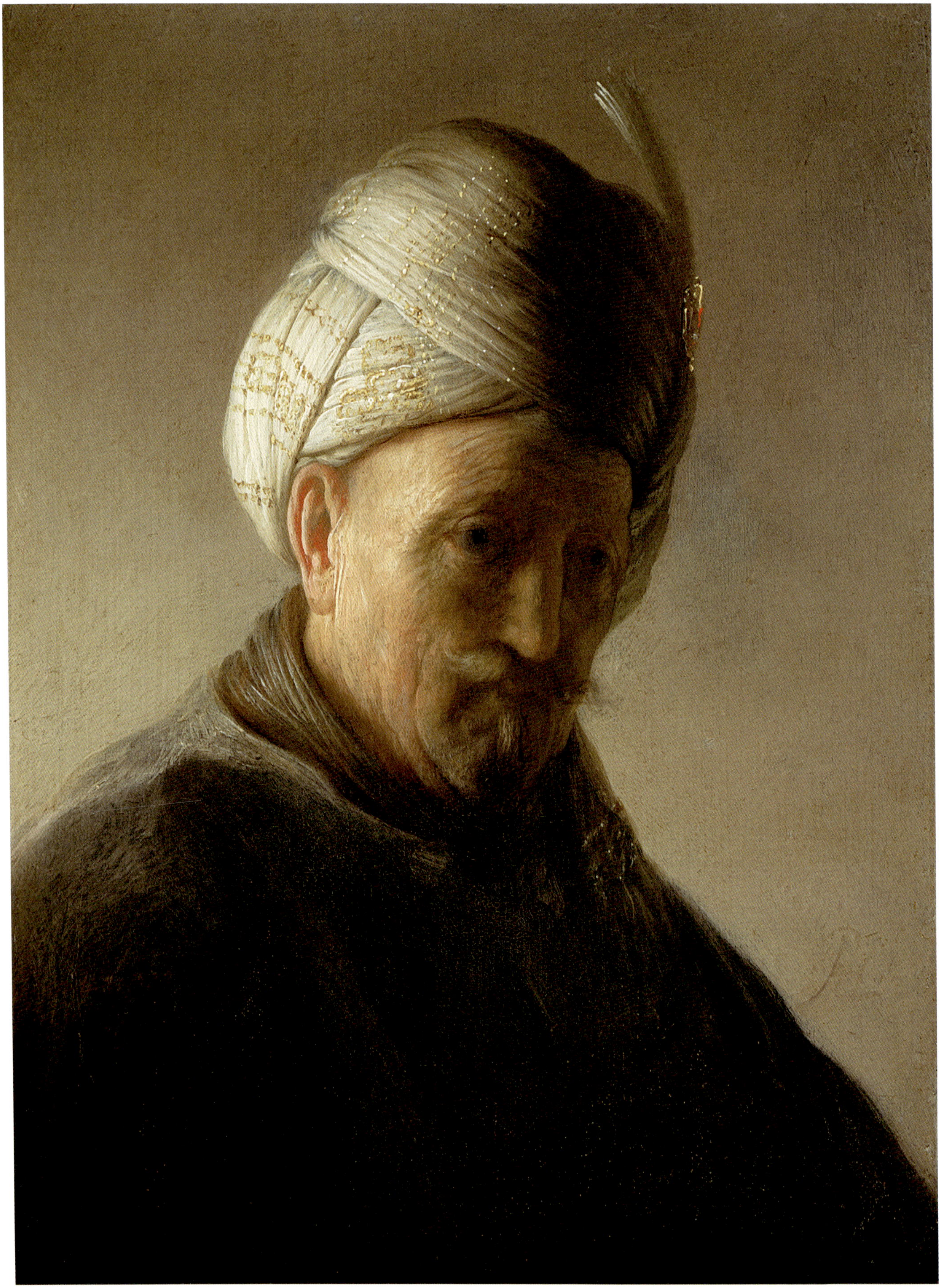

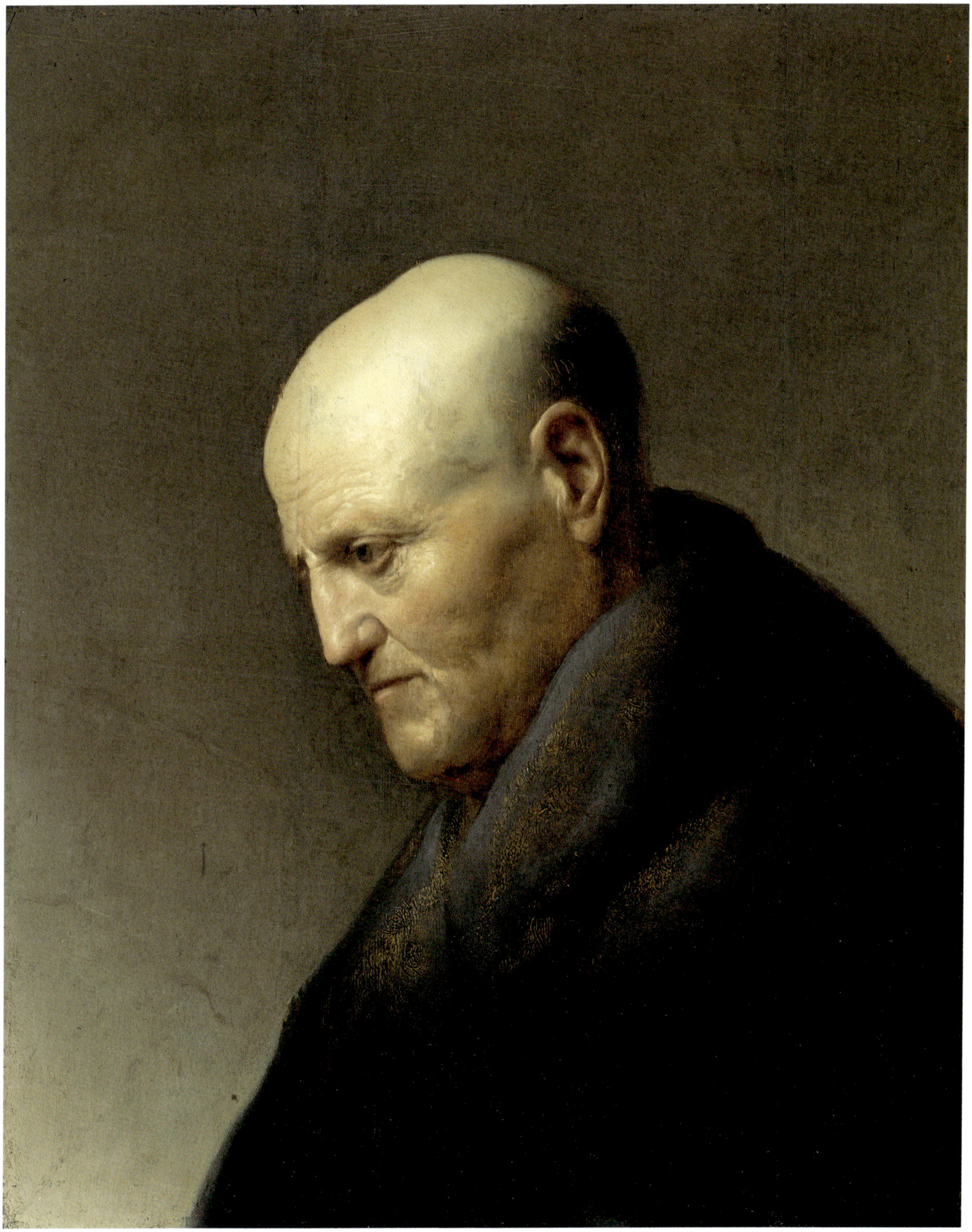

FIG. 109
Rembrandt,
Bust of an Old Man with Turban, 1627–1628, oil on panel, The Kremer Collection, New York

FIG. 110
Jan Lievens,
Head of an Old Man, c. 1629, oil on panel, National Gallery of Ireland, Dublin, NGI.607

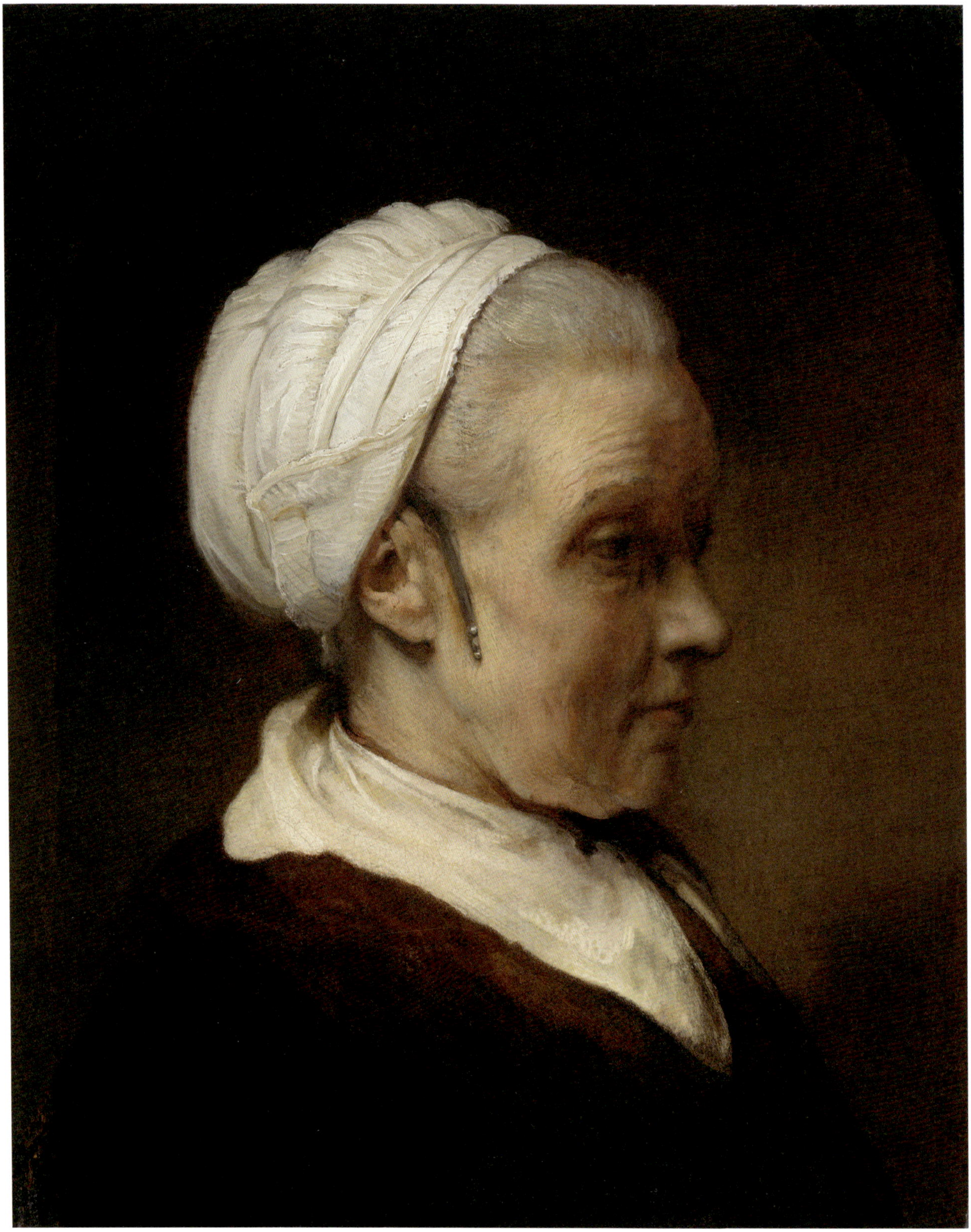

FIG. 111
Rembrandt,
Study of a Woman in a White Cap,
1632, oil on panel,
The Leiden Collection,
New York, RR-101

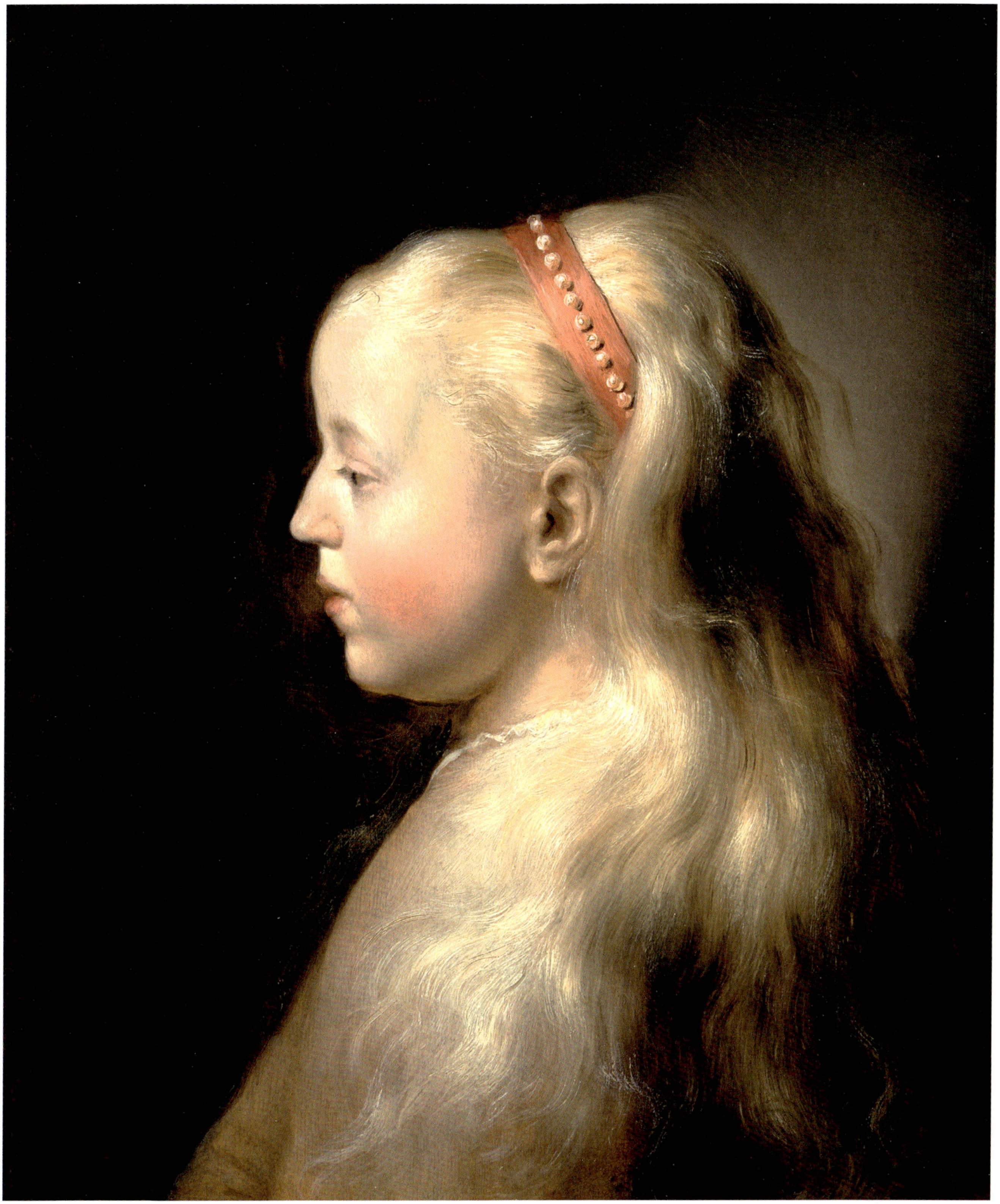

FIG. 112
Jan Lievens, *Head of a Young Girl in Profile*, c. 1631–1632, oil on panel, Museum of Fine Arts, Boston, gift of Rose-Marie and Eijk van Otterloo, in support of the Center for Netherlandish Art, 20.192.085

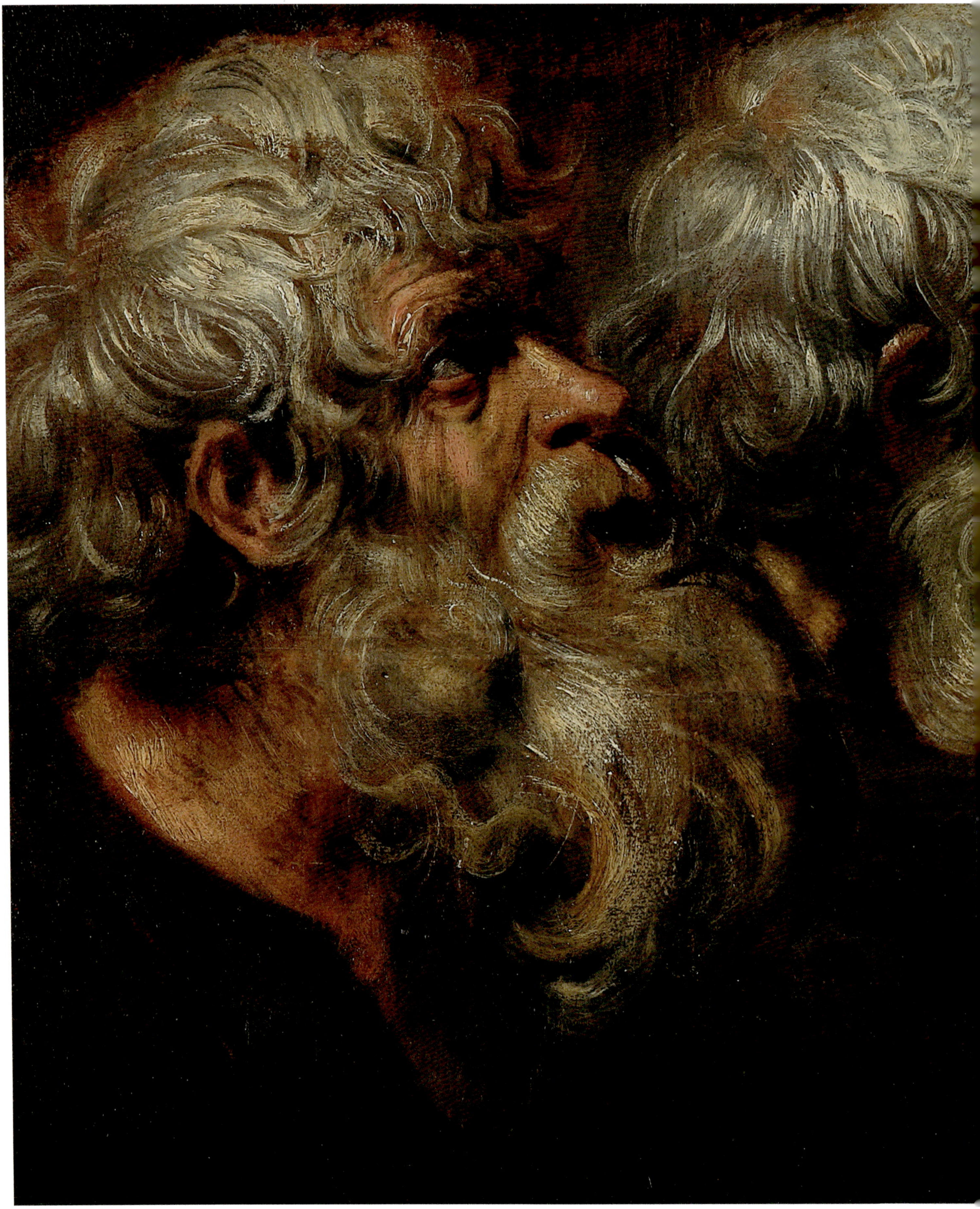

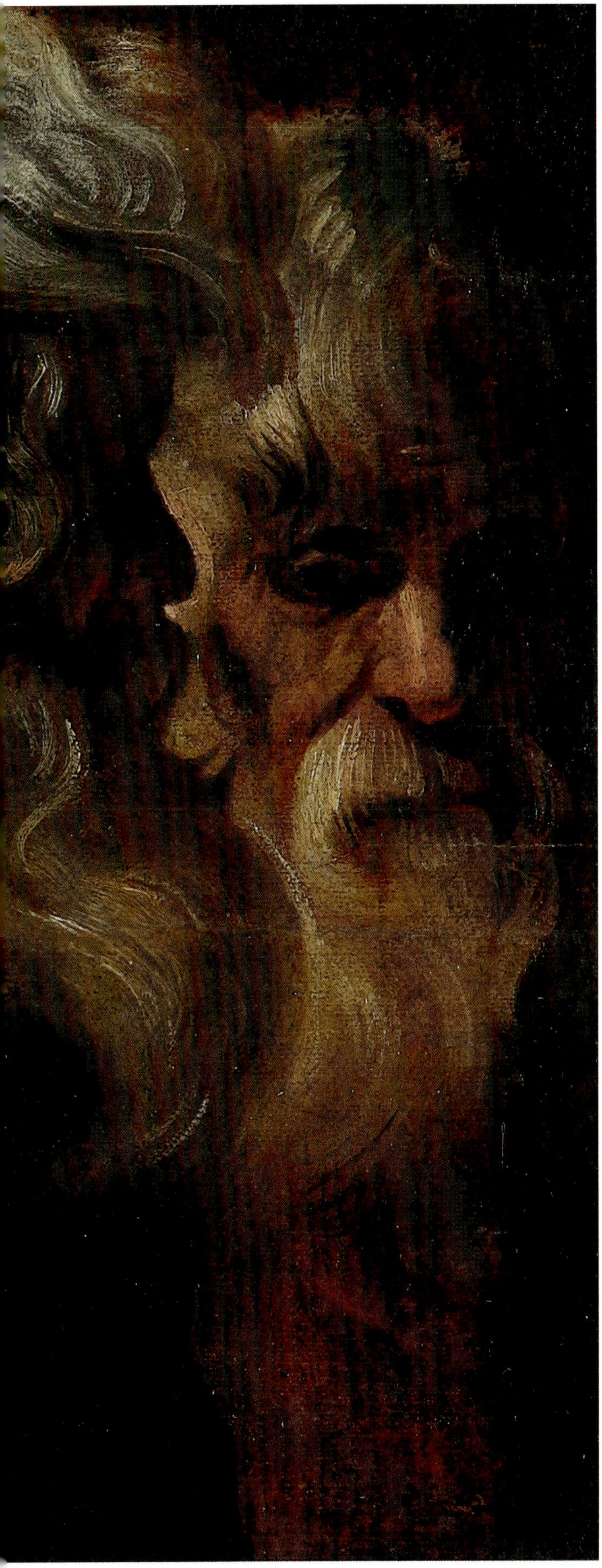

FIG. 113
Peter Paul Rubens,
Three Head Studies of a Bearded Old Man,
c. 1609–1610, paper glued on panel,
Musée des Beaux-Arts de Libourne, MI1313

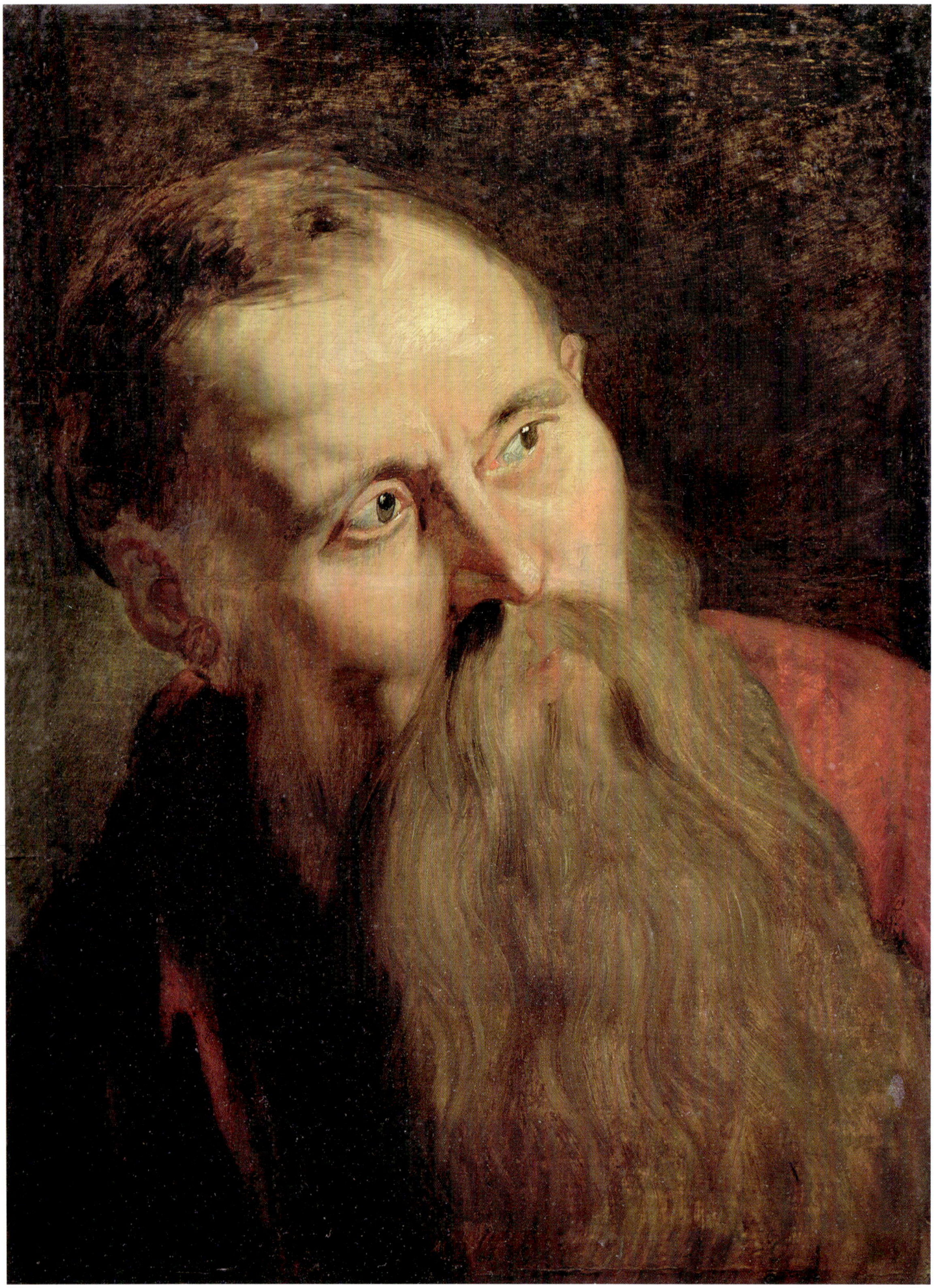

FIG. 114
Peter Paul Rubens, *Head Study of a Man*, 1611–1612, oil on panel, private collection, Madrid

FIG. 115
Peter Paul Rubens, *Head Study of a Man in Profile*, 1611–1612, oil on panel, National Gallery, Prague, DO 4377

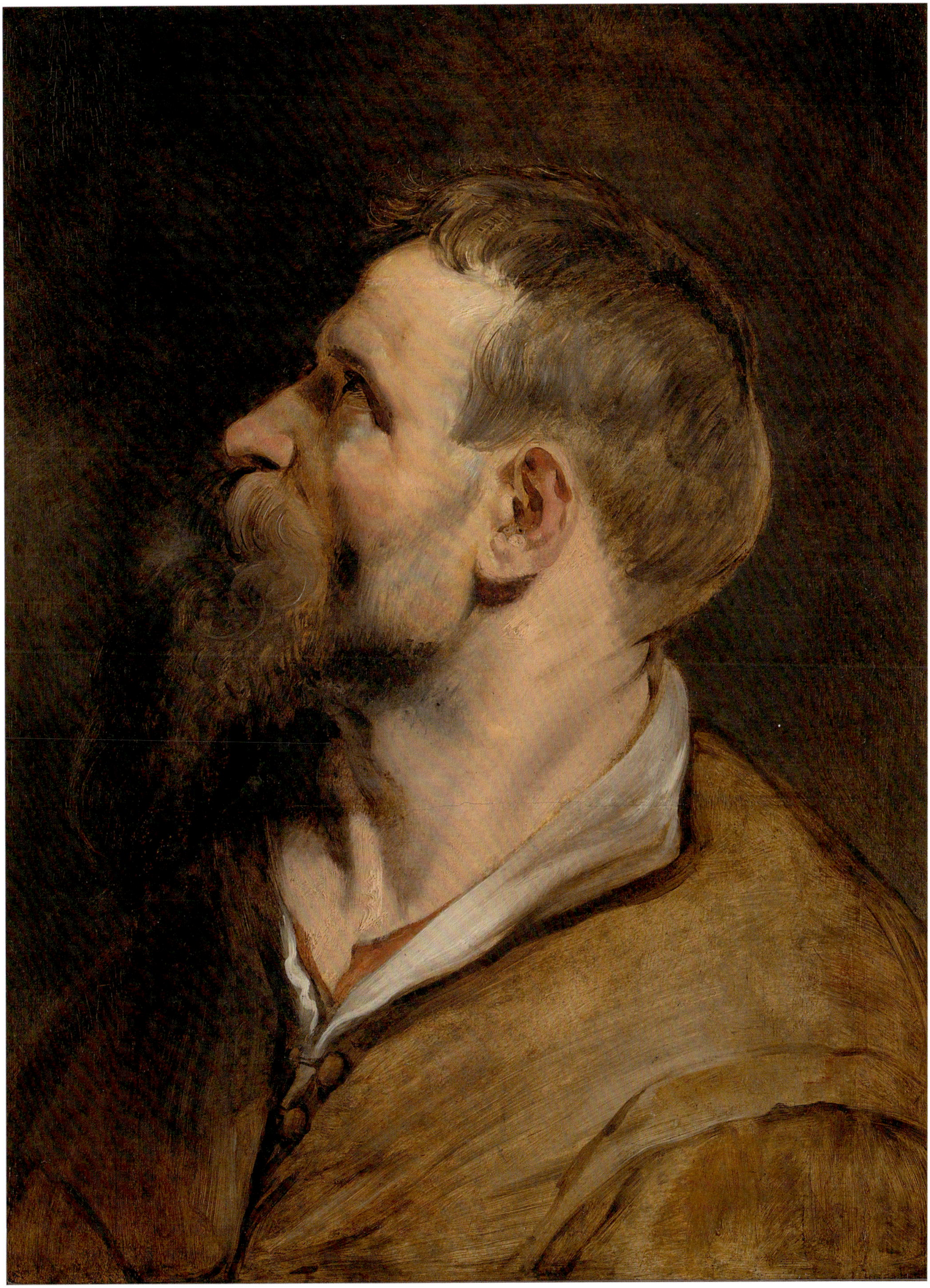

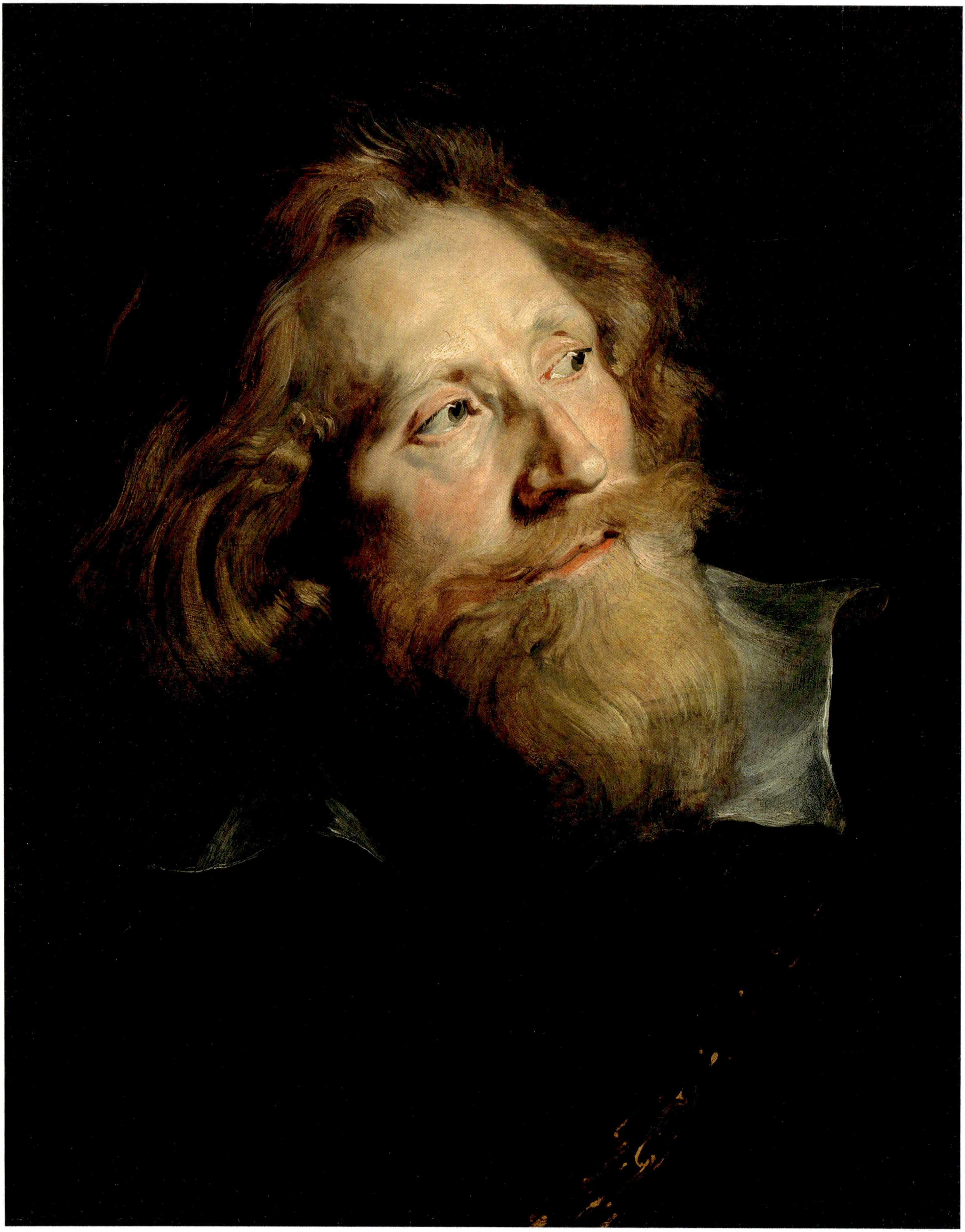

FIG. 116
Peter Paul Rubens, *Head Study of a Bearded Man*, 1622–1624, oil on panel, National Gallery of Ireland, Dublin, NGI.2016.21

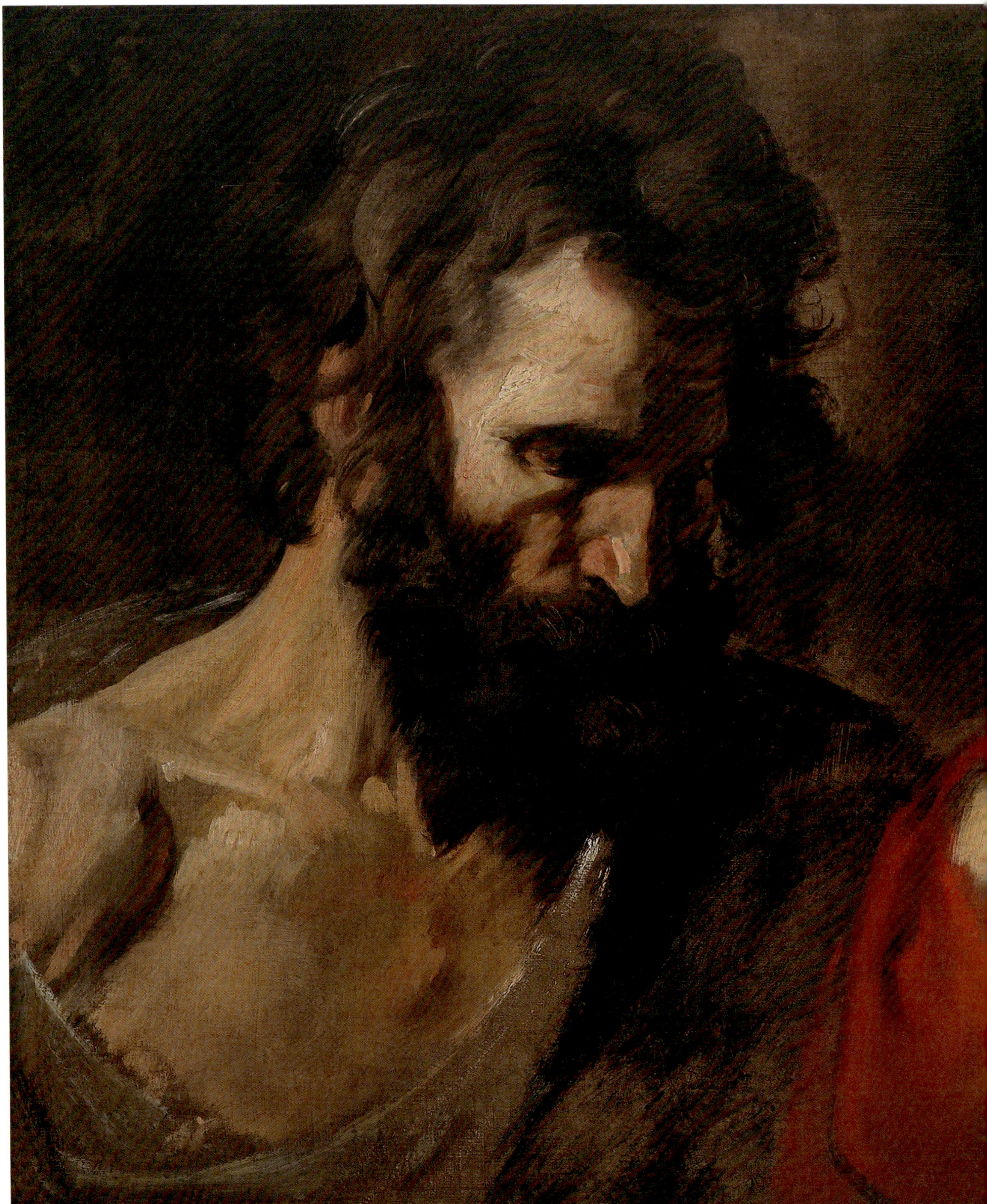

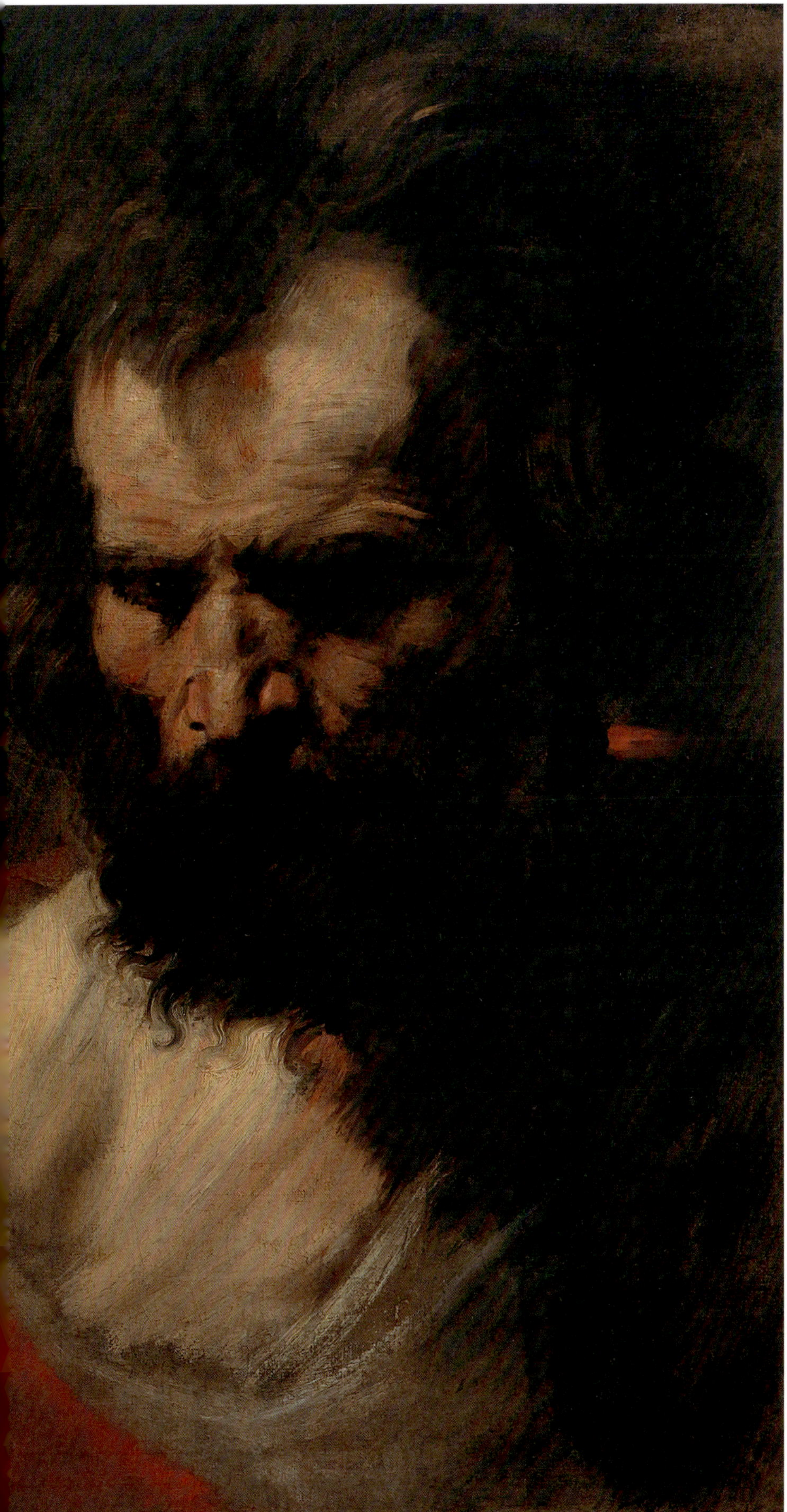

FIG. 117
Anthony van Dyck,
Two Head Studies of a Bearded Man, 1618–1620, oil on canvas, private collection

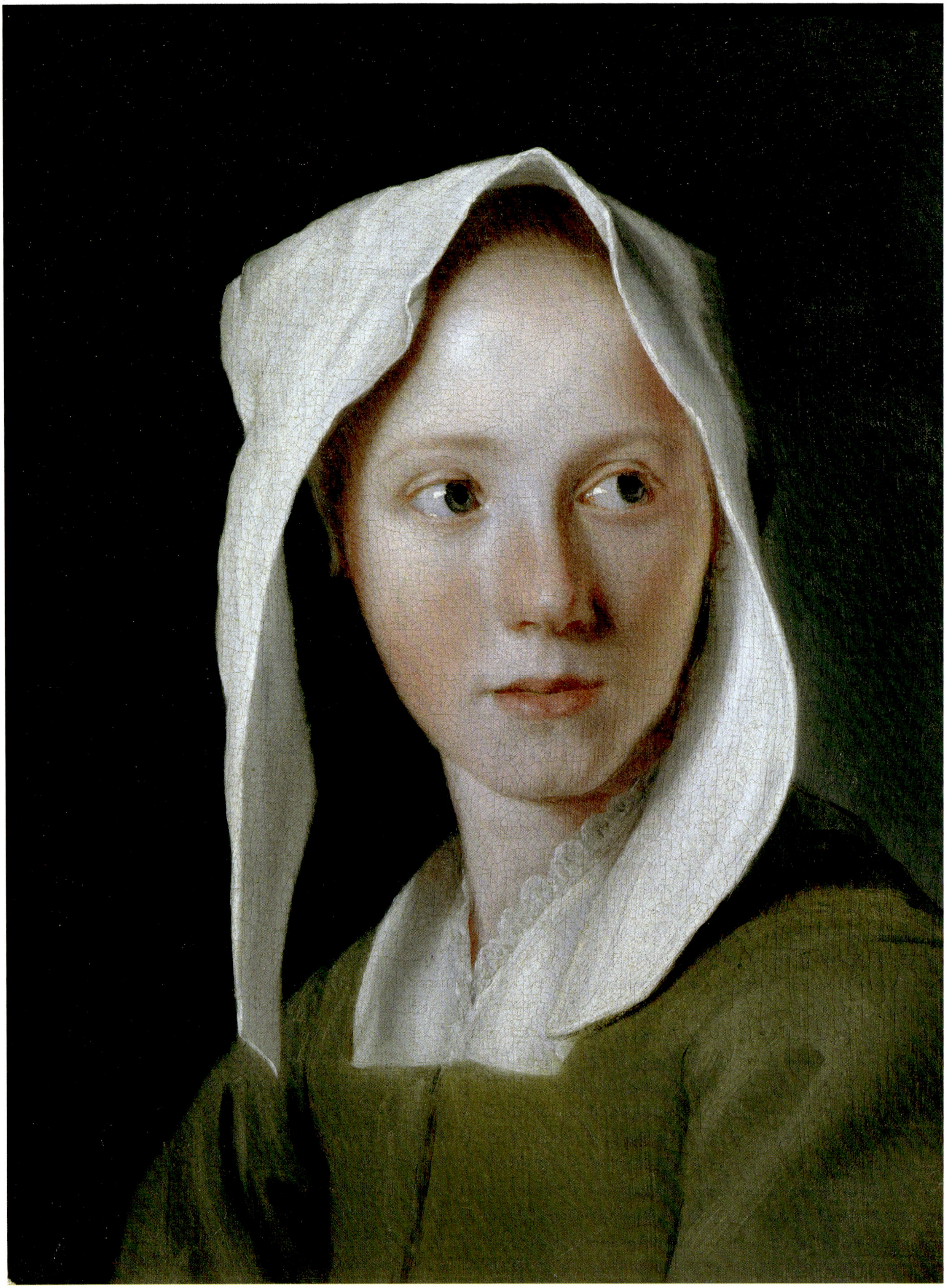

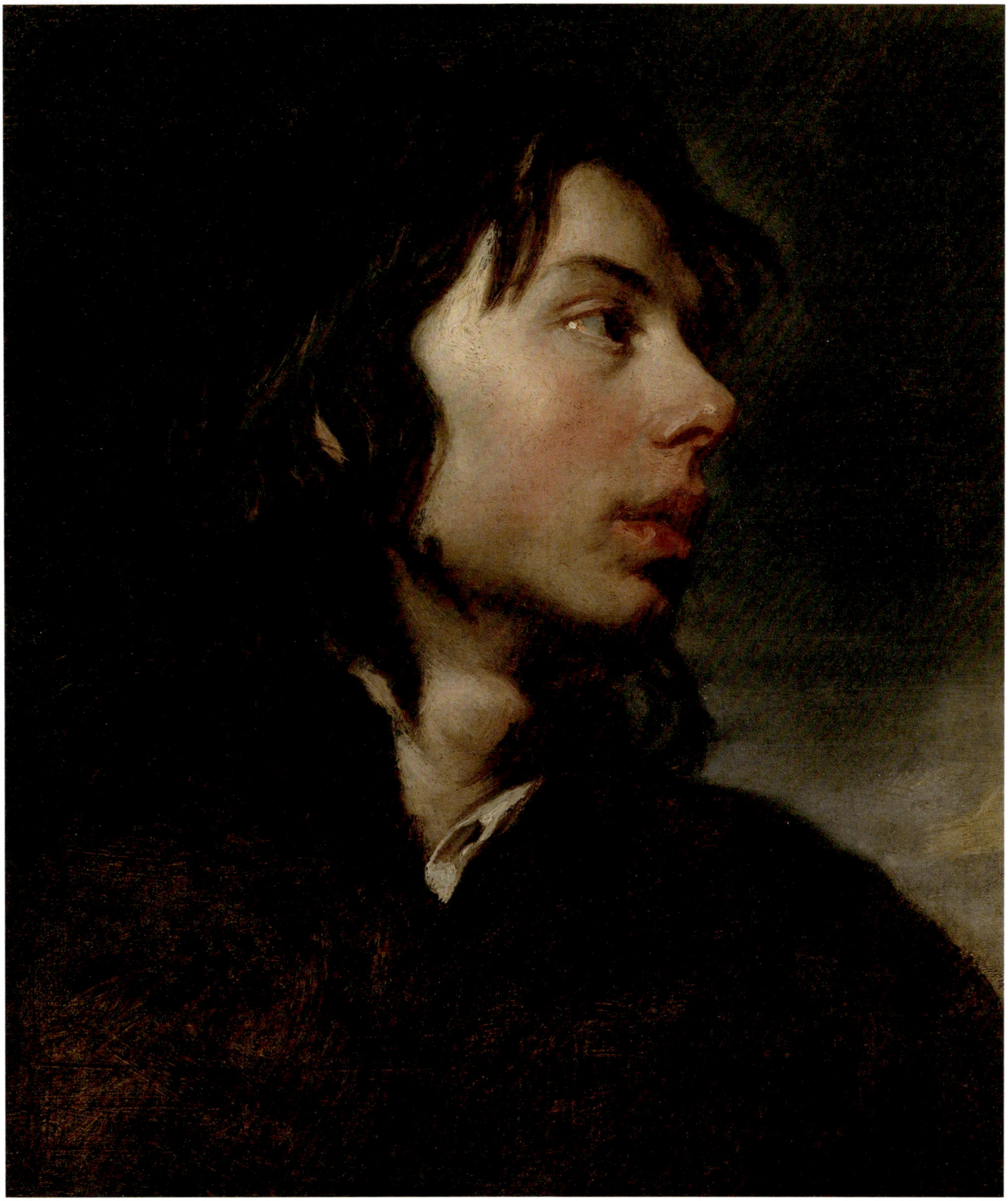

FIG. 118
Michael Sweerts, *Head of a Girl*, c. 1654, oil on canvas, Leicester Museum and Art Gallery, L.F201.1975.0.0

FIG. 119
Jacob van Oost the Younger, *Bust of a Young Man in Profile*, c. 1665, oil on canvas, Mauritshuis, The Hague, 297

FIG. 120
Johannes Vermeer,
Girl with the Red Hat,
c. 1665–1667, oil on
panel, National Gallery
of Art, Washington DC,
1937.1.53

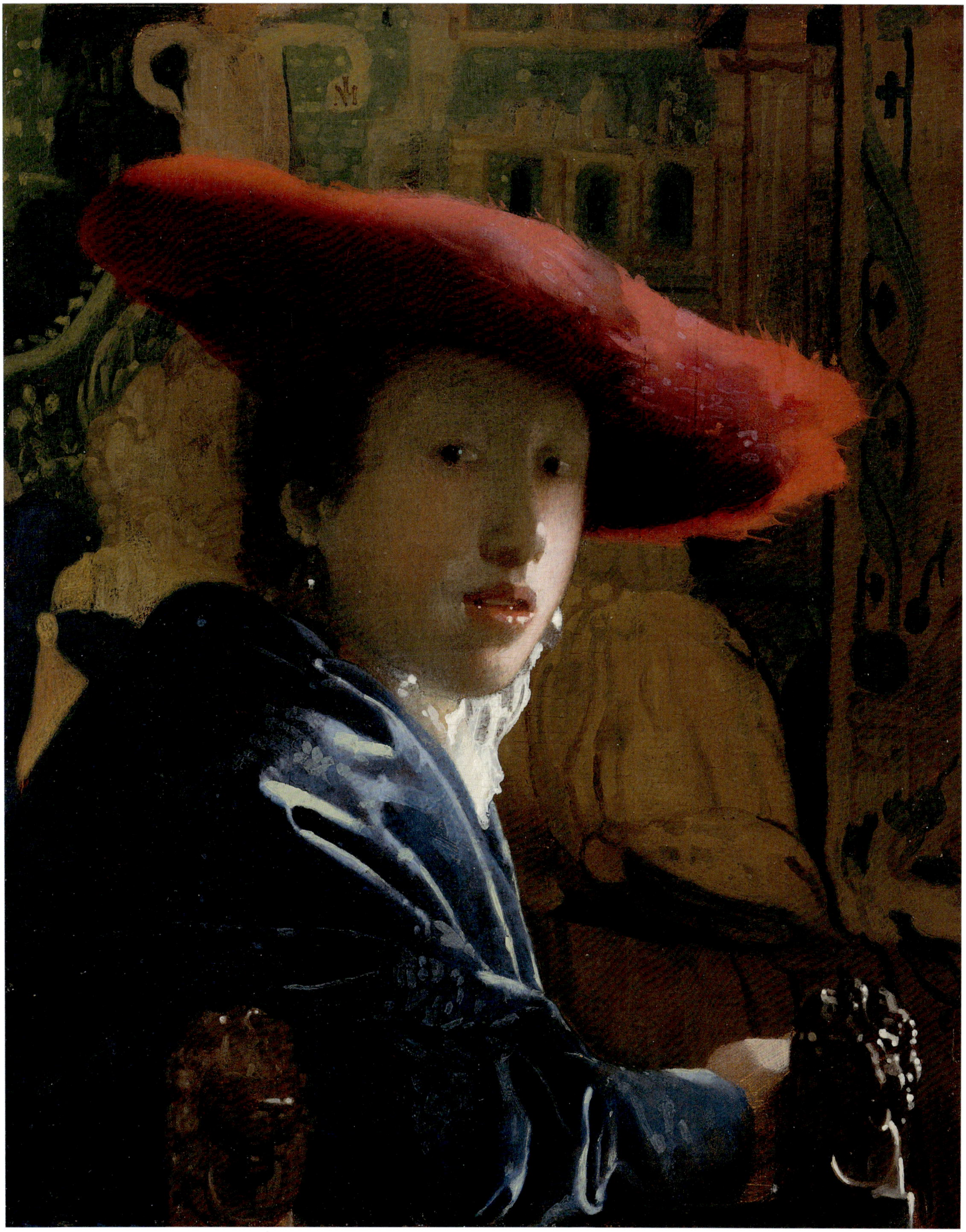

INDEX OF NAMES

BIBLIOGRAPHY

S.n. 2007
s.n. Woordenboek der Nederlandsche Taal, online:<ivdnt.org/woordenboeken/woordenboek-der-nederlandsche-taal/>, 2007, accessed 13 June 2023.

Akdeniz, Toker and Atli 2018
Gulsum Akdeniz, Sila Toker and Ibrahim Atli, 'Neural mechanisms underlying visual pareidolia processing: An fMRI study', in: *Pakistan Journal of Medical Sciences*, 34 (2018), pp. 1560–1566.

Alberti (ed. Grayson) 1972
Leon Battista Alberti. On Painting and On Sculpture. The Latin Texts of *De Pictura* and *De Statua* edited with translations and notes by Cecil Grayson, London, 1972.

Anderson and Kehoe 2023
Carrie Anderson and Marsley L. Kehoe, *JHNA*, 15, vol. 1 (2023).

Angel, Hoyle and Miedema 1996
Philips Angel, Michael Hoyle and Hessel Miedema, 'Praise of Painting', in: *Simiolus*, 24, no. 2/3 (1996).

Arasse 1998
Daniel Arasse, *Leonardo da Vinci: the Rythm of the World.* Translated from the French by Rosetta Translations, Old Saybrook, 1998.

Aristotle/Hett 1936
Aristotle, *Minor Works. On Colours; On Things Heard; Physiognomics; On Plants; On Marvellous Things Heard; Mechanical Problems: On Indivisible Lines; Situations and Names of Winds; On Melissus, Xenophanes, and Gorgias*, English translation by W.S. Hett, Cambridge, Mass./London, 1936.

Atkins 2018
Chris Atkins, 'The Painter's Painter', in: Katrien Lichtert (ed.), *Adriaen Brouwer. Master of Emotions between Rubens and Rembrandt*, exhib. cat. (MOU), Amsterdam, 2018, pp. 115–125.

Bambach 2019
Carmen C. Bambach, *Leonardo da Vinci Rediscovered*, 4 vols., New Haven, 2019.

Barnes et al. 2004
S. Barnes, N. De Poorter, O. Millar, H. Vey, *Van Dyck, A Complete Catalogue of the Paintings*, New Haven-London, 2004.

Barret 2012
Kerry Barrett, *Pieter Soutman. Life and oeuvre* (Oculi: studies in the arts of the Low Countries, 12), Amsterdam, 2012.

Belting 2017
Hans Belting, *Face and Mask. A Double History*, (translated by Thomas S. Hansen and Abby J. Hansen), Princeton (NJ), 2017.

Bettella 2005
Patrizia Bettella, *The Ugly Woman. Transgressive Aesthetic Models in Italian Poetry from the Middle Ages to the Baroque*, Toronto-Buffalo-London, 2005.

Bialostocki 1959
Jan Bialostocki, '"Opus quinque dierum": Dürer's "Christ among the doctors and its sources"*,* in: *Journal of the Warburg and Courtauld Institutes*, XXII (1959), pp. 17–34.

Bodmer 1931
Heinrich Bodmer, *Leonardo, des Meisters Gemälde und Zeichnungen in 360 Abbildungen*, Stuttgart, 1931.

Bos 2010
Jacques Bos, 'Between physiognomy and pathognomy: theoretical perspectives on the representation of characters and emotions in the seventeenth century', in: Katlijne van der Stighelen, Hannelore Magnus and Bert Watteeuw (eds.), *Pokerfaced. Flemish and Dutch Baroque Faces Unveiled*, Turnhout, 2010, pp. 11–24.

Bramly 1991
Serge Bramly, *Leonardo da Vinci. The Artist and the Man.* Translated by Sian Reynolds, London, 1991.

Breukink-Peeze, 1989
Margaret Breukink-Peeze, '"Eene fraaie kleeding, van den turkschen dragt ontleent". Turkse kleding en mode "à la turque" in Nederland', in: Hans Theunissen, Annelies Abelmann and Wim Meulenkamp (eds.), *Topkapı en Turkomanie: Turks-Nederlandse ontmoetingen sinds 1600*, Amsterdam, 1989.

Brown 1993
David Alan Brown, 'The Idealized Portrait in Milan', in: *Arte Lombarda*, no. 67 (1983/1984), pp. 102–116.

Brown 1994
David Alan Brown, 'Leonardo's "Head of an Old Man" in Turin: Portrait or Self-portrait?', in: Miklós Boskovits et al., *Studi di storia dell'arte in onore di Mina Gregori*, Cinisello Balsamo, 1994, pp. 75–77.

Bruce and Young 2012
Vicky Bruce and Andy Young, *Face Perception*, London-New York, 2012.

Bruegel, 1658
Pieter Bruegel, *Toonneel des wereldts: Ontdeckende de ongestuymigheden en ydelheden in woorden ende wercken deser verdorvene eeuwe*, Weesp, 1658.

Brusati, 2021
Celeste Brusati, *Samuel van Hoogstraten's 'Introduction to the Academy of Painting; or, The Visible World'*, translated by Jaap Jacobs, Los Angeles, 2021.

Bruyn et al. 1982
Josua Bruyn, Bob Haak, Simon Levie, Pieter van Thiel and Ernst van de Wetering, *A Corpus of Rembrandt Paintings I*, 1625–1631 The Hague-Boston-London, 1982.

Bückling 2006
Maraike Bückling, 'Der Gähner', in: Frankfurt am Main 2006, exhib. cat., pp. 154–161.

Bulckens 2023
Koen Bulckens, *The Workshop of Peter Paul Rubens (1577–1640)*, Brown University, 2023.

Butterfield 1997
Andrew Butterfield, *The Sculptures of Andrea del Verrocchio*, New Haven-London, 1997.

Butterfield 2001
Andrew Butterfield, 'Verrocchio and the bronze statuette', in: Debra Pincus (ed.), *Small Bronzes in the Renaissance* (Studies in the History of Art, vol. 52), Washington-New Haven, 2001.

Büttner 2006
Nils Büttner, *Landscape Painting: a History*, New York-London, 2006.

Cadogan 1983
Jean K. Cadogan, 'Verrocchio's Drawings Reconsidered', in: *Zeitschrift für Kunstgeschichte*, 46 H. 4 (1983), pp. 367–400.

Caglioti 2008
Francesco Caglioti, 'Fifteenth-century reliefs of ancient emperors and empresses in Florence: production and collecting', in: Nicholas Penny and Eike D. Schmidt (eds.), *Collecting Sculpture in Early Modern Europe*, New Haven 2008, pp. 67–109.

Caglioti 2011
Francesco Caglioti, 'Andrea del Verrocchio e i profili di condottieri antichi per Mattia Corvino', in: Péter Farbaky and Louis A. Waldman (eds.), *Italy & Hungary: humanism and art in the early Renaissance*, Florence, 2011, pp. 505–551.

Capron 2023
Emma Capron (ed.), *The Ugly Duchess. Beauty and Satire in the Renaissance*, exhib. cat. (London – The National Gallery), London, 2023.

Chapman 2010
H. Perry Chapman, 'Reclaiming the Inner Rembrandt: Passion and the Early Self-Portraits', in: Dickey and Roodenburg, 2010, pp. 233–261.

Clark 1988 (1939)
Kenneth Clark, *Leonardo da Vinci*. Introduction by Martin Kemp, London, 1988.

Clark and Pedretti 1968–1969
Kenneth Clark and Carlo Pedretti, *The Drawings of Leonardo da Vinci in the Collection of Her Majesty the Queen at Windsor Castle,* 2nd revised edition, 3 vols., London, 1968–1969.

Corry 2013
Maya Corry, 'The Alluring Beauty of a Leonardesque Ideal: Masculinity and Spirituality in Renaissance Milan', in: *Gender & History*, vol. 25, no. 3, 2013, pp. 565–589.

Cunnally 1993
John Cunnally, 'Numismatic Sources for Leonardo's Equestrian Monuments', in: *Achademia Leonardi Vinci. Journal of Leonardo Studies & Bibliography of Vinciana*, vol. 6 (1993), pp. 67–78.

De Beatis (ed. Pastor) 1905
Die Reise des Cardinals Luigi d'Aragona durch Deutschland, die Niederlande, Frankreich und Oberitalien, 1517–1518 / beschrieben von Antonio de Beatis. Transcribed and annotated by Ludwig Pastor, Freiburg in Breisgau, 1905.

De Clippel 2004
Karolien De Clippel, 'Rubens meets Brouwer', in: *Netherlands Yearbook for History of Art*, 55 (2004).

De Clippel 2006
Karolien De Clippel, 'Two Sides of the Same Coin? Genre Painting in the North and South during the Sixteenth and the Seventeenth Centuries', in: *Simiolus: Netherlands Quarterly for the History of Art*, 32 (2006), pp. 17–34.

De Smet 1977
R. de Smet, 'Een nauwkeuriger datering van Rubens' eerste reis naar Holland in 1612', in: *Jaarboek van het Koninklijk Museum voor Schone Kunsten Antwerpen* (1977).

Devisscher and Vlieghe 2014
Hans Devisscher and Hans Vlieghe, *Corpus Rubenianum Ludwig Burchard: Part V (1): The Life of Christ Before the Passion*, London, 2014.

De Vries 1989
Lyckle de Vries, 'Tronies and Other Single Figured Netherlandish Paintings', in: *Leids Kunsthistorisch Jaarboek*, 8 (1989), pp. 185–202.

De Winkel 2006
Marieke de Winkel, *Fashion and Fancy: Dress and Meaning in Rembrandt's Paintings*, Amsterdam, 2006.

De Witt 2020
David de Witt, 'Study of a Woman in a White Cap', in: Arthur K. Wheelock Jr. and Lara Yeager-Crasselt (eds.), *The Leiden Collection Catalogue*, 3rd edition, 2020, https://theleidencollection.com/artwork/study-of-a-woman-in-a-white-cap/ (accessed March 2023).

Dickey and Roodenburg 2010
Stephanie S. Dickey and Herman Roodenburg, 'Introduction: The Motions of the Mind', in: *The Passions in the Arts of the Early Modern Netherlands*, Nederlands Kunsthistorisch Jaarboek, 60 (2010), pp. 7–16.

D'Hulst 1974
Roger-A. d'Hulst, *Jordaens Drawings* (Monographs of the Nationaal Centrum voor de Plastische Kunsten van de XVIde and XVIIde eeuw V), Brussels, 1974.

Duparc, Dierckx and Neff 2011
Frits Duparc, Femke Diercks and Terry Ann R. Neff, *Golden: Dutch and Flemish masterworks from the Rose-Marie and Eijk van Otterloo Collection*, exhib. cat. (Salem – Peabody Essex Museum – San Francisco, Fine Arts Museums – Houston, Museum of Fine Arts), Salem, 2011.

Duverger 1973
E. Duverger, 'Arnout Vinckenborch, een weinig bekend schilder te Antwerpen uit het begin van de XVIIde eeuw', in: *Jaarboek Koninklijk Museum voor Schone Kunsten Antwerpen* (1973).

Duverger 2001
Erik Duverger, *Antwerpse Kunstinventarissen uit de Zeventiende Eeuw II 1680–1689*, Brussels, 2001.

Duverger 2002
Erik Duverger, *Antwerpse kunstinventarissen uit de Zeventiende Eeuw 12 (1690–1699)*, Brussels, 2002.

Eaker 2015
Adam Eaker, 'Van Dyck between Master and Model', in: *Art Bulletin*, 97, no. 2 (June 2015).

Edinburgh/London 2002-2003
Martin Clayton (ed.), *Leonardo da Vinci. The divine and the grotesque*, exhib. cat. (The Queen's Gallery – Holyroodhouse; Edinburgh – The Queen's Gallery; London – Buckingham Palace), 2002–2003.

Eisenberg 2019
Elizabeth A. Eisenberg, 'A Verrocchio Sculpture as a Source for Leonardo and Raphael: The Evidence of Drawings', in: *Master Drawings*, 57, no. 1 (2019), pp. 5–32.

Ekkart et al. s.d.
Rudi Ekkart, Michel Franken, Anne van Grevenstein and Maud Lankester (eds.), *De Oranjezaal. Catalogus en Documentatie*, online: <htttp://oranjezaal.rkd monographs.nl/>, accessed 1 July 2018

Esposito 2020
Teresa Esposito, 'Black Ethiopians and the Origin of "materia Prima". Rubens' Images of Creation', in: *Oud Holland*, 133, 2020 (1), pp. 10–32.

Farago 1992
Claire J. Farago, *Leonardo da Vinci's* 'Paragone'. *A Critical Interpretation with a New Edition of the Text in the Codex Urbinas*, Leiden-New York-Copenhagen-Cologne, 1992.

Filarete (ed. Spencer) 1965
Treatise on Architecture; being the Treatise by Antonio di Piero Averlino, Known as Filarete. Translated with an Introduction and Notes by John R. Spencer, 2 vols., New Haven-London, 1965.

Florence 2005
Vanna Arrighi, Anna Bellinazzi and Edoardo Villata (eds.), *Leonardo da Vinci. La vera imagine. Documenti e testimonianze sulla vita e sull'opera*, exhib. cat. (Florence – Archivio di Stato) Florence, 2005.

Florence 2006
Paulo Galuzzi et al. (eds.), *The Mind of Leonardo* [*The Universal Genius at Work*], exhib. cat. (Florence – Galleria degli Uffizi), Florence, 2006 (*La mente di Leonardo.* [*Nel laboratorio del Genio Universale*], 2006).

Florence 2019
Francesco Cagliotti and Andrea De Marchi (eds.), *Verrocchio. Maestro di Leonardo*, exhib. cat. (Florence – Palazzo Strozzi & Museo Nazionale del Bargello), Venice, 2019.

Frankfurt am Main 2006-2007
Maraike Bückling (ed.), *Die phantastischen Köpfe des Franz Xaver Messerschmidt*, exhib. cat. (Liebieghaus, Skulpturensammlung), Frankfurt am Main, 2006–2007

Freedberg 1984
David Freedberg, *The Life of Christ after the Passion* (Corpus Rubenianum Ludwig Burchard VI), Turnhout-London, 1984.

Galesloot 1868
L. Galesloot, 'Un procès pour une vente de tableaux attribués à Antoine van Dyck', in: *Annales de l'Académie d'archéologie de Belgique*, XXIV (1868), pp. 561–565.

Goeree 1670
Wilhelmus Goeree, *Inleydingh tot de practijck der algemeene schilder-konst*, Middelburg, 1670, pp. 50–51.

Gombrich 1976
Ernst H. Gombrich, 'The Grotesque Heads', in: *The Heritage of Apelles. Studies in the art of the Renaissance*, Oxford, 1976, pp. 57–75.

Gottwald 2011
Franziska Gottwald, *Das Tronie. Muster, Studie und Meisterwerk. Die Genese Einer Gattung der Malerei vom 15. Jahrhundert bis zu Rembrandt* (Kunstwissenschaftlichen Studien 184), Berlin-Munich, 2011.

Grollemund 2013
Hélène Grollemund, in: Blaise Ducos, Olivia Savatier Sjöholm et al. (eds.), *Un Allemand à la cour de Louis XIV. De Dürer à Van Dyck, la collection nordique d'Everhard Jabach*, exhib. cat. (Paris – Musée du Louvre), Paris, 2013.

Haarlem 2018
Michael W. Kwakkelstein with Michiel Plomp, *Leonardo da Vinci. The Language of Faces*, exhib. cat. (Haarlem – Teylers Museum), Bussum, 2018.

Held 1965
Julius S. Held, 'Notes on Jacob Jordaens', in: *Oud Holland*, 80 (1965), pp. 112–122.

Held 1979
Julius S. Held, 'Rubens and Aguilonius: New Points of Contact', in: *The Art Bulletin*, 61 (1979), pp. 257–264.

Held 1982
Julius S. Held, *Rubens and his Circle: Studies*. Princeton, 1982.

Hemmer 2015
Marloes W. Hemmer, 'Artistic transmission in the Low Countries. De Grebber's creative imitation of Rubens', in: *De Zeventiende Eeuw*, 31 (2015) 1.

Hinterding and Rutgers 2013
Erik Hinterding and Jaco Rutgers, *Rembrandt I, 1625-1635. The New Hollstein Dutch & Flemish Etchings, Engravings and Woodcuts 1450–1700*, Oudekerk aan den IJsel, 2013.

Hirschfelder 2008
Dagmar Hirschfelder, *Tronie und Porträt in der Niederländischen Malerei des 17. Jahrhunderts*, Berlin, 2008.

Hirschfelder 2009
Dagmar Hirschfelder, 'Tronie und bürgerliches Kostümporträt im Werk Rembrandts und seiner Nachfolger', in: *Jahrbuch der Berliner Museen*, new series 51, supplement, 2009.

Hirschfelder and Krempel 2014
Dagmar Hirschfelder and León Krempel, eds., *Tronies: Das Gesicht der Frühen Neuzeit*, Berlin, 2014.

Hirschmann 1920
Otto Hirschmann, 'Balthasar Gerbiers Eer ende Claght-dight ter eeren van Henricus Goltius', in: *Oud Holland*, 1920, vol. 38 (1920).

Hollander 2011
Martha Hollander, 'Vermeer's Robe: Costume, Commerce, and Fantasy in the Early Modern Netherlands', in: *Dutch Crossing,* 35, no. 2 (2011).

Horn and Van Leeuwen, 2021
Hendrick J. Horn and Rieke van Leeuwen, *Houbraken Translated. Arnold Houbraken's Great Theatre of the Netherlandish Painters and Paintresses*, vol. 1 (2021) 261, https://houbraken-translated.rkdstudies.nl/1-240-289/page-250-259/ (accessed March 2023).

Houbraken 1718
Arnold Houbraken, *De groote schouburgh der Nederlantsche konstschilders en schilderessen*, vol. 1, Amsterdam, 1718.

Huvenne 2020
Paul Huvenne, 'Minerva', in: Katharina Van Cauteren (ed.), *From Memling to Rubens: The Golden Age of Flanders,* Antwerp-Veurne, 2020.

Huygens 1987
Constantijn Huygens, *Mijn jeugd*, ed. C.L. Heesakkers, Amsterdam, 1987.

Hymans 1882
H. Hymans, 'Un voyage artistique de Rubens ignoré', in: *Bulletin de l'Académie royale de Belgique*, 3rd series, XXIV (1882).

Ilsink et al. 2016
Matthijs Ilsink et al., *Hieronymus Bosch painter and draughtsman: catalogue raisonné* (translated by Ted Alkins; 's-Hertogenbosch Bosch Research and Conservation Project), Brussels, 2016.

Isaacson 2017
Walter Isaacson, *Leonardo da Vinci*, New York, 2017.

Jombert 1773
Charles-Antoine Jombert, *Théorie de la figure humaine, considérée dans ses principes, soit en repos ou movement*, Paris, 1773.

Judson 2000
Richard J. Judson, *The Passion of Christ* (Corpus Rubenianum Ludwig Burchard VII), Turnhout-London, 2000.

Kelch 1986
Jan Kelch, *Der Man mit dem Goldhelm: Eine Dokumentation der Gemäldegalerie in Zusammenarbeit mit dem Rathgen-Forschungslabor SMPK und dem Hahn-Meitner-Institut Berlin*, Berlin, 1986.

Kemp 2006
Martin Kemp, *Leonardo da Vinci. The Marvellous Works of Nature and Man*, Oxford, 2006 (first edition 1981).

Kemp and Barone 2010
Martin Kemp and Juliana Barone, *I Disegni di Leonardo da Vinci e della sua Cerchia nelle Collezioni della Gran Bretagna*, Florence, 2010.

Kemp and Walker 1989
Martin Kemp and Margaret Walker (eds.), *Leonardo on Painting: An Anthology of Writings*, New Haven-London, 1989.

Kern 2014
Ulrike Kern, *Light and Shade in Dutch and Flemish Art. A History of Chiaroscuro in Art Theory and Artistic Practice in the Netherlands of the Seventeenth and Eighteenth Centuries* (Art Theory (1400–1800) 7), Turnhout, 2014.

Kirchner 2014
Thomas Kirchner, 'Ausdruckstheorien von der Antike bis zum 18. Jahrhundert', in: Dagmar Hirschfelder and Léon Krempel (eds.), *Tronies. Das Gesicht in der Frühen Neuzeit*, Berlin, 2014, pp. 11–24.

Kirchner 2006
Thomas Kirchner, 'Franz Xaver Messerschmidt und die Konstruktion des Ausdrucks', in: Maraike Bückling (ed.), *Die phantastischen Köpfe des Franz Xaver Messerschmidt*, exhib. cat. (Frankfurt am Main – Liebieghaus Skulpturensammlung), Munich, 2006, pp. 266-281.

Kleinert 2006
Katja Kleinert, *Atelierdarstellungen in der niederländischen Genremalerei. Realistisches Abbild oder glaubwürdiger Schein?* (Studien zur internationalen Architektur und Kunstgeschichte), Petersberg, 2006.

Kolfin 2008
Elmer Kolfin, 'Zwarte modellen in de Nederlandse kunst tussen 1580 en 1800. Feit en fictie', in: Elmer Kolfin and Esther Schreuder, *Black is Beautiful. Rubens tot Dumas*, exhib. cat. (Amsterdam – De Nieuwe Kerk), Zwolle, 2008, pp. 70–87.

Kolfin 2017
Elmer Kolfin, 'When Africans Became Black. Dürer, Rubens and the Changing Image of Africans in Northern Europe', in: *Print Quarterly*, 34, no. 4 (December 2017), pp. 379–392.

Kolfin 2020
Elmer Kolfin, 'Black in the Art of Rembrandt's Time', in: Elmer Kolfin and Epco Runia (eds.), *Black in Rembrandt's Time*, exhib. cat. (Amsterdam – Museum Het Rembrandthuis), Zwolle: WBOOKS, 2020, pp. 12–37.

Koreny 2002
Fritz Koreny (ed.), *Early Netherlandish Drawings from Jan van Eyck to Hiëronymus Bosch*, Antwerp, 2002.

Kultzen 1996
Rolf Kultzen, *Michael Sweerts: Brussels 1618 – Goa 1664* (Aetas Aurea: Monographs on Dutch & Flemish Painting 12), Doornspijk, 1996.

Kwakkelstein 1991
Michael W. Kwakkelstein, 'Leonardo da Vinci's grotesque heads and the breaking of the physiognomic mould', in: *Journal of the Warburg and Courtauld Institutes*, vol. 54, 1991, pp. 127–136

Kwakkelstein 2014a
Michael W. Kwakkelstein, *Leonardo da Vinci as a physiognomist. Theory and Drawing Practice*, Leiden, 2014 (first edition 1994).

Kwakkelstein 2014b
Michael W. Kwakkelstein, 'Leonardo da Vinci's Recurrent Use of Patterns of Individual Limbs, Stock Poses, and Facial Stereotypes' in: Ingrid Ciulisová (ed.), *Artistic Innovations and Cultural Zones* (Spectrum Slovakia Series, Vol. 7), Frankfurt am Main, 2014, pp. 45–61.

Kwakkelstein 2019
Michael W. Kwakkelstein, 'Disegni di volti mostruosi di uomini e donne anziani come critica morale', in: Annalise Perissa Torrini (ed.), *Leonardo da Vinci. L'uomo modello del mondo*, exhib. cat. (Venice – Gallerie dell' Accademia), Venice, 2019, pp. 43–51

Kwakkelstein 2023
Michael W. Kwakkelstein, 'Leonardo da Vinci's Drawings of Busts of Old Men and Women with Monstrous Faces: Satire as Moral Criticism', Lucia Tantardini and Rebecca Norris (eds.), *Grotesque and Caricature: Leonardo to Bernini* (Brill Studies on Art, Art History, and Intellectual History, vol. 68), Leiden/Toronto, 2023, pp. 13–37.

Lammertse 2002
Friso Lammertse, 'Van Dyck's Apostle series, Hendrick Uylenburgh and Sigismund III', in: *The Burlington Magazine*, 144, no. 1188 (March 2002), pp. 140–146.

Lange 1911
Julius Lange, *Studien über Leonardo da Vinci*, translated from Danish by Ida Jacob-Anders, Strasbourg, 1911.

Larsen 1988
Erik Larsen, *The Paintings of Anthony van Dyck*, vol. 2. Freren, 1988.

Laurenza 2001
Domenico Laurenza, *De figura umana: fisiognomica, anatomia ed arte in Leonardo* (Biblioteca di Nuncius. Studi e testi), Florence, 2001.

Lavater 1775-1778
Johann Kaspar Lavater, *Physiognomische Fragmente zur Beförderung der Menschenkenntnis und Menschenliebe*, Leipzig and Winterthur, 1775–1778.

Leonardo/McMahon 1956
Leonardo da Vinci, *Treatise on Painting* [*Codex Urbinas Latinus 1270*], Translated and annotated by A. Philip McMahon with an introduction by Ludwig H. Heydenreich, 2 vols., New Jersey, 1956.

Libby et al. 2022
Alexandra Libby, Melanie Gifford, Dina Anchin, Marjorie E. Wieseman, Kathryn A. Dooley, Lisha Deming Glinsman and John K. Delaney, 'Experimentation and Innovation in Vermeer's *Girl with the Red Hat*: New Findings from the National Gallery of Art', in: *Journal of Historians of Netherlandish Art*, 14.2 (2022), online: <doi:10.5092/jhna.2022.14.2.2>, accessed 17 March 2023.

Libby 2022
Alexandra Libby, 'Johannes Vermeer/ Girl with the Red Hat/ c. 1669', in: *Dutch Paintings of the Seventeenth Century* (NGA Online Editions, 2022), https://purl.org/nga/collection/artobject/60 (accessed February 2023).

Lichtert 2018
Katrien Lichtert, 'Adriaen Brouwer. Master of Emotions', in: Katrien Lichtert (ed.), *Adriaen Brouwer. Master of Emotions between Rubens and Rembrandt*, exhib. cat. (Oudenaarde – MOU), Amsterdam, 2018, pp. 79–95.

Little et al. 2011
Anthony C. Little, Benedict C. Jones and Lisa M. DeBruine, 'The many Faces of Research on Face Perception', in: *Philosophical Transaction of the Royal Society. Biological Sciences,* 366 (2011).

Lohse Belkin 1980
Kristin Lohse Belkin, *Corpus Rubenianum Ludwig Burchard: Part XXIV: The Costume Book*, Brussels, 1980.

Lomazzo 1584
Giovanni Paulo Lomazzo, *Trattato Dell' Arte Della Pittura, Scultura et Architetettura*, Milan, 1584.

London 1989
Martin Kemp and Jane Roberts (eds.) *Leonardo da Vinci*, exhib. cat. (London – Hayward Gallery), New Haven-London, 1989.

London 1996-1997
Martin Clayton (ed.), *Leonardo da Vinci. A Curious Vision*, exhib. cat. (London – The Queen's Gallery, Buckingham Palace), London, 1996.

London 2010
Hugo Chapman and Marzia Faietti (eds.), *Fra Angelico to Leonardo. Italian Renaissance Drawings*, exhib. cat. (London – The British Museum), London, 2010.

London 2011
Luke Syson and Larry Keith et al. (eds.), *Leonardo da Vinci. Painter at the Court of Milan*, exhib. cat. (London – The National Gallery), London, 2011.

London 2023
Emma Capron (ed.), with essays by Martin Clayton and Charlotte Wytema, *The Ugly Duchess: beauty and satire in the Renaissance*, exhib. cat. (London – The National Gallery), New Haven-London 2023.

Lugano 1998
Giulio Bora, Manuela Kahn-Rossi, Francesco Porzio et al. (eds.), *Rabisch. Il grottesco nell'arte del Cinquecento; l'Accademia della Val di Blenio, Lomazzo e l'ambiente milanese*, exhib. cat. (Lugano – Museo Cantonale d'Arte), Milan, 1998.

Magurn 1955
Ruth Saunders Magurn (ed.), *The Letters of Peter Paul Rubens*, Cambridge (MA), 1955 (reprinted 1977).

Manuth et al. 2016
Volker Manuth, 'Der Maler als Heiliger: Aspekte des Künstler-"portrait historié"', in: Volker Manuth, Rudie van Leeuwen and Jos Koldeweij (eds.), *Example or Alter Ego? Aspects of the 'Portrait historié' in Western Art from Antiquity to the Present*, Turnhout, 2016.

Marcaida 2014
José Ramón Marcaida, 'Rubens and the Bird of Paradise. Painting Natural Knowledge in the Early Seventeenth Century', in: *Renaissance Studies*, 28, no. 1 (2014).

McGrath 2008
Elizabeth McGrath, 'Rubens and his Black Kings', in: *Rubens bulletin. Koninklijk Museum voor Schone Kunsten Antwerpen*, II, 2008, pp. 87–101.

Meij and De Haan 2001
A.W.F.M. Meij and Maartje de Haan (eds.), *Rubens, Jordaens, Van Dyck and Their Circle: Flemish Master Drawings from the Museum Boijmans van Beuningen*, Rotterdam, 2001.

Melion 2022
Walter S. Melion, *Karel van Mander and his Foundation of the Noble Free Art of Painting*, Leiden, 2022.

Meller 1963
Peter Meller, 'Physiognomical theory in Renaissance heroic portraits', in: *The Renaissance and Mannerism. Studies in Western Art. Acts of the 20th International congress of the history of art*, New Jersey, vol. 2, 1963, pp. 53–69.

Mendola 1999
Giovanni Mendola, 'Van Dyck in Sicily', in: *Van Dyck (1599–1641)*, exhib. cat., Antwerp-London, 1999, p. 61, noot 18.

Merle du Bourg and Joubert 2012
Alexis Merle du Bourg and Caroline Joubert, 'Un modèle et ses peintres', in: C. Joubert, A. Merle du Bourg (ed.), *Jacob Jordaens et son modèle Abraham Grapheus – l'oeuvre en question – 8*, Caen-Ghent, 2012, pp. 4–34.

Metzger 2019
Christof Metzger, 'The Heller Altarpiece', in: Christof Metzger and Julia Zaunbauer, *Albrecht Dürer*, exhib. cat., Vienna, 2019, pp. 302–315.

Miedema 2017
Hessel Miedema, *Theorie En Praktijk. Teksten over Schilderkunst in de Gouden Eeuw van de Noordelijke Nederlanden*, Hilversum, 2017.

Moes 1886
E.W. Moes, 'Gerard ter Borch en zijne familie', in: *Oud Holland*, 4 (1886), pp. 146–163.

Muller Hofstede 1965
Justus Müller Hofstede, 'Beiträge Zum Zeichnerischen Werk von Rubens', in: *Wallraf-Richartz-Jahrbuch*, 27 (1965), pp. 259–365.

Muylle 2001
Jan Muylle, 'Tronies toegeschreven aan Pieter Bruegel. Fysionomie en expressie (1)', in: *De Zeventiende Eeuw*, 17 (2001), pp. 174–204.

Muylle 2002
Jan Muylle, 'Tronies toegeschreven aan Pieter Bruegel. Fysionomie en Expressie (2)': in: *De Zeventiende Eeuw*, 18 (2002).

Muylle 2011
Jan Muylle, 'Ethos en pathos. De literaire appreciatie van expressie in het werk van Metsijs en Bruegel', in: *Netherlands Yearbook for Art History*, 60 (2011), pp. 19–33.

Muylle 2014
Jan Muylle, 'Von Tronies antiker Philosophen. Lagneau und Rembrandt', in: Hirschfelder/Krempel, 2014, pp. 81–87.

Nathan 2002
Johannes Nathan, 'Motiv und Methode: zur Wechselwirkung von Arbeitspraxis und Denkweise bei Leonardo da Vinci', in: Frank Fehrenbach (ed.), *Leonardo da Vinci: Natur im Übergang: Beiträge zu Wissenschaft, Kunst und Technik*, Munich, 2002, pp. 347-370.

Nicholl 2004
C. Nicholl, *Leonardo da Vinci. The Flights of the Mind*, London, 2004.

Nuttall 2021
Paula Nuttall, 'Low Life in High Society: a Group of Comic-Grotesque Drawings by Verrocchio', in: *Renaissance Studies*, 2, vol. 35, 2021, pp. 287–317.

Oberthaler 2018
Elke Oberthaler, Sabine Pénot, Manfred Sellink, Ron Spronk, Sabine Haag (ed.), *Bruegel: The Hand of the Master*, exhib. cat. (Vienna – Kunsthistorisches Museum), Vienna-Veurne, 2018, passim.

Pade 2008
Marianne Pade, 'The Reception of Plutarch's Lives in Fifteenth-Century Italy', in: *Renaissance Quarterly*, vol. 61, no. 2 (summer 2008), pp. 499–501.

Palmer and Clifford 2020
Colin J. Palmer and Colin W.G. Clifford, 'Face Pareidolia Recruits Mechanisms for Detecting Human Social Attention', in: *Psychological Science*, 31 (2020), online <https://doi.org/10.1177/0956797620924814>.

Panofsky 1948
Erwin Panofsky, *Albrecht Dürer*, Princeton (NJ), 1948.

Panofsky 1955
Erwin Panofsky, *The Life and Art of Albrecht Dürer*, Princeton (NJ), 1955

Parshall 2013
Peter Parshall, 'Graphic Knowledge: Albrecht Dürer and the Imagination', in: *The Art Bulletin*, 95, 3 (September 2013), pp. 393–410.

Payne 1978
Robert Payne, *Leonardo*, New York, 1978.

Pedretti 1977
Carlo Pedretti, *The Literary Works of Leonardo da Vinci compiled and edited from the original manuscripts by Jean Paul Richter. Commentary*, 2 vols., Oxford, 1977.

Pedretti and Vecce 1995
Carlo Pedretti and Carlo Vecce (eds.), *Leonardo da Vinci, Libro di Pittura: Codice Urbinate lat. 1270 nella Biblioteca Apostolica Vaticana*. 2 vols. Florence, 1995.

Planiscig 1927
Leo Planiscig, 'Leonardos Porträte und Aristoteles', in: *Festschrift für Julius Schlosser zum 60. geburtstage herausgegeben von Árpád Weixlgärtner und Leo Planiscig*, Zürich, 1927.

Pliny the Elder 2005
Pliny the Elder, *De wereld. Naturalis historia*, Dutch translation by Joost van Gelder, Mark Nieuwenhuis and Ton Peters, Amsterdam, 2005.

Pliny/Rackham 1938
Pliny, *Natural History*, translation by H. Rackham, 10 volumes (Loeb Classical Library, vol. IX, books 33–35), London-Cambridge, Mass., 1938.

Plutarch/Perrin 1926
Plutarch, *Lives: Aratus. Artaxerxes. Galba. Otho.* Translation Bernadotte Perrin (Loeb Classical Library, vol. XI), London-Cambridge Mass., 1926.

Popham 1994 (1945)
Arthur E. Popham, *The Drawings of Leonardo da Vinci.* Revised and with a new introductory essay by Martin Kemp, London, 1994.

Potterton 1986
Homan Potterton, *Dutch Seventeenth and Eighteenth Century Paintings in the National Gallery of Ireland*, Dublin, 1986.

Pousão-Smith 2001
Maria-Isabella Pousão-Smith, 'Quinten Matsys and Seventeenth-Century Antwerp: An artist and his uses', in: *Jaarboek Koninklijk Museum voor Schone Kunsten Antwerpen* (2001), pp. 137–189.

Price 2003
David Hotchkiss Price, *Albrecht Dürer's Renaissance: humanism, reformation and the art of faith*, Ann Arbor, 2003.

Ribeiro 2017
Aileen Ribeiro, *Clothing Art: The Visual Culture of Fashion, 1600–1914*, New Haven-London, 2017.

Richter 1970
Jean Paul Richter, *The Literary Works of Leonardo da Vinci compiled and edited from the original manuscripts*, 2 volumes, London, 1970 (first edition 1883).

Ripa 1603
Cesare Ripa, *Iconologia: Overo descrittione di diverse imagini cauate dall'antichita, & di propria inuentione*, Rome, 1603.

Ripa and Tempest 1709
Cesare Ripa and P. Tempest, *Iconologia: Or, Moral Emblems*, London, 1709.

Robinson 2018
William W. Robinson, 'A Book of Indian Drawings, by Rembrandt, 25 in Number', in: Stephanie Schrader (ed.), *Rembrandt and the Inspiration of India*, exhib. cat. (Malibu – The J. Paul Getty Museum), Los Angeles, 2018.

Roelofs 2023a
Pieter Roelofs, 'Closer to Vermeer: A Look Inside the Family Home of the Delft Painter', in: Pieter Roelofs and Gregor J.M. Weber (eds.), *Vermeer*, exhib. cat. (Amsterdam – Rijksmuseum), Amsterdam-Veurne, 2023.

Roelofs 2023b
Pieter Roelofs, 'Vermeer's Tronies: An Outward Gaze of Connection', in: Pieter Roelofs and Gregor J.M. Weber (eds.), *Vermeer*, exhib. cat. (Amsterdam – Rijksmuseum), Amsterdam-Veurne, 2023.

Roelofs and Weber 2023
Pieter Roelofs and Gregor J.M. Weber, *Vermeer*, exhib. cat. (Amsterdam – Rijksmuseum), Amsterdam-Veurne, 2023

Roland 1984
Margaret Roland, 'Van Dyck's Early Workshop, the "Apostle" Series, and the "Drunken Silenus"', in: *Art Bulletin*, LXVI (1984), pp. 211–223.

Rooses-Ruelens 1887-1909
Max Rooses and Charles Ruelens (eds.), *Correspondance de Rubens et documents épistolaires concernant sa vie et ses oeuvres*, I-VI, Antwerp, 1887–1909.

Rublack 2021
Ulinka Rublack, 'Befeathering the European: Feathers as Matter in the European Renaissance', in: *American Historical Review*, 126, vol. 1 (2021).

Rupprich 1956
Hans Rupprich, *Dürers Schriftlicher Nachlass*, Berlin, 1956.

Sander and Schulz 2013
Jochen Sander and Johann Schulz, '"I will make something that not many can equal". Dürer and the *Heller Altarpiece*', in: Jochen Sander (ed.), *Albrecht Dürer. His Art in Context*, Frankfurt, 2013.

Scheller 1995
Robert W. Scheller, *Exemplum. Model-Book Drawings and the Practice of Artistic Transmission in the Middle Ages (ca. 900–ca. 1470)*, Amsterdam, 1995.

Schnackenburg 2001
Bernhard Schnackenburg, 'Young Rembrandt's "Rough Manner": A Painting Style and Its Sources', in: Ernst van de Wetering and Bernhard Schnackenburg (eds.), *The Mystery of the Young Rembrandt*, exhib. cat. (Kassel – Museum Schloss Wilhelmshöhe, Gemäldegalerie Alte Meister; Amsterdam – Museum Het Rembrandthuis), Wolfratshausen, 2001.

Schütt 2021
Friederike Schütt, *Quentin Massys. Bildstrategien der Affekterzeugung*, Petersberg, 2021.

Schwartz 1989
Frederic Schwartz, '"The Motions of the Countenance": Rembrandt's Early Portraits and the Tronie', in: *Anthropology and Aesthetics*, 17/18 (spring–autumn, 1989).

Schwartz 2014
Gary Schwartz, 'Emotions: Pain and Pleasure in Dutch Painting of the Golden Age', in: *Emotions. Pain and Pleasure in Dutch Painting of the Golden Age*, exhib. cat. (Haarlem – Frans Hals Museum), Haarlem-Rotterdam, 2014, pp. 10–88.

Schwartz 2020
Gary Schwartz, 'Convention and Uniqueness: Rembrandt's Response to the East', in: Bodo Brinkmann et al. (eds.), *Rembrandt's Orient: West Meets East in Dutch Art of the 17th Century*, exhib. cat. (Basel – Kunstmuseum Basel; Potsdam – Museum Barberini), Munich-London-New York, 2020.

Scott and Hillyard 2019
Jennifer Scott and Helen Hillyard (eds.), *Rembrandt's Light*, exhib. cat. (London – Dulwich Picture Gallery; Amsterdam – Museum Rembrandthuis), London, 2019.

Sellink 2007
Manfred Sellink, *Bruegel: The Complete Paintings, Drawings and Prints*, Ghent, 2007.

Sellink 2012
Manfred Sellink, *Bruegel. Het volledige werk*, Ghent, 2012.

Siegfried 1995
Susan L. Siegfried, *The Art of Louis-Léopold Boilly. Modern Life in Napoleonic France*, New Haven, 1995.

Silver 1984
Larry Silver, *The Paintings of Quentin Massys with Catalogue raisonné*, Oxford, 1984.

Silver 2006
Larry Silver, *Peasant Scenes and Landscapes. The Rise of Pictorial Genres in the Antwerp Art Market*, Philadelphia, 2006.

Silver 2014
Larry Silver, 'Leonardo in the lowlands', in: Ingrid Ciulisová (ed.), *Artistic innovations and cultural zones*, Frankfurt am Main, 2014.

Sluijter 1991
Eric Jan Sluijter, 'Vertumnus en Pomona door Hendrick Goltzius (1613) en Jan Tengnagel (1617). Constanten en Contrasten in vorm en inhoud', in: *Bulletin van het Rijksmuseum*, 39 (1991).

Surh s.d.
Dominique Surh, 'Self-Portrait (?) at an Easel', in: Arthur Wheelock Jr. and Yeager-Crasselt, *The Leiden Collection Catalogue*, https://theleidencollection.com/artwork/self-portrait-at-an-easel/ (accessed March 2023).

Swan 2021
Claudia Swan, *Rarities of These Lands: Art, Trade, and Diplomacy in the Dutch Republic*, Princeton-Oxford, 2021.

Taylor 1992
Paul Taylor, 'The Concept of *Houding* in Dutch Art Theory', in: *Journal of the Warburg and Courtauld Institutes*, 55 (1992), pp. 210–232.

Taylor 1998
Paul Taylor, 'The Glow in Late Sixteenth and Seventeenth Century Dutch Paintings', in: *Leids Kunsthistorisch Jaarboek,* 11 (1998), pp. 159–178.

Taylor 2008
Paul Taylor, 'Flatness in Dutch Art: Theory and Practice', in: *Oud Holland*, 121 (2008), pp. 153–184.

Van Thiel-Stroman s.d.
Irene van Thiel-Stroman, 'De documenten over Frans Hals. Geschreven en gedrukte bronnen, 1582–1679', in: Slive, *Frans Hals*, s.d.

Van Thiel-Stroman 1989-1990
Irene van Thiel-Stroman, 'Chronologie', in: Seymour Slive (ed.), *Frans Hals*, exhib. cat. (Washington – National Gallery of Art; London – Royal Academy of Arts; Haarlem – Frans Halsmuseum), 1989–1990.

Van Thiel-Stroman 2006
Irene van Thiel-Stroman, 'Frans Pietersz. De Grebber' and 'Pieter Fransz. De Grebber', in: Neeltje Köhler (ed.), *Painting in Haarlem 1500–1850. The collection of the Frans Halsmuseum*, Ghent, 2006, pp. 163–164 and 168.

Thiis 1913
Jens Thiis, *Leonardo da Vinci. The Florentine years of Leonardo & Verrocchio*, translated by Jessie Muir, London, 1913.

Thomson 2001
Katrina Thomson, *From the Madonna to the Moulin Rouge: Drawings Recently Acquired for the National Gallery of Scotland*, Edinburgh, 2001.

Tieze 2009
Agnes Tieze, *Flämische Gemälde im Städel Museum 1550–1800*, vol. 1 (Kataloge der Gemälde im Städel Museum, Frankfurt am Main, 10, ed. Jochen Sander and Max Hollein), Petersberg, 2009, pp. 101–112.

Tinagli 1997
Paolo Tinagli, *Women in Italian Renaissance art: gender, representation, identity*, Manchester-New York, 1997.

Treanor, 2008-2009
Virginia C. Treanor, 'Man in Oriental Costume ("Sultan Soliman")', in: Arthur K. Wheelock Jr. et al. (eds.), *Jan Lievens: A Dutch Master Rediscovered*, exhib. cat. (Washington – National Gallery of Art; Milwaukee – Milwaukee Art Museum; Amsterdam – Museum Het Rembrandthuis), New Haven-London, 2008–2009.

Trentelman 2014
Karen Trentelman, 'Rembrandt's "An Old Man in Military Costume: The Underlying Image Re-Examined', in: *Applied Physics A*, 121 (2014).

Turin 2011
Carlo Pedretti, Paolo Salvi, Clara Vitulo, Pietro C. Marani, Renato Barilli and Arnaldo Colasanti (eds.), *Leonardo: il Genio il Mito*, exhib. cat. (Turin – Venaria Reale, Reggia di Venaria; Turin – Cinisello Balsamo), 2011.

Turin 2019
Enrica Pagella, Francesco Paolo di Teodoro and Paola Salvi (eds.), *Leonardo da Vinci. Disegnare i l futuro,* exhib. cat. (Turin – Musei Reali, Galleria Sabauda), Cinisello Balsamo, 2019.

Turner 1993
A. Richard Turner, *Inventing Leonardo*, Berkeley-Los Angeles, 1993.

Underhill 2017
Justin Underhill, 'Peter Paul Rubens and the Rationalization of Light', in: *Journal for Art History,* 87 (2018), pp. 1–22.

Van Alewijn, s.d.
Inventory of Frederick van Alewijn, lot 0014, https://research.frick.org/montias/details/400 (accessed March 2023).

Van den Boogert 1999
Bob van den Boogert (ed.), *Rembrandt's Treasures*, exhib. cat. (Amsterdam – Museum Het Rembrandthuis) Amsterdam-Zwolle, 1999–2000.

Vandenbroeck 1984
Paul Vandenbroeck, 'Verbeeck's peasant weddings: a study of iconography and social function', in: *Simiolus: Netherlands Quarterly for the History of Art*, 14 (1984), pp. 106–108.

Van der Coelen and Lammertse 2015
Peter van der Coelen and Friso Lammertse, 'Inleiding', in: Peter van der Coelen and Friso Lammertse (eds.), *De ontdekking van het dagelijkse leven. Van Bosch tot Bruegel*, exhib. cat. (Rotterdam – Museum Boijmans Van Beuningen), Rotterdam, 2012, pp. 9–29.

Van der Vinde 2007
Lea Van der Vinde, *Children in the Mauritshuis*, Waanders, 2007.

Van de Wetering 2015
Ernst van de Wetering, *Rembrandt's Paintings Revisited. A Complete Survey* (A Corpus of Rembrandt Paintings VI), Dordrecht, 2015.

Van Eikema Hommes 2013
Margriet van Eikema Hommes, 'Een Triomfstoet Belicht. De Werkelijke En de Geschilderde Lichtinval in de Oranjezaal', in: Margriet van Eikema Hommes and Elmer Kolfin (eds.), *De Oranjezaal in Huis Ten Bosch. Een Zaal Uit Loutere Liefde*, Zwolle, 2013.

Van Fornenberg 1658
Alexander Van Fornenbergh, *Den Antwerpschen Protheus, ofte Cyclopshen Apelles; dat is; Het Leven, ende Konst-rijcke Daden, des Uyt-nemenden, ende Hoogh-beroemden, Mr. Quinten Matsys*, Antwerp, 1658, pp. 16–18.

Van Gelder 1950–1951
G. Van Gelder, 'Rubens in Holland in de zeventiende eeuw', in: *Nederlands Kunsthistorisch Jaarboek (NKJ) / Netherlands Yearbook for History of Art*, vol. 3 (1950–1951).

Van Haute 2015
Bernadette van Haute, 'Black "Tronies" in Seventeenth-Century Flemish Art and the African Presence', in: *De Arte,* 91 (2015), pp. 18–38.

Van Hoogstraten 1678
Samuel van Hoogstraten, *Inleyding tot de hooge schoole der schilderkonst: Anders de zichtbaere werelt*, Rotterdam, 1678.

Van Hout 2020
Nico Van Hout, Rubens. *Study Heads and Anatomical Studies* (Corpus Rubenianum Ludwig Burchard, XX, 2). Turnhout-London, 2020.

Van Mander 1604
Karel van Mander, *Het Schilderboeck*, Paschier van Wesebvsch, Haarlem, 1604.

Van Mander 1604 [Hoecker 1916]
R. Hoecker, *Das Lehrgedicht des Karel van Mander. Text, Übersetzung und Kommentar nebst Anhang über Manders Geschichtskonstruktion und Kunsttheorie* (Quellenstudien zur Holländischen Kunstgeschichte VIII), C. Hofstede de Groot (ed.), The Hague, 1916.

Vecce 2021
Carlo Vecce (ed.), *La Biblioteca di Leonardo*, Florence, 2021.

Venice 2019
Annalisa Perissa Torrini, *Leonardo da Vinci. L'uomo modello del mondo*, exhib. cat. (Venice – Gallerie dell'Accademia), Cinisello Balsamo, 2019.

Vermeylen 2001
Filip Vermeylen, *Painting for the Market. Commercialization of Art in Antwerp's Golden Age*, Turnhout, 2001.

Vermeylen and De Clippel 2012
Filip Vermeylen and Karolien de Clippel, 'Rubens and Goltzius in dialogue. Artistic exchanges between Antwerp and Haarlem during the revolt', in: *De Zeventiende Eeuw*, 28 (2), 2012.

Vienna 2003
Klaus Albrecht Schröder, Maria Luise Sternath et. al. (eds.), *Albrecht Dürer*, exhib. cat. (Vienna – Albertina), Ostfildern, 2003.

Voghtherr 1538
Heinrich Vogtherr, *Ein fremdes und wunderbares kunstbüchlein*, Straatsburg, 1538.

Von Bode 1906
Wilhelm von Bode, 'Anton van Dyck als Mitarbeiter des Peter Paul Rubens', in: *Rembrandt und seine Zeitgenossen*, Leipzig, 1906, pp. 264–265.

Von Sandrart 1675
Joachim von Sandrart, *L'Academia Todesca della Architectura, Scultura & Pittura: Oder Teutsche Academie der Edlen Bau-Bild- und Mahlerey-Künste*. Band 2. Nuremberg, 1675.

Vrolijk 2020
Arnould Vrolijk, 'Knowledge of the East: Collecting Oriental Manuscripts in the Dutch Republic in the Age of Rembrandt', in: Bodo Brinkmann et al. (eds.) *Rembrandt's Orient: West Meets East in Dutch Art of the 17th Century*, exhib. cat. (Basel – Kunstmuseum Basel; Potsdam – Museum Barberini), Munich-London-New York, 2020.

Wadum and de la Fuente Pedersen 2008
Jørgen Wadum and Eva de la Fuente Pedersen (eds.), *Jordaens. The Making of a Masterpiece*, Copenhagen, 2008.

Washington 2001
David Alan Brown et al., *Virtue and Beauty. Leonardo's Ginevra de' Benci and Renaissance Portraits of Women*, exhib. cat. (Washington – National Gallery of Art), Washington, 2001.

Washington 2019
Charles Demsey et al. (eds.), *Verrocchio: sculptor and painter of Renaissance Florence*, exhib. cat. (Washington – National Gallery), Princeton, 2019.

Watteeuw 2015
Bert Watteeuw, 'Household Names? Domestic Staff in Rubens's Home', translated by Ted Alkins, in: *Rubens in Private: The Master Portrays his Family*, exhib. cat. (Antwerp – Rubenshuis), Antwerp, 2015.

Weber 2022
Gregor Weber, *Johannes Vermeer. Geloof, Licht en Reflectie*. Amsterdam, 2022.

Weissert 2016
Caecilie Weissert, 'Charles le Bruns *Expression des Passions* und die *Têtes d'expression* im Kontext physiologischer Betrachtungen', in: Anna Pawlak, Lars Zieke and Isabella Augart (eds.), *Ars – Visus – Affectus. Visuelle Kulturen des Affektiven in der Frühen Neuzeit*, Berlin-Boston, 2016, pp. 251–272.

Wohl, Wohl and Montanari 2005
Alice Sedgwick Wohl, Hellmut Wohl and Tomaso Montanari, *Giovan Pietro Bellori. The Lives of the Modern Painters, Sculptors and Architects. A New Translation and Critical Edition*, Cambridge, 2005.

Worp 1916
Jacob Adolf Worp, *De Briefwisseling van Constantijn Huygens, Deel 5: 1649–1663,* The Hague, 1916.

Wouk 2018
Edward H. Wouk, *Frans Floris (1519/20–1570). Imagining a Northern Renaissance*, Leiden-Boston, 2018.

Yarbus 1967
Al'fred Luk'yanocivh Yarbus, *Eye Movements and Vision*, London-New York, 1967.

Zöllner 1992
Frank Zöllner, '"Ogni Pittore Dipinge Sé". Leonardo da Vinci and "Automimesis"', in: Matthias Winner (ed.), *Der Künstler über sich in seinem Werk*, Weinheim 1992, pp. 137–160.

Zöllner 2019
Frank Zöllner, *Leonardo da Vinci: 1452–1519. The Complete Paintings and Drawings*, Cologne, 2019.

Zöllner 2022
Frank Zöllner, 'Leonardo da Vinci on painting: from the use of types to the criticism of types", in: *Leonardo da Vinci e la lingua della pittura in Europa (secoli XIV-XVII). Atti del Convegno internazionale di studi (Parigi-Torino, 4–5 aprile e 27–29 novembre 2019)*, Florence, 2023, passim.

PHOTO CREDITS

Front cover: RMN-Grand Palais (Musée du Louvre) / Thierry Ollivier
Back cover: Leicester Museums & Galleries / Bridgeman Images

Accepted by HM Government in lieu of inheritance tax and allocated to the National Gallery of Scotland, 2000 (p. 93)
Alamy (p. 21)
Albertina, Vienna (p. 41)
Art in Flanders (p. 151)
bpk / Bayerische Staatsgemäldesammlungen (p. 30)
bpk / Gemäldegalerie, SMB / Jörg P. Anders (p. 12)
bpk / Hessen Kassel Heritage (p. 98)
bpk / Herzog Anton Ulrich-Museum (p. 95)
bpk / Lutz Braun (p. 111)
Stephane Boudin (p. 101)
Bridgeman Images (p. 170)
Christie's Images / Bridgeman Images (pp. 17, 82, 142–143)
Dorotheum, Vienna (p. 15)
Erfgoedbibliotheek Hendrik Conscience, Antwerp (p. 60 bottom)
FENIX, Rotterdam (pp. 116, 117)
Florent Gardin – Musée des Beaux-Arts, Nîmes, France (p. 145)
Liza François (p. 131)
Gallerie degli Uffizi – Gabinetto Fotografico (p. 40 top left)
G.A.VE – Archivio fotografico – "su concessione del Ministero della Cultura" (pp. 36, 44)
J. Paul Getty Museum (pp. 31, 110, 115)
Hermitage, Saint Petersburg (p. 14)
KBC Bank NV, Antwerp, Snijders&Rockoxhuis (pp. 62, 83)
KMSKA – Vlaamse Gemeenschap, photo Rik Klein Gotink (pp. 25, 34, 89, 118, 119)
KMSKA – Vlaamse Gemeenschap, photo Hugo Maertens (pp. 16, 73)
KMSKA – Vlaamse Gemeenschap, photo Dominique Provost (p. 87)
David Laing Bequest to the Royal Scottish Academy transferred 1910 (p. 39 bottom left)
Leicester Museums & Galleries / Bridgeman Images (p. 176)
Liechtenstein, The Princely Collections, Vaduz-Vienna (pp. 9, 134)
Kunstmuseum Basel (p. 53)
Mauritshuis, The Hague (pp. 10, 28, 125, 133, 177)
Su concessione del MiC-Musei Reali (p. 38)
Coll. MUba Eugene Leroy, Tourcoing, photo Musenor (p. 146)
MSK, Museum voor Schone Kunsten, Ghent (pp. 26–27, 54–55)
Musée de la Chartreuse, Douai (p. 84)
Musée du Louvre au Musée des Beaux-Arts de Libourne, photo Jean-Christophe Garcia (pp. 168–169)
Musée des Beaux-Arts de Nancy (pp. 78–79)
Musée du Louvre, Dist. RMN-Grand Palais / Martine Beck-Coppola (p. 147)
Museo Nacional del Prado (pp. 85, 97, 112)
Museo Thyssen-Bornemisza, Madrid (pp. 56–57)
Museum Boijmans Van Beuningen, Rotterdam, from the estate of F.J.O. Boijmans 1847, photo Studio Tromp (p. 152)
Museum of Fine Arts, Budapest, 2023 (p. 144)
Museum of Fine Arts, Boston (p. 167)
National Gallery of Ireland, Dublin (pp. 71, 96, 106–107, 113, 148, 165, 172)
National Gallery, London (p. 32)
National Gallery, Prague 2023 (pp. 105, 171)
National Gallery of Art, Washington (pp. 139, 179)
Noord-Hollands Archief (p. 103)
Private collection, New York (p. 33)
Private collection, New York (pp. 69, 174–175)
Private collection (pp. 76, 124, 135)
Public domain (pp. 127, 128)
Preußische Schlösser und Gärten Berlin-Brandenburg (SPSG), photo Daniel Lindner (p. 114)
Rembrandthuis, Amsterdam (pp. 160–161)
Rijksmuseum (pp. 20, 29, 58–59, 102 bottom, 123, 140, 159, 162, 163)
RMN-Grand Palais (Musée du Louvre) / Mathieu Rabeau (p. 74)
RMN-Grand Palais (Musée du Louvre) / Michèle Bello (p. 66)
RMN-Grand Palais (Musée du Louvre) / Michel Urtado (pp. 80, 150)
RMN-Grand Palais (Musée du Louvre) / Thierry Le Mage (p. 86)
RMN-Grand Palais (Musée du Louvre) / Thierry Ollivier (pp. 61, 137)
Royal Collection Trust / His Majesty King Charles III 2023 (pp. 39 top left, 40 bottom right, 42, 43, 46, 65)
Royal Library of Belgium, Brussels (pp. 60 top, 102 top, 141)
Royal Museums of Fine Arts, Brussels (pp. 19, 126)
Staatliche Museen zu Berlin, Gemäldegalerie / Property of Kaiser Friedrich Museumsverein / Christoph Schmidt (pp. 90, 109)
Städel Museum, Frankfurt am Main (pp. 120, 138)
The Governing Body of Christ Church, Oxford (p. 48)
The Kremer Collection, New York (p. 164)
The Leiden Collection (p. 166)
The Metropolitan Museum of Art, New York (p. 39 right, 94)
The Phoebus Foundation, Antwerp (pp. 75, 77, 104)
The Trustees of the British Museum (p. 81)
The Wallace Collection, London (p. 153)
Stephan Vanfleteren (p. 157)

COLOPHON

This publication accompanies the exhibition *Turning Heads – Bruegel, Rubens and Rembrandt* from 20 October 2023 to 24 January 2024 at the KMSKA, Antwerp, and *Turning Heads* from 24 February to 26 May 2024 at the National Gallery of Ireland, Dublin.

KMSKA Chairman
Luk Lemmens

KMSKA Managing Director
Carmen Willems

National Gallery of Ireland Director
Caroline Campbell

Exhibition curators
Nico Van Hout and Koen Bulckens [KMSKA]
Lizzie Marx [NGI]

KMSKA Publications Manager
Frédéric Jonckheere

KMSKA Publication Coordinator
Véronique Van Passel

Texts
Nico Van Hout
Koen Bulckens
Michael W. Kwakkelstein
Lizzie Marx
Friederike Schütt

With contributions from
Vicki Bruce and Andy Young
Sara De Bosschere
Cian McLoughlin
Elvis Pompilio
Stephan Vanfleteren

With thanks to the staff of the KMSKA

Translation
Ted Alkins

Copy-editing
Derek Scoins

Project management Hannibal Books
Sofie Meert
Hadewych Van den Bossche

Design
Thomas Soete

Image research
Madeleine ter Kuile [KMSKA]
Eline Wellens [KMSKA]
Séverine Lacante [Hannibal Books]

Image editing
Pascal Van den Abbeele [die Keure]

Printing
die Keure, Bruges, Belgium

Binding
Brepols, Turnhout, Belgium

Publisher
Gautier Platteau

ISBN 978 94 6466 678 6
D/2023/11922/61
NUR 646

HANNIBAL

KMSKA

Vlaanderen
is toerisme

The exhibition was made possible thanks to the support of the exhibition partners

DCA + MEER DAN BOUWEN

nationale loterij
MEER DAN SPELEN

and many others

Front cover image:
Joos van Craesbeeck,
The Smoker [detail], 1630–1640,
oil on canvas, Musée du
Louvre, Paris, M.I.906

Back cover image:
Michael Sweerts,
Head of a Girl [detail],
c. 1654, oil on canvas,
Leicester Museum and
Art Gallery, L.F201.1975.0.0